In February of 1718, Governor Bienville of Louisiana set out to pick a spot on the banks of the Mississippi River for a new settlement. The governor chose a site on the east bank about a hundred miles from the Gulf of Mexico—a fortunate selection, for that position astride the river allowed New Orleans to develop into a major port and eventually to exercise economic hegemony over a vast area to the north.

In this detailed economic history, Professor John G. Clark explores the ever-expanding commercial world of New Orleans and the Louisiana colony during their first century of development.

During the formative period, the author notes, both New Orleans and the colony struggled on the edge of economic disaster. France was unwilling and at times unable to send sufficient money, supplies, and colonists to Louisiana, and the efforts of private companies to develop the colony failed. Nevertheless, some gains were made—plantations were established, marketable crops were grown, and domestic and foreign trade systems were developed.

Under the Spanish, New Orleans emerged as a major port and assumed an urban identity. Spain, unable to fully assimilate Louisiana into her colonial system, was compelled to allow Louisiana to operate outside of the system. This freedom, says Clark, allowed English and American commerce to flourish in the port city and contributed greatly to its economic progress between 1765 and 1803.

With the transfer of Louisiana to the United States, New Orleans—free of colonial economic restrictions—was soon assimilated into the world's largest free trade area. Banks, insurance companies, and other capitalist enterprises followed the American flag to New Orleans, and new avenues of economic expansion opened up.

The volume contains tables which illustrate New Orleans' trade activities during the period.

NEW ORLEANS, 1718–1812

NEW ORLEANS
1718-1812

An Economic History

JOHN G. CLARK

LOUISIANA STATE UNIVERSITY PRESS   *Baton Rouge*

To my wife Lois

Preface

My interest in New Orleans derives from an earlier study of the
grain trade in the Old Northwest. During several decades of the
nineteenth century, New Orleans was a major grain distributing
center for farmers north of the Ohio River—indeed, the only accessible center for many farmers for many years. While working
on the grain trade, I thought it would be interesting to try to discover how the grain and provisions trade of New Orleans fitted
into the total economy of the city; to isolate the factors that contributed to the rapid growth of New Orleans; and to understand
why the city grew in the directions that it did, rather than in some
other directions.

My original intention was to focus on the American period, 1803–
1861, and to devote an introductory chapter to the French and
Spanish periods, based largely on secondary sources. However, I
soon learned that, while much information was available relative to
the political and social history of colonial New Orleans particularly
during the Spanish period, little work had been done on its economic
history, and still less on the economic relationship between New
Orleans and its successive mother countries. The opportunity to
trace the growth of the city from its birth intrigued me, as the
colonial era soon did, and the result was this volume. A second
volume, hopefully, will follow, carrying the city's development to
the Civil War.

I used whatever sources I could put my hands on. The resulting
work is as much a synthesis of the work of other scholars as it is the
fruit of original research. I hope that the ingredients were used in a
sufficiently interesting way to produce a work of some relevance

both to specialists and generalists in the fields of economic, urban, colonial, Louisiana, and United States history. I might add here that the decision to eliminate most of the footnotes was done at my request.

Numerous individuals and institutions provided the necessary services and time to research and write this book. The University of Kansas provided research support for two summers. The Department of History at Louisiana State University, Baton Rouge, in adopting me as a visiting teacher for a summer and an academic year, provided an indispensable opportunity to spend a full year working the archives located in Louisiana and Mississippi. The National Endowment for the Humanities awarded me a nine-month fellowship which allowed me to start and complete the first draft. The staff at numerous libraries made the research work a pleasant experience. Special thanks are due Mrs. Connie Griffith, Director, Manuscript Division, Tulane University Library, and Vergil Bedsole, former Archivist, Louisiana State University Library. Among other libraries which provided significant aid were: the New York Public Library; the New Orleans Public Library; the Mississippi Department of Archives and History; the Library of Congress; the Henry E. Huntington Library; and the Archives Nationale, Paris. Professors Jo Ann Carrigan of the University of Nebraska at Omaha and James D. Hardy of Louisiana State University provided sympathetic and knowledgeable criticism at various stages of the project, as did Professor Charles Stansifer, University of Kansas. The shortcomings of the volume are my responsibility alone. A great debt is owed to my wife Lois, who typed and retyped, read and proofread, the successive drafts of this work.

Contents

Tables

NEW ORLEANS, 1718–1812

1

Planting a Delta Town

IN February, 1718, Jean Baptiste Le Moyne, Sieur de Bienville, Governor of Louisiana, set out to select a place on the banks of the Mississippi River for a new settlement. Departing in small vessels from Dauphin Island, at the entrance of Mobile Bay, his party of several score navigated the shallow coastal waters of the Gulf without difficulty, passed the bar, took soundings at the mouth of the Mississippi, and began the tedious ascent of the river. The marshlands, the high-pitched cries of the wild birds, the glare of a low horizon—all of this was familiar to Bienville from a prior journey. Moving slowly against the rapid current, deftly avoiding the swirling debris of unknown northern storms and floods, the convoy for many days sought out a suitable tract of land on which to establish a settlement. Some one hundred miles from the Gulf, where the winding river changes from its east-southeastern course, turns almost due north and then jogs back to the southeast, a likely spot was found on the east bank at the elbow of the jog.

The locale was wet, heavily forested and, even then, clouded by mosquitoes, but it had certain advantages over other possible sites. The terrain was generally higher than it was along most of the river and only a narrow strip of land, traversed part way by a bayou, separated the site from Lake Pontchartrain. Access to the spot— named New Orleans—from the Gulf was afforded by Lakes Borgne and Pontchartrain as well as by the river. Indeed, it was thought that the lake route would be paramount. Bienville left fifty men to clear the land and build some houses and returned temporarily to Dauphin Island.

The development of New Orleans proceeded fitfully. Although

the earlier headquarters of the colony at Dauphin Island, Mobile Bay, and Old and New Biloxi were recognized to be inadequate as ports, there was considerable reluctance to move the colony's administrative center to the Mississippi River. But the Company of the Indies finally determined upon the move in 1722. At the site Le Blond de la Tour and Adrien de Pauger, engineers responsible for the building of the town, were laboring against a serious shortage of labor and supplies, recurrent hurricanes, and general poor health and morale to provide accommodations for the troops and anticipated settlers. When the *Dromadaire* hove to before New Orleans in 1722 with supplies and colonists for the settlement, its crew was treated to a rather unimposing sight.[1] Barracks for the troops were still not complete. Most people were living in low houses covered with large pieces of bark and strong reeds.

In 1723, the earthen levee thrown up to protect the city against the river was deemed inadequate; by 1727 the levee's thickness had been doubled and extended for eighteen hundred yards in front of the settlement. Buildings were put up more rapidly following the hurricane of 1722. A large warehouse was completed in 1724 and the town could boast of a hundred cabins and two or three more sumptuous dwellings. Most of the dwellings were placed close to the river and provided with ample space for gardens. Streets were laid out and the outlines of an orderly, developed settlement could be detected. Work was begun on the palisades which would eventually protect the city on three sides. The Rue de Chartres became the "government row" of the town. All of this was achieved at a cost of fifty thousand livres.

The population of New Orleans and vicinity during the 1720s is difficult to determine, although it appears to have grown from some 1,250 in 1721, with 250 in New Orleans, to roughly 3,000 in 1727, while the overall population of Louisiana decreased. A census of population in 1727 listed 938 residents of New Orleans proper. Moreover, the composition of New Orleans' population changed

---

[1] Frequent desertions plagued the resident engineers; and hurricanes in 1721 and 1722 destroyed a new church, hospital, and thirty other buildings while demolishing most of the vessels then in port.

significantly between 1721 and 1727. Services were available at the later date which had been unavailable earlier. In 1721, 49 individuals—40 of whom were company employees—were credited with possessing skill in 16 different crafts. Six years later, 159 men were pursuing 37 crafts, in addition to an unknown number of company craftsmen. Expansion in the private sector of the town's economy made available new services of critical importance. Shipbuilders, wheelwrights, sailmakers, masons, nailmakers, and roofers took up residence. An innkeeper and four surgeons moved to New Orleans, although the value of the latter is in dispute. The number of carpenters rose from 4 to 21, joiners from 5 to 13, blacksmiths from 1 to 7, and coopers from 1 to 4. A town whose major function was to facilitate the movement of staple crops and other raw materials demanded the presence of such skills.

Louisiana did not demonstrate great vitality in the first three decades of formal occupation by France. Frenchmen considered it more amenable to colonization than Canada because of the docility of the natives and the richness of the soil. There was no empirical proof of this, however, only conjecture. Also, there was an assumption that the establishment of the colony would guarantee French mastery of the continent through a chain of posts stretching from the Gulf to the Great Lakes, but the British and their Indian allies would have something to say about this development. The British were always a critical factor in the history of Louisiana and its principal city, no less so in the initial phases of French control than in the final decision to cede the colony to Spain.

By the mid-seventeenth century the clash of contending European powers was worldwide in scope but was of greater intensity in Atlantic and Caribbean waters than in the waters of the Indian and Pacific oceans. This was less a conscious decision than a factor of power availability. Given the military and naval technology of the time, it was obviously easier to bring force to bear on the Caribbean islands than on the Moluccas. In the early stages of the century of war initiated between the great powers in Europe in 1688, dynastic and continental ambitions ruled with but desultory conflict in the colonies. But as one war followed another during the eighteenth century, colonial pretensions grew in importance and ultimately dominated the purposes of France and Great Britain, the major contending powers.

Anglo-French colonial rivalry has a long and bloody history, inextricably bound into colonial patterns. It was precipitated by the successful Norman conquest of England, complicated by the continental and colonial ambitions and accomplishments of Portugal, Spain, and the United Provinces, as well as the struggles between the Austrian Hapsburgs and the Turks. It reached a first denouement only in 1765. During the sixteenth century England, France, and the Netherlands, too weak to undertake successful colonizing ventures of their own, had preyed upon Spanish lines of communication between the New World and the Peninsula. By the mid-seventeenth century, the three challengers to Spanish hegemony were all in the colonial game and the remaining West Indian islands and North America were staked out and more or less occupied.

France was reasonably well positioned in colonizing the Western Hemisphere by the mid-seventeenth century. Although repulsed by the Portuguese in Brazil, the French were firmly established in Canada, the Lesser Antilles and, by the end of the century, in the French half of Hispaniola (St. Domingue). France and her rivals were cognizant of the necessity of controlling the trade of their own colonies and the advantages of monopolizing to the maximum degree both the legal and illegal trade between Spain and her colonies. The French had managed, with the active aid of the English, effectively to challenge Dutch power in the Caribbean by the 1670s. Not only was France able to seize control of the increasingly lucrative commerce of her own colonies but a tenacious rival for the Spanish trade was virtually eliminated. However, England, the strongest maritime state and the most dangerous adversary, remained with augmented power to confront the French at all points between Hudson Bay and Martinique.

From 1688 to 1815 France fought Great Britain in seven wars lasting sixty years. French interest in the Lower Mississippi Valley must be viewed from within the context of these conflicts which were the dominant factors in French history and, at times, in the history of Europe and the Western Hemisphere. The first French endeavors in Louisiana coincided with the outbreak of the War of the League of Augsburg (1688–97), followed by a five-year peace which was shattered by the War of the Spanish Succession (1702–13). France, sensitive to English pressures along the St. Lawrence, in the area of Hudson Bay, and in the Ohio River Valley, received information that the English planned to seize the mouth of the Mississippi and reacted by dispatching Pierre Le Moyne, Sieur de Iberville's fleet to the Mississippi in 1698. The sea approach to the Mississippi Valley was secured in the following year.

French purposes were apparently twofold: on the one hand, the security of Canada was believed dependent upon the possession of the Mississippi River; on the other, the French viewed Louisiana as a staging point from which to penetrate Spain's colonies both by sea and land and thus seize a lion's share of the Spanish trade. These not mutually exclusive purposes were pursued with some diligence for more than sixty years. Success was neither completely attainable nor totally elusive.

French fears regarding English encroachments into Canada and the Mississippi Valley were well founded. The English were dominant in trade and influence among the Louisiana Indians when Iberville planted his first settlement at Biloxi. Basic elements of French policy were developed to meet this threat. With the support of the Choctaws, the Alabamas, and other anti-English tribes, the small French population managed to hold the enemy at bay in the Lower Valley for almost seventy years. When disaster came, it was experienced in Canada rather than Louisiana. But this may have also proved, somewhat academically for the French, that the security of Canada was not in fact dependent upon the occupation of Louisiana and control of the Mississippi Valley. Louisiana and Canada could well have survived the presence of the English between them as the Illinois country was not critical to the existence of either. But the emphasis placed on the fur trade of the Upper Mississippi and Ohio valleys clouded the thoughts of French governments and predisposed them to a policy which linked the fortunes of Canada and Louisiana at the most vulnerable point in French North America, the Illinois.

The interval between the Treaty of Ryswick (1697) and the outbreak of the War of the Spanish Succession afforded France the respite necessary for Iberville's venture. But the peace was only a truce and the moment too short for the French to ensconce themselves solidly in Louisiana. Before the small party left by Iberville could accomplish even basic tasks, Louis XIV attempted to place a Bourbon prince on the recently vacated Spanish throne. It was in response to this and other French policies, including an alliance with Spain and Portugal, that Austria, England, and the Netherlands concluded an alliance and commenced hostilities in 1702.

While the debilitating contest raged in Europe, the West Indies, Canada, and elsewhere, the French colonies were without succor from the mother country because England controlled the seas. Isolation produced almost unbearable hardship in Louisiana, the colony least able to withstand it. The colony, now under Bienville's command, was unprepared for war in 1703. Occasional vessels reached Louisiana until 1708 and then none arrived until 1711. The Spanish and French colonials aided each other when possible. Limited supplies reached Louisiana from Vera Cruz and the French sent military aid and supplies to Florida. Disaster in Louisiana was narrowly avoided: an epidemic took thirty-five lives in 1705, the Indians showed signs of hostility, and famine threatened from 1708 to 1710.[2]

Louisiana's survival of the war period was due as much to the unrelenting efforts of Bienville as to any other factor; that is, a population of some three hundred survived in scattered posts from Mobile to the Mississippi, by subsisting with or as the Indians. Bienville, harassed by political opponents, hemmed in by unfriendly Indians, unable to maintain discipline among the troops or colonists, and uncertain as to the future of the colony or himself, addressed a long, plaintive, and pessimistic letter to Comte Jerome de Pontchartrain, Secretary of State of the Marine, pleading with the government not to abandon the colony. Eleven months later the crown ceded Louisiana to Antoine Crozat and in 1713 Bienville's authority was superseded by that of de la Mothe Cadillac.

    2 Marcel Giraud, "La France et la Louisiane au début du XVIII siècle," *Revue historique*, CCIV (October–December, 1950), 185–208, points out that conditions in France, to a small degree, mirrored those in Louisiana during the war and that poor harvests in France made all the more uncertain the availability of provisions for Louisiana.

Peace came to France and Crozat's regime came to Louisiana, a combination that did not bring prosperity to the colony. France, too weak and perhaps too indifferent to sustain Louisiana, found it convenient to turn the entire colony over to a private entrepreneur. But the task was beyond the capabilities of an individual, however wealthy and powerful he might be. The colony, almost totally undeveloped, needed massive injections of people, money, and goods and required a guaranteed market for its products. Crozat could supply none of these. After heavy expenditure, he relinquished his privileges to the crown, which was no more prepared to develop the colony in 1717 than it had been in 1712. The regency wished to place the colony in the hands of a company. John Law, Scottish financier and soon to be among the most powerful men in France, obliged the regency with the formation of the Company of the West and Louisiana passed into Law's hands.

The company under Law engaged itself heavily in Louisiana and achieved some success until the original Company of the Indies collapsed under the weight of its fiscal responsibilities. Certainly its accomplishments in Louisiana were not sufficient to transform the colony overnight into a paradise, but one must remember that the task which confronted it in Louisiana was extremely complicated. Critics of the company and its policies in Louisiana need only look cursorily at the problems of today's undeveloped and underdeveloped nations to learn that large investments do not necessarily result in immediate tangible and measureable improvement. Development is a long-run process. The company had only a short-run existence.

The company's problems were aggravated not only by its multiple commitments in France but by conditions there and the foreign policy pursued by the regency. In 1719, at the peak of the company's efforts in Louisiana, France went to war with Spain. This was not a great war and the Spanish were quickly cowed into a temporary acceptance of the Treaty of Utrecht, but it came at an inopportune moment for Louisiana.

At the conclusion of hostilities, the colony, now centered at New Orleans, was in frightful condition. The war, the fall of John Law, the chaos of the period during which the company was reorganized

all militated against substantial progress. In 1721 a month's supply
of flour remained and—even more intolerable—there was no wine in
the colony. The Indians' corn crops had failed and no aid could be
expected from that source. The same conditions prevailed throughout the decade. So precarious was the colony's condition, so finely
balanced between minimal sufficiency and famine, that the colony
tipped constantly like a see-saw from one state to the other and was
thrown into a state of shock by the loss of a single vessel, the
Bellone, in 1725.[3]

New Orleans, then, was not founded under particularly auspi-
cious circumstances. Great difficulties faced those groups, public
and private, which interested themselves in the fortunes of the
colony. Its future depended upon the willingness and ability of its
rulers to subsidize it. Without large subsidization the natural wealth
of the area could not be exploited. For the colony and its capital to
succeed, one basic problem had to be resolved—the unwillingness of
Frenchmen to move to Louisiana. A company official, in a memoir
to the regent and directors of the company, acknowledged the need
to destroy the false ideas that the public held of Louisiana. He wrote:
"In the first place it is certain that the country of Louisiana has a
very poor reputation, and that few people in the world have other
than false and frightful ideas of the land, so much so that when a
man condemned to death is portrayed on the stage, an equivalent
punishment is judged to be his banishment to the Mississippi." [4]
Law's collapse worsened the problem.

The colony served certain strategic purposes and held out the
promise of economic gain. It was for this reason that Law and the
Company of the Indies involved themselves in Louisiana. The company had not only the privilege of economic exploitation but the
duties of colonization, administration, defense, and subsistence. Before it could return substantial profits to the investors, the colony
required services and expenditures. As for New Orleans, its develop-

---

[3] The vessel sank off Dauphin Island with the total export of the colony, prin-
cipally indigo, in its hold. Sunk also were the hopes of the colony, for the sale of
the rich cargo was expected to bring much-needed relief to Louisiana.

[4] Purry to "Son Altesse Royale Monseigneur le duc d'Orleans" and to "Messieurs
les Directeurs de la Compagnie des Indes," 1719, Purry Mémoire (Photostat in
Tulane University Library, Manuscript Division, New Orleans).

ment beyond the role of a petty administrative center was dependent upon the exploitation of its hinterlands. Unlike the cities of St. Domingue or Havana, New Orleans could not hope to achieve significance as a major center of government or as a major port of call in the trade between mother country and colony. Unlike Vera Cruz, there was no established, productive civilization existing at the rear of New Orleans.

The development of a mainland city, planted for commercial purposes by a colonial power, demands the utilization and exploitation of a hinterland. In the case of New Orleans one can define two hinterlands, the natural and the artificial. The natural would include those areas settled by or under the hegemony of the various Indian societies present at the time of initial settlement. The artificial hinterland refers to those rural settlements and posts established and sustained by the French. The two are susceptible to geographic delimitation. During most of the French period, reasonable control was exercised south of a line running from Natchitoches through Natchez to Fort Toulouse, the post on the Alabama River. With the exception of sporadic Indian incursions, this was a fairly secure area and thus open to agricultural development.

North of the line was the natural hinterland—Indian country— which stretched beyond the Ohio to the Great Lakes. A French enclave existed in Illinois, functioning both as a part of the artificial hinterland of New Orleans and also as a part of the natural hinterland of New France and Louisiana. Large sums were expended to control the natural area so as to exclude from it the ubiquitous English traders and thus monopolize the fur trade. It is possible that efforts disproportionate to potential results went into this policy and that the French lacked the resources both to develop the artificial hinterland and control the natural to the extent desired. Such diffused efforts retarded the progress of the settled areas. The experience of Canada indicated that an undue emphasis on the fur trade had deleterious effects upon the achievement of agricultural self-sufficiency. In any event, the rulers of Louisiana, whether private, corporate, or governmental, were confronted by serious difficulties in their efforts to plant a permanent, stable, self-sufficient, and economically progressive colony in Louisiana.

The extraordinary expense of waging the militarily unsuccessful War of the Spanish Succession and the general governmental indifference toward the struggling colony of Louisiana led to a decision to lodge responsibility for the project in the hands of a private company. Antoine Crozat, wealthy financier and merchant, submitted an acceptable proposal to the crown. Letters patent were issued on September 14, 1712, granting Crozat exclusive commercial and developmental privileges in Louisiana for fifteen years. In his instructions to Cadillac, appointed governor-general of the colony, Louis XIV graciously enjoined the governor to keep the people healthy and happy, in union and in peace, thus procuring for them the greatest possible accommodation. The crown had hopefully placed primary responsibility for Louisiana in other hands.

Ample precedents for such action existed in the prior century of French colonial history. It was early recognized that the risks of overseas trade were too great for the private individual to bear alone. Associations of merchants, generally partnerships, became the normal means of sharing the manifold risks. But such arrangements, involving relatively small amounts of capital and few vessels, did not suffice when colonization and exploration were intended. Larger concentrations of capital and manpower were desirable to secure permanent footholds and lasting economic penetration in such areas as India and North America. While it may be true that the origins of France's Atlantic empire resulted from the initiative of private individuals, it is also true that France, impressed by the unexampled success of the Dutch East India Company, quickly turned to the chartered company as a primary device for exploiting old and new colonies. The success of these organizations may be doubted, but not the tenacious hold of this method upon official French thinking.

Commercial companies, an intrinsic part of French economic policy during the seventeenth century, were designed to further that doctrine of exclusivism which European nations commonly followed in seeking to monopolize the economic potential of their colonies. Sporadic interest was expressed in colonization and monopolistic companies prior to the advent of Cardinal Richelieu in 1624. Richelieu brought focus and purpose to French overseas efforts, but the classical age of the French companies coincided with the ministry of Colbert, who fostered a colonial area second only to Spain in extent and which was viewed with hostility by England.

By the end of Colbert's ministry (1683), the organizational structure of the companies was fixed; so closely directed were they that they can hardly be attributed independent existence. Active intervention by the government was necessary to the initial organization of the companies as commerce was not held in high esteem in France during the seventeenth and early eighteenth centuries. With industry and commerce retarded by the lack of both investment capital and social and political incentives, the promotion of large-scale commercial enterprise was accomplished by exerting governmental pressure and, in effect, imposing the chartered companies upon frequently unwilling investors.

Royal interests were protected and royal wishes were promoted in all facets of a company's affairs, regardless of the true interests of the subscribers. The companies were dependent upon royal support for the fulfillment of their economic and noneconomic purposes.[5] Although the availability of government support did not guarantee success, the withdrawal of that aid meant certain death. If the crown's favor could overcome the most difficult problems with loans, tariff privileges, or military and diplomatic pressures, the companies were also expected to contribute resources—men and materials during a war—to further royal policies, thus frequently diverting scarce resources from valid commercial objectives.

Even though the companies generally failed in their commercial

[5] Nominally, the purpose of most companies was to promote commerce in stipulated parts of the world, but this frequently involved the organizations in paramilitary activities in which they served as a political arm of the state to the detriment of legitimate commercial pursuits. Many companies also engaged in colonization, especially if the area to be exploited economically was without an established, sedentary, native society which produced goods marketable in Europe. A distinction may be made between the purposes of the East India Company, or the Dutch and the English East India companies for that matter, and those of the companies which came and went in New France and those engaged in Louisiana. Although the former were organized strictly for trading purposes, the latter were compelled to devote a portion of their resources to development and settlement in order to create a trade which had no pre-existence. Both, however, could find themselves suddenly performing tasks for the sovereign.

purposes because of poor administration, foreign wars, smuggling, inadequate resources, and unrealistic objectives, their overall impact may be viewed in positive terms, if one is not thoroughly intoxicated with a laissez-faire view of economic development. Precedents for monopolistic control led more or less naturally to the granting of Louisiana, first to Crozat and then to John Law's Company of the West.

The system of commercial privilege in France was not under vigorous attack in the first years of the eighteenth century. Although the bourgeoisie were increasing both in numbers and economic power, they were not economic liberals who demanded free trade and the end to privilege. When they called for the lifting of restrictions, they were normally concerned only with those impinging upon their own operations. They were quite willing to see other merchants and other ports restricted, limited, and hamstrung whenever possible. Each port had its specialty; each pattern of trade was buttressed by privilege. The ports were not passive when liberalization would result in the sharing of privileges with other ports. Economic parochialism, evident in all sectors of the economy, did not supply hospitable surroundings for the application of liberal ideas.

Because the commercial company was so obviously in harmony with the royal government and as yet unchallenged by a united body of public opinion, it was natural that the government should grant Louisiana to Crozat after the Spanish rejected a French offer to exchange it for the Spanish portion of St. Domingue. Crozat, a successful businessman and one of a number of powerful capitalists who became more powerful through their financial services to the crown during the War of the Spanish Succession, took Louisiana on speculation. He possessed a knowledge of trade and finance, had engaged profitably in the slave trade, commanded a considerable capital, and had access to the French government. That he was a man of small views and short-term hopes, if true, places him foursquare among the generality of mankind within which the merchant classes also fall; that he was not the man to found an empire, while probably true, is irrelevant. Indeed, had he been such a man, he would likely have perished in some faroff wilderness rather than remain at home amassing a fortune and risking a portion of it in such a questionable venture as Louisiana.[6]

The letters patent of September, 1712, inaugurated a period of company control in Louisiana that lacked one year of surviving two decades. Crozat's monopoly represents the first phase; John Law's Companies of the West and of the Indies, 1717–21, the second phase; the reorganization of the Company of the Indies, 1721–23, more or less an interregnum, the third phase; and the reorganized Company of the Indies, 1723–31, the last phase.

Crozat's company was basically an entrepreneurial effort, resembling many of the companies organized in the pre-Colbert period in that it held no particular economic implications for the nation at large and was not expected to assume a major role in the foreign policy of the state. It was thus significantly different in its scope or purposes from the Law organizations. Crozat's privileges reflect a fair assessment of the exploitable potential of a colony about which relatively little was known. The charter was not unduly influenced by romantic dreams but rather summarized contemporary notions about what one should expect to do and find in a colony in a particular part of the world.[7]

Crozat's company must be viewed as a failure if for no other reason than the financial reverses it experienced in operating the colony. Crozat placed his hopes for profit on the discovery of mineral resources and the development of lucrative commercial ties with the Spanish, both by sea and overland via New Mexico. These were certainly legitimate and rational goals that happen to have failed of achievement. His financial and technological resources were too limited to accomplish much in the way of bringing out minerals because they were located far up the Mississippi in a region where the Indians were hostile. But the minerals—lead and copper— were there, later forming a part of the commerce of the Upper

[6] Giraud, "La France et la Louisiane," 195, generally hostile to Crozat's efforts, regrets that Crozat lacked the abilities necessary for empire building.

[7] The charter granted Crozat vast commercial, mineral, and fur trading privileges and authorized him to bring in one vessel of Negroes annually for sale to the colonists. He was obligated to send two vessels of colonists to Louisiana each year and to assume the expense of administration and defense in the tenth year—a year that failed to materialize for Crozat's monopoly.

Valley. As for the Spanish trade in which Crozat invested consider-able funds, his agents found the ports of Spain's colonies effectively closed to foreign commerce. This was not his failure but essentially that of Louis XIV, who was instrumental in establishing a dynasty in Spain capable of enforcing to an unprecedented degree the his-toric Spanish policy of exclusivism. Growing Franco-Spanish en-mity resulted in losses for French merchants other than Crozat during those years.

These dual failures, in addition to the unprofitability of the fur trade and general Indian trade, precluded any major effort at colo-nization by Crozat, who was relying on commercial profits to sup-ply the necessary capital. His only reliable market consisted of the seven hundred colonists scattered about Louisiana. He may indeed have been guilty of exploiting these captives by charging exorbitant prices for his goods while allowing low prices for colonial products. However, the costs of transportation were high and the risks many, making necessary large markups if expenses were to be made. Crozat has been criticized for his policies toward the colonists. From a humanitarian point of view, a more liberal policy would have been desirable but it would not have increased the probability of success. In any event, he suffered a financial blow in 1716 that compelled him, the following January, to relinquish his privileges in Louisiana.

In 1717, however, the regency was in no better position to assume the responsibility for Louisiana than Louis XIV had been in 1712. The French war debt stood at more than 3 billion livres in 1715. Beginning in 1713 the French government resorted to various ex-pedients to diminish her contracted debt. New offices and patents of nobility were sold, new taxes were promulgated, monetary ma-nipulations deflated the value of coin, and a repudiationist policy reduced the value of outstanding state paper from 600 million livres to 250 million. The violence and capriciousness of these measures reverberated throughout the French economy, destroying business confidence, causing the hoarding of specie funds, increasing the rate of business failures and, in general, producing an atmosphere of stark crisis.

Of the myriad reform proposals which the crisis stimulated, the idea of chartering a bank as a stabilizing mechanism was a common suggestion. John Law happened to have plans for such a bank in hand, ready for implementation, and the regency proved receptive to the ideas of the Scotsman. In May, 1716, letters patent were issued chartering a *Banque Générale* for twenty years, capitalized at six million livres and authorized to act as a bank of deposit, of discount, and as a clearing house. This bank became the nuclear agency of a concentration of economic power unparalleled in European history.[8]

Once the success of the *Banque Générale* was proven, Law was ready to initiate a new project, backed by the strength of his bank, designed to open up fresh opportunities for the investment of French capital and to transform a neglected wilderness into a flourishing civilization. Law, ever alert to achieve a more total and rational mobilization of French resources, was not remiss in his assessment of the significance of Crozat's retrocession of Louisiana. In a memoir of 1715 Law suggested that the failure of individual companies of commerce resulted from the inadequate and uneconomic use of available resources. He proposed to merge all existing companies into a single, centrally directed *compagnie générale du commerce maritime*. In spite of some opposition but with the welcome support of numerous deputies of commerce from the Atlantic ports and the Council of the Marine, letters patent were issued in August, 1717, establishing the Company of the West, endowed with the exclusive commerce of Louisiana and the beaver trade of Canada.

Shortly thereafter, the *Banque Générale* became a major stockholder in the Company of the West. By thus uniting the two operations, the company became involved in the fiscal services which the bank performed for the regency, forcing Law to secure permanent sources of operating revenue for the company. Thus began a process of accumulation of privileges which transformed an essentially commercial undertaking into a hydra-headed corporation whose basic nature was fiscal. The pyramiding of privileges and

---

[8] Unlike the Bank of England, the *Banque Générale* was not a bank of issue; that is, its bills could only be issued against deposits. These bills, while not considered legal tender, were receivable in payment of taxes.

obligations resulted in the destruction of Law's financial edifice while leaving the commercial largely intact. An era of French history occurred during the three years of the system's life.

Law's search for sources of revenue resulted in securing for the Company of the West the tobacco farm (which made the company sole distributor of that crop in France) for nine years beginning in September, 1718.[9] In December of that year the Company of Senegal was absorbed to provide the means of supplying Negroes to Louisiana. In the same month, the *Banque Générale* was transformed into the *Banque Royale*. The system continued to grow. In May, 1719, the Company of the West absorbed the Companies of the East Indies and of China, changed its name to the Company of the Indies, and offered a new stock issue. Within another month, the Company of the Indies received the privileges of the Company of Africa and the Company of Cape Nègre. In 1720 Law's behemoth then obtained the rights to the Argentine trade and sole trade with St. Domingue and the coast of Africa from the Sierra Leone River to the Cape of Good Hope.

The system achieved final unity in 1719, the year of its destruction. The details of its collapse in a frenzy of speculation are beyond the purview of this study. Suffice it to say that the shock, coinciding in time with the excesses connected with Britain's South Sea Bubble, destroyed fortunes overnight and paralyzed the economy. But within five years, France entered into a period of prosperity unprecedented in her history. Law's fall did not bring utter ruin; nor was the system without permanent benefits; nor were the troubles that followed wholly attributable to Law.

Throughout the period of repudiation and reorganization that followed Law's fall, the Company of the Indies remained intact, although shorn of its recent splendor. By July, 1721, all privileges were taken from the company, now reduced to the carrying trade, while Louisiana, in the meantime, was governed by commissioners appointed by the crown. Finally, in 1723 a reorganized company emerged with its capital resources, Louisiana, the tobacco monopoly, and other fiscal and commercial privileges restored to it. Now ready

---

[9] Law counted heavily on the establishment of tobacco culture in Louisiana to turn this to account.

to resume the business of exploiting its monopoly of the East Indies, St. Domingue, West Africa, and Louisiana trades, the company was no longer committed to underwriting the economic development of the latter as had been the case during Law's time.

Law recognized an economic potential in Louisiana that required the channeling of much material and human resources into the colony. His system was to be the agency which was to marshal the money, credit, materials, and men necessary to sustain such an undertaking, operating, as he projected the plan, within a France liberated from many feudal restraints upon trade and from the shackles of specie money. Unfortunately, Law's purposes frequently ran counter to the government's preeminent concern with its fiscal status as well as to the general inertia of a tradition-bound society. The purposes of the reorganized company were much less exalted.

Given the relative value of the trades open to the reorganized company, it is not surprising that Louisiana received diminishing attention. The most important area of exploitation was India. Between 1725 and 1736 the company purchased 51 million livres worth of Indian goods which sold in France for more than 100 million livres. Next in importance came China and the West Indies. The Louisiana trade was relatively insignificant. In an inventory of resources conducted in 1722, the value of vessels and cargoes at sea, exclusive of those to Louisiana, was set at 22 million livres; those to Louisiana were valued at 314,000 livres.

Louisiana was a burden to the Company of the Indies, which quickly decided to remove itself from the Louisiana trade. Indeed, the company gave up most of its privileges in America between 1724 and 1731. In 1724 it renounced its commercial privileges in St. Domingue and in 1730 the tobacco privilege was leased to the Farmers General. Louisiana was restored to the crown in 1731, leaving only the trade in beaver and slaves in company hands. The company thereafter concentrated on the Eastern trade and functioned profitably until its liquidation in 1769.

Students of Louisiana history frequently deplore the performance of the company in Louisiana. For some, the mere presence of monopoly is sufficient to condemn the effort. The working assumption here is that crown control would somehow result in greater concern for the welfare of Louisiana than was possible under the rule of special interests searching for immediate profits. Others, more universal in their criticism, attack the French (and after that the Spanish) system of colonial government. They are indignant with France for its negligence in attending to the wants of the colony and for the restrictions placed upon its economic development. From the point of view of Louisiana, the only satisfactory condition was economic freedom.

What is frequently forgotten is that the view cannot realistically be confined to the vantage point of Louisiana. France operated a vast empire, generating many conflicts and tensions resolvable only at the highest level of government. The colonies existed to service the mother country whose views must necessarily be preemptive. While Louisianians might view their particular corner of the empire as its center, this restricted and provincial attitude could not be accepted in France. Louisiana was or was not assigned a high priority by the crown, depending upon the interplay of many variables. As it turned out, Louisiana was of but small concern and ultimately expendable. But this decision was to be made at the top. France was the center of the empire.

2

The Monopolies in Action
1712–1731

I N 1720, while rioting occurred daily in the Rue Quincampoix
and tens of thousands of people converged on Paris seeking to
make a quick killing in company stock, a company ad-man
wrote rhapsodically, and probably in total ignorance, of the wonders
and riches to be derived from Louisiana. While admitting the enormous task of establishing the colony and acknowledging that some
time must elapse before the sweet fruits were harvested, he drew the
reader's attention to the tobacco, silk, indigo, and silver already
taken from the colony. "Consider," the writer continued, "the pleas-
ing climate in which it [Louisiana] is situated; the fertility of its
lands, the options available throughout its vast extent, the soft manners of its natural inhabitants; the number of plantations that rich
individuals and companies establish daily which one hopes to see in
a short time more flourishing than the establishments of our neighbors...." [1]

The writer was not far from the truth. Hurricanes and floods did
not strike every year. The Indians were peaceful when not at war
with other tribes or with the Europeans. Individuals of quality and
wealth had founded concessions, some even in person. Tobacco was
exported from Louisiana, although it had been grown in New Spain.
Mulberry trees grew wild in the woods, apparently providing a
natural habitat for the silkworm. Indigo grew wild and cultured
indigo seeds were coming from St. Domingue. As for the silver, a

---

[1] Mémoire instructif des profits et avantages des intéressez dans la Compagnie des
Indes & de Mississippy [1720], in Rosemonde E. and Emile Kuntz Collection (Tulane University Library, Manuscript Division).

tolerant attitude may allow us to believe that the memorialist meant lead.

The reality of Louisiana had little to do with public attitudes. Few of the masses caught up in the Mississippi fever would come closer to the colony than Rue Quincampoix. Accurate knowledge of the colony was unavailable to the public. When one who possessed such knowledge, like ex-Governor La Mothe Cadillac, expounded on the horrors of the place, the Bastille welcomed him. Little that happened in Louisiana had any effect on the steady inflation and rapid decline in the market value of the company's stock. The ad-man knew this and it is reflected in his presentation. He did not refer to Louisiana as a source of immediate profit. Rather he emphasized the large resources available from the fixed revenues and the tax farms assigned to the company.[2] Sources of profit embraced not only these but the bank and trade with both Indies and China. Louisiana was potential.

As noted earlier, Law realized that large numbers of people must be planted in Louisiana if this potential was to become reality. The Company of the West was a company of colonization. It was enjoined to transport no less than six thousand whites and three thousand Negroes before the expiration of the charter. Colonization was encouraged by other sections of the charter. Residents of Louisiana were guaranteed all the liberties and immunities of the mother country; the customs of Paris were established as the law of the land; and colonists were exempted from all taxes on personal and real property.

The company was authorized to sell and grant lands. It offered free transportation and board to Louisiana, and it would provide subsistence and equipment at fair prices until the immigrant was securely established. These terms applied to men of both large and

---

[2] The Farmers General, a group of financiers, purchased from the state the right to collect the indirect taxes (referred to separately as a tax farm). The state was thus guaranteed a fixed sum from which the farmers sought to turn a profit by collecting more in taxes than they had paid for the privilege. The sale of tobacco was a government monopoly. It was sublet to a tax farm which was granted the monopoly of importing and distributing tobacco in return for paying the crown a lump sum of money.

small means; to individuals thinking in terms of thousands of acres as well as men who thought in tens and hundreds. These were not illiberal terms and compare favorably with the conditions of settlement used to attract colonists to other portions of North America. It was Law's hope that such attractions would encourage a large migration.

Law created the capital necessary to move large numbers of immigrants but found that Frenchmen were not anxious to leave their homeland. His best success resulted from an intensive promotional campaign in Switzerland and in Germany but this was inadequate. Law was compelled to use force and undertook the transportation of criminals and indigents to Louisiana. This practice, attended by considerable violence throughout France, was abandoned with the fall of the system. Whatever the inducements, the fate that awaited many immigrants was not one to be envied.

In 1717 three ships loaded with some eight hundred colonists left La Rochelle for Louisiana. Vessels arrived from La Rochelle, Le Havre, and other ports with increasing frequency between 1718 and 1722, carrying troops, owners and managers of concessions, contract laborers, criminals, orphan girls, slaves, and company officials. Always the story was the same: too many people in relation to available supplies. Many died in French ports awaiting embarkation; epidemics and starvation struck down many others. In 1721 it was reported that more than two thousand individuals remained at New Biloxi awaiting transportation to eleven concessions. Vessels were under construction but competent skilled labor and hardware were lacking. The halt and the lame were in abundance, suffering was extensive, and only slowly were the surviving colonists distributed to concessions and farms.

All who were familiar with the colony agreed that Negro slaves were urgently required. In 1720 the entire French slave trade fell into the hands of the Company of the Indies, which plunged energetically into the job of providing slaves for Louisiana. Large numbers of them arrived throughout 1722, more than 2,500 in all, placing an additional strain on the already slender resources of the colony. Throughout the decade at least thirteen company vessels plied the slave trade between Africa and Louisiana.[3] According to the company some 6,000 Negroes were landed in Louisiana prior to 1731. Importation virtually ceased at that point, to the great dismay of Louisiana planters, even though the most active period in the French slave trade commenced at this time.

Company policy both as to price and credit was fair. Since cash was scarce, the company accepted tobacco, rice, lead, or other goods in payment for Negroes spread out over a few years. Nevertheless, complaints and recriminations followed from both sides. The colonists grumbled that company directives regarding the planting of various crops were unrealistic, given the inadequate labor force at their disposal. They demanded more Negroes. The Superior Council of Louisiana warned them that no more Negroes could be expected until the slaves received earlier were paid for. Both sides had a point that was not resolved to the satisfaction of either. The company could not continue to supply slaves if payment was not forthcoming. The planters could not produce the means of payment without additional slaves.

Therefore, the company adopted the policy of distributing Negroes to those it believed best able to afford them. An investigation in 1726 produced a list of responsible planters and the number of slaves they desired. Credit was extended. When vessels arrived at New Orleans in late 1728 and early 1729, company officials gave preference to those planters who had met earlier obligations. This caused considerable dissatisfaction. Bienville informed the company in 1725–26 that less than 25 percent of the population in Louisiana owned any slaves and that no more than fifteen colonists (including himself) owned more than twenty. Most of the larger planters or concessions were in the neighborhood of New Orleans, with some large operations scattered about, such as the Diron Concession at Baton Rouge and the Cantillon Concession at the junction of the

---

[3] Private merchant vessels may have also engaged in the trade because in 1725 licenses were available on payment of 20 livres per head to the company. French merchants did make the Antilles run but it is unlikely that many came to Louisiana as prices in the West Indies were considerably higher than in Louisiana and the voyage was shorter. Some Louisianians sought to purchase slaves for resale in St. Domingue but the company prohibited this practice in 1722. As subsequent chapters will show, the more profitable West Indian market frequently worked a hardship on Louisiana.

Red and Ouachita rivers. Long after the Company of the Indies withdrew from Louisiana, its agents at New Orleans labored to collect debts incurred for the purchase of slaves prior to 1731.

New Orleans in the mid-1720s was not an impressive town nor did it grow rapidly. It appeared as an appendage to some of the surrounding plantations rather than as the center of a thriving agricultural community. Most of the colonists who survived their arrival during the early 1720s were distributed among the various concessions or earned a precarious existence as small farmers. There was really no domestic market for them to tap, although a limited amount of vegetables or fruits and the like could be vended in New Orleans. *Voyageurs* from the up-country wandered in and out of town. The crews of a few vessels in port increased the population temporarily, along with the tempo of life. Local Indians and slaves roamed the town selling faggots, fruits, and ashes. *Engagées* and slaves frequently drove cattle and hogs into town where they were slaughtered and bled in the open. Little more could be expected since New Orleans was not only in its infancy but was also a company town. Company vessels loaded and unloaded company goods in company stores while the distribution and handling of the goods was supervised by company agents. There were neither *négociants* nor *armateurs* in town because the company was the *négociant-armateur*. In addition to company personnel there were the troops. These were the two most important elements within the community which transformed itself from a military-administrative center into a commercial town only in the years following the company's retrocession of Louisiana to the crown.

New Orleans' future was developing beyond its palisades in the plantations and agricultural settlements that were struggling for survival up and down the Mississippi River, even as far as the Illinois country and to the west. The company was prepared to grant large tracts of land to those who would commit themselves to putting the land into production. Most of the land was granted free or with a nominal charge. Regulations spelled out the obligations of the *concessionnaires* regarding settlement and improvement. These were rarely enforced while the distribution system was chaotic. Company officials in Paris and Louisiana granted and staked out concessions for themselves and others without much attention to the resources available to develop the land. Many of the great concessions were never operative. On occasion the company decided to rationalize the land system on the basis of use and performance, but this was difficult to accomplish and more often than not confused the issue by raising the question of titles.

Under frontier conditions, abuses and disputes relative to the operation of the land system were normal. Large tracts were claimed but uncultivated, as was the case for the valuable river frontage immediately above and below New Orleans. Company officials selected choice sites for themselves and imposed feudal terms on the *habitants* settled on their lands. Many plantations, however, were established and demonstrated substantial growth during the 1730s. Most of the successful units were located within a radius of twenty-five miles from New Orleans. As the radius expanded, so too did the concentration of landholding and by the Spanish period most of the small farmers were forced out.[4]

The largest *concessionnaires* did not normally journey to Louisiana to oversee their properties. Instead they equipped vessels, contracted with *engagées*, and purchased Negroes, delegating the actual operation of the estate to stewards. Several large plantations were begun between 1719 and 1721, most belonging to individuals connected with the company or wielding influence in Paris. Law's concession at the Arkansas River was the most ambitious but it disintegrated with his fall. Two of the largest were the Paris-Duvernay Concession at Bayagoula (Bayou Goula), some eight miles above New Orleans, owned by an archopponent of the system; and the de Mézières Concession, owned jointly by the Marquis de Mézières and the Marquis de Marches. Both concessions were aided by the company at various times by generous extensions of credit and other preferential treatment while resident officials intervened quite regularly to facilitate their development. These and

---

[4] An ordinance of the king (1719) prohibited governors, lieutenant governors, and intendants from owning plantations. Governors Bienville, de la Chaise, and Perier all operated concessions. In 1728 land laws cancelled all concessions between Bayou Manchac and the Gulf while providing for the legalization of those holdings which could be justified. Eleven years later, Bienville was still engaged in efforts to obtain title to his lands.

other concessions experimented with silkworm raising and mining but finally developed into staple plantations.[5]

One of the most prosperous and heavily cultivated regions in the colony was the district between New Orleans and Cannes Brûlées, including Chapitoulas (Tchoupitoulas). Owners in this region utilized relatively large numbers of both *engagées* and slaves in the fields. Plantations were cleared along Lake Pontchartrain and Bayou St. John, below the town to the English Turn, and on the west bank of the Mississippi. By the end of the 1720s New Orleans was surrounded by a network of plantations, any two of which were probably larger economic units than the city itself. But at least there was a local hinterland to tap and the city could provide minimal storage and transportation facilities for plantation produce.[6]

During the same period, other settlements upriver and to the west took root and established commercial relations with New Orleans. On the west bank, some twenty-five miles upriver and extending for another thirty to forty miles, the German Coast was settled by Germans during the Law period, supplying New Orleans and neighboring plantations with foodstuffs but lacking the labor necessary to engage in staple farming other than tobacco. Scattered and largely undeveloped plantations existed between Cannes Brûlées and Baton Rouge. At Natchez, Fort Rosalie formed the nucleus of a town around which several concessions were organized. The Company of the Indies decided to develop tobacco at Natchez, which had a population of 350 soldiers and concessionnaires by 1721. Natchez tobacco enjoyed an excellent reputation, but its development was retarded by labor scarcities and by difficulties in packaging and shipping the crop. These problems, while not insurmountable, became academic in 1729 when the Natchez Indians rose against the

[5] Herbert Lüthy, *La banque protestante en France de la révocation de l'Édit de Nantes à la Révolution* (2 vols.; Paris, 1959–61), I, 294, points out the interesting connection between the Oglethorpe family and these two noblemen. Two sisters of James Oglethorpe, founder of Georgia, married the two Frenchmen. The de Mézières' home in Paris became a gathering place for those speculating in the Law system and the South Sea Company.

[6] The largest establishment in the area appears to have been the Chauvin plantation with 87 slaves and twice the number of livestock of any other plantation. Sr. Du Breuil, who will be discussed in various circumstances in later chapters, worked a plantation of 46 slaves and more than 100 head of stock in 1727, representing significant growth over 1721.

French. The garrison and settlers were decimated and the survivors abandoned their lands in fleeing to New Orleans. This blow, coupled with the Indian wars which followed, drained the colony of resources which it could hardly spare during the subsequent decade. The farthest removed of the settlements within the present-day borders of Louisiana was Natchitoches, from where corn was shipped to the workers at New Orleans as early as 1719. A few struggling concessions existed in an area supporting some three hundred whites and Negroes during the 1720s and 1730s, while the Spanish, always sensitive to the proximity of potential intruders, occupied a post a few leagues from the French at Los Adaes.

New Orleans' artificial hinterland comprised areas suitable for agricultural exploitation; the problem was to discover the crops best adapted to particular locales and capable of cultivation with the limited human and technological resources available. Crozat achieved some success along the Gulf Coast in the establishment of a lumber industry, pitch and tar production, and the export of skins and pelts drawn from the upper Alabama River country. The smallness of the population thwarted all efforts to develop a domestic food supply or cash crops, while minimal efforts to introduce livestock failed to guarantee a local meat supply.

The Company of the Indies enjoyed somewhat greater success in charting the possibilities for agricultural development, although there were still some doubts as to priorities at the end of the company's reign. One of the major tasks of the crown was to set up priorities through the creation of bounties and other incentives favoring the production of certain crops. The company's primary objective was to develop crops or other commodities marketable in France, thus providing the colonists with a means of exchange for imported goods.

Rice was quickly developed as a major food crop, the more important—under both French and Spanish rule—because of the failure of wheat crops in Illinois and the uncertainty of flour supplies arriving from overseas. Even good rice yields failed to resolve the problem of subsistence which plagued the colony throughout the entire French period and into the Spanish. Garden products relieved some of the pressure but even these were normally scarce and expensive until the opening up of the Atakapas and Opelousas districts.

Of the cash crops, indigo, tobacco, and lumber products provided the colonists with the best returns and were, with the exception of lumber, readily accepted for export to France. Indigo became the principal cash crop of, and was largely confined to, the larger plantations around New Orleans because it required both a large initial capital outlay for machinery and a substantial labor force. Most planters, lacking the means to establish this culture, depended upon tobacco while supplementing their incomes with lumber whenever possible.

Tobacco, suitable to both small farms and plantations, quickly became the major money crop in the area between New Orleans and Natchez. Its growth was encouraged by the company through the distribution of Negroes, bounties for new areas of cultivation, quality controls, and similar measures. In an effort to overcome transportation difficulties at Natchez, the company in 1724 established a tobacco factory to construct hogsheads and press the tobacco for shipment. These hopeful beginnings were nullified in 1729 by the Natchez massacre, and the confusion was compounded by the company's retrocession of Louisiana to the crown which required new procedures for the marketing of tobacco and other commodities.

Early voyagers to Louisiana were struck by the lumber potential of the area. It was thought that the abundant stands of pitch pine, cypress, cedar, and oak could fulfill West Indian demands for construction timber and barrel staves, as well as provide the raw materials necessary for local shipyards. Although the West Indies drew some lumber from the colony during the 1720s, inadequate transportation and the bulky nature of the goods retarded the advance of the industry. As the plantations became more highly specialized, skilled Negroes fabricated lumber products more suitable for the small vessels engaged in the island trade, and in the post-company period the crown promoted the production of pitch and tar.

While New Orleans was developing the capacity to serve an expanding artificial hinterland, similar services were provided for its natural hinterland, including in the Southeast most of the present-day states of Georgia, Alabama, southern Tennessee and Mississippi, and to the north the Illinois or Wabash country. This entire area was in dispute between the British, French, and Spanish, each in alliance with one or more of the several Indian tribes who exercised a tenuous sovereignty over various portions of these lands. Furs, skins, and security were the prizes sought after along this frontier.

French strategy, devised by Bienville, was to maintain a chain of outposts from Mobile to Fort Toulouse across to Natchez, and up the Mississippi to the Yazoo, the Arkansas, and the Illinois country in order to protect Louisiana proper, isolate the Choctaw from the British and maintain control of the Mississippi River. At stake were fifty thousand deerskins in addition to the valuable pelts obtained from the Upper Mississippi and Indian auxiliaries during times of European conflict. Success in this chaotic field of Indian diplomacy shifted back and forth between the British and the French. The explosion at Natchez temporarily disrupted the French strategy.[7]

Special value was placed by the French on the Illinois country, strategically located between New France and the Lower Mississippi Valley, potentially capable of dominating the fur traffic of both the Upper Mississippi and Lower Ohio rivers, thought to contain unrivalled mineral wealth, and to be suitable for the large-scale production of wheat required in lower Louisiana. The Company of the Indies, recognizing the importance of the Illinois, succeeded in having the area attached to Louisiana in 1717. A small population (estimated at two hundred in 1728) which limited agricultural productivity in the area; the distance and uncertainties of traffic with New Orleans; and recurrent Indian crises which hampered the fur trade and the development of mining operations all combined to lessen the actual value of Illinois to lower Louisiana. The full potential of the relationship would emerge only with the increases in settlement and agricultural productivity that followed the American Revolution.

The uprising against the French in 1729 destroyed the settlement

[7] Illinois supplied lower Louisiana with occasional shipments of flour, lead, and copper, drew about 11,000 livres worth of goods from New Orleans during the 1720s, and shipped about that much fur to company officials at New Orleans.

around Fort Rosalie and at the Yazoo and severed communications via the Mississippi. The revolt was part of a British-supported conspiracy that almost included the Choctaw, who backed out only at the last minute. With Choctaw assistance, the French took their vengeance against the Natchez, who were eliminated as a tribe, leaving only remnants operating out of Chickasaw country against the French. For a brief moment in December the French believed the conspiracy to be general. Alarm and consternation prevailed at New Orleans as planters and traders streamed into the town for protection. Communications with the Illinois were cut and, although soon reopened, remained extremely hazardous during the decade of Indian wars that followed. The fur trade was damaged, men and supplies were diverted from productive purposes to the punishment of the Natchez and Chickasaw coconspirators. It was at this point that the company gave up an increasingly expensive colony to the crown.

New Orleans possessed a hinterland of infinite possibilties and almost limitless extent. As of 1730 few of the possibilities had been realized. Not without products suitable for export to France, the colony, however, lacked the manpower to produce these goods in quantities large and valuable enough to pay for imports and guarantee profitable returns for those engaged in the carrying trade. Only a tiny portion of the artificial hinterland was cleared and settled, and its yields hardly sufficed to fill even two or three of the small merchantmen that plied the Louisiana route from France.

Even though the Company of the Indies achieved economic success in areas where the prerequisites for trade antedated their presence, the reorganized company, shorn of much power, could not cope with the demands and exigencies of so immense an undeveloped region. While the colonists were struggling to tame the settled and contiguous lands of Louisiana, chaos ruled in the natural hinterland. Prepared to trade with the Indians, the company was, on the other hand, ill equipped to pursue diplomatic and military competition with the British to guarantee that trade. Even less was the company competent to engage in a diplomacy reflecting the colonial and European aspirations of the French government.

Nonetheless, both Crozat's company and the Company of the

Indies created a foundation in Louisiana upon which a substantial commerce could be raised. A major port had been built on the Mississippi. Certain crops had proved more advantageous than others. Patterns of trade had evolved with various parts of the world and rudimentary facilities for the handling of imports and exports existed in New Orleans. In short, an economy, however primitive, did exist when the crown gained control of the colony.

The letters patent of August, 1717, establishing the Company of the West, endowed the corporation with virtually complete political and economic authority in Louisiana. Supplemented by liberal commercial benefits in France which became almost all-inclusive as the company added to its interests, the charter was more than adequate to the fulfillment of company objectives. The Company of the Indies exercised a fuller sovereignty more efficiently than had Crozat his lesser powers. It must also be noted that the company used its authority with greater liberality under Law than after the collapse of the system.

As the companies were commercial organizations, procedures had to be evolved for the achievement of economic ends. This involved more than putting people in the colony, a task which Crozat could not perform and which the Company of the West may have performed through methods too swift, arbitrary, and disorganized to allow for efficient assimilation and distribution. The purpose of both companies was to extract profits from the sale of marketable colonial produce in France and elsewhere; to sell manufactured and other goods in the colony; to control all phases of the above both in the colony and in France; and to provide any and all services which might further these purposes either directly or indirectly. Although primarily concerned with economic factors, the companies could not ignore the noneconomic. Indeed, because the companies were in reality establishing societies with the raw materials of people, place, and time, it is unrewarding to attempt a distinction between noneconomic and economic factors.

In order to take profits out of Louisiana, the companies had to provide the means of production, incentives to production, and production priorities. The corporations possessed the authority to establish price schedules for colonial and imported goods received at company depots. An acceptable currency had to be supplied in Louisiana for purposes of local exchange and receivable in payment for remittances on France. A system of distribution had to be established to handle imports and exports which involved marketing and quality controls as well as details such as packaging and warehousing. Absolutely essential were the concomitant requirements of adequate shipping at reasonable freights and markets for the disposal of the goods. The companies had also to guarantee the equitable treatment of the colonists and protect company interests by controlling and limiting the private initiative of company officials in the colony. This latter goal was more in the realm of a wish than a possibility because the officials functioned with power and privilege in an economy of scarcity.

For our purposes, the basic political problems of this government were factionalism, which caused economic favoritism, and the inability of either Crozat or his successors, in spite of repeated efforts, to prevent their appointed officials from engaging in private economic ventures at the expense of both employer and colony. Factionalism and intracolonial strife were chronic in Louisiana from 1712 to the retrocession. The central figure in the political warfare was Bienville, at all times jealous of his prerogatives and economic interests and dogmatic regarding the making of policy for the colony. Conditions did not improve when Bienville was recalled to France and replaced by Perier in 1726, a move accompanied by a shake-up in the Superior Council in which Bienville's friends were replaced by other officials.[8]

Many of the influences which made factionalism part of the daily life of the New Orleans government derived from company policies and company failures to meet urgent needs. Company failures can,

[8] Most historians of Louisiana view Perier's administration as a disaster for the colony. They view the shake-up of 1726 as caused by internal conditions in Louisiana. See Pierre Heinrich, *La Louisiane sous la Compagnie des Indes, 1717–1731* (Paris, 1908), 190–91; Walter Adolphe Roberts, *Lake Pontchartrain* (Indianapolis, 1946), 51–57. Professor James D. Hardy, Jr., of Louisiana State University, engaged in a much-needed study of Bienville, suggests that the removals of 1726 might best be explained through reference to the end of the regency, the accession of Louis XV and Fleury, and the efforts of the new administration to sweep both old Law supporters and antagonists out of office.

at least partially, be ascribed to influences and developments beyond the control of the corporations. Crozat, for example, did not succeed in meeting even the most basic needs of the colony. His rule was heavy handed; the monopoly he enjoyed was used with neither ingenuity nor sensitivity to the legitimate needs of the colonists. He exercised his control rigidly but to no avail and finally lost his investment. The record of the Company of the West and its heirs was somewhat more constructive. All, however, confronted similar problems, some of which went unresolved during the entire French period. Many of these problems reflect more precisely the difficulty of establishing a colony rather than any inherent defects in monopolistic organizations. A series of interrelated problems concerning a monetary system, exchange, and price structures required solutions that neither company was capable of evolving.

Of all the areas of colonial life where the monopolistic corporations intervened, few were so crucial as the area of exchange and prices. The general practice was to set prices on all goods exchanged between the companies and the colonists and to keep in company hands the control of all phases of the commerce. Crozat's policies burdened the fragile economy of the colony with price schedules which fixed high prices for imported goods and low prices for colonial produce. However, shipping and distribution costs were too high and market and productive capacities in Louisiana too small to warrant a feasible alternative for Crozat.

Strung out along the Gulf, the colonists were virtually without the means of paying for imports. Lumber, pitch and tar, skins and furs were not available in sufficient quantities nor valuable enough to balance out accounts. Money was almost unobtainable. Inflation, near famine conditions, no means of exchange, dissidence in the colony—all created a situation which Crozat failed to resolve largely because his resources were not ample enough and because he failed to establish a trade with the Spanish.

The Company of the Indies exercised a more effective and total control over the economy of Louisiana. During the Law period, when the organization was engaged in the colonization of Louisiana and the economic center shifted to New Orleans, the company established its basic price and exchange policies. Reaffirmed during the period of reorganization, the policies were subject to occasional and slight modification by colonial officials. Seeking profit as had Crozat, the company was willing to accept lower prices from the colonists for imported goods while paying higher prices for colonial produce. The company also provided currency for the colony but was unable to protect it from serious depreciation.

Prices were set in Louisiana—for Negroes, crops, other colonial products, and imported goods—according to the difficulty of accessibility of certain districts. In New Orleans and the Gulf settlements, goods were sold at a 50 percent markup upon the invoice price; at the Illinois at 100 percent. Purchases of all imports were restricted to company stores at New Orleans, Mobile, and Biloxi. By 1725 the latter two derived most of their stock from New Orleans, the center of distribution for the colony.[9]

In the period of Law most of these regulations were irrelevant because there were virtually no crops for export, nor were there any vessels to distribute them locally, nor a consumer market with the ability to pay for the goods. But by 1722 or 1723 the surviving immigrants were located on farms or on concessions with strong resources and good locations producing cash crops, and a degree of stability settled on Louisiana. Company affairs in France were put in order. New Orleans with its own small domestic market was developing facilities to handle the import and export trade. A pricing system became operative and the immediate target of vocal criticism by the colonists, who demanded adequate supplies of staple items, additional Negroes, and company purchase of their produce at the same margin of profit obtained by the organization on its sales to the planters. Depreciation of colonial money and the predictable shortage, if not absence, of specie threatened the stability of the structure.

In 1717 the French government announced the issue of paper money for Louisiana, New France, and Martinique. By 1719 some 25 million livres in notes were available for circulation in Louisiana, redeemable in bills of exchange on France but nontransferable. By

---

[9] Packaging regulations were established under which the company assumed responsibility for establishing the quality of all goods and providing compensation to the colonists if packaging expenses were high. With the exception of tobacco, beaver pelts, and deerskins, the colonists were permitted to make private shipments to France at company freight rates.

the end of the year they had depreciated 100 percent. The reorganized Company of the Indies attempted to provide a sound currency by first introducing copper money, as a marginal currency, and card money. After a shaky start, the copper circulated with some success, although at a depreciated value that was stabilized in 1725 by amending price schedules to reflect the depreciation of the currency.

The stabilization policy prevented further depreciation until 1727 when copper money was made legal tender in France. Copper fled the colony just as had specie, leaving Louisiana again without any medium of exchange. Treasury notes were issued by local officials but since no specie was received, these could be negotiated only at great discount and then only when vessels were in port. As more paper was issued to meet current debts, its value further declined and business was carried on only with difficulty. Resident officials were compelled to accept produce in payment of company debts while the company, in an effort to retire the paper, directed additional cargoes of goods to the colony which could be purchased with paper at 50 percent of face value. Little paper remained in circulation when Louisiana became a crown colony but the problem of money and exchange remained unresolved.

Under the most favorable conditions during the next three decades, remittances to France were never regularized. Debtors in Louisiana wished to meet their obligations in produce or in the current money and creditors demanded specie or letters of exchange on the royal treasury. Merchants in France lacked enthusiasm for the New Orleans trade because of the uncertainty of remittances. They found it difficult to collect debts in Louisiana and to remit the proceeds to France. In 1731 when the crown faced the problem of convincing French merchants that a profitable trade was possible with New Orleans, it had to offer some guarantees that remittances to France would be facilitated. These endeavors will form the subject matter of chapter 4.

Although Law tried to interest private merchants in the Louisiana trade, French merchants were unwilling to venture their capital in Louisiana and the colony was dependent upon the company fleet for its sustenance. The adequacy of shipping available to the colony has been challenged.[10] Full shipping statistics relative to the Louisiana trade are lacking for the period 1713–30, but the sources utilized in this study have yielded what I believe to be a fairly complete list of vessels—summarized in Table I—which made voyages to Louisiana.

TABLE I

Annual Arrivals of Vessels in Louisiana,
1713–30, with Incidental Information

1713..4	1722..12 (6 positively company ships, 2 probable)
1714..6 (1 smuggler seized)	1723.. 4 (3 positively company ships, 1 probable)
1715..2	1724.. 5 (4 positively company ships, 1 probable)
1716..4	1725.. 7 (all company)
1717..3	1726.. 3 (all company)
1718..9	1727.. 6 (all company)
1719..12 (including 6 warships)	1728.. 7 (all company)
1720..29 (including 8 warships)	1729.. 8 (7 positively company ships, 1 possibly a Rasteau slaver)*
1721..16 (11 positively company ships, 2 probable)	1730.. 6 (all company)

* The Rasteaus were La Rochelle merchants who will be treated extensively in chapter 4 and other sections

After the Treaty of Utrecht, the merchant fleet of France experienced rapid growth, employing in 1730 more than 5,000 vessels and 40,000 seamen in a foreign trade which had quadrupled in value since 1716. The Company of the Indies possessed an impressive fleet during this period. By 1720, 105 vessels displayed the company pennant. During the remainder of the decade, 75 to 85 vessels, not counting coasters and smaller vessels, composed the fleet. Sailings

[10] See N. M. Miller Surrey, *The Commerce of Louisiana during the French Regime, 1699–1763, Columbia University Studies in History, Economics, and Public Law,* LXXI (New York, 1916), 77.

were mostly from Lorient and Nantes. About 50 percent of these vessels were at sea during any given year, say 40 vessels each year between 1729 and 1730, and 50 before that. With this in mind, it appears from Table I that a high proportion of these resources was directed to Louisiana in 1720–21; 42 percent in 1720 and 26 percent in 1721. This more than served Louisiana's needs and most of these vessels left the colony in ballast. The question of available tonnage is not so easily resolvable for the period subsequent to 1721 and the data available hardly justify more than an educated guess.

It is not enough to know how many vessels arrived at New Orleans in each year after 1721. Information is required relative to the tonnage of the vessels and the season of their arrival. Vessels departing New Orleans before the harvest or arriving after the bulk of it was carried off had little impact on the export trade, although their inbound cargoes may have been in great demand. Most vessels about which information is available departed France in the spring—in order to arrive in the Gulf before the hurricane season—frequently stopping at St. Domingue or Martinique before continuing on to New Orleans. They then lay over in New Orleans until the fall crop came in, putting to sea again in November and December, arriving in France eight weeks later. The schedule was fairly routine during the company period but was subject to great variation when Louisiana was opened up to private merchants. Most of the company vessels engaged in the New Orleans trade were between 450 and 600 tons while the private vessels engaged during the crown period averaged about 250 tons.

Information relative to the value of inbound cargoes is scanty and is concentrated largely in 1720 and 1721. But these were the two years in which the organization commanded its greatest assets and made its supreme effort to colonize the area. Of some thirty-four company arrivals in 1720–21, six carried either colonists and their belongings, slaves, or supplies for concessions. Twelve vessels ranging in size from 340 to 520 tons carried cargoes averaging 185,000 livres in value. This appears to be about half the average value of cargoes carried in company ships to other destinations. It is assumed that the average cargo to Louisiana remained constant between 1723 and 1730. If this is the case, forty-six arrivals during the above years carried 8.5 million livres worth of goods to New Orleans, or an average annual import of a million livres. This figure formed .007 percent of average annual French exports from 1721 to 1723.

There are no figures available that measure the value of colonial exports. Yet something, however conjectural, must be said on this score. The company (and private merchants later) completed their cargoes with difficulty, many vessels taking on bricks or other ballast, and headed for the French islands for a cargo. The company ordered Governor Perier not to allow empty vessels to leave New Orleans but to fill their holds with lumber. Moreover, colonial exports were of a bulky nature and of proportionately less value per cargo than imports. On the basis of such subjective evidence, it is suggested that colonial exports were worth about half the imports, or some 500,000 livres annually. Four or five vessels were sufficient to carry the exports to France. At least this number arrived in New Orleans in each year between 1718 and 1730 except 1726. This is not to say that shipping was always available but that it generally was.[11]

Both the colonists and the company, then, had reasons for dissatisfaction with shipping conditions at New Orleans. Year in and year out, between 1723 and 1730, the company allocated close to 15 percent of its seaborne fleet to the service of Louisiana while Louisiana returns formed no more than 5 percent of total receipts. Moreover, the company lost at least six vessels in Gulf waters during this period. On the other hand, there is no question as to the frequency of food shortages in New Orleans. It did not take the colonists long—after the retrocession—to learn that the company's performance compared quite closely with the crown's.

Although Louisiana's productivity did not support a large trade with France, it was in fact established and regularly pursued to the degree that production and consumption in Louisiana warranted. By

[11] In 1722 the appearance of the *Profond* in the roadstead of Ship Island provoked jubilation in New Orleans and the singing of a *Te Deum* in thanks for the coming succor. In March, 1724, the company store at New Orleans held large quantities of Natchez tobacco because no shipping was available to France. Two months later the *Gironde* reached New Orleans, followed closely by the *Bellone* and the *St. André*. The *Bellone* took the available cargo, departed, and sank. The *Gironde* went to St. Domingue. When last heard of, the *St. André* had landed its crew to cut wood for lack of other useful employment.

no means affluent, nevertheless, plantations in the Lower Mississippi Valley returned profits to their owners and supplied New Orleans with provisions sufficient to insure the continuation of the export trade with France and the slow growth of a trade with the West Indies and certain Spanish colonies. However, the company derived little, if any, profit from the connection; colonists stood indebted to it for some millions of livres in 1731. The corporation recognized the marginal value of Louisiana after 1722; that is, after reorganization ended the developmental purposes of the organization in Louisiana. Mindful of the proximity of its colony to those of Spain, the company hoped to develop commercial relations between the colonies that would compensate for the paucity of trade between Louisiana and France.

Certain general features of the trade with the Spanish colonies are clear. Goods of French or foreign manufacture, rather than Louisiana goods, were the major items in the trade which was conducted by French merchantmen with French crews under the orders of French *négociants* and at their expense and risk. New Orleans served as a depot for this trade and for the most part New Orleans merchants so engaged acted as agents for mercantile houses in France. Profits from the trade did not remain in the port, which cannot be described even as a middleman in the trade because the goods and monies involved were not owned by the merchants of the city. Indeed, French merchants developed the custom of sending to New Orleans goods more suitable for the Spanish trade than for Louisiana and sending goods to the French West Indies for resale in Louisiana. The French islands served as middlemen in this trade. The company, as the sole merchant in New Orleans, initiated these patterns, which were not especially advantageous to the municipality.

Crozat and the Company of the Indies, after 1722, assigned considerable priority to the opening of trade via Louisiana with the Spanish colonies which were thought to be accessible to Louisiana by both land and sea. Crozat focused his attentions on the overland route via Natchitoches into East Texas and, hopefully, New Mexico, the latter also thought to be approachable from bases along the

Arkansas and Missouri Rivers to the north, but little profit resulted from expeditions sent out from those points.

Threats to Spanish exclusionist policies via the Gulf were more serious and more successful. This was the traditional base for the interloping trade with the French headquartered at St. Domingue and Martinique, the British at Jamaica, and the Dutch at Curaçao. Occupation of Louisiana afforded the French a potentially excellent site, on the flank of Spain's empire, from which to carry on the contraband trade. Such trade was Crozat's goal and it was implemented whenever possible by his agents in Louisiana, although not always to his profit and normally without profit. Spanish coast guard vessels stopped and pillaged French vessels on the open sea, assuming their purpose to be illicit trade with Spain's possessions. A small commerce was carried on with Spanish Florida, but the French were usually thwarted in their efforts to introduce goods into Havana and Vera Cruz. By the end of 1716 Crozat owned at least 2,000,000 livres worth of Spanish trade goods but was unable to dispose of them.

Under Law, the company subordinated the Spanish trade to the principal objective of populating Louisiana. The reorganized Company of the Indies upgraded the importance of this trade and experimented with a new approach—that of attracting Spanish vessels to Louisiana rather than seeking entry to Spanish ports. It was decided to establish a depot for this purpose at the Balize rather than to allow or compel Spanish ships to push on to New Orleans. This presumed the existence of a permanent and well-chosen inventory of goods, for the Spanish might appear off the Balize at any moment. Unfortunately, the inventory was frequently depleted. In 1727 and 1728 Spanish vessels crossed and recrossed the bar without leaving their piastres.

In 1728 there was an attempt to regularize the trade by sending an agent, François Chastang, who was responsible for establishing the commerce on a sound basis. He and the major resident officials, Perier and de la Chaise, were instructed to gather information as to Spanish needs and to inform themselves of exchange rates and Spanish weights and measures. Credit was denied the Spanish but allowance was made for an exchange of goods marketable in France. Chastang arrived at New Orleans but his job, as well as the company's program for the Spanish trade, went up in smoke along with Fort Rosalie at the Natchez post.

The crown patterned its approach to the Spanish trade upon that of the company while a few of the French merchants who agreed to enter into the trade with New Orleans did so, at least partially, with the possibility of the Spanish trade in mind. The pace of the trade accelerated during the years of crown control, aided and abetted by Anglo-Spanish hostilities, but it was never safe commerce, even by the standards of the eighteenth century.

A mutually advantageous connection seemed possible between Louisiana and the French West Indies, which drew many of their supplies through a contraband trade with New England. Louisiana loomed as a potential source of lumber, brick and tile, foodstuff, and livestock. However, Crozat did little to develop a connection with the islands and, although the Company of the Indies adopted a more liberal view toward the coasting trade, most of the commerce involved the forwarding of supplies from the islands to Louisiana. Some lumber and Negroes were exchanged, but the uncertainty of remittances from Louisiana plagued this trade just as it did that with France and the Spanish. Agents in St. Domingue informed de la Chaise in 1727 that no shipments of cattle to Louisiana were possible because return cargoes were unavailable.

The Company of the Indies conducted a much more extensive trade with the islands than with Louisiana. Virtually all of its vessels that headed for Louisiana touched first at the islands, returning again on the voyage to France. This pattern provided some transportation to the islands but the practice was not to the benefit of Louisiana. The company frequently unloaded its cargoes in the islands, normally Cap Français, St. Domingue, or St. Pierre, Martinique, declining to continue the voyage to Louisiana because of the availability of return cargoes in the islands. This not only delayed the arrival of goods in New Orleans but their reshipment increased costs for both the company and the colonists. The practice, adopted by private merchants, harmed Louisiana, although it created a more or less regular traffic between the colonies. It meant that French merchants sold their goods to island traders, who then reexported to Louisiana what could not be sold locally and at a higher price than would have prevailed in a direct commerce between France and New Orleans. Louisianians complained and the French government sought remedies, but the natural character of the trade led in this direction. It was a problem which New Orleans could not fully solve even in the American period.

The Natchez uprising and consequent Indian wars placed the company in an impossible financial situation. Denying its ability to finance a general Indian war or to provide for the defense of the colony, the company requested that the crown assume control of Louisiana.[12]

At the time of retrocession and even before, the company admitted that its past efforts in Louisiana had not met with unalloyed success. Laying most of the blame on the British and their machinations among the Indians, which compelled the company to divert much money to defense and Indian diplomacy, the corporation maintained that this obligation properly belonged to the crown. This evaluation, also reached by the crown after 1731, recognized that the Indian trade held little economic potential and was mainly a matter of security. After Natchez, it was obvious that posts did not guarantee security against British and Indian penetration. Only large numbers of colonists could accomplish this. If Louisiana possessed strategic assets in the contest for empire with Great Britain, the company argued that the crown to that degree should assume the burden of exploiting those advantages.

Critics emphasized questions about numerous errors and failures in the administration of Louisiana, most of which the company could partially answer. They maintained that plural leadership in Louisiana created factionalism and inefficiency, to which the company replied that the division of responsibilities between a governor and *ordonnateur* and the existence of a Superior Council was the norm

[12] Between 1722 and 1730 company expenditures in Louisiana averaged 502,000 livres for salaries, Indian presents and trade, and administrative charges. This did not include monies advanced in credits and bounties to create a commerce in the colony. The Natchez uprising forced the 1731 budget up to 786,000 livres. Under Crozat, administrative expenses during his last four years averaged 92,000 livres annually.

in French colonial government. The company, the critics further pointed out, failed to utilize Louisiana's admirable position to develop trade with Spain's colonies by sea and through Natchitoches. Admitting both the potential and the irregularity of its efforts to maintain goods in Louisiana to attract Spanish merchants, the company could offer some defense by emphasizing the difficulty of the seaborne commerce caused by the vigilance of Spanish officials. As for building up the overland trade, that was only a vision and hardly worth the effort. In any event, the benefits to Louisiana of such trade were problematical because the merchandise was neither produced nor owned by colonists.

The company appeared especially vulnerable to charges of short-sightedness and illiberality in nurturing the agricultural resources of Louisiana. If it diverted sufficient resources to tobacco and paid a fair price, Louisiana could relieve France of the need to enrich the British by purchasing their tobacco. Then, some critics claimed, tobacco should be emphasized. Other commentators who might frequently agree on this point, censured the company for not fostering production of silk, indigo, lumber, pitch and tar, hides and furs, hemp and flax, waxberries, and cotton. It was damned for not paying sufficient attention to tobacco and damned for emphasizing tobacco at the expense of indigo or some other crop or mineral. How, inquired critics, could any agricultural progress occur when labor was in short supply? How, responded the company, could it be expected to supply Negroes to Louisiana's planters who already owed upwards of 3 million livres for prior shipments of slaves and goods?

As for agriculture, the company perceived quite clearly the benefits of both a staple policy and agricultural diversification. It had established a conveniently located market town on the Mississippi River and extended large credits to colonists. Concentration upon tobacco alone would lead to economic disaster in Louisiana should prices ever decline. Louisiana tobacco was more expensive and of poorer quality than English varieties. And the tobacco industry required price supports in the form of drawbacks or bounties on shipments which the commercial company could not afford. Vessels carrying nothing but tobacco could not meet expenses because the value of the weed was small in proportion to its bulk. The same was true for lumber and pelts.

The sum of these problems was more than the company could cope with. Only the national government possessed resources sufficient to the task, a task that would be less demanding than that which confronted either Crozat or the Company of the Indies. Plantations, the nucleus of a city, patterns of trade, and crop possibilities had been experimented with and established. As a single unit in a multiunit empire of worldwide extent, the question was the priority to be assigned Louisiana.

3

New Orleans and Its Hinterlands
1730–1760

THE decade 1730–40 was one of distress for New Orleans which events during the 1740s did little to relieve. Recurrent failures of both cash and food crops caused occasional suffering, persistent hardship for planters, and grave difficulties for French merchants who had succumbed to the blandishments of the Minister of the Marine and engaged in the Louisiana trade. Devastating hurricanes, heavy rains, and flooding in 1732, 1734, and 1740 alternated with years of drought to destroy promising crops. The repercussions of natural calamity which might be overcome with time and patience lingered on, nourished by the man-made disasters following in the wake of the Natchez massacre. Few Frenchmen remained at Natchez, which had furnished the bulk of Louisiana's tobacco. The colony girded itself for a war that dragged on with inconspicuous success until its skirmishes were swallowed up in the War of the Austrian Succession (1744–48). Acts of God and acts of man, the deadly rise of prices throughout the two decades, shortages of supplies and funds from France, paper money issues and rapid depreciation, dissension in the colony, mutual distrust among officials form the somber setting for the isolated French colony. Through 1763 peace, real security, and a touch of prosperity favored the colony only during the eight-year interval between 1748 and the outbreak of the Seven Years' War in 1756.

During most of the period, the colony fortunately enjoyed experienced leadership in the persons of Bienville, who returned as governor in 1733; Edine Gatien Salmon, the *ordonnateur* who served from 1731 to 1743; the Marquis de la Vaudreuil, successor to Bienville; and Governor Louis Billouart, Chevalier de Kerlérec (1752–

63), who followed Vaudreuil. All but Kerlérec served under the competent administration of Jean-Frédéric Phélypeaux, Comte de Maurepas and Pontchartrain, Minister of the Marine from 1723 to 1749. None managed to do more than maintain a precarious equilibrium in the colony, save Vaudreuil who guided the colony into its one happy period, leaving a relatively thriving community to Kerlérec.

The colony was in miserable shape when Governor Vaudreuil, sick with dysentery and fever, arrived off the Balize in May, 1743. Colonial finances were chaotic because of the extraordinary expenses incurred in warring against the Chickasaw and a rebel band of Choctaw. Bienville and, especially, Salmon were made the scapegoats for this situation. Salmon, replaced by Lénormant as *ordonnateur*, returned to France in disgrace. The experiences of the newcomers in New Orleans, blighted by mutual distrust and dislike, were no more rewarding than those of their predecessors. Lénormant arrived during an inflationary crisis. Flour, normally retailing for 30 to 35 livres the barrel, was selling for 365 livres. Lénormant's assignment, which will be treated separately in chapter 6, was to liquidate the depreciated paper then circulating. Vaudreuil, not yet in office a year, received news of the French declaration of war against Great Britain in March, 1744.

The War of the Austrian Succession inevitably engaged France and Britain as antagonists in the general contest. For Louisiana, the French declaration meant more of the same treatment, but much more. New Orleans already felt the impact of Anglo-Spanish hostilities as several French vessels had been seized by the belligerents in Caribbean and Gulf waters. New Orleans, in the fall of 1741, buzzed with facts and fiction regarding the British seige of Santiago de Cuba, Georgia's attacks on St. Augustine, and the intentions of the British Admiral Vernon toward the French, should the contest involve both nations.

Shipping between France and New Orleans became increasingly hazardous from 1740 to 1743. Not only did Britain patrol the approaches to Spain's colonies, capturing numerous French vessels bringing supplies to the Spanish, but some French vessels, which succeeded in finding protection under the guns of Cuban forts, suffered confiscation by Spanish officials who refused to allow the war to serve as a pretext for the introduction of prohibited goods. Capture by either antagonist aggravated the deteriorating economic conditions in Louisiana and its capital. Then, with the coming of French belligerency, the reality of war with the foremost naval power in the world was experienced by New Orleans in July, 1744.

On the thirtieth of that month, the frail wooden buildings of the capital were shaken by the reverberations of cannon fire. Civilians flocked to the levee, the militia and troops were mustered, dragging rusty cannon into place, as the town was spectator to a naval battle between three British privateers and two French merchantmen. After two hours the attacking vessels, buffeted by the swift current and unable to maneuver effectively against the broadsides of the moored French vessels, withdrew, abandoning one severely damaged ship. The French lost two sailors and—how, it is unknown—a woman of quality with child. Although the enemy was repulsed, the penetration itself could only contribute to a sense of insecurity and isolation that intensified as the war progressed and as all efforts to achieve a modicum of security against the British and Indians seemed incapable of achievement.

During the long years of war, Vaudreuil's letters to his superiors mournfully reiterate the hardships experienced by the colonists because the lack of supplies and the virtual absence of contact with the mother country. A similar quality permeates letters to France during the Seven Years' War. The capture of the king's ship *L'Éléphant* by the British in 1745, with the ill-starred Salmon aboard, on its return voyage to France dealt a blow to the colony no less severe than that suffered at the loss of the *Bellone* two decades earlier. *S. M. L'Éléphant* carried a rich cargo of deerskins, tobacco, and indigo, in addition to almost 26,000 piastres and a large sum in letters of exchange. Expressions of foreboding and desperate appeals for aid had particular relevance to the state of Franco-Indian relations. Always short of the necessary Indian trade goods, colonial officials uttered dire predictions of future disaster if the Indians were not cared for.

And so it went. Indian wars, absorbed into a European conflict, were followed by the news of peace in 1749, touching off lively demonstrations in New Orleans, the chanting of a *Te Deum*, and mass pledges of service to His Majesty. An all too brief respite—tinged with prosperity—came, only to disappear when news of another war reached the settlements. After this war, there was to be no new beginning for the French in Louisiana. The flag of another nation was to grace the staff in the Place d'Armes.

When the crown took possession of Louisiana in 1731, the royal wealth was not noticeably augmented. The total population of the territory stood at about five thousand, including three thousand slaves with most colonists concentrated in New Orleans or nearby and a thousand soldiers and male civilians in the town proper. The total population of the colony may well have decreased through 1745 while New Orleans' population remained fairly stable. Troop reinforcements, people drifting in from surrounding areas, and a few immigrants compensated for losses caused by epidemic, natural death, or other causes. Sickness in 1740 carried off close to 10 percent of the population. Between 1745 and 1763 the white population grew, particularly in New Orleans, and at the close of the Seven Years' War, the number of residents in the town approached five thousand whites and Negroes. Most of the increase came between 1748 and 1756 when the crown made some effort to stimulate immigration to Louisiana. The Negro population of the colony was variously estimated at four thousand in 1741 and between six thousand and ten thousand in 1763. The latter seems unrealistic and even the lower figure is probably high.

Because stone was very scarce and generally imported, the town's construction was largely of wood. The number of brick homes increased and provided a market for the production of three kilns located at the city's gates. Limestone was available from the infinite supply of shells on Lake Pontchartrain's beaches. Shells also provided the first surfacing material for city streets. The city formed a crescent of close to a league's circumference, backed up on the river with only sporadic palisading. Basically the town was open and without defense. Spacious enough streets, laid out in straight lines, probably afforded passage for more boats than vehicles when the levee gave way, as in 1735. Pedestrians and livestock were in

little danger from wild drivers until the 1750s, when most towns-
men of means owned carriages. Small shops, residences, chapels of
the religious orders, the Ursuline hospital, the king's few buildings,
and the shed serving as the market building were the prominent
structures in the frontier community. The town had not really begun to sprawl and push back the plantations which extended to the
city gates. Aside from the few manufactories located on the out-
skirts of the city, the waterfront and cabarets were the centers of
greatest activity in town.

The port of New Orleans handled a substantial and increasing
amount of traffic between 1730 and 1760, although it was by no
means comparable to that of the late Spanish period and thereafter.
Before New Orleans, the river was nearly a mile wide and in places
close to sixty fathoms deep, providing anchorages where vessels of
up to a thousand tons could ride with their sides close to the levees.
At this time there was no real problem of crowding, but occasionally
four or five vessels would appear together, all eager to unload, take
on cargo, and depart. Traffic of smaller vessels was normally quite
heavy, with canoes, dugouts, pirogues, batteaux or flats of various
sizes and shapes, and some river sailing vessels crowding the levee
front bringing farmers and their produce to market. The market,
the king's storehouses, and the intendant's quarters were directly in
front of the anchorage. This was the nerve center of the colony—
the site of congregation for merchants and planters, for Negro long-
shoremen, for the peddlers of the town, and for the incoming seamen, anxious to sample the recreational delights offered in the city.

The Balize was a serious bottleneck, expensive to maintain, but it
was necessary for navigation both in approaching the river's mouth
and for crossing the bar. Northerly winds or low water caused
serious delays and occasional disaster to vessels headed for New
Orleans. *S. M. Le Chariot Royal*, after a trip of seventy-five days
from France, was detained at the Balize for six weeks by contrary
winds. The post there, with some cannon and a normal garrison of
fifty, served also as a prison where the inmates manufactured brick.
As a fort, it was of little value, its major function being headquarters
for the river pilots. Although the Balize was abandoned in 1761, the
problem of maintaining an efficient pilot corps at the mouth could

not be evaded and became more pressing than ever during the Spanish period.

New Orleans served as a frontier market town, a seaport, provincial capital, and military center. As such, its population, even while small, was hardly homogeneous or tranquil. It possessed its portion of craftsmen, shopkeepers, and bourgeoisie who, if affluent enough, might socialize with officers and government officials. The bourgeois merchants were the international set, accustomed to dealing with faroff places and voyaging across the seas. They gave the town whatever stability it had. Other civilizing groups were the Ursuline nuns, the Capuchins, and Jesuits who operated establishments in and near the city, giving religious instruction, performing the ceremonies necessary to life and death, and providing care for the orphaned, sick, and indigent. Some of the religious were enterprising and innovative and carried on useful experiments with various crops.

One traveller to New Orleans, Jean Bernard Bossu, perhaps unconsciously affected by some miasmic malady, spoke of its residents as enjoying it "as an enchanted abode." [1] Vaudreuil thought it turbulent; *ordonnateur* Michel thought it riotous and its citizens debauched. Officials in New Orleans frequently sought to bring order to the community, usually without avail. Tavern owners sold their drink to all comers. Slaves peddled their wares openly at day and assembled for song and dance at night. Some slaves carried weapons and defended themselves against the insolence of whites; others, runaways called *marrons*, hid in the woods and raided plantations at night.

A new police code of 1751 had little measurable effect because the city lacked a permanent local police force. Even after the code reduced the number of legitimate taverns to six and restricted soldiers to two canteens, those Indians, slaves, and soldiers with the price could purchase *guildive*, a rot-gut type of rum, at numerous establishments designed to service the natural drives of man. [2] Later

[1] [Jean Bernard] Bossu, *Travels through that part of North America formerly called Louisiana*, tr. John R. Forster (2 vols.; London, 1771), I, 24.
[2] Ordonnateur Michel blamed the troops for much of the turbulence. Because the garrison at New Orleans increased from 200 in 1744 to almost 1,000 in 1751, thus greatly straining local facilities, some credibility may be granted Michel's complaints.

Spanish and American officials faced and failed to resolve similar problems on a much larger scale.

Small though it was, the town early assumed its cosmopolitan character. Red men, Negroes, and whites of various nationalities mixed their blood in New Orleans. But most people in the city and the colony were hardly the *nonchalants* Michel inveighed against. Up until 1748 the population was composed largely of the survivors and children of those sent over by Law. Immigration was as negligible as it was necessary. Officials at New Orleans recognized the value as colonists of certain state criminals such as salt smugglers, occasionally exiled to remote places like Louisiana. However, the crown sent only a few small groups and officially frowned on intercolonial migration. Only after 1748 did the French government demonstrate some interest in the settlement of Louisiana, but after a few boatloads were sent over, the policy received no further encouragement.

Patterns of settlement in New Orleans' hinterlands changed little during the thirty years following the company's departure. New plantations were established while many older ones were in a flourishing condition by the 1750s, and small farms proliferated between the English Turn and the German Coast. It remained relatively easy for newcomers to obtain grants of land and assistance during the difficult stage of farm making. By 1763 it was common practice to grant land only upon the condition that it be placed in production within one year on pain of forfeiture, that timber rights remained with the crown, and that levees and roads along the river frontage be maintained by the grantee.

Among the largest and best equipped plantations were those of De Noyan, Lieutenant of the King at New Orleans—valued at more than 200,000 livres in 1763; Jean de Pradel, named captain of the marines in 1720; and Du Breuil, *Entrepreneur Générale des Travaux du Roy* during the 1730s and 1740s. All three plantations were industrial as well as agricultural units, containing facilities and providing services that resulted in complete self-sufficiency. Both the De Noyan and Du Breuil operations, for instance, contained excellent systems of drainage and canals for lumber operations and for the operation of indigo factories. Drainage canals used for irrigation and runoff were especially sophisticated on Du Breuil's rice lands. For all three, indigo was apparently the major cash crop, with other activities providing supplementary income and the efficient use of labor during all seasons of the year. Each maintained large herds of cattle, raised corn and vegetables, and employed large numbers of slaves. Du Breuil, with more than two hundred slaves, was the largest slaveowner in the colony. De Pradel's labor force is not known, but in 1755, with the aid of Governor Kerlérec, he purchased twenty at less than the current price, having just completed clearing twenty arpents of new land for indigo.

These plantations were probably much more highly developed than most, although one memoir in 1746 stated that there were some twenty colonists in the New Orleans area possessing estates valued at between 100,000 and 300,000 livres. A high density of plantations extended from English Turn to Pointe Coupée, with an admixture of small farms and settlements particularly at the German Coast and Pointe Coupée. The plantations at Pointe Coupée were not flourishing in the 1760s but the smaller farms, supporting some two hundred families, produced substantial quantities of tobacco and corn and floated lumber to New Orleans.

Below Pointe Coupée and about twenty-five miles above New Orleans, the German Coast sustained upwards of one hundred families and two hundred Negroes in 1746, a number which may have doubled by 1760. New Orleans derived most of its vegetables and large quantities of meat from the truck farms of that area. By the mid-1750s, a large enough surplus was produced in the area to allow exports of produce to the French West Indies. From Pointe Coupée to Natchez there were few establishments, and Natchez did not recover from the Indian revolt of 1729 until it became part of British West Florida in 1763. Then it developed into one of the major agricultural centers dependent upon New Orleans. Far up the Red River, Natchitoches contained some sixty families, two hundred Negroes, and a garrison of soldiers. It sent some tobacco into New Orleans and followed a fitful trade with the Spanish. South of the Red River, population filtered in slowly until the Acadian dispersal.

Agricultural staples were the major items in the export trade of New Orleans from the 1720s through the nineteenth century. The

French had fairly well determined the crop possibilities by the end of their domain. These crops composed the bulk of New Orleans receipts until the Americans moved into the Upper Mississippi Valley at the close of the American Revolution and poured a new group of staples into New Orleans. For a time in the first decades of the nineteenth century, these staples—wheat, flour, corn and corn derivatives such as pork and bacon—would make up the largest portion of receipts at New Orleans. Then the movement of masses of men and slaves into the Lower Valley following the Treaty of Ghent initiated a boom in southern staples, especially cotton, that toppled northern produce from its premier position in the economy of New Orleans.

To say that the possibilities were understood is not to say that the knowledge was acted upon successfully. Conditions in Louisiana were early recognized as favoring the culture of cotton, sugarcane, and silk. Efforts at cotton culture foundered due to the lack of an efficient gin. Sugar was no more successful, although several individuals experimented with its cultivation during the French period. Neither cotton nor sugar took hold until the later years of the Spanish regime.[3] As for silk, one could be sure that, in whatever strange lands Frenchmen found themselves during their imperial phase, included among the things they sought for would be the mulberry tree. In Louisiana, the black-berried variety grew wild from the mouth of the Mississippi to the Arkansas and for half a century the French shipped silkworms and silkworkers to Louisiana, but extensive experiments invariably resulted in dead worms and no silk.

Most planters in Louisiana concentrated their efforts on the more bountiful crops such as tobacco, indigo, rice, corn, and lumber—the staples of the French and Spanish periods. Production was always hindered by the lack of slave labor and frequently damaged by the vagaries of the climate and river. But by and large, Louisiana shipped some quantity of all of these from New Orleans each year. The 1730s were very bad years: floods, freezing weather, drought, the worm, and hurricanes—some one or another hazard endangered crops during the entire decade. There was simply no counting on

[3] Du Breuil and the Jesuit Father Beaubois both contrived unsuccessful cotton gins and Du Breuil experimented with sugar planting and refining.

success at just the time the French government was making a concerted effort to interest French merchants in the Louisiana trade. Conditions improved between 1740 and 1744, but the war and resulting isolation discouraged planters until peace again revived their hopes. Aside from 1750, a year of violent storms, the years between 1748 and 1756 appear as the most fruitful of the entire French period. The renewal of hostilities between Britain and France in 1756 ended the brief agricultural renaissance until the solidification of Spanish control in 1769.

Tobacco was the most popular cash crop; indigo the most valuable; rice was the principal food staple; lumber, pitch, and tar were significant products for export as was, for a time, myrtle wax. The commitment to the major cash crops was generally consistent during the period to 1765, with indigo suffering from erratic planter interest more than tobacco because of the greater difficulty and expense involved in its production. Before it was determined that indigo culture should confine itself to the vicinity of New Orleans and tobacco farther to the north, there was some competition between the crops. Prior to 1748 a tendency existed, noted by Bienville and Salmon, for indigo planters who were discouraged by the vicissitudes of its culture to move north to Pointe Coupée or beyond and turn to tobacco growing. Subsequent to the peace of Aix-la-Chapelle in 1748, with the improvement of prices and transport, a reverse trend occurred. Successful tobacco planters moved south to engage in indigo cultivation. This planter or crop mobility manifested itself in later years between cotton and sugarcane.

A memoir on tobacco of 1750 maintained—probably correctly—that tobacco production in Louisiana declined between 1730 and 1750 largely because of the destruction of Fort Rosalie.[4] One event which impinged upon its cultivation was the cession of Louisiana to the crown in 1731, which necessitated a readjustment in the marketing system for tobacco. These negotiations will be treated in chapter 4, but it may be noted here that the colonists were not particularly pleased with the ensuing price schedule or the methods used by

---

[4] Mémoire sur l'État présent des habitants de la Louisiane relativements au projet d'y introduire des nègres et d'en sortir du tabac [1750], in French Colonial Documents (Library of Congress).

French merchants in exchanging their goods for the staples of the colony. In spite of dissatisfaction, most planters had no alternative to turn to. Even with a lower price than the Company of the Indies paid for the crop, it was the one commodity with a guaranteed sale in France.

Indigo required a large field labor force, certain skilled workers familiar with the dye-making process, an investment in buildings and machinery, and sufficient acreage in cultivation to make the investment worthwhile. Its cultivation, at first favored by the Company of the Indies, was later downgraded as the company sought to capitalize on its monopoly in tobacco, a crop requiring much less initial investment on the part of planters and company alike. Prices for indigo rose during the 1730s from 3 livres per pound in 1732 to 7 livres in 1740, and 9 livres in 1744. This, in addition to its acceptability by French merchants, was sufficient to induce increased production in spite of the shortage of labor. Du Breuil and Father Beaubois improved the method of cultivating the crop and the final reduction process. Even though the price dropped from a peak of 9 livres per pound in 1744 to 5 livres between 1750 and 1754, possibly as a result of greatly augmented quantities reaching Europe from South Carolina, production also increased in Louisiana. Those who could, planted indigo because, at a minimum, one Negro could cultivate 60 pounds, yielding 300 livres at the lowest price. So reasoned de Pradel, when he purchased twenty-three Negroes and constructed an *indigoterie* in 1755, and the Jesuits, whose plantation concentrated on indigo in 1761.

Most of the indigo plantations below New Orleans planted rice for the subsistence of their Negroes, marketing any surplus in New Orleans, where colonial officials purchased quantities for the subsistence of the troops. Small amounts were occasionally exported to the French West Indies and the Florida posts of Spain. But by the 1750s the crop was of small commercial value, although, like corn, it was a basic part of the colonial diet. Similarly, the indigo planters maintained cattle herds which, along with animals raised at Mobile, the German Coast, and elsewhere, supplied New Orleans with meat. The meat supply was uncertain; public contractors were used; prices were regulated in the city; and in 1745 an ordinance was passed requiring planters to bring two beeves each week for the troops. Herds were depleted in the 1750s after an epidemic disease struck for three years running, and the meat supply of New Orleans was more uncertain than usual until livestock farming took a firm hold in the Atakapas and Opelousas country. Occasional shipments of salted meats from the Illinois supplemented the short supplies. The wax obtained from the wax myrtle tree also furnished a supplemental income to numerous indigo planters during the 1740s and 1750s and several individuals opened wax plantations in 1752. Du Breuil planted six thousand trees and de Pradel two thousand in 1752. De Pradel manufactured about 150 pounds of wax daily during the harvest in December through February, which was sold at 15 sols (a sol was valued at 1/20th of a livre) per pound in France and netted de Pradel about 3,000 livres.

During the entire period from 1720 to 1765, the lumber industry supplied New Orleans with a large portion of its exports. Lumber products were the Louisiana staple in the trade with the French West Indies and, when possible, Havana. Efforts were made by the colonists to open the French market to Louisiana lumber. In 1736 Du Breuil began the construction of a canal connecting the Mississippi with Barataria Bay. This venturesome colonist hoped to develop the timber resources of the bay area by the export of ships timbers to France and the development of a shipbuilding industry at New Orleans. A few shipments to the naval yards at Rochefort and Brest convinced French officials that this was an uneconomic commerce. Nor was Du Breuil successful, in spite of support from Bienville, Salmon, and Vaudreuil, in stimulating the industry locally. The obstacles were too numerous: lack of ships carpenters and other skilled workers, the need to import the ironwork, rigging and other component parts of a vessel, and a lack of funds. Du Breuil did complete several vessels but lost his entire investment. Shipbuilding never became a major industry at New Orleans during the eighteenth or nineteenth centuries.

Along with lumber, the pitch and tar industry furnished New Orleans with a valuable export. The crown favored the development of this extractive industry by establishing a remunerative price schedule on shipments to France and allowing free passage for the product on public vessels. Further incentives were granted manufacturers through the extension of money advances to initiate production. Toward the late 1730s a few tarworks were built outside of New Orleans which handled shipments for the entire colony. French merchants preferred to load tobacco at New Orleans, taking pitch and tar as a last resort, and if they planned a stopover at St. Domingue, they preferred to take bricks or lumber as ballast. For this reason, free passage on the king's ships was provided. By the end of the 1730s, and as a result of subsidization, the industry was well established. French merchants overcame some of their initial reluctance to take pitch and tar as cargo because they were received at French naval yards without difficulty.

Besides these products of the plantation and forests, New Orleans received from and distributed goods to the small posts and settlements located far to the north and southeast. The line of normal security for the artificial hinterland of the town was pushed back rather than extended during the period before 1765, while the strength of French settlement in the natural hinterland remained stable. As was noted earlier, just when the Chickasaws seemed disposed to withdraw from the enervating and inconclusive war which followed the Natchez uprising, the War of the Austrian Succession began. The French managed to maintain the status quo against the British and their Indian allies until peace in Europe brought some relief. By the time Kerlérec reached Louisiana, the situation had returned to its normal danger point, thanks in part to a devastating Choctaw offensive against the Chickasaws in 1751.

Vaudreuil and Kerlérec, as Bienville before them, recognized that the key to the situation was control of the Indian trade. This was difficult to achieve, given the resources at hand. Not only was the value of trade goods at the disposal of French officials inadequate—Vaudreuil sought more than 100,000 livres worth of goods and received less than 50,000 in 1747—but French goods even in adequate supply could not compete with English goods. Anglo-American traders, consequently, received the best furs and pelts, fastened more tightly their economic hold upon the Indians, and increased Indian dissatisfaction with the French.

Largely in the hands of private individuals who purchased their goods at New Orleans and the various posts, the French trade was ill organized and virtually uncontrollable. Theoretically, the commanders at the various posts exercised some regulatory authority over the trade, but in practice, they and the garrisons engaged in such traffic whenever possible, even though it was forbidden to them. Almost anyone with the will and a little capital could pursue the commerce not only with the Indians but with the British as well. Vaudreuil's solution, as the free trade established in 1731 was not working, was to organize trading companies to monopolize the Indian trade.

In 1732–34, Bienville and Salmon had supported a proposal to organize the trade more centrally but nothing came of it. In 1744 Vaudreuil initiated his own effort by granting exclusive privileges to a New Orleans merchant, Deruisseau, to pursue the Indian trade along the Missouri River.[5] Vaudreuil's objectives—the effective organization of the trade and the exclusion of Canadians and English from the Missouri region—were not satisfied. Canadians and others apparently moved at will throughout the Upper Mississippi Valley. Furs and skins were routed to New Orleans by individuals often acting in concert with such merchants in New Orleans as the Rochelais, Testar, Chantalou (Chief Clerk of the Superior Council, Royal Notary, and Attorney of Vacant Estates), St. Denis, and Ancelin.

The idea of monopoly, however, did not die, for in 1762 a vast privilege in the Missouri country was granted to Maxent, Laclède, and Company. Out of this came the founding of St. Louis, the rise of the Chouteau family in St. Louis, and a future connection with John Jacob Astor's American Fur Company.

The Illinois was only of occasional value to New Orleans. Productive capacities there were normally unequal to the task of feeding New Orleans, although in 1741 and 1752 the area did ship sufficient flour to meet the needs of the Lower Valley. In 1752, a peak year in flour production, an estimated 800,000 pounds, or 2,500 barrels, of flour were exported downriver. Most estimates of flour production placed this quantity at three times local consump-

---

[5] Deruisseau was permitted to route beaver and martin pelts to Canada but all other pelts had to be shipped to New Orleans. Illinois traders were excluded from the Missouri country in an effort to confine the *voyageurs* to their farms.

tion needs while the population of New Orleans was more than four times greater than that of Illinois. Moreover, production was uncertain and the river route to New Orleans was vulnerable to Indian attack. Illinois was isolated during the last two wars of the French period, causing a decline in the value of the fur trade and making it all but impossible to exploit the rich lead and copper mines properly. In short, while Illinois possessed great potential value to the Lower Mississippi Valley just as the latter possessed potential value for France, the French regime came to a close before these potentials were realized.

While Louisianians might apply a commendable amount of ingenuity and resolution to their environment, more was required if the full measure of economic value was to be extracted from the colony. To match crop with area; to establish a conveniently located market town; to maintain security, however uncertain, against the Indians—all this might be done with local resources. Certainly such individuals as Father Beaubois, Du Breuil, Bienville, Salmon, Vaudreuil, and Kerlérec brought to the environment courage, innovative qualities, and perseverance. But this was not sufficient. France and Frenchmen must be made aware of Louisiana; they must be convinced that support was useful and profitable. No other group was more essential to the province than the French merchants. It was the duty of the crown to make the hard sell to the skeptical and conservative French *négociant* and *armateur*. Maurepas undertook this task in 1731.

4

France and the Louisiana Trade

ESIDENTS of New Orleans and its environs in the mid-1730s slaked their thirst with an annual per capita consumption of 416 pints of wine, brandy, and other liquors. Bordelais reds and the brandies of Cognac were preferred. One hundred tons of flour, thousands of ells of cloth, olive oil, tin and pewterware, spices, and a hundred other items composed the yearly wants of New Orleans and its hinterlands. All of these goods were obtainable only in France, and when the Company of the Indies turned Louisiana over to the crown in 1731, it became the duty of the latter to see that these minimal needs were met. The colonists could pay for these goods with the products of their farms and plantations, but Negroes were desperately needed if the colonists were to derive full value from the rich lands. Profitable trading opportunities existed with the neighboring French islands and Spanish colonies. In reorganizing the trade of Louisiana, the crown had to maintain a balance among the interests of the producers, suppliers, and the realm.

Food and immediate assurance of the interest of the crown in the fate of the colony were the most pressing needs in 1731. The king's vessels were outfitted rapidly with provisions and ordered to New Orleans. But doubts on a score of urgent problems could be alleviated only by action. Would the crown act swiftly to engage French merchants in the trade and at whose expense? What would be the terms of the reorganized tobacco trade? Would adequate shipping be available to carry off Louisiana's production? When would new supplies of slaves appear? Would credits be available and distribution equitable? Would the colonists continue in their debt-ridden condition with 75 percent of each crop encumbered by prior obligations? The answer to some of these questions arrived in December, 1731, with the ship *St. Paul*, 150 tons, owned by the merchant Rasteau of La Rochelle, followed in April by the *St. Laurent*, owned by Jean Jung of Bordeaux, the first fruits of the crown's campaign to commit French merchants to the Louisiana trade.

Times seemed propitious for the solid organization of the Louisiana trade. The coming to power of Fleury in 1726 ushered in a period described as unadventurous in foreign policy and conducive to economic advance. A generation of peace broken only by the War of the Polish Succession (1733–38), which had little impact on colonial affairs, provided a setting in which the natural strengths of the French economy developed at their own tempo. The decades prior to French involvement in the War of the Austrian Succession were the most prosperous experienced in France to that time. Monetary stabilization, achieved in 1726, and adequate specie supplies, a thoughtful program of internal improvements, an enlarged naval force, a less restrictive commercial policy, industrial growth, especially in the woolens industry, testified to the vigor of the economy. French maritime commerce prospered as never before, based as it was on the valuable sugar trade with the French Antilles, while France captured the sugar market of Europe.

The quickened pace evident at all the French ports from the Mediterranean to the Channel was to a large extent grounded in the dramatic prosperity which peace brought to the French islands. At the beginning of Louis XV's reign, the foreign trade of France stood at approximately 215 million livres annually. By 1740 the figure had risen to 430 million and between 1749 and 1755 the average annual total reached 616 million. Bordeaux, Nantes, and La Rochelle concentrated on the island trade, reexporting a large part of the imports throughout Europe. Those ports and Marseilles supported numerous sugar refineries. In the 1740s these ports, plus others such as St. Malo, Le Havre, and La Bayonne, outfitted a fleet of more than five hundred vessels engaged in the island trade. In one year, 1729, 123 Bordelais vessels returned from the Indies with 7.5 million livres in goods, 80 percent in sugars, with at least two-thirds of the sugar destined for reexport to foreign ports. If shipping was lacking at

New Orleans, it was not because of any general shortage in France.

The colonial commerce of France was more tightly regulated than that of Great Britain but considerably less restricted than that of Spain. The system theoretically guaranteed French monopoly of the colonial trade through the restriction of that trade to various privileged ports and through the concentration of certain facets of the trade in certain ports. During the period 1688–1783 only the ports of Marseilles, Dunkirk, and La Bayonne, designated as the *ports franc*, could handle merchandise destined for foreigners without the payment of import and export duties. Efforts on the part of any one port to gain this privilege were vigorously contested by the other ports. Prior to 1700 the ports authorized to engage in the colonial trade were Bordeaux, La Rochelle, Marseilles, Nantes, and Rouen. Dunkirk, La Bayonne, and the ports of Languedoc gained entry between 1704 and 1716. In the following year, the crown issued a revision of colonial regulations which served as the basic code during the remainder of the *Ancien Régime*.

The letters patent of 1717 codified existing regulations, extended the list of privileged ports to which others were added in subsequent years, renewed *arrêts* of prior years concerning the importation of foreign goods, and exempted provisions and merchandise of French manufacture from tariffs if destined for the colonies. Detailed procedures were established for the reexport trade, especially in sugar. The underlying rule of the letters applied the principle that vessels trading with the colonies must return directly to the port of departure, thereby avoiding the possibility that foreign goods would gain entry into France.[1]

This principle was difficult to apply consistently because of the frequency of wars and resulting colonial needs and the recurrent shortages in France of various provisions required in the colonies. The most significant exception to the rule of direct passage applied to provisions for the colonies, particularly Irish salt beef. In *Arrêts du Conseil* of 1723, 1727, 1730–38, 1741 and 1748, French merchants were allowed to travel directly to Ireland, or import free of

---

[1] This was liberalized in 1726 when French merchants were allowed to carry colonial produce to Marseilles or, excepting sugar, to Spain and thence to the port of origin.

duty therefrom, salt beef and fish, lard, tallow, and candles destined for the colonies. The principle of direct return was suspended during the War of the Austrian Succession and the Seven Years' War.

In 1731 and 1732 the privileges and exemptions granted in the letters of 1717 were applied to Louisiana in *arrêts* of January 23, 1731, and September 30, 1732. By the terms of these *arrêts*, trade with Louisiana was thrown open to all the ports privileged to deal with the French colonies, except for the beaver trade and the commerce in Negroes which remained in the hands of the Company of the Indies. The *arrêts* of 1732 were extended in 1741 and 1751 for ten years. In addition, the obligation which compelled French merchantmen to carry *engagées* and arms on each voyage to the colonies was lifted for the Louisiana trade in 1731 and 1738, reinstated from 1744 to 1748, and again lifted in 1748.[2] It remained to be seen whether the royal government could build these privileges into a regular and direct commerce between New Orleans and the ports of France.

The ports of France in 1731 were, as remarked above, on the eve of extraordinary prosperity. The six major ports in the colonial trade in order of importance were Bordeaux, Nantes, Le Havre, La Rochelle, Marseilles, and La Bayonne. During the period 1749–55 these ports sent an average of 392 vessels annually to the American colonies. For the same years, the four ports most interested in the Canadian trade, Le Havre, Bordeaux, Marseilles, and La Rochelle, routed an average of 130 merchant vessels annually to either Louisbourg or Quebec. Of the six dominant ports, Bordeaux and La Rochelle, both experienced in the West Indian and the slave trades, appeared as the most likely candidates for the Louisiana trade.

Bordeaux rose to first rank as an entrepot for the colonial trade during the late seventeenth and early eighteenth centuries, controlling a major portion of the trade with St. Domingue by the mid-eighteenth century. While in 1685 the West Indian fleet of La Rochelle was twice the size of that of Bordeaux, by 1750 the fleet of Bordeaux was three times the size of La Rochelle's. The total

2 Vaudreuil and Michel were not entirely in favor of renewing the exemption from carrying *engagées*, maintaining that it was but a small burden for the shipowners and of great assistance to Louisiana.

foreign trade of Bordeaux rose from 12.7 million livres in 1717 to 74 million in 1749, while the value of sugar imports tripled between 1740 and 1753. Returns from Holland and the French West Indies accounted for more than half the value of the port's foreign trade. In 1730 Bordeaux, recovering from a period of recession, supported more than one hundred vessels in the West Indian trade. Without doubt, the port possessed the requisite facilities and experience, but it was difficult to foresee the reaction of her merchants to the freeing of the Louisiana trade.

During the days of Colbert, La Rochelle profited from the great minister's enthusiasm for overseas trade and maritime strength, but

TABLE II

The Merchant Fleet of La Rochelle, 1664–1759*

	Total Ships Owned	Tonnage	Ships to All Colonies	Ships to Canada
1664	32	4,000		
1682	89			
1683	92	10,731		
1685	81		49	
1687	65			
1690	36			
1718	52			
1748	81	18,000		
1749	104		59	10
1750	112		39	14
1751	118	26,090	32	16
1752			47	16
1753			33	17
1754			44	15
1755			36	16
1756				17
1757				20
1758				9
1759				1

* See Table IV for Rochelais vessels arriving at New Orleans.

his death, wars, and the revocation of the Edict of Nantes in 1685 sent the Huguenot port spinning into a depression lasting until the 1720s. Almost half a century passed before the fleet again reached the size of 1683. By the 1720s the commerce of La Rochelle was demonstrating new energy. Scores of vessels were outfitted for the West Indies and Canada while others sought slaves along the Guinea Coast of Africa. By 1736 the foreign trade of the port reached 14 million livres, about 50 percent with the colonies. This figure had doubled by the early 1750s and declined thereafter. Some twenty sugar refineries were kept active after 1730, when at least one of every two Rochelais vessels brought sugar back from the West Indies. Maurepas sought to divert a portion of this strength to the service of Louisiana.

Aside from Rochefort, the other major privileged ports demonstrated no particular interest in the New Orleans trade during the French period. Le Havre and Nantes annually sent about as many vessels to the West Indies as did La Rochelle and plied a significant slave trade. Marseilles' focus was on North Africa, although considerable trade developed in the eighteenth century with St. Domingue while Rouen, St. Malo, and Lorient each had a special interest. Rochefort, as a major naval base, prospered under the patronage of Maurepas, who allocated significant sums to improve the naval yards. Most of the royal vessels arriving at New Orleans originated at Rochefort and most of Louisiana's pitch and tar was marketed there.

In the eighteenth century, as in the seventeenth, the merchants of the French ports operated largely as individuals or as members of familial associations with the two methods not mutually exclusive. Each member of a family firm was free to engage his own capital in private ventures or to associate in partnership with some other merchant in a venture while simultaneously participating in the profits and losses of family projects. Partnerships were generally limited to a specific purpose, with the association coming to an end when that purpose was achieved. As with the Rasteaus of La Rochelle in the eighteenth century, the capital of the family firm was not treated as a unit belonging to the firm but was constantly being divided among the participants. Each Rasteau could then commit whatever portion of his capital that he wished to the next venture and receive profits proportionate to his investment.

Capital was used in ways as various as there were mercantile opportunities. The guiding principle in days when each venture faced numerous hazards was to spread the capital among as many operations as possible. Multiple ownership of vessels was a common form of sharing risks and merchants might place cargoes on vessels besides the one they had an interest in. The Rasteaus owned vessels in common as well as with other merchants. By the mid-eighteenth century, private and familial ownership of vessels was normal. Other investment opportunities available to merchants included lending operating capital to venturers without participating in the risks of the commerce, underwriting insurance on vessels, the leasing of vessels to merchants, or putting the entire vessel in freight while retaining command, and so on. All could be done simultaneously. The desideratum was to decrease the probabilities of loss even at the expense of accepting a lower margin of profit.

Merchant contacts were as diverse as the possibilities of trade. Magon de la Balue of St. Malo traded in slaves, associated with a London merchant in trade with Mexico, owned an interest in the ship *François*, joined with a Nantes merchant to send a cargo to St. Domingue to exchange for indigo, owned in whole the *Louis Erasmé*, and leased the Rasteau's *Comte de Maurepas*. Magon and the Rasteaus often acted as commission merchants for merchants of other French ports and usually performed the same function for numerous colonists. Augustin Seigne, a Nantes merchant, normally routed goods from Louisiana through the Rasteaus during the 1730s, and the Rasteaus, who had agents in the West Indies and in New Orleans, bought and sold colonial goods at the account and risk of many Rochelais businessmen. The Rasteaus—who owned numerous vessels commanded by members of the family—retained family agents throughout the French American colonies and enjoyed contacts with the French government. They were in an excellent position to undertake the Louisiana trade if it were made sufficiently attractive.[3]

[3] These general remarks on French merchants are meant only to touch upon those aspects of their operations which were relevant to the New Orleans trade.

Minister of the Marine Maurepas engaged in extended negotiations with French ports in 1731 in order to stimulate their interest in the trade with New Orleans. The merchants of the realm, as an outline of the negotiations will make clear, were not ready to initiate this trade without certain guarantees and privileges additional to those granted by royal *arrêts*. While the advantages of the trade were crystal clear to officials in New Orleans, the merchants of France were dubious: there were unanswered questions regarding incentives, tobacco prices, government freights, and remittances to France. Some of these could be negotiated by Maurepas and the merchants; others involved the Farmers General and the financial policy to prevail in Louisiana.

Maurepas contacted resident Marine officials in La Rochelle, Bordeaux, Nantes, and St. Malo in April and May, 1731, instructing them to convey to the merchants of the port information relative to the Louisiana trade. Maurepas offered as a minimal attraction a bonus per ton of cargo delivered at New Orleans. The discussions began at that point. The Chamber of Commerce of La Rochelle responded to the feeler by requesting more details on the subsidy and assurances that the Farmers General would take Louisiana tobacco at a reasonable price. The latter was essential, for the Farmers General sold all the tobacco entering France. In response to Maurepas' general promises relative to the fixing of prices for Louisiana tobacco sold in France, the La Rochelle chamber submitted a set of concrete proposals in June, 1731.

In making the legitimate point that the present value of trade with Louisiana was small, the chamber asserted the indispensability of government financial support to assure its success. It then proposed a subsidy of 50 livres per ton of goods sent to New Orleans, payable at departure and retained in case the vessel was lost; a price of 50 livres per hundredweight for tobacco of good quality; 60 livres passage money for soldiers transported to Louisiana; aid in equipping for the voyages; exemption from export and import duties on goods destined for Louisiana or the vessel's outfit; and the certainty that debts owed the Company of the Indies would not take precedence over debts to individual merchants. Maurepas countered with an offer of 25 to 30 livres subsidy, agreed to the passage rates,

promised aid in equipping vessels, calmed the apprehension of chamber members regarding the Company of the Indies, and noted that
talks were progressing with the Farmers General about tobacco
prices. Maurepas had approached the Farmers to secure a higher
price for Louisiana than for British leaf. The Minister shrewdly
emphasized various hidden advantages in the trade such as the opportunity to obtain specie through contraband trade with the Spanish and through the natural process by which gold sent to Louisiana
to cover royal expenses would pass into the hands of the merchants.
Remittance of the specie to France, he added, would be facilitated
by the availability of letters of exchange on the Treasury of the
Marine.

Rochelais merchants responded by demanding 40 livres subsidy
per ton, which Maurepas accepted, and repeated their fears concerning tobacco, although they recognized that Maurepas could not
solve this problem unilaterally. Maurepas explained the penalty of
double restitution of the bonus if the cargoes destined for Louisiana
were sold elsewhere, making clear that it was meant only to prevent
fraud and denying that it was designed to penalize vessels forced off
course or vessels unable to sell their cargoes in the colony. He was
persuaded that good sales would meet well-assorted cargoes in New
Orleans and that sufficient silver was available to meet the needs of
the trade. Sometime in July, 1731, the Rasteaus of La Rochelle accepted the conditions tendered and prepared the *St. Paul* for departure to New Orleans. Negotiations went less smoothly at other
ports, although Jean Jung, the merchant from Bordeaux, and one
Frotin from St. Malo finally accepted the government's terms. In
September, 1731, the first vessel, Rasteau's *St. Paul*, was on its way to
New Orleans; Jung's *St. Laurent* followed in December; and Frotin's *St. René* left soon after.

The full weight of the Ministry of the Marine exerted itself to
hasten the departure of the *St. Paul*. Maurepas ignored nothing that
would increase the profitability of the voyage, convinced as he was
that Rasteau's success would motivate other merchants to take up
the trade. Letters were written to the proper officials admonishing
them to give Rasteau all possible aid. Salmon, in New Orleans, was
informed of the vessel's departure and instructed to make the trip

successful. The *ordonnateur* was to furnish the vessel's captain all the letters of exchange requested. Rasteau was promised good prices for tobacco carried back to France. When Jung readied his vessel for the trip, he experienced similar cooperation, as did Frotin.

As a rule, Maurepas acted rapidly and favorably to merchant requests for aid. His knowledge of the details of the trade was complete as information regarding all its phases daily crossed his desk, much of it requiring his decisions. Not an ell of limbourg cloth moved nor a pot of brandy loaded, a crew enlisted nor an anchor weighed without his personal approval. One can, of course, criticize the inherent bureaucracy and centralization of the process but one can also admire the ability and perseverance of a man overwhelmed with details of extraordinary variety.

Maurepas' role in the Louisiana trade began with the movement of goods from centers of production to the ports. Responsible for the supply of the French colonial establishment and the maintenance of the royal fleet on the seas and in the naval yards—and for the yards as well—only Maurepas could smooth the path of merchants' goods from points in France to the ports and thence overseas. He negotiated contracts or ratified those made by subordinates with individuals throughout France for the delivery of goods and foodstuffs required in Louisiana. Time and time again during the 1730s and 1740s he was forced to intercede on behalf of various merchants to insure prompt delivery. Royal passports were issued by him to speed delivery and he was always prepared to fire off a terse letter to the Farmers General or to enlist the aid of Comptroller-General Orry in freeing as many goods as possible from the payment of duties.

His consistent policy was to evade duties whenever feasible, arguing, as he did to Orry in 1732, that the trade needed this form of encouragement. When Rasteau's ship *St. Paul* returned to France in June, 1732, customs officials at La Rochelle exacted the *domaine d'occident*, a 3.5 percent tax on all goods coming from America. Maurepas requested and received exemption for Rasteau and others from this duty on the basis of the *arrêts* regulating trade with Louisiana and the letters patent of 1717. A decade later, the Rasteaus engaged the Farmers General in disputation regarding goods purchased in Amsterdam and transported to France in Rasteau's *Lion d'Or* for shipment to Louisiana. At the same time other merchants were experiencing trouble with the farm and Maurepas was irritated at the obstacles placed in the way of the Louisiana trade. Maurepas recommended—indeed peremptorily ordered—that the farm interpret those clauses exempting Louisiana goods from import and export duties to include foreign goods, in particular Rasteau's. Rasteau received his exemption. In this special case the vessel in question embarked on a voyage ostensibly to New Orleans but in reality to trade at Vera Cruz. Maurepas was in on this venture from the beginning.

The scope of his activity was all encompassing: he secured a crew for Rasteau in 1734 and Jung in 1737, cheap water casks for Rasteau in 1737, and an outfit for the Rochelais merchant Bourgine's *Reine des Anges* in 1741. In other words, the merchants were in an absolute dependence upon the minister who used his great authority with reasonable moderation and equity, seeking always to further the interests of the merchants while servicing Louisiana's needs and protecting the proper interest of the crown. In matters of government freight and the scheduling of departures for New Orleans, Maurepas frequently had to reconcile these potentially competitive interests.

Government freight was lucrative and much sought after by the Louisiana traders. Maurepas procured freights for the *St. Paul* on its first trip to the Mississippi. Thereafter, all the merchants expected similar treatment and, although this was not Maurepas' intention, he used the lure of government freight to interest merchants in the trade. Rasteau's vessel received 120 livres per ton for a government freight of 54 tons which, combined with the subsidy of 40 livres per ton on the 136 tons of private cargo, netted him 12,035 livres paid in advance before the vessel ever left the harbor. Jung's *Comte de Maurepas*, carrying 204 tons of private goods and 139 tons of government freight, received 13,746 in subsidies and charges. These sums were close to 35 percent of the invoice value of the private goods and, given the problem of remittances which quickly developed in spite of Maurepas' earlier assurances, acted as a necessary cushion against the possibilities of poor sales in New Orleans. The-

oretically, government freight was available only if royal ships were
not, but he juggled cargoes whenever possible to fit the needs of
merchant vessels about to depart for New Orleans. It was not, as
Maurepas ingenuously explained to Rostan at Bordeaux, just coincidence that government flour was embarked on Rasteau's vessel,
for the flour was taken from a royal ship headed for St. Domingue
and Louisiana.

During the 1730s and 1740s government cargoes were obtained
readily enough to stimulate competition between merchants and
ports. These freights became the more desirable in 1735 when the
bonus system was revised so as to pay a sum of 20 livres per ton of
goods destined for Louisiana and a similar sum for Louisiana goods
carried to France. In effect, this lowered the bonus received by
merchants because a given tonnage of French goods took less space
than the same tonnage of Louisiana produce. Full freights at New
Orleans were frequently unavailable. Competition for government
freight thus increased after 1735, resulting in a decline in rates and
providing Maurepas with the opportunity to seek competitive bids
for cargoes. When Bourgine of La Rochelle approached Belamy in
1732 concerning the outfitting of his 450-ton *Ste. Anne* for Louisiana, government freight was available at 100 livres per ton. By 1736
Rasteau could contract only at 90 livres and obtained this only by
underbidding Bourgine. In 1739, annoyed at the continued high
rates demanded by La Rochelle's shipowners, Maurepas instructed
his subordinates to give preference to Bordeaux and to place contracts at La Rochelle only as a last resort. Rates by this time were
down to 85 livres per ton, or a 30 percent reduction since 1731.

Vessels could not depart for Louisiana without the permission of
Maurepas. During the early years of the trade, Maurepas ran a tidy
schedule that attempted to provide adequate shipping at New Orleans while preventing too many vessels from glutting the market
and discouraging the trade. In 1733 he delayed the sailing of a St.
Malo vessel so that a Rasteau ship could get a good start. Rasteau had
received Jung's concurrence for this departure as Jung's vessel held
priority in the scheduling. In October, 1735, with three merchant
ships at New Orleans and one just returned to France, Maurepas
delayed the departure of Jean Ferchaud's *Marie Elisabeth* from

Bordeaux. By the end of the decade, he had loosened the traces a bit, confining himself to the dissemination of shipping information and allowing the merchants to decide departure times for themselves.

Maurepas' free-wheeling authority in these affairs was neither oppressive nor arbitrary, and his intervention with other government agencies on behalf of the shippers was beneficial. In some instances he was forced by circumstance to act precipitately. In 1736 and 1737, when Bienville was preparing his first Chickasaw campaign, Maurepas committed large quantities of government supplies and numerous troops to various shipowners, only to cancel out abruptly when news arrived from Louisiana that matters were not quite so urgent as he had thought. He did attempt to divide available freight among those preparing vessels for New Orleans, although they received substantially less than the original agreements stipulated.

By and large, Maurepas acted to advance the interest of the trade. In certain areas his authority was restricted by prior decisions on general policy or by authority vested in or shared with other government or quasi-public agencies. Moreover his ability to ease the process of equipping vessels for Louisiana was greater than his ability to assure the merchants a satisfactory market in New Orleans. This dilution of authority is apparent in the question of remittances to France and the price received for certain Louisiana goods in France.

Jean Jung's *St. Laurent* reached New Orleans in April, 1732, but there was no return cargo available as the *St. Paul* had carried off all the tobacco available. The captain was compelled to carry brick and lumber to the French West Indies, leaving his Louisiana goods in New Orleans for sale, and return to New Orleans, hopefully to obtain a supply of new tobacco. By the time the *St. Laurent* returned to New Orleans its cargo was sold, but the commodities available for export were worth considerably less than the proceeds derived from the sale of the French goods. Part of the proceeds were received in silver, part in credits and notes, and part in goods. Some method was necessary to expedite the transfer to France of funds received in Louisiana. Maurepas provided this service by allowing the *ordonnateur* to draw 150,000 livres annually in letters of exchange upon the Treasury of the Marine. The merchant could substitute at no cost letters of exchange for his specie and colonial notes and then cash or otherwise negotiate the letters elsewhere.

It quickly became clear that the annual quota of letters was grossly inadequate. The problem became more urgent during the late 1730s and 1740s as the expenses of colonial administration rose far above receipts, necessitating the circulation of treasury notes which depreciated rapidly and dragged the value of current paper money down with them. These untoward events complicated the problem of remittances, which was difficult enough to resolve under the normal conditions of a growing trade.

This difficulty confronted both the French merchant engaged in the Louisiana trade and the colonist, whether a merchant in New Orleans or a planter. None of the parties involved could well afford to have his capital tied up for long periods of time. While the system of bonuses moderated the problem somewhat for French merchants, they were often unable, as Jung had been, to find adequate or suitable produce in New Orleans. Letters of exchange were issued by the *ordonnateur*, as Maurepas explained it, to facilitate the return of funds earned from the sale of cargoes. He also recognized that the solution to the problem lay in the increased production of cash crops in Louisiana. But he evidently did not anticipate the inadequacy of the quota of letters or the reluctance of French merchants to load colonial produce even when it was available.

During the first year of the trade, French merchants received letters payable in ninety days. Salmon followed instructions to issue these at the request of the merchants. By 1733 the limit of 150,000 livres was exceeded and Salmon was forced into issuing letters on the next year's quota. The arrival of a few vessels was sufficient to take up the entire quota. In 1734 Jung's *Comte de Maurepas*, Touron's *Dauphin*, Bordeaux, and Bourgine's *L'Alexis* drew over 80,000 livres in letters prior to the arrival in September of three more vessels. Jung's vessel alone arrived with 120,000 livres worth of goods, a portion of which had to be stored in New Orleans for later sale. Salmon wrote Maurepas in February, 1736, that he had already drawn 100,000 livres and would soon be compelled to draw on 1737 funds as Rasteau required more than 120,000 livres because his ship had loaded entirely with colonial produce. Three vessels were in port, Salmon continued, and could sell only for specie or bills as no products were available. The 150,000-livre limit, Salmon declared, hampered commerce.

Merchants suffered grave inconvenience under this system. Letters of exchange obtained were payable according to the year's quota under which they were drawn. Rasteau found that letters obtained in 1736 would be acceptable for payment only in March of 1737 and 1738. Maurepas refused his request for early payment just as he refused a similar inquiry from Jung. By 1739 both merchants had considerable sums tied up in New Orleans—at least seventy thousand livres in Jung's case and the proceeds from the sale of a cargo in Rasteau's case. Other merchants experienced similar difficulties, but when they importuned Maurepas for payment, they received similar replies. However, Maurepas could move when he wished to, quota or no quota. When Rasteau suggested a potentially lucrative venture to Vera Cruz in 1742, Maurepas instructed Salmon to draw letters immediately at short sight so that Rasteau would have operating capital. Salmon normally bore the brunt of criticism over this problem. He received a steady flow of orders to act liberally toward merchant requests for letters and a stream of criticism for exceeding the annual quota.

Remittance difficulties were aggravated by the nature of colonial produce and the preferences of French merchants. Salmon informed Maurepas in 1734 that the merchants were not disposed to take on colonial products, preferring letters of exchange. This freed the vessels to take on a cargo for the islands or even to go in ballast, purchase Antillean staples, and return to France. In 1733–34 Rasteau's *St. Paul* sold its cargo in New Orleans at good prices and purchased tobacco but chose to embark lumber, bricks, pitch, and tar for St. Domingue, leaving the tobacco to be loaded on a royal vessel. But Salmon, refusing to give space to Rasteau on royal vessels in 1734 or 1735, pointed out that the *St. Paul* could easily enough have carried the tobacco. The king's ships, he added, were the only certain means of transportation available to the colonists, given the reluctance of French shippers to load colonial produce. Maurepas sustained Salmon's decision against Rasteau's objections.

The disinclination of French merchants to load colonial produce at New Orleans was based on indisputable economic facts. Bienville pointed them out in 1735 and Du Breuil again in 1752. A vessel of two hundred tons carried goods worth about 100,000 livres to Louisiana. A full cargo of tobacco weighing some one hundred tons brought 25,000 livres in France. Pitch and tar, lumber, or pelts were no more valuable. In lieu of more valuable and less bulky goods, only adequate amounts of letters of exchange could make up the difference. Thus, the colonists were justified in complaining about the lack of shipping for their crops, largely tobacco, even though sufficient tonnage arrived yearly at New Orleans to carry off every ounce of the colony's production. French merchants adopted the practice of shipping goods bound for Louisiana to the French West Indies where Indies vessels carried them to New Orleans and sold them at higher prices than paid in the direct French-Louisiana trade. Moreover, the colonists were compelled to route their exports via the French islands, receiving lower prices and paying proportionately higher freight rates on the vessels used in this trade, which were smaller than those engaged in the direct trade.

French merchants wished to sell their goods for specie or letters of exchange, and the colonists naturally preferred to pay in goods or in the money current in the colony. Obviously neither interest was fully satisfied. Considerable quantities of all the marketable products of Louisiana were embarked on vessels at New Orleans and sold with profit in France. Much depended upon the precise time the exchange occurred. Pressed for payment, the colonists accepted low prices for tobacco, reasoning that it was better to accept a low price in New Orleans than to consign their goods to a merchant in France and await payment. They needed cash in hand. In 1733 Frotin's vessel, *St. René*, selling wine and brandy at double the normal price, obtained a full cargo of tobacco and 49,140 livres in letters of exchange This was the general pattern. The merchants took a sufficient quantity of colonial produce to support a request for letters of exchange while the colonists paid as much in kind as possible, sending any surplus on consignment to France via a royal ship. Colonial planters and merchants alike were faced with the problem until they developed a close relationship with a French correspondent. French merchants soon discovered that, with considerable sums tied up in Louisiana in the form of credits or colonial money, agents on the spot could best deal with the situation. In 1736 Rasteau sent his youngest son Paul to New Orleans to handle the firm's affairs.

When Maurepas first approached the merchants of the French ports, proposing that they enter the Louisiana trade, a question of major concern was the price tobacco would receive in France. Maurepas promised that the price would be fair but could be no more specific because he could not resolve the question unilaterally. He then initiated talks with the Farmers General, who held the monopoly of imports and sales of tobacco. The sale of tobacco in France had belonged to a monopolistic group since 1674 when Colbert first farmed it out to a syndicate of financiers. Imports, sales, and the manufacture of tobacco remained in the hands of the farm until 1718 when it was turned over to the Company of the Indies. In 1730 the company leased the tobacco trade to the Farmers General, with the company retaining the original lease until 1747. In that year the French government, seeking revenue to finance the War of the Austrian Succession, withdrew the lease from the company and restored receipts to the government amounting annually to 30 million livres by 1789.

The preference of the tobacco farm for British leaf was well known in France and subject to much criticism. This policy was believed to damage the interests of France and its colonies while funneling French silver into British coffers. It was frequently pointed out that tobacco from the French colonies should be substituted and that Louisiana alone could meet French needs with proper encouragement. But prices for British tobacco were substantially less than for inferior leaf from the West Indies or good tobacco from Louisiana. The farm argued that it could hardly meet its obligations to the crown if forced to pay the 30 livres per quintal (hundredweight) demanded by French merchants.

French merchants with whom Maurepas conferred asked that the price of Louisiana tobacco be set at 30 to 35 livres per quintal in Louisiana and 40 to 45 livres in France as the tobacco cost the merchants 6 sols per pound in Louisiana plus the costs of transportation. Hearing from Salmon that Rasteau paid less than 6 sols per pound, Maurepas believed that the merchants could do with less than they demanded. He also believed that the farm could afford at best 25 livres per quintal. It was decided to fix prices in France on a sliding scale: 35 livres per quintal for 1732–33; 30 livres for 1734–35; 27 livres 10 sols for 1736–37; and 25 livres thereafter with the government paying that part of the cost above 25 livres. Maurepas hoped that the favorable prices would stimulate production during the first years and that the sale of larger crops would compensate for the fall in prices. However, the system was inequitable for the planters and merchants of Louisiana in view of the fact that the price of only one item in the trade was fixed at only one point in the exchange.

Bienville and Salmon contended that the colonists derived little advantage from the favorable price in France because of the high prices French merchants demanded for their goods. Having neither the shipping nor the time to allow direct sales in France, the colonists were forced to exchange their tobacco for imported goods. This criticism was entirely justified. Merchants purchased wine in France for 100 livres per barrel and sold it in New Orleans for as much as 300 livres. A colonist who received 4 sols per pound for his tobacco paid the equivalent of 15 quintals of tobacco, or just under two standard barrels or casks of tobacco, for the wine. The merchant then carried the 15 quintals of tobacco to France, received 525 livres, and purchased five barrels of wine; two barrels of tobacco purchased one barrel of wine at New Orleans and five barrels in France. Of course, the merchant had freight charges both ways but 20 quintals of tobacco, or roughly a ton, cost only 25 to 50 livres to move to France. And, as the price of tobacco declined in France, so did it in Louisiana while wine prices actually rose. Little wonder that Bienville and Salmon in 1737 relayed to Maurepas the disgust of Pointe Coupée's residents over the exchange value of tobacco.

After the agreement, the Farmers General made considerable

difficulty for the merchants regarding the packaging and quality of the tobacco. The Farmers, in agreeing to the price schedule, stipulated that only leaf tobacco would be accepted and that each shipment must contain no less than a third first quality tobacco and no more than half of second quality, packed in separate containers. Both colonists and merchants preferred to send semiprocessed or pressed tobacco because more tobacco could then be loaded in a given vessel. In 1734 pressed tobacco brought to Bordeaux by Jung's *Comte de Maurepas* was rejected by the farm until Maurepas interceded with Orry and the Farmers General. But in 1735 Maurepas was unable, if he even tried, to obtain a similar concession for Bourgine. Rasteau experienced a similar rejection in 1739. Tobacco that was rejected by the farm could only be sold in Canada or Guinea. The packaging standards worked a hardship on Louisianians because the leaf frequently suffered damage or deterioration, while, as Vaudreuil said in 1748, the higher freight rates cut into the already small profits of the planters.

Quality control proved difficult to achieve in Louisiana and it does appear that the farm acted arbitrarily on occasion in determining the quality of Louisiana tobacco. Maurepas instructed Bienville and Salmon to maintain the quality of exported leaf. Several inspectors were appointed but the procedure established was not very successful. The farm rejected large portions of various shipments on the grounds that the leaf was of poor quality. The merchants complained to Maurepas but there was little that he could do unless the farm's decision appeared inconsistent or arbitrary. Rasteau brought in a cargo, a portion of which the farm declined to purchase; a higher official of the Farmers General even rejected half of that originally accepted. Maurepas then endeavored successfully to return the acceptable quantity to that initially established and also convinced the farm to make Rasteau an offer of 16 livres per quintal for the poor tobacco. But generally the minister could not intervene—nor should he have—for the quality was often substandard.

Officials in Louisiana blamed poor packaging and the absence of a qualified individual to replace the tobacco inspector who had died. They assured Maurepas that a more rigid control would be established which would provide for the inspection of all tobacco before packaging and require each planter to identify his product by a registered mark. An ordinance to this effect was issued in 1740, followed by another in 1741 requiring a stamp for each cask attesting to the quality, weight, origin, and date of curing. This system was efficient during Salmon's period but fell into disuse when war came and was only revived by Vaudreuil in 1748.

The relationship between the French government and Farmers General precluded any substantial improvement in the tobacco industry in Louisiana. So long as the sale of tobacco in France contributed a significant portion of government revenues through the farming-out system, the government would sanction the purchase of tobacco in the cheapest market. Cumulative financial burdens resulting from two wars between 1744 and 1763 made it unlikely that any changes would be forthcoming. The tobacco industry of Louisiana crystallized as of 1740–44 and demonstrated no measurable progress until new rulers implemented new policies in 1777. Shortly thereafter, in the late 1780s, tobacco from the American settlements in the Upper Mississippi Valley began arriving at New Orleans, inaugurating a new era in the tobacco trade of the town.

Tobacco, waiting on the levee or wharf for transportation, poorly packed in wide-seamed casks and subject to the alternating attacks of the sun's rays or the penetrating rain, often spoiled, loosing a pungent odor that carried clear to the back of the town. Piled around the casks of decaying leaf, barrels of tar and its residue, pitch, impervious to rain, burst their staves during many days of waiting in the glare of the sun. The thick, dark liquids expanded in the heat, became oozy and steamy, and blended in with the gases from the spoiled tobacco to produce an interesting aroma. Unfortunately, this major export commodity of New Orleans reacted similarly in the oven-hot holds of the vessels which carried the product to France. It arrived in a thin, syrupy state useless for caulking or the weathering of cordage. When the pitch and tar arrived in good condition, it was generally judged as good quality, although occasionally the tar was too thick. Whether too thick or too thin, this product of Gulf pine barrens was favored by Maurepas and produced in fairly large quantities, especially in Mobile and across Lake Pontchartrain from New Orleans.

In 1734, the Ministry of the Marine advised officials in New Orleans that pitch and tar would be accepted at the naval yards of France at 10 livres per gallon or 40 livres per barrel, exempted it from freight charges on royal vessels, and increased the price paid private merchants to compensate for shipping expenses. The colonists received this news with pleasure and made plans to step up production. At least four new tar manufactories were established in 1734. Bienville and Salmon immediately applied themselves to the task of augmenting production by arranging for space on royal ships, by advancing money to would-be manufacturers, and by purchasing tar and pitch for the account of the King from individuals who could not wait for remittances from France. One question bothered them: Because French merchants preferred even tobacco to pitch and tar, how would an expanded production get to France?

This was a problem but how serious a one is uncertain. As with all other commodities, the production data are conjectural. An annual figure somewhere between 6,000 and 15,000 barrels of pitch and tar seems to fit the estimates of Bienville and Salmon and might be accepted tentatively as the norm except during times of war. Because vessels of around 250 tons burden were standard for the trade and could carry a full cargo of about 1,250 barrels of pitch and tar, five to fifteen vessels could carry off the total manufacture. But, of course, other products competed for space and there is no indication that at any time a single vessel took only this product. It is also known that vessels left in ballast rather than carry Louisiana products. Shipping then was a grave problem and it is likely that production hovered closer to the lower estimate.

Nonetheless, according to Maurepas, the incentives granted to this commodity resulted in a flood of pitch and tar into Rochefort. By 1738 the stores there overflowed with a quantity of the product far beyond need. Part was sold at a loss. Prices paid to exporters were lowered to 6 livres per gallon for tar and to 6.5 per gallon for pitch. There is little evidence that lower prices resulted in a decline in production. Rasteau, Jung, Bourgine, and other merchants continued to carry the product to France even at the lower price but shipments via the king's ships seem to have tapered off. Like tobacco, the industry probably did not expand after 1740.

As for the other products of Louisiana, only shipments of beaver required Maurepas' sporadic intervention as its sale remained the monopoly of the Company of the Indies. The minister used his influence with the company on behalf of Rasteau, assuring him that the company would accept the beaver carried on the *St. Paul*'s first journey, informing him that the price paid in other ports was no more than that received at La Rochelle, and advising him to apply to the Company of the Indies for the permission Rasteau sought to sell a quantity of beaver in Holland. The planting and mercantile public in Louisiana and the French merchant took their own risks in buying and selling other commodities.

Maurepas, Bienville, and Salmon expressed disappointment in 1741 over the results of the campaign to interest French merchants in the Louisiana trade. But the actual results, as shown in Table III, do not warrant labeling the effort a total failure.

Arrivals from French ports between 1731 and 1748 are believed to be reasonably accurate but, if anything, low.[4] Less certainty is claimed for those arrivals between 1749 and 1755 as officials in France and Louisiana were much less precise in detailing individual arrivals. Few specific West Indian arrivals were noted in the correspondence of the time, although frequent mention is made of "a number" of West Indian vessels in the roadstead before New Orleans, so these figures probably are much too low. The number of arrivals took an upward turn in 1740 as a result of the increased

[4] A check was possible for the figures on French arrivals between 1731 and 1742. When the Company of the Indies retroceded Louisiana to the Crown, it obligated itself to a payment of 1,450,000 livres to the Ministry of the Marine to provide for the needs of the colony. The sum was payable in ten years. Out of this sum, 313,969 livres were expended in bonus payments to French merchants shipping goods to Louisiana and returning with Louisiana produce. The subsidy of 40 livres per ton on goods to Louisiana was quickly replaced by a subsidy of 20 livres per ton on exports and 20 livres per ton for imported Louisiana goods. The total bonus paid subsidized 10,698 tons of goods. Most private exports ran between 80 and 120 tons with as many under 80 as over 120, so 100 tons was used. Fifty tons of inbound merchandise was the norm. The subsidy paid for each voyage carrying 150 tons would allow 71 roundtrips. Table III lists 72 arrivals including seven of unknown origin.

TABLE III

Annual Arrivals at New Orleans by Port of Origin, 1731–55, 1765

	La Rochelle	Bordeaux	St. Malo	L'Orient	Nantes	Marseilles	La Bayonne	King's	Other[b]	French West Indies	Un-known	Total
1731	1	1						4			1	8
1732	1	1		1				1		1	1	6
1733	2	3	2	1				2		1		10
1734	2	2	1					3		1		9
1735	5	3						4			1	13
1736	4	2						1			1	8
1737	5							3	1			9
1738	5	11	1		1			3		1		12
1739	6	2						1				9
1740	4		1					3		5	3	16
1741	6	1						4	1			12
1742	11	1						1		12[d]		25
1743	15				1					1	1	18
1744	3		1		2			1		20		27
1745	3	2						2				7
1746	5							3				8
1747[a]	6	2					1	3			2	14
1748							1	3	1		1	6
1749	5	1				1		1			1	9
1750	2	2				2	1	1	4[c]			12
1751	9	1				1	1	1		1		14
1752	3					1	1	2	5[c]			12
1753	5							2				7
1754	6	2									1	9
1755	5	2					2					9
1764	3	1					3	1	5	4	4	21

[a] Convoy
[b] Dunkirk, Le Havre, Rouen, and Beauvais
[c] Four Spanish vessels
[d] A similar figure is probably applicable to 1741 and 1743 and the period between 1748 and 1754.

participation and virtual monopoly of La Rochelle in the trade. French involvement in the War of the Austrian Succession obstructed further growth.[5]

The increase noticeable in 1740 and subsequent years was probably stimulated in the first place by the War of Jenkins' Ear and the general European war that followed which forced Spain to open up her colonial ports to French vessels. Maurepas grasped at this opportunity even though he was sensitive to the adverse impact it had on New Orleans. For New Orleans the invigorated Spanish trade resulted in more arrivals but fewer goods. Enhanced risks attended fresh opportunities. Spanish possession of Florida was threatened, a possibility which frightened the French, for a British conquest of that peninsula would create bases from which Great Britain could control the Gulf and prevent contact between France and the West Indies.

British war vessels and privateers, operating against the Spanish, infested the sea approaches to Havana, St. Domingue, and the Gulf Coast. With increasing frequency between 1740 and 1744 British vessels stopped, searched and occasionally seized French ships suspected of trading with the Spanish colonies. A large French fleet sent to West Indian waters in 1740 accomplished little except to cause Great Britain to augment the strength of her West Indian squadrons. It was unusual for a French vessel to sail from France to Louisiana without a sighting of or encounter with British ships. From 1738 to 1743 at least sixteen vessels bound to or from New Orleans were stopped and searched, half ultimately suffering condemnation. Many sighted British cruisers but managed to slip away. Less fortunate were Jung's *Comte de Maurepas*, looted by a Jamaican privateer in 1739; Bourgine's *Reine des Anges*, whose cargo was confiscated in 1740; Rasteau and Paul Vivier's *St. Jean de Baptiste*

[5] Emile Garnault, *Le commerce Rochelais au XVII siècle d'apres les documents composant les anciennes archives de la Chambre de Commerce de la Rochelle* (4 vols.; La Rochelle, 1888–98), III, 52–53. Garnault lists 48 clearances from La Rochelle to Louisiana from 1731 to 1744 inclusive. Table III lists 68 arrivals from La Rochelle, which I believe accurate. The estimates of all arrivals at New Orleans from 1744 to 1749 in Surrey, *The Commerce of Louisiana*, 202, 205–206, cite 26 arrivals in the seven years. Table III lists 71 arrivals for the same seven years; *ibid.*, 211–13, lists only 38 arrivals for the five year period 1750–54, compared to 54 in Table III.

and *Triton*, both condemned in 1741. Such harassment, often justified by the nature of the cargoes, added to the difficulties of making remittances to France and supplying Louisiana. But these losses were slight compared to those suffered when harassment gave way to war.

During the War of the Austrian Succession, France lost 2,185 vessels to Great Britain. The West Indian fleet of some 600 vessels was cut by one half. Marseilles alone lost vessels and cargoes valued at 40 million livres, while La Rochelle merchants in 1744 and 1745 lost 30 vessels with ships and cargoes valued at 8.5 million livres. La Rochelle's losses included four of Rasteau's ships and cargoes worth 2,373,425 livres. Not included in these losses were twelve additional Rochelais vessels destined for or departing from Louisiana, three belonging to Rasteau, and other ships from La Rochelle headed to Canada or the West Indies. New Orleans was also hit hard by the loss of several royal vessels laden with supplies for the colony or carrying off valuable cargoes of goods and piastres.

Vaudreuil was most energetic in his efforts to obtain supplies from the French islands and neighboring Spanish. One merchant, Grenier, was sent out in 1745 to search all possible ports for flour. Long periods went by with New Orleans in total isolation and neither Vaudreuil nor Maurepas aware of the needs or actions of the other. While Grenier was playing the role of the Flying Dutchman, seeking flour rather than judgment, Maurepas sought ships and shippers willing to venture to New Orleans. La Rochelle remained the best source and numerous contracts were made with Rasteau, Bourgine, Pierre Hardy, and others to carry government freight at rates 60 percent higher than those of peacetime. Bordeaux contributed a few vessels.

Some of these vessels traveled in the convoys organized to supply the colonies in 1745, 1746, and 1747. Severe penalties were applicable to shippers departing alone when an escort was available but permission could be obtained from Maurepas to circumvent this requirement. The great convoy of 1747 containing 250 merchantmen and 10 war vessels, including 49 Rochelais vessels—four destined for New Orleans—departed in October 1747. This convoy escaped an attempted British interception off Cape Finistere but lost an estimated third of the merchantmen and two warships. One Louisiana-bound vessel was captured by the British, while most of those which ventured out alone gained New Orleans.

Merchantmen did not try a direct run to New Orleans during the war. Risks were lessened by aiming at St. Domingue, slipping from there to Havana, and then attempting the final run to the Mississippi. This route was reversed for the homeward voyage in an effort to join the annual convoys which departed from St. Domingue for France. Occasionally, the Spanish furnished an escort either to or from New Orleans. The La Rochelle vessel *Suédre* and another ship received an escort of Spanish warships from Havana to New Orleans while the Nantes vessel *Josué*, out of New Orleans, was accompanied from Havana to St. Domingue by Spanish warships. The security to be gained from this practice was less the motivating force than was the chance of trading in Havana.

The evolution of this expedient practice into a system was much commented upon in subsequent years. Most observers, among them Lénormant, Vaudreuil, and Du Breuil, pointed out its prejudicial effects upon Louisiana. During the war, ships laden for New Orleans sold what they could in the French and Spanish ports touched at and arrived in New Orleans to sell the remainder or to deposit their specie for the duration of the war. Peace brought traditional Spanish restrictiveness into operation again but the trade was conducted around it, although seizures often occurred. More and more of New Orleans' imports arrived in West Indian vessels and much merchandise coming to New Orleans was proper only for the Spanish trade.

The nature and quantity of Louisiana's products, the latter a factor of a stable population, and the location of the colony were major determinants in shaping the role of Louisiana and its port in the French empire. In the last analysis, the French merchant had to be the judge of Louisiana's economic significance. If he prized the trade, he would pursue it as Rasteau and Jung did consistently during the 1730s and 1740s and as others were to do after Aix-la-Chapelle. But most French merchants did not assign the trade a high priority and those that did were as much concerned with the exploitation of New Orleans as an advanced base from which to engage in other trades. They were content to deliver merchandise consumed in Louisiana to West Indian merchants who then made final sales on their own account or as agents of the French merchants. West Indians and French both worked increasingly through correspondents and agents in New Orleans whether for the purpose of direct trade or to seek markets in the Spanish colonies. Diminishing direct contact between French shipowners and Louisiana planters expanded the role and widened the economic horizons of the New Orleans merchant.

5

The New Orleans Merchant During the French Period

WHILE performing functions similar to those of merchants in the French ports, the colonial merchant viewed the world of trade from a different vantage point. The field within which he operated was more narrowly defined and afforded fewer opportunities or alternative modes of action. Typically, the colonial merchant worked both the import and export trade. He marketed French goods in his or other colonies and gathered colonial produce for sale in France to meet his obligations and to provide a means of payment to the planter for goods and services purchased from both colonial and French merchants. In these activities the colonial merchant exercised less control over the entire process than his colleague at home. The vigor of the domestic colonial market and the demand for consumer goods were determined not only by local crop conditions but by the demand for those crops elsewhere. This, of course, was the general case in France as well, but in France, the variety of goods was greater and a shortage of one caused mercantile interest to shift to others while opening up a field for speculation in the commodity in short supply. In the colonies, where the staple crops were few in number and cultivated within the same general area, conditions causing a failure in one crop could well damage all crops. In Louisiana, flooding and high winds could destroy or shorten indigo and rice crops below New Orleans as well as tobacco crops at Pointe Coupée.

Colonial merchants also sought the patronage of a relatively small number of people as buyers or suppliers. The colonial economy was inelastic compared to that of the mother country, where merchants could compensate for stagnant commerce in one region by focusing upon another. In the colonies, the economy operated virtually as a one-celled organism and a blow at one area of the body reverberated with equal force throughout the whole. Through the 1730s and 1740s a succession of poor crops, especially of tobacco, cast a pall over the commerce of Louisiana, severely limiting the extent of its trade. The merchant at New Orleans could not ride out these bad years by revising his plan of operations because he had few alternatives. He could not initiate a direct trade with foreign markets as this was forbidden. To ignore legalities was difficult as vessels were lacking and suitable goods obtainable only in France. He could not lower expenses by shipping goods to France on his own vessels for this was prohibited. While he could use his own vessels in the Indies and Gulf trades, their cost was great, if he had to buy them, and the facilities for the construction of such vessels were largely nonexistent. He could not develop an interest in manufacturing because it was proscribed for certain items, capital and labor were scarce, and the domestic market was too small. He could not adapt to conditions but only be borne along by them. His flexibility may have been attenuated to a greater degree than that of the planter who could at least retrogress into subsistence agriculture.

Merchants who composed the business community of New Orleans were subject, then, to diverse pressures. The French colonial system was certainly central to the problem of the merchant, but it was not so restrictive or impossible of circumvention that all ills became explicable solely in terms of the system. It may be true, as Richard Pares suggests, that the monopoly of colonial trade impinged more heavily on the French than on the British colonist because the British economy was better suited to fill the needs of the colonies than the French.[1] Suggested here is that the staples of the colonies would have flowed largely toward Britain regardless of the system and that those of the French colonies may have been unnaturally directed toward France by the system. But this may be another way of saying that colonies were more important to Great Britain than they were to France and that greater human and capital resources were thus made available to them both within and without

[1] Richard Pares, *War and Trade in the West Indies, 1739–1763* (Oxford, 1936), 326.

the system. So far as Louisiana was concerned, the system was directed wherever possible to the stimulation of growth in the colony. It was the private sector of the French economy that failed to exploit the openings available to it, not because of a prejudice against colonial trade or lack of experience but because of the low level of profits derivable from that trade compared to other trades.

Victim of a system of priorities evolved in France, the New Orleans merchant did not accept his condition with passivity. Surmounting the stultifying conditions of an economy of scarcity was arduous, but it was accomplished by numbers of merchants in New Orleans and a vigorous mercantile establishment existed at the end of the French regime. Extreme hardship, experienced during the 1730s as a result of recurrent crop failures and inflation, eased in the early 1740s, reappeared during the War of the Austrian Succession, and was dissipated by the good times which followed 1748. A certain amount of opulence and splendor clothed New Orleans, evidenced by an increasing demand for luxury items, especially among the successful planters. Women dressed in high style; the consumption of wine and brandy, always large, became larger; more horses and carriages appeared on the streets; colonial officials complained of salaries inadequate to sustain a proper style of living; and consistently active markets greeted the arriving merchant vessels from France and the West Indies. There existed in the colony by the 1750s, as there had not two decades earlier, a domestic market which increasingly turned to the merchants of New Orleans for the satisfaction of its wants.

Like most colonial merchants, those of New Orleans—a fairly homogeneous group in interests and origins—would buy from and sell to anyone, anywhere, regardless of regulations to the contrary. The problem of illicit trade was not of grave proportions at the capital because the English and Dutch did not habitually frequent the place, due perhaps to the difficulties of approach, while trade with the Spanish was fostered by the French government. English vessels coasted off Gulf shores occasionally, attempting with some success to sell Indian trade goods at Mobile, but to move up the Mississippi was a different problem. At New Orleans, success for English or

Dutch traders depended upon the sanction of the resident officials. During a period such as 1744–48, when the colony had only sporadic contact with the mother country, a certain amount of illicit trade might be countenanced. In 1744 and 1746 Vaudreuil, as other colonial governors, allowed foreign ships to sell goods in New Orleans, concerned as he was more with procuring supplies than with the niceties of trade regulations. In 1746 he permitted, over the opposition of Lénormant, a Dutch vessel to sell its goods at New Orleans. Mortified by an official reprimand from Maurepas for his conduct, Vaudreuil justified his action on the basis of the colony's need and denied that it caused any damage to French or colonial interests. Maurepas, concerned with English and Dutch efforts to obtain Louisiana indigo, refused to permit any trade with foreigners. The activity of English smugglers increased during the Seven Years' War and in the confused period between the cession of Louisiana to Spain and the establishment of firm Spanish control. The English took possession of West Florida at that time.

Most of the merchants and traders located in New Orleans through 1763 were French: most had come directly from France and had established themselves after 1731. Major exceptions were the Company of the Indies, the largest single mercantile unit in New Orleans and represented by agents continuously during the French regime; those French officials who survived the retrocession and used their positions to further their economic interests; and the Jesuit and Capuchin establishments, particularly the former who conducted a large trade with the Illinois country.

A commonly encountered tendency among many officials, the religious groups, and a shifting group of individuals was the combination of planting and mercantile pursuits. This was normal during the entire French period but seems to have been less usual after the Peace of Aix-la-Chapelle. By then, there were sufficient business specialists in New Orleans, including planter-merchants, to perform all services required in moving the crops and distributing imports. In this connection, it is pertinent to remark that businessmen in New Orleans in both the eighteenth and nineteenth centuries frequently utilized commercial profits to set themselves up in planting. This became most common in the nineteenth century, following the Louisiana Purchase and the commitment of lower Louisiana to the sugar staple.

The government official as merchant- or businessman-planter recurs frequently during the eighteenth century. It was usual for the governor to purchase and work an estate. Governor Vaudreuil supplemented his income by working two extensive tracts of land, one the Bienville Concession, and by operating a wholesale drug outlet. Such Superior Council members as Gerard Pery, Fleuriau, Roguet, and Councillor Assessor of the Superior Council Augustin Chantalou were among the foremost merchants in New Orleans at various times. Mixing business and politics was even more pronounced during the Spanish period, when most members of the Cabildo were prominent New Orleans merchants, a tendency that continued unabated in the City Council of New Orleans during the American period. There is no particular evidence during the French period that such men used their offices to improve their competitive position in the trade of the colony. One may assume that they made an effort in this direction, but the absence of complaints by other merchants, French and colonial, and the fact that other merchants without official connections competed successfully leads to the conclusion that such efforts were not crowned with great success—or, that the gains were shared with other merchants.

Most merchants in New Orleans seem to have come as agents or as partners of merchants in France with the right to trade on their own account. Several were petty tradesmen in 1730 who expanded their operations with the arrival of the first merchant vessels following the retrocession. Among the most successful of the latter was J. B. Piemont, in whose hands Jean Jung of Bordeaux placed a large quantity of wine to be sold when prices improved. Described by Salmon as one of the richest merchants in New Orleans, Piemont served as a principal agent of several La Rochelle shipowners, including Bourgine. Gerard Pery also acted as an agent for Jung as well as Jacques Rasteau *pere* of La Rochelle. For the most part, the early traders to New Orleans depended upon their ship's captain for the sale of merchandise and the procurement of a cargo. The organization of the Rasteaus was most tightly knit because Captain Provost of the *St. Paul* was a brother-in-law of Jacques Rasteau, while two sons, Pierre Isaac and Eli, also commanded vessels making the Louisiana run, and the youngest son, Paul, settled in New Orleans in 1736 as his father's direct agent.[2]

Commanders of merchant vessels performed a variety of crucial services for the shipowner in France, sometimes in conjunction with a resident agent at New Orleans and sometimes on their own responsibility. Not infrequently the captain was the owner and in at least one case, that of Mayeaux de Lormaison of Beauvais, brought his vessel to New Orleans in 1734 and remained as a merchant. For the most part the captains served under the orders of and contracted in the name of an absentee owner or lessee. Whether acting for an owner or lessee in a charter-party contract, the captain's responsibilities were to the owners of the goods in his charge. While usually acting under written instructions detailing the route of the voyage, possible cargoes to take on, minimal conditions for sales, credit procedures and such, the instructions were frequently obsolete before the vessel reached its destination, thus compelling the captains to use their own best judgment. At New Orleans the captains frequently instituted suits for the collection of debts in the name of the shipowner and normally devoted considerable effort to obtaining a cargo for a run to the French West Indies or elsewhere. The major objective was to keep the vessel in service, and many of the legal actions taken at New Orleans involving a ship's captain centered around the issue of time, for time was expense. Captain Joseph Ricard, in a petition to the Superior Council, sued the lessees of the schooner *Marie* for expenses in failing to provide a cargo within the eight days agreed upon and causing a two-month delay at New Orleans. Most contracts specified the penalties to be imposed in case of delay on the part of lessee or lessor but they required litigation to compel payment.

The most suitable method of minimizing the responsibilities of the ship's captain was to work through a resident agent. Rasteau sent his son, as did the merchant Mathieu Teissere of Grenoble in 1755;

[2] A Jung and a Bourgine were in business in New Orleans during the 1760s, but their relationship with Jean Jung of Bordeaux and Rochelais shipowner Bourgine is unknown.

Augustin Seigne, merchant of Nantes operated through his brother
Dauberville; Bourgine, Jung, and others utilized the services of
Pery, Piemont, and Paul Rasteau; one group of merchants banded
together to send Fuselier de la Claire to New Orleans as their agent;
and a joint stock company chartered in Geneva in 1746 sent François Caminada of Geneva and Gaspard Pictet of Nantes, two stockholders, to New Orleans to act for the company.

Agents such as these, acting on either their own account or for
the account of the fostering organization, served as middlemen between the planter and the French merchant. Few planters shipped
their crops to France on their own account, consigned to a French
merchant upon whom the planter drew bills roughly equivalent to
anticipated returns. This practice was not unknown among large
planters such as de Pradel and Du Breuil, but it did not enjoy such
currency as in the English islands. It became more common toward
the end of the eighteenth century and was quite widespread in the
nineteenth, but during the French period the planter normally delivered up his crop to a New Orleans merchant who kept the account current.

Credits flowed from the French merchant to the New Orleans
merchant and from the latter to the planter. This was more expensive for the planter but it was advantageous for the merchant in
New Orleans who could act immediately to protect his capital or
the capital of his French employer. J. Piemont in 1740 sold on
Bourgine's account 25,000 livres worth of goods at Pointe Coupée,
collecting tobacco in exchange with 13,000 livres and commiting
the debtors to turn over to him the crop of 1741. When a debtor
defaulted in 1741, Piemont obtained a judgment against him in the
Superior Council.

Piemont and the other merchants bought and sold on their own
account as well. Gerard Pery contracted to outfit the vessel *Marie
Elisabeth* for a commission of 5 percent on all purchases, contracted
with various individuals to receive all their furs, while furnishing
them with French goods, contracted with two individuals to receive
their total production of pitch and tar deliverable at New Orleans,
and purchased campeachy wood (logwood) from a Spanish vessel
to send to Jung on consignment. Jean Baptiste Prevost, agent of the

Company of the Indies at New Orleans, not only handled the affairs of the company, which were quite complicated after 1731, but acted on occasion as a commission merchant for businessmen of La Rochelle and shipped large quantities of furs on his own account to France. Prevost also received provisions from the Illinois, marketing them in New Orleans among the planters, and to incoming vessels. Prevost, as late as 1764, sold tobacco and indigo to a La Bayonne merchant who agreed to ship manufactured items to Prevost.

Outlets for Louisiana's wares were sought in markets other than the mother country, primarily the French West Indies. Most of this trade was carried by West Indian shipping, with West Indian merchants providing French goods in exchange for lumber, rice, and other products vendable in France. The organization of this trade was quite similar to that with France. Some mercantile associations were for particular ventures, as when Pierre Ancelin, wholesale merchant of New Orleans, entered into a partnership with Louis Delaunay to purchase the entire cargo of a vessel from St. Domingue. Others were of longer duration such as the arrangement between Jacques Malvesin, owner of *L'Élizabet*, to carry goods between the Roussillons of New Orleans and Sr. Rondes of Martinique. The Spanish trade was predominantly in the hands of the French merchants, who either carried goods directly to Spanish ports or placed them in the hands of their agents for sale to the Spanish.

Scattered information is extant concerning the dealings of a large number of merchants in New Orleans but the total impact received from a description of their activities would be less satisfactory than an account of a few merchants and associations for whom the data are more comprehensive and concentrated. The routines of the various trades can be followed through the operations of the Rasteaus and the partnership between Chantalou and Testar, a La Rochelle merchant, both of whom acted with and for the Rasteaus as well as independently of them.

The Rasteaus were one of the premier mercantile families in La Rochelle during the eighteenth century. They appear to have risen to prominence in that Protestant stronghold during the late seventeenth or early eighteenth centuries. By the end of the War of the Spanish Succession, they appear quite frequently in the shipping annals of the port, sending vessels to Guinea for slaves and to the French West Indies. Both of these trades remained central to the Rasteau operations during the period in which they were involved in the Louisiana commerce. The family was large and the business included, as far as can be ascertained at this point, at least three sons of Jacques Rasteau, Pierre Isaac (the oldest), Eli, and Paul. Gabriel and Daniel Rasteau, Jacques' brothers, were heavily engaged in the family's business ventures and appear in Louisiana during the 1760s. Another of Jacques' brothers, Jean Benjamin, was located in Cap Français, handling the West Indian end of the operations. At least two Rasteaus, Jean Benjamin and Eli, were ship's captains. One of the Rasteau daughters married into the Allard Bellin family of La Rochelle merchants and another married the merchant Vivier. Both Bellin and Vivier ventured with the Rasteaus and both worked through Paul in New Orleans. Another important connection resulted from the marriage of Gabriel Rasteau to the sister of the Parisian banker Jean Cottin.

Various members of the family served in the La Rochelle Chamber of Commerce during the eighteenth century and in the La Rochelle militia and, in 1777, Pierre Isaac was honored by becoming the first Protestant elected as a deputy to the Council of Commerce, a national advisory body responsible to the crown. The Rasteaus were also subscribers to the *Compagnie d'assurances générales*, founded in 1750 with a capital of 12 million livres, and Pierre Isaac was named a director of the branch office in La Rochelle, along with Vivier. The Rasteaus also had dealings with the powerful English capitalist Lawrence Woulfe, one of the most significant underwriters of maritime insurance during the period 1740–60. Connections of the family extended into the Spanish empire, particularly at Vera Cruz, but the precise nature of the association is unknown at this time. This was a powerful merchant family, heavily committed to commerce with the western hemisphere and patronized by the French government.

Jacques Rasteau's earliest ventures in Louisiana involved the shipment of goods via the *St. Paul*, the *Perle*, the *Comte de Maurepas*, and the *Flore* to New Orleans, under the direction of the ship's captains, to be exchanged for local goods. Market conditions in

New Orleans prevented immediate sales of some of these early cargoes, thus requiring that the goods be placed in the charge of a local merchant. On the very first trip, a large part of the cargo of the *St. Paul* was sold in a block to a group of New Orleans merchants associated for that purpose. Portions of later cargoes were delivered to one Tixerant and other local merchants on consignment. The return cargoes consisted of tobacco, pitch and tar, furs and skins, bear's grease, and small quantities of other items. As pointed out in chapter 4, letters of exchange, which became difficult to obtain, composed a major portion of the returns to France. Most of the vessels returned via St. Domingue where additional goods were freighted. In 1736 Jacques Rasteau apparently decided that it would be expedient to locate a member of the firm in New Orleans to handle the family's business.

Between 1736 and his death in 1747 Paul Rasteau managed the affairs of the Rasteau family in New Orleans, married the daughter of the wealthy planter Broutin, and became a powerful force in the economic life of the city. Paul's early operations were largely confined to servicing the family's affairs: receiving imports from the twelve Rasteau vessels that plied the trade; gathering produce for export to France; collecting debts; running the retail store and warehouse in New Orleans; and relaying current economic information to La Rochelle. Rasteau *fils* associated with Pierre Voisin, a merchant in New Orleans, in distributing imported goods throughout the colony. In addition, Rasteau received an increasing quantity of goods from various merchants in La Rochelle to be sold on consignment. These operations, expanded during the late 1730s and thereafter, were distinct from the family's business.

By 1739 Paul not only received goods from merchants in La Rochelle, Rouen, Bordeaux, and Amsterdam via Rasteau vessels but sent goods on his own account to various individuals in La Rochelle, Bordeaux, and the French West Indies. A letter from a merchant in La Rochelle, soliciting cargoes from Rasteau in New Orleans, and other transactions, leads to the conclusion that the family organization in La Rochelle did not take Paul's Louisiana goods on consignment; his private shipments were separate from the family business while he continued to receive his father's goods. Rasteau's private ventures to La Rochelle were successful on the whole, although numerous letters reached Paul demanding that he make remittances and take care of debts in La Rochelle. It was not always a simple matter to remit either in goods, letters of exchange, or specie, and the young Rasteau must have been as hard pressed as other merchants on occasion. But he accumulated sufficient capital to indulge in large-scale real estate speculation in Louisiana and carried on a substantial trade with St. Domingue. Yet in the years after Paul's death by drowning off Florida, his father referred often to the confusion of Paul's affairs in New Orleans and indicated sadly that more had been expected from him. He left sizable debts in La Rochelle, La Bayonne, and New Orleans which left his succession in confusion through the 1760s.

At the very time several individuals in La Rochelle wrote urgent letters to Paul Rasteau requesting remittances, he was engaged in a large real estate operation in association with Jean Baptiste Prevost, Gerard Pery, and the merchant Couturier. The associates first purchased the entire estates of Labro and Marsilly at prices well below their true value. The partners took advantage of the uneasy military situation vis-a-vis the Chickasaw and the inflated currency to offer Marsilly 14,000 livres for an estate valued at close to 26,000 payable in letters of exchange which the partners purchased with depreciated card money. Labro received 50,000 livres. They then bought an estate from Bobé Descloseaux for 50,000 livres which the latter had only recently obtained. The partners paid the transportation of Labro and Marsilly to France, promising not to resell the lands or effects until payment had been remitted to France. Shortly after the original owners left, the partners sold off some Negroes to meet the first installment to Descloseaux and followed with the sale of all the slaves at a great profit, more than sufficient to pay off the debts of the association. Couturier used his profits to establish a plantation at Pointe Coupée while the others turned the card money into specie at less than the prevailing discount. Evidently this large monetary transaction temporarily reversed the inflationary trend in New Orleans and the partners made their exchange at just that precise moment.

While Salmon deplored the entire transaction, which resulted in the abandoning of three plantations, the profits became available to Paul at a most opportune moment. Jacques Rasteau, in conjunction with Eli and Paul and with the cooperation of Maurepas, undertook a heavily capitalized trading sortie to Vera Cruz and the Campeachy Coast. The story of this venture is better told in chapter 7, in connection with the general Louisiana-Spanish trade, but Paul accompanied the *Lion d'Or*, Eli Rasteau captain, as the first officer and supercargo and invested heavily in the operation from which much was anticipated and not a little gained.

Rasteau's other areas of trade included Mobile and the West Indies. In the former, Rasteau cooperated with Prevost and dealt largely in pitch and tar. Mobile enjoyed little direct contact with France, being supplied via New Orleans and carrying on a random trade with Spanish Florida. Rasteau utilized the proximity of Mobile to Florida to establish a trade with Pensacola and St. Augustine. In the spring of 1747 Rasteau accompanied a family vessel, *L'Irondelle*, to Florida with a cargo obtained from St. Domingue. It may well have been on this voyage, or a similar one undertaken shortly thereafter, that the young Rasteau perished.

In the West Indies, Rasteau corresponded with his uncle and traded on his own account. He usually did not purchase French goods at St. Domingue as these could be obtained at home, but he did receive such goods on consignment from West Indian merchants as well as purchase refined sugars, syrups, and taffia for his own account. For the most part, Rasteau serviced the lumber requirements of the island's merchants by exporting such items to his uncle on joint ventures and to other traders of the islands on order. In May, 1747, Rasteau and several others invested 16,000 livres in a lumber shipment to Martinique, the purpose of which was to purchase slaves for resale in Louisiana. The vessel left New Orleans in August. Three months later Paul Rasteau was dead.

After 1748 the Rasteaus' major purpose in New Orleans was to liquidate Paul's affairs. The La Rochelle firm sent an occasional vessel to New Orleans and odd assortments of merchandise on various other vessels. Some of these were joint ventures with Testar of La Rochelle and most were consigned to Chantalou, the latter's partner in New Orleans and the executor of the Rasteau succession.

Chantalou and Testar used each other's services as early as 1748 but the relationship remained intermittent until sometime between 1751 and 1752. Even after the two merchants formed a partnership in 1751, Testar dealt with other New Orleans merchants whenever it seemed expedient and Chantalou acted similarly with several merchants in La Rochelle and Nantes. Chantalou was one of the more active businessmen in New Orleans between 1740 and 1765, combining widespread mercantile operations with official positions as Attorney of Vacant Estates, Chief Clerk of the Superior Council, and Royal Notary after 1758. Testar's involvement with New Orleans may have begun with a shipment aboard the Rasteaus' *Lion d'Or* in 1742 and it continued to at least 1758.

From the several score of letters that passed between the two men in 1751 and 1752, it appears that all goods addressed to one another were on joint account. The merchandise was typical of the trade: indigo, tobacco, and furs were the preferred items from New Orleans. A great variety of soft and hard goods, especially high cost items such as brocades, linens, silks, velvets, and beaver hats was addressed to Chantalou. Each merchant kept the other fully informed as to changing market conditions and suggested the proper reaction to price changes, freight rates, consumer demand, and the like. Testar in March, 1753, informed Chantalou that the Company of the Indies increased the price of beaver, requiring an additional markup on the price of beaver hats in New Orleans. Rumors of war, the number of vessels in port, a killing frost, the spoilage of cheese—such mundane items are the essence of their communications.

Testar's responsibilities were the greater of the two in the mutual exchange of goods. Now in Bordeaux, on to Nantes, then to Rochefort, he buzzed from port to port purchasing goods, arranging for their freight, and forming opinions as to where remittances from Louisiana should be directed. He owned at least one vessel, *L'Ajax*, but most goods were carried by others, with Testar making arrangements for return cargoes on the basis of the most recent information received from Chantalou. Chantalou, of course, could not always conform to his partner's expectations but used his own discretion as to the best return, again on the basis of Testar's evaluation of market conditions in the various ports of France. Regular correspondence was essential and Testar at one time chided his associate for allowing a vessel to leave New Orleans without a letter to La Rochelle. Testar required exact information regarding incoming cargoes since he made the insurance for both out and inbound vessels.

During the period 1749–54 insurance was fairly cheap and readily available in the French ports through either French or English underwriters. Rates to Louisiana from the Atlantic ports ran between 3 and 5 percent; Testar normally paid 4.5 percent at La Rochelle and Bordeaux. When Testar was ignorant of Chantalou's intentions, he usually acted prudently by taking out a time policy for a month costing a half percent of the anticipated wholesale cost of the cargo. Rumors of war, ominous fleet movements from Britain, or seizures in West Indian waters all precipitated instant rate increases. A declaration of war pushed rates up to 50 percent and even higher. During the War of the Austrian Succession and the Seven Years' War, London underwriters continued to insure French vessels at low rates and issued passports to the insured which were generally honored by British cruisers.

The Testar-Chantalou partnership operated somewhat more formally than the normal New Orleans-France business association. In most cases, the accounts were balanced with the termination of each transaction. When Testar forwarded goods worth 1,250 livres to *ordonnateur* Salmon in New Orleans, Salmon's remittance was credited to his account and any surplus or deficit appeared in the next shipment. If an account was current, one party was usually in the debt of the other, the sum varying, depending upon the flow of goods. Testar and Chantalou worked with a fixed capital in both La Rochelle and New Orleans with profits, which ran between 20 and 30 percent net, distributed in proportion to the capital contributed. Both men seem to have maintained equivalent sums active in the partnership; a sum which was increased in 1752.

Neither partner ever referred to the advantages of this arrangement but they may be partially determined by reviewing the nature and chronological pattern of remittances. Testar commonly made at least one shipment per month to New Orleans valued at between 3,000 and 5,000 livres. Chantalou, operating in a society geared to the harvest of staple crops, disposed of the French goods at all seasons but made his remittances when the crops were in or when the Illinois convoys appeared at the levee. At those critical periods, Chantalou utilized the partnership's capital resources to make purchases far in excess of the credits granted to various planters. At such a time, the operations of most merchants in New Orleans were restricted to an amount roughly equal to credits extended to planters and anticipated credits from French sources. Chantalou adapted his purchases and remittances to crop conditions in Louisiana and market conditions in France. Because the harvest of Louisiana staples did not as yet affect European prices for those crops, Chantalou on one occasion was able to make heavy purchases of a bumper indigo crop on the basis of prices current received from Testar, without the apprehension that the large crop would drive prices down in France. When purchases of staples seemed unprofitable, Chantalou remitted letters of exchange, enabling Testar to send additional goods quickly to New Orleans. When the former was pressed for funds in 1753 because of heavy debts owed him by the country, Testar temporarily increased his share of funds active in the partnership. Through such arrangements Chantalou was always in funds and on top of the market.[3]

How common this sort of arrangement was in New Orleans is not clear. Company organizations existed, such as Thibaudeau and Company, whose capital fluctuated with the state of business but their overseas connections are unknown. Paul Rasteau's connections with the interlocking network of Rasteau firms in La Rochelle and St. Domingue guaranteed him access to funds which allowed him to act with capital resources which were constantly replenished. The firm Pictet and Caminada was a more sophisticated version of the Chantalou and Testar partnership but only odd bits of information were uncovered concerning their operations. Undoubtedly, the Company of the Indies was the largest of the permanently capitalized units operating in New Orleans.

The charter of Pictet and Caminada established a capital of 300,000 livres of which 172,000 was actually subscribed. One of the

---

[3] Chantalou resigned his office as Chief Clerk of the Superior Council to Jean Baptiste Garic in 1763. His accounts were in disorder and he was ordered to present full accounts before departing for France.

heaviest subscribers, Pierre Hardy of La Rochelle, invested 10,000 livres. Hardy, a large shipowner in La Rochelle, devoted five vessels to the trade between 1746 and 1751, having earlier engaged in joint shipments with the Rasteau family. Most of the goods received by Pictet and Caminada were freighted aboard Hardy's vessels and charged to the company. Gaspard Pictet's relations with New Orleans antedated the organization of Pictet and Caminada. In 1745 Pictet sent and received goods through François Chastang of New Orleans. The partners were in New Orleans by 1747, Caminada arriving via *S. M. Le Parham*.

Pictet and Caminada received imports and forwarded agricultural products to France on account of the company and on their own account. Herbert Lüthy has documented five separate shipments on the company's account between 1753 and 1755 valued at 155,062 livres.[4] In addition, at least three other remittances valued at 90,000 livres were made during this period, but only one reference was found to a cargo prior to 1753. No other single firm or individual about whom information is available remitted such large cargoes during this period. The annual value of the firm's shipments exceeded by about three times the value of Chantalou's exports to Testar.

The charter of Pictet and Caminada expired in 1752 and was not renewed. Most of the shipments noted above were designed to fulfill obligations to the company but the liquidation, interrupted by the Seven Years' War, was not concluded until 1765. Pictet and Caminada remained in New Orleans to service the company's accounts but also operated on their own behalf and in association. Caminada purchased two tobacco plantations in 1757 and with Pictet sent large indigo cargoes to France. Caminada sold real estate in New Orleans in 1765 and was still operating in 1767. Pictet died at New Orleans in 1776.

The Company of the Indies continued on in New Orleans, not out of fond hopes for profit but in an effort to liquidate its affairs and collect debts which were in excess of 500,000 livres in 1742. Many obstacles faced the company in its collection efforts, most serious being the reluctance and inability of the debtors to meet

4 Lüthy, *La banque protestante en France*, II, 121–23.

their obligations, most of which antedated 1731 and involved the purchase of Negroes. Hardly less serious was the lukewarm, if not hostile, attitude of government officials in New Orleans and the lack of consistent support from Maurepas.

When Louisiana rejoined the crown's domains, all of the company's physical possessions, including plantations, buildings, Negroes, and brick works, became crown property. In addition to these properties, valued at several hundred thousand livres, the company agreed, as noted in reference to shipping bonuses, to pay the crown 1.4 million livres in ten annual payments. At least 2 million livres were involved in the retrocession and the company hoped that debts collected in Louisiana would provide part of the sum due to the crown. But company efforts in Louisiana were immediately obstructed by a demand by the colonists that the total debt be scaled down by 50 percent.

Salmon supported the debtors' position, arguing that full repayment would ruin the colony and that the company, if it wished to realize anything, would have to scale down the debt. The *ordonnateur* also maintained that the company should receive produce in part payment of its debts. Salmon's program prevailed against the objections of the company, the latter pointing out that members of the Superior Council who initiated the demand for a reduction were among the most considerable debtors to the company. The company finally agreed to allow Salmon to control the liquidation of up to 40 percent of the debt. He accomplished this by fixing the prices of various products used by the debtors to meet their obligations at a level above that current when the debts were mostly accrued and at about the level current in 1735. Currency depreciation in Louisiana in the late 1730s operated to scale down the debts even further.

The resident agent of the company in New Orleans worked to gain the acknowledgement of debtors for their obligations and to prescribe the method of payment in each case. The company wished to receive as much cash as possible and remit funds to France in letters of exchange. But the French government used the excuse of a shortage of letters to compel the company to remit in produce whenever possible. This was obviously more advantageous to the debtor than to the creditor. In 1740 and 1741 Maurepas instructed

Salmon to cease issuing letters to the company, suggesting that the latter remit in tobacco. By 1742 the company held some 267,000 livres in New Orleans for which Salmon would issue only 130,000 livres in letters. The remainder had to be invested in goods for shipment to France. The company was still trying to get its funds to France in the 1750s and Louisiana officials continued to object to its collection methods.

Few merchants in New Orleans controlled capital resources equal to those of Paul Rasteau, Augustin Chantalou, or Pictet and Caminada. Most companies operated more traditionally, sending a venture now to La Rochelle or to Nantes and soliciting the business of French merchants, while gathering what produce they could from the planters and farmers or *voyageurs*. Their ventures were smaller than Rasteau's or Chantalou's, thus spreading risk as widely as possible and maintaining their limited capital in constant use but with relatively small sums involved in a single transaction. Not a few combined merchandising with planting and amassed considerable fortunes by the end of the French period. Chantalou accumulated sufficient capital to make a loan of 60,000 livres to Flamand in 1760; Louis Rançon, who became attorney general of Spanish Louisiana in 1770, frequently loaned money in the 1760s; Nicholas Forstall, who migrated to Louisiana from Martinique in the 1740s, was a wealthy man and prominent official in the 1760s and 1770s and his heirs maintained their prominence into the pre-Civil War decades. Those New Orleans merchants whose business activities continued during the Spanish period generally initiated their operations in New Orleans after 1748. Certain families span the periods, such as the Fleuriaus, Pontalbas, Jungs, La Vergnes, Le Brettons, and Thibaudeaus, providing continuity and much of the local leadership between 1765 and 1803. Fleuriau *père*, a merchant in 1738, served as *Procureur Général* of the Superior Council until his death in 1752. His son, a lieutenant of troops in 1752, continued the business and served on the Cabildo in 1770.

As a group, merchants in New Orleans were probably quite similar to those found in any French colonial port, or indeed any European port. They were vigorous and adventurous in the management of their trade, exploiting to the full the opportunities available to them. Some may have been more innovative than others in creating opportunities but value judgments here are tenuous because great risk attended even the most conventional forms of trade. When possible they invested in real estate or engaged in planting, both of which provided returns in security and status. They appeared to be about as law abiding in their relations with one another and outside merchants as conditions demanded. As in any other entrepot, the local judicial bodies dealt largely with business affairs. The Superior Council and the *ordonnateur* devoted most of their time to the arbitration of commercial disputes. French merchants occasionally complained of prejudicial treatment but this was not the norm. During Maurepas' administration, the Minister intervened when necessary to obtain justice for French merchants. Usually, the *ordonnateur* and the governor guaranteed equitable treatment for all. One *ordonnateur*, Rochemore, was dismissed in 1760 after a comprehensive indictment by a group of New Orleans merchants. Others may have been controversial figures, as was Lénormant, but there is no evidence questioning their honesty. According to one scholar, the process of justice moved more rapidly and with less expense in Louisiana than in France.[5]

While the colonists may have enjoyed reasonably just treatment at the hands of local judicial bodies, both justice and security seemed sadly lacking in financial and monetary matters. In these affairs, the locals were at the mercy of and constantly threatened by the arbitrary acts of officials seated comfortably at Court. Nothing plagued the colony more consistently than specie scarcity and the depreciation of colonial money. It was neither a problem resolvable by the colony alone nor a problem of great moment to French officials. The priority assigned to Louisiana did not include taking the action required to place and maintain colonial finances in order. Thus, they were generally in disorder.

---

[5] James D. Hardy, Jr., "Law in French Louisiana," in *Proceedings of the Ninth Annual Genealogical Institute* (Baton Rouge, 1966), 9–10.

6

The Problem of Colonial Finances and Money

N 1720 a Boston merchant complained that the "medium of exchange, the only thing which gives life to Business . . . is so exhausted, that in a little time we shall not have wherewith to Buy our Daily Bread, much less to pay our Debts or Taxes." [1] Far to the south, along the banks of the Lower Mississippi, a planter, de Pradel, about a decade later wrote pessimistically to his brother in France that specie was becoming so exceedingly scarce in the colony that it was doubtful that the troops or government officials could be paid. His observations were confirmed by a royal official who informed his superior that there was no specie in the colony. The same planter, richer by far, voiced similar fears three decades later. In describing the rampant inflation sweeping the colony, he explained that he guarded against monetary depreciation by investing in improvements on his plantation and by acquiring a new farm.

The North American colonies of Britain and France, from Canada through the Atlantic Coast provinces to Louisiana, suffered from a chronic shortage of exchange that was more burdensome and damaging at some times than others but which was always present and always inconvenient. Monetary conditions varied among the English colonies but led at one time or another to the emission of fiat money by virtually all of the provincial governments. Such issues were necessary if the colonies were to have a medium of exchange sufficient to service ordinary business demands. Hard money or specie

[1] John Colman, *The Distressed State of the Town of Boston, &c. Considered, in a Letter from a Gentleman in the Town, to his Friend in the Country* (Boston, 1720) quoted in Stuart Bruchey (ed.), *The Colonial Merchant: Sources and Readings* (New York, 1966), 83.

tended to flow out of the colonies, which normally bought more than they sold in international markets. Certain English colonies, notably Massachusetts, New York, and Pennsylvania, were able to lessen their balance of payment deficits by means of a thriving carrying trade and by operating outside of the colonial system. The staple colonies, operating within the system imposed by the Navigation Acts, became chronically and heavily indebted to British merchants while benefiting to an extent by the preferential treatment granted to the major staples and from the large credits extended to the agricultural sector by British capitalists.

The French plantation colonists of Louisiana were subject to all the ills experienced by their British antagonists to the northeast and more. Adequate supplies of free men and bondsmen were harder to come by, thus hampering efforts to increase agricultural productivity and reducing the incentives necessary to tempt French merchants to develop the trade. Markets and credits were less accessible to Louisianians than to their planting equivalents in South Carolina or Martinique. However persistently and justifiably citizens of the latter colonies might criticize their governments for sacrificing colonial interest to home interests, they functioned at the center of the system rather than at the periphery, as did Louisiana. Carolinians had their rice and indigo to sell while sugar from Martinique, Guadeloupe, and St. Domingue sweetened tables throughout Europe. Factors and commission merchants might siphon off the middleman's profits through their control of marketing processes, shipping, and credits, but this did not prohibit, for example, the purchase by planters of an endless supply of slaves.

Europe wanted the indigo and sugar that Carolina and Martinique produced. Those crops would be moved to market whatever the internal condition of the colony. The local supply of hard money, the specie value of paper money, and the current value of the staple might determine profit margins for producers and shippers. The availability of shipping, freight rates, insurance premiums, conditions in Europe also were variables which affected profits and the rate at which the crops flowed to markets. But if a crop was harvested, the crop was moved, the colonists were supplied, and credits were extended for another year. Louisiana lacked as yet the productive capacity of the more highly developed colonies which served to induce merchants to make the trade in spite of local conditions. One of the least attractive attributes of Louisiana, and one which dampened mercantile interest in her fortunes from 1731 forward, was the consistently uncertain state of colonial finances. An inconvenience in more mature colonies, financial conditions acted as a repellent to merchants and as a barrier to growth in Louisiana.

By the eighteenth century the management of currency was one of the unchallenged prerogatives of the state. States manipulated the currency by altering the specie content of coinage, and through its position as the primary debtor of the nation, the state could influence monetary circulation. During the sixteenth and seventeenth centuries the nations of Western Europe expended much energy securing stocks of precious metals, an adequate supply of which was believed indispensable to national power. In the succeeding century, Europe enjoyed a greater abundance and more certain supply of specie, obtained in various ways from the mines of the New World. But the larger scope and augmented expenses of frequent wars and the burgeoning demands of commerce and infant industries for capital continued to exert pressure on the monetary supply.

Satisfying the ever-present monetary requirements of an exuberantly expansive commercial capitalism which operated in the world at large and contributed the wherewithal by which states pursued national aims became an ascendant objective during the eighteenth century. Whatever the rubric used to define economic thought and policy in the sixteenth and seventeenth centuries, dynastic power had been exalted at the expense of the welfare of the nation. In the seventeenth century, however, the power syndrome, responding to the forces of nationalism and internationalism, was penetrated by the truth that the state is subsumed in a nation and that the nation is a congeries of conflicting interests demanding satisfaction and requiring the mediatory efforts of the state. Mercantilism became, according to Curtis P. Nettels, "a rationalization of the special interests of dominant groups of the time." [2] As Jacob Viner phrases it, a har-

---

[2] Curtis P. Nettels, "British Mercantilism and the Economic Development of the Thirteen Colonies," *Journal of Economic History*, XII (Spring, 1952), 105.

mony was achieved between "the pursuit of power and the pursuit of plenty," with the latter defined by the economic elite.[3]

The melding of Nettels' definition with Viner's concept provides an interesting perspective from which to view the response of the French state to the melange of interests that formed the nation and, more specifically, to the commercial portion of those interests. It is erroneous, as Viner and others point out, to accept the absolutist structure of the French government at face value and thus underestimate the sensitivity of the government to commercial interests. Whatever the motives of Maurepas, he devoted an inordinate amount of time to the organization of trade with Louisiana and to resolving the problems faced by the merchants. Nonetheless, the eighteenth-century merchants and industrialists of France did not participate as fully in the policy-making processes of the state as did their equivalents in Great Britain. Individual capitalists might achieve elitist status politically, but as a class the capitalists were denied entrance to the establishment. They might petition and memorialize but they could not demand. Dynastic or state interests, stratagems to further French power continentally and *outre-mer*, problems of land defense and security, fiscal schemes to prevent royal bankruptcy—such concerns held sway in France to the ultimate retardation of commercial growth.[4]

In the broad areas of money and credit, the French government did not demonstrate that sympathy and support for commercial interests so noticeable in Great Britain. While the regency government sanctioned and lavished great privileges upon John Law and his projects, the motivation was largely fiscal and not necessarily complimentary to the broader commercial and industrial purposes of Law. The inflationary content of the system of managed currency that Law attempted to implement did not take root in France, which rejected both his ideas and his institutions following his fall. Monetary policies and credit facilities in France were inferior to those of England, which not only supported commerce but the state

---

[3] Jacob Viner, "Power Versus Plenty as Objectives of Foreign Policy in the Seventeenth and Eighteenth Centuries," *World Politics*, I (1948), 11.

[4] Penfield Roberts, *The Quest for Security, 1715–1740* (New York, 1947), 4, defines the "dynasty" as a rather large group consisting of "sovereign, royal family, court, government, high business and financial circles."

as well during times of crisis. The great prosperity of France between 1725 and 1755 depended to a large degree upon the staples of her colonial possessions which achieved preeminent positions in European markets. Great Britain, jealous of French ascendancy in certain staple markets, was less dependent than France upon her formal empire for profits and more successful in penetrating the empires of other powers—thus establishing a vast informal empire and busily creating a broad industrial plant at home.[5]

France, then, lagged behind Britain as well as the Netherlands in the development of money, banking, and credit resources. France shared the larger supply of specie money available in the eighteenth century, just as she participated in the use of newer methods of remittances such as letters of exchange, bills of credit, brokerage and exchange services, and other similar devices. But without central banking institutions and with a system of privilege that fed on the fiscal embarrassments of the royal government, France did not have available capital to meet colonial demands. Capital was sufficient but not for those areas. Should a colony fall into fiscal difficulties, it could hope for little assistance from the metropole beyond the emission of colonial money that lacked the active support of liquid capital resources.

With the exception of brief interludes, French Louisiana possessed dangerously inadequate supplies of money and received minimal financial backing from France. Various expedients were tried to provide a circulating medium but a dearth existed regardless of the particular expedient. Specie money obtained in piastres from the Spanish fled the colony in payment for imports. This was the logical consequence of a relationship between developed and undeveloped economies and was applicable to the relationship between Louisiana and the more advanced economies of the French West Indies. To ameliorate the monetary problem, France had either to step up purchases from Louisiana, extend long-term credits, or inject large sums of capital directly into the economy through government spending to compensate for the relative absence of capital formation in the

[5] I am indebted to Professor Richard Sheridan of the Department of Economics at the University of Kansas, Lawrence, for an introduction to the concept of the informal empire. This seems especially relevant to the situation in Spanish Louisiana between 1763 and 1779.

colony. The French government was unwilling to appropriate the funds necessary to development in Louisiana. Indeed, the government even failed to provide sufficient money to expedite remittances to France.

French merchants, as chapter 4 indicated, suffered grave inconvenience because of remittance difficulties stemming from scarcities of both currency and produce. In the sugar islands of France, French merchants extended credits and received payment in kind, not so much because currency was lacking, as one scholar suggests, but in anticipation of a future crop marketable to advantage in France.[6] The crop drew shippers to the islands. In Louisiana, an inadequate currency posed an altogether different problem, for products were not easily obtainable and thus credits were extended only at great risk.

During the years immediately following retrocession to the crown, the currency problem did not reach a critical stage, but by 1735 the symptoms of future ills were apparent and producing an effect. The French government sent to Louisiana specie which covered expenses and circulated in the colony. Letters of exchange could be drawn by the *ordonnateur* to an amount not exceeding 150,000 livres annually to provide a means of return to the merchants newly engaged in the trade. This arrangement proved adequate for only a short period. Between April 1, 1732, and April 1, 1734, Salmon overdrew the quota for letters by 61,000 livres but retained a specie reserve of some 140,000 livres. By 1735 specie was in short supply and letters of exchange were issued in amounts significantly above the quota. The specie drain left the colony without the means to carry on its normal affairs. Merchants in New Orleans, unable to gather sufficient produce to pay for imports, were hard put to meet their obligations, while French merchants were unable to obtain large enough sums in letters of exchange to remit the proceeds from sales to France. Salmon was pressed to overdraw each annual quota with the overdrawals applied against future quotas. By 1734 Bienville and Salmon were discussing with Maurepas

[6] Louis-Philippe May, *Histoire economique de la Martinique, 1635–1763* (Paris, 1930), 193–94.

the efficacy of issuing card money to provide the colony with the currency necessary to a normal economic life.

Maurepas initiated the discussion in the fall of 1733 by describing the progress of the card money issued recently in Canada to the amount of 600,000 livres. That emission, he maintained, was successful in reviving the internal commerce of Canada which had been stagnant for more than a decade because of the absence of a circulating medium. Maurepas offered similar advantages to Louisiana. Referring to the inevitability of specie flow to France, he explained that it was inconvenient for the government to make specie advances to Louisiana in order to sustain its commerce. Card money would provide sufficient currency to handle the domestic trade. Maurepas recognized that the Louisiana experience with *billets de caisse* issued by the Company of the Indies had been unfortunate, but that was the company's fault. It had damaged the money by refusing to receive it for all transactions and by raising prices when it was received. The new issue would be legal tender in the king's stores without an additional markup and would be transmittable to France in letters of exchange at specie value. Maurepas requested an opinion from Bienville and Salmon before he proceeded further with the proposal.

The response of Bienville and Salmon was subdued and questioning. They admitted the need but believed that no issue would be better than one improperly sustained. Colonial experience with the company's money would be the chief obstacle to a successful emission and a general lack of confidence in the value of the money would result in rapid depreciation. The colonists must be convinced of the acceptability of the cards in all commercial transactions. Moreover, even if the colonists demonstrated a willingness to accept the money, the problem of circulation would not necessarily be resolved. Just as specie normally passed to France via the merchant vessels, so too would the card money pass into the hands of the French traders who would convert it into letters of exchange on France. The success of an issue hinged upon the attitude of the French merchant.

The ambivalent reply from Louisiana neither deterred the crown nor elicited from it assurances that the French merchant would be provided for. An ordinance was published in February, 1735, authorizing the issue of 200,000 livres in various denominations to be received at par in all transactions. An interpretive memoir addressed to Bienville and Salmon accompanied the ordinance. Reviewing its efforts to establish the commerce of Louisiana by subsidies to French merchants and the granting of privileges to various Louisiana products, the crown viewed the issue of card money as a supplement to those measures and an assurance of their success. The ordinance, it was explained, followed the suggestions of Bienville and Salmon to proportion the value of the money to that of the Spanish piastre current in Louisiana at five livres per piastre and to increase the amount of smaller denominations. On the critical issue of letters of exchange, the memoir fell far short of dissipating the apprehensions voiced by the colonial officials. Instead, the crown stated explicitly that the quota would remain at 150,000 livres yearly. Salmon was instructed to distribute the letters equitably but only to those remitting in card money so as to establish the new issue securely. In a barbed aside, the memoir reminded Salmon that he had only 53,000 livres remaining of the 1735 quota. This was in February.

Bienville and Salmon were well aware of the shortcomings of the new monetary system. While they assured Maurepas in letters of February and May, 1737, that there was no opposition to the card money, they were not prepared to assess its impact on the colony. Instead, they stated explicitly that the card money would be favored by merchants to the degree that letters of exchange were made available. In spite of the obvious fact that an unfilled demand for letters of exchange would drive down the value of the card money, the crown was unwilling to increase its capital investment in Louisiana by raising the annual quota of letters of exchange drawable on France. Salmon adopted the only policy available by issuing letters in excess of the quota which sustained the value of the card money for a short time in 1736 and 1737. But an escalation of the war against the Chickasaws, pressed intermittently since 1730, created pressures which the static money supply of the colony could not withstand. Card money was virtually worthless by 1743–44. Colonial expenses rose to unprecedented levels and were carried on colonial accounts as unpaid encumbrances.

Pressure on the monetary supply was serious by 1739 as the expenses of the Indian war mounted. Salmon and Bienville notified Maurepas of their inability to keep within the stipulated amount of letters because of the war. They observed that money was growing scarce and that the paper money fell into discredit because of the lack of letters. As a measure of the depreciation, they singled out the rise in the price of the livre-value of piastres from five livres to eight. They insisted that the expenses of the war could be met only by increasing the quota for letters and through the issue of 200,000 livres in new card money. Salmon, lacking cash to meet the augmented expenses, had recourse to the issue of treasury notes to the creditors of the colony. These passed as money in the colony but were subject to the same depreciatory influences as the card money—that is, their value depended upon their ability to purchase letters of exchange.

Maurepas expressed great displeasure over the circulation of treasury notes and the overdrawal of letters. He would, however, neither sanction an increase in the quota, send additional specie money, nor admit the necessity for a new issue of card money. Instead, he communicated his hope that Salmon could recall the notes and get along with available resources. This was impossible in 1739 and continued so until 1743. By the later date, the expenses for the Chickasaw wars exceeded 4 million livres while the colonial debt surpassed 2 million. In 1741 Salmon was drawing letters on the quota of 1744 and was a favorite target of Maurepas' criticism. The minister was of no help whatsoever in this financial crisis and placed the entire responsibility upon Salmon. Maurepas understood the nature and extent of the problem quite well as Bienville and Salmon kept him fully informed of each new deepening of the crisis. Thus, Salmon communicated increases in the amount of notes outstanding in January and May, 1740, and Bienville in March, 1741, analyzed the seriousness of the emergency. Letters were so scarce, Bienville wrote, that speculation in those issued caused continued depreciation of the card money while the price of necessary provisions increased.

Inflation hit hard. French merchants doubled the price of their goods, eliciting a similar response from the colonists. The piastre, in

1743, brought 12.5 livres, two and one-half times its normal value. All staple provisions were scarce and dear: flour, usually at 30 livres per barrel, rose to 70 livres in 1740 and 365 livres in 1744; wine, normally 200 livres per barrel, sold for 500 livres in Spanish silver and 800 livres colonial paper in 1741. The impact of inflation on commercial transactions is apparent in the sale by Du Breuil and Dalcour of eleven slaves in 1743 to Bobé Descloseaux for 32,450 livres, or about 1,000 livres per slave above their value in a non-inflated market. The cost of living rose so sharply that government officials and employees extracted a promise from Maurepas to pay half of their salaries in France. Such an expedient was of no consequence to the permanent residents of the colony who were destined to receive ill treatment at the hands of Maurepas when he finally decided to intervene in the financial crisis.

Until 1743 Maurepas was content to direct severe criticisms at Salmon for financial mismanagement. Extreme dissatisfaction and an accurate description of the condition of the colony formed the substance of the minister's communications to Salmon. In the detail of his criticism, Maurepas was frequently accurate. It was true that Salmon was far behind in his accounts and that he possessed no accurate knowledge of the amount of debt outstanding or the total amount of treasury notes issued. He was not following proper administrative procedure in these matters. Such criticisms hardly went to the root of the matter. Maurepas ordered Salmon to call in the various notes issued for conversion into a single kind of note and ordinances to this effect were published in May, 1741, and January, 1743. The earlier ordinance had little effect but the second resulted in the conversion of about 933,000 livres in *billets de trésorier* into *bons de caisse*. The new bills were worth no more than the old. The total paper issue, not including 200,000 livres in card money, climbed to over one million livres by 1744. Maurepas had, by this time, made his decision regarding the new policy to implement.

In the meantime Vaudreuil had replaced Bienville as Governor of Louisiana and Salmon's time was measured. Both Vaudreuil and Salmon recognized the need to retire the paper outstanding and forwarded concrete proposals to Maurepas covering three major points. The quota of letters of exchange should be doubled; the crown should send two or three cargoes of slaves to be paid for in paper at prices proportionate to the depreciation of the money; and if liquidation was determined upon, a distinction should be made between those who received the paper prior to June, 1739, after which date depreciation became serious, and between those with card money and those with the new *bons de caisse*. In these last points, Vaudreuil and Salmon were attempting to protect the interests of merchants like Rasteau, Bourgine, and Jung who had traded with Louisiana since 1731.

These proposals were discussed in the Ministry of the Marine and rejected categorically. Vaudreuil and Salmon sought to moderate the impact upon Louisiana of the inevitable liquidation. Insensitive to this objective, the crown thought more in terms of convenience, mitigation of risk, and avoidance of losses to the royal treasury. France stood on the threshold of war with Great Britain as the steadying hand of Cardinal Fleury was replaced in 1743 by the mailed fists of adherents of the war party. With war in the offing, Maurepas' councilors advised against the transportation at the king's risk of slave cargoes to Louisiana, turned down an increase in letters of exchange which would draw specie from the Marine treasury at an impropitious moment, and advised a simple liquidation. In discussing the details of conversion, it was decided to refrain from making the distinctions between holders of the money suggested by Vaudreuil and Salmon. As to the critical question of the extent of the reduction, the final decision prescribed the conversion of Louisiana's paper into letters of exchange at two-fifths of face value; a note for 100 livres paper would purchase a letter of exchange of 40 livres. Sebastian-François-Ange Lénormant de Mezy, late of St. Domingue and son of an influential Farmer General, was chosen to execute the liquidation.

The departures of Bienville, whose association with Louisiana was as old as the colony, and Salmon, *ordonnateur* for more than a decade, should have signaled the end of an era. The arrival of the new men, Vaudreuil and Lénormant, with new ideas and fresh enthusiasms, should have heralded the start of a new one. Unfortunately, this was not the case and it was at best more of the same for the two decades left to France in Louisiana.

Lénormant and the war arrived in Louisiana together and it is difficult to make a judgment as to their relative impacts. Certainly the war made his task more difficult, not only because of the effective isolation of Louisiana from France and the consequent shortage of supplies, but because of the increased expenses forced upon the colonial government. It may also be that certain of Lénormant's difficulties were of his own creation, the result of a too literal adherence to parts of his instructions and a concomitant unfamiliarity with the unique problems of Louisiana. These weaknesses may also explain the ire and dislike he aroused in Governor Vaudreuil.

There are two aspects of his administration to consider. One is the process of liquidation carried out by the *ordonnateur*. Lénormant executed decisions made at higher levels and carried out instructions that left little room for discretionary activities. The liquidation may well have been draconic, but this was not his responsibility. In the matter of retrenchment and economy, however, Lénormant's instructions were general, leaving to his judgment the manner in which he followed Maurepas' instructions to cut expenses. Lénormant's zeal in paring expenses and his ignorance of colonial affairs combined with the uncertainties caused by the war to produce serious discord between the governor and the *ordonnateur*.

The method of liquidation was a closely guarded secret, unknown even to Vaudreuil until Lénormant published the king's order on January 2, 1745. The expenses of 1744 were met by further issues of *bons de caisse*, which raised the total paper outstanding to some one million livres. Two months were allowed to holders of colonial money to present their bills for redemption in letters of exchange at a rate of five livres for two or piastres at a rate of twelve livres per piastre. Additional time was allowed the distant posts to send in their paper but the amounts outstanding were small as the New Orleans area held most of the paper. By March, 1745, close to 850,000 livres in paper were redeemed and burned. The New Orleans area turned in 775,000 livres of this sum. In October, 1745, Lénormant reported that only 5,000 livres remained outstanding.

Vaudreuil's reaction to the terms was unfavorable. He opposed the severity and suddenness of the plan, although recognizing the necessity for a recall of the paper. The merchants of New Orleans, he wrote, were especially resentful of the recall of the card money which was issued by authority of the crown, the withdrawal of which left the colony bereft of all money. Vaudreuil also criticized the extremity of the reduction at a time when bills were passing at ten livres per piastre rather than the conversion rate of twelve to one. The governor advised Maurepas, as Bienville and Salmon had many times before, that the drawing of letters of exchange payable only two years from date tied up capital for an unreasonable period of time and resulted inevitably in speculation as merchants attempted to negotiate the letters to meet short-term obligations. The capture of *S. M. L'Éléphant* and Rasteau's *Lion d'Or* in the summer of 1745 with more than 350,000 livres in letters of exchange and piastres aboard the two vessels jarred the colony and added to the general confusion by compelling the temporary suspension of payment of Louisiana bills of exchange.

Vaudreuil's hands were tied except insofar as he could convince Lénormant to relax the terms of redemption for certain individuals. He was able to do this in at least two cases, but as the individuals involved were among the most wealthy in the colony, little can be said regarding the distribution and equity of Vaudreuil's interventions. In one instance, one Castanier, a director of the Company of the Indies, remitted 53,000 piastres in letters of exchange purchased at five livres to the piastre. At the official rate of conversion, Castanier's livres would have purchased 22,000 piastres. In addition, freight for specie shipped by Castanier aboard *S. M. Le Chaneau* was set at 2 percent when the prevailing rate was 4 percent. The second case arose from the sale of slaves by Du Breuil and Dalcour to Descloseaux. The purchase price for eleven slaves in 1743 was 32,450 livres colonial money. With devaluation this amounted to 13,980 livres or, if used to purchase piastres, 13,000 livres in France. Descloseaux wished to pay at the devalued rate and the vendors brought suit in the Superior Council, where Vaudreuil used his influence to gain a more favorable settlement for the slave traders. Descloseaux was ordered to pay 1,800 livres per slave at five piastres per livre, netting 19,800 livres for Dalcour and Du Breuil in France. It is unlikely that many experienced such tender treatment.

In dealing with the continuing expenses of Louisiana, Lénormant utilized the inherent powers of his office in ways which the governor considered pernicious in their effect upon the colony. Lénormant's justification resided in his orders to reduce expenses, but in so doing he ignored the legitimate needs of established policies, especially with regard to the Indians and the French garrisons in Indian territory. From 1745 through 1747 Vaudreuil opposed Lénormant's policy of retrenchment, blaming most of the colony's troubles upon the *ordonnateur*. Such criticism was almost as extreme as Lénormant's policies for the fault lay with the royal government rather than the *ordonnateur*. Lénormant merely attempted to shave expenses from a budget that was and had been inadequate since the retrocession.

Total expenses in Louisiana for the fourteen years 1731–44 were approximately 10 million livres, of which 4.4 million were incurred during the Chickasaw wars. Budgeted or ordinary expenses composed the other 5.6 million, or an average of some 390,000 livres annually. Until 1744, when ordinary expenses mounted to 523,645 livres, expenses did not exceed 400,000 livres in any year. Expenses rose sharply after 1744 from 444,906 livres in 1746 to 534,160 in 1748 and 930,767 livres in 1752. These sums, whether the average between 1731 and 1744 or the figure for 1752, were insignificant in a royal budget that reached 203 million livres for fiscal 1739–40 and rose to higher levels during the succeeding decades of war.

The Louisiana budget was, however, a major item to the starved Ministry of the Marine. Maurepas received 9 million livres annually from 1730 to 1743. In 1744, when a rupture with Britain was imminent, he requested 20 million and received 10 to mobilize the fleet. Maurepas' budgets, the product of the economy-minded Cardinal Fleury and Comptroller Orry, had to support both the naval establishment and the colonies. Over the fourteen-year period, about 8 percent of the funds received by the Ministry of the Marine was expended in Louisiana. This was not an insignificant sum to a department whose commitments stretched from India and the Indian Ocean to the Mississippi and St. Lawrence rivers.

When Lénormant, then, suddenly reduced by 50 percent the flour rations of public officials and troops in 1744 and doubled the price of goods destined for both the outlying garrisons and the Indian trade in 1745, he may be faulted for acting unwisely. Vaudreuil, objecting strenuously to these acts, described Lénormant as an official new to the country, without a clear idea of its problems and unwilling to consult with experienced officials. Lénormant was performing his task in the best bureaucratic tradition. Told to economize, he did so by cutting into the largest item in the budget—supplies for the posts and Indian presents. If this caused further dissension among the already disaffected Choctaw, if increased prices caused a small mutiny among the troops in the Alabama country, and if the English were the beneficiaries of a sagging French reputation among the tribes, this was not his problem. He was simply carrying out the orders of Maurepas, who issued them in a desperate effort to stretch his budget as far as possible. Maurepas or his functionaries in Louisiana were not responsible for these crises. The source of the difficulty was twofold: a system of priorities in France which subordinated naval and colonial matters to continental concerns and, even more crucial, the inefficient, oppressive, and expensive tax structure of the Old Regime.

Vaudreuil was undoubtedly relieved when Lénormant left Louisiana in 1748 but his satisfaction was short lived, for the new *ordonnateur* Honoré Michel de la Rouvillière proved less acceptable to Vaudreuil than his predecessor. A bitter feud developed between the two men, lasting from May, 1749, until the death of Michel in December, 1752. Among the root causes of the enmity were the ever-present monetary problems of the colony.[7]

Certain students of Louisiana's history have noted that the specie supply of Louisiana improved during the War of the Austrian Succession and particularly between 1744 and 1748.[8] French vessels stopping to trade at Spanish ports on their way to Louisiana carried large quantities of silver to New Orleans, and after French involvement in the war, French merchants in the West Indies shipped

[7] Guy Frégault, *Le Grand Marquis, Pierre de Rigaud de Vaudreuil et la Louisiane* (Montreal, 1952), 272–75, 304, is the consistent champion of Vaudreuil in his feuds with Lenormant and Michel. To the former's policies, he attributes the credit for Louisiana's prosperity between 1748 and 1753; obstructionism and disaffection fall to the lot of the *ordonnateurs*.

[8] Surrey, *The Commerce of Louisiana*, 106–107; Frégault, *Vaudreuil et la Louisiane*, 393, 401–402.

silver to New Orleans for letters of exchange on France in order to avoid the loss of specie to British warships. The arrival in New Orleans of large amounts of silver is presumed to have greatly augmented the sum of specie circulating in the colony. But the constant complaints of Bienville, Salmon, Vaudreuil, Lénormant, and Michel about specie scarcity and the known inadequacy of letters of exchange, which compelled owners of specie to ship as much as possible aboard royal vessels, cast doubt on the benefits the colony received from the specie imports.

Specie gained through the Spanish trade during the 1740s did not ease the tight money situation in Louisiana. Spanish silver did not remain in Louisiana and was not the result of sales of Louisiana goods and services. It was obtained with French goods carried in French and Spanish vessels. While the transactions occurred in New Orleans and some silver filtered into temporary circulation through commissions and the outfitting of vessels, the real fruits of the trade passed to France in specie or letters of exchange. Letters were already in short supply and the added demand for them may well have hampered the traditional patterns of trade by forcing New Orleans merchants to share the inadequate quota with the owners of Spanish silver. Such owners were interested in remitting the specie to France rather than in purchasing Louisiana products. This development was terminated shortly after the conclusion of peace in 1748 when Spain closed her ports to legitimate trade, although the contraband trade continued to bring some silver into New Orleans. In 1749–50 Vaudreuil and Michel informed Rouillé that the commerce of Louisiana was much damaged by the shortage of specie and low quota for letters of exchange. This could come as no revelation to the minister.

Change for the better in monetary affairs was not possible because Louisiana still suffered a balance of payments deficit which could only be overcome by a substantial increase in exports along with growth in the internal market. The tempo of trade accelerated between the wars but not sufficiently to have an impact on Louisiana's trade balance. Nor was the increase in the annual quota of letters to 200,000 livres more than a palliative, as Michel and Vaudreuil informed Minister of the Marine Rouillé. Merchants were still unable to obtain letters of exchange adequate to their needs, a condition which persisted through 1759 when commerce was really brought to a halt by the suspension of payments on letters of exchange for the duration of the war. Indeed, by 1751 the inflationary conditions of the early 1740s had returned.

After the liquidation of the card money in 1745, the colony was without a local currency. A new issue of card money was planned in 1744 but never implemented. Expenses rose more quickly than receipts, placing Michel in a position similar to that of Salmon in 1737–38. By February, 1750, Michel felt compelled to issue treasury notes which circulated as legal tender and which amounted to 379,000 livres by November of that year. Michel did not consult Vaudreuil regarding the initial issue and the governor signed the ordinance only in order to create confidence in the paper. For a time, the notes circulated at close to par value as commercial activity between New Orleans, the French West Indies, and the Spanish colonies brought money into the colony. The Chevalier de Pradel, remarking in April, 1753, that goods were in plentiful supply and letters of exchange obtainable without difficulty, noted that many vessels plied their trade between St. Domingue, Martinique, and New Orleans. However, doubt as to the ultimate fate of the notes persisted. In February, 1753, the merchants of Louisiana memorialized Governor Kerlérec and *ordonnateur* Dauberville, expressing their great uncertainty regarding the real value of the money and informing the officials of their hesitancy in accepting the notes in payment of debts. The Seven Years' War and its catastrophic impact on the French colonial empire in general, and Louisiana in particular, proved these forebodings to be not without substance.

Governor Vaudreuil was transferred to the governorship of Canada in 1752 to preside over the demise of the French empire in North America. His replacement in Louisiana, Louis Billouart de Kerlérec, arrived in 1753 to fulfill a similar unanticipated role in Louisiana. Kerlérec's administration, uneventful until 1756, was a victim of the Seven Years' War. In the years from 1752 to 1766 the *ordonnateurs* Dauberville, Bobé Descloseaux, Rochemore, and Dabbadie resorted to the old expedients of adding to the quantity of notes earlier placed in circulation by Michel. Rochemore found, on his arrival at New Orleans in 1758, that 1.8 million in notes was outstanding in addition to letters of exchange amounting to 1.4 million. His appeals to retire the notes by substituting increased amounts of letters of exchange, followed by a new emission of card money, were ignored by the French government.

French finances were in a deplorable state and relief was unlikely. But even the status quo would have better served Louisiana than the suspension of payment of 1759. Provision was made in a series of *arrêts* for payment after the war. During the interim, the letters outstanding were to be converted into bills (*reconnaissances*) on the issuing agency, bearing interest of 5 percent. An *arrêt* of 1765 provided for the payment of the state's creditors holding notes and certificates of debt other than letters of exchange. These events destroyed whatever solvency existed in Louisiana, for no mention was made of the treasury notes and everyone anticipated some kind of repudiation after the war. This belief was turned into a virtual certainty when the sad news of the colony's cession to Spain reached New Orleans. To the question of how France would liquidate its financial obligations in Louisiana was added the larger question of Spain's intentions regarding the economy of the colony and its money supply. With such uncertainty and pessimism prevalent throughout the colony, careful men grew more cautious and sought means to protect themselves against serious losses. One bright prospect was the possibility of improved access to Spanish sources of specie.

In the meantime, inflation swept through the colony and involved many in considerable losses. In early 1763 a 4,000-livre treasury note purchased a 1,000-livre letter of exchange; at the end of the year the same letter required 5,000 livres. In October, 1763, Governor Kerlérec, preparing to leave New Orleans, placed 210,143 livres in colonial notes in the hands of Dabbadie for safekeeping pending the final settlement of colonial finances. Few could afford to so dispose of their funds. Speculation was a common pastime among the adventurous who were willing to gamble on the final terms of the settlement. The notes were regarded not as money but as merchandise, and the letters of exchange gained or lost value depending upon the most recent rumor regarding the crown's intentions. Business was conducted only with difficulty. Cézaire le Breton's determination to export 25,000 livres in colonial produce was dampened by a sudden increase in crop prices and he decided to wait until colonial finances were in order. Only those with substantial property to mortgage could obtain credit and then the terms of repayment could not be defined. Beaujeux borrowed 22,000 livres from la Frenière in 1765, promising to repay according to the settlement the crown made regarding colonial finances.

Confusion gripped New Orleans from September, 1764, when news of the cession was received, until the arrival of General O'Reilly in July, 1769. Had it not been for the British present in West Florida and the trade initiated by them, the colony most certainly would have lost the hard-won achievements of a half century. British ships, goods, and credit injected new vigor into the economic life of New Orleans, transforming a potentially disastrous financial situation into one that, while remaining serious, was resilient enough to survive whatever settlement the bankrupt Bourbon king of France had in mind.

7

_____

Major Patterns of Trade

EW ORLEANS was located on the north central edge of
one of the vital trade areas in the world. Lying due north
of Cape Catoche at the tip of the Yucatan Peninsula, it
was within easy sailing of Tampico, Vera Cruz, Havana, and points
beyond in the Antilles and on the Spanish Main. I have pointed out
that during the French period, the growth of the town was retarded
by weaknesses in its agricultural hinterland caused by an inadequate
supply of labor and the inability of all but a few wealthy planters
to expand their agricultural operations. The products gathered at
New Orleans for shipment abroad were not sufficiently valuable to
support a large trade with France, and the risks of the trade and its
normal costs were high enough to compel French merchants to seek
methods of exploiting the value of New Orleans other than a direct
trade to that port.

Commercial connection with France did not disappear, of course,
because Louisiana could hardly exist without the goods, services,
and markets of the mother country. Nor did direct contact come to
any absolute end. Rather, the commercial relationship developed a
new focus centering upon the French Antilles, which determined
that the direct trade between New Orleans and France would be
less important after the mid-1740s than it had been in the past.[1] The
two Anglo-French wars between 1744 and 1763, while important
factors in the emergence of this new pattern, were not the primary
cause. The size of the market at New Orleans did not warrant the

[1] Table III does not reflect this adequately except in the years 1742 and 1744. It
is probable that annual arrivals at New Orleans from the French West Indies did
not dip much below 10 or 12 ships during the period 1740–63 and there may indeed have been more.

diversion of Atlantic shipping to that port while the vessels of West Indian merchants were capable of undertaking the trade. The fact that an indirect trade with France via the Antilles was not wholly advantageous to Louisiana did not enter into the calculations, because Louisiana lacked the economic power to make effective demands on the colonial system. Although not adequate to sustain a large direct commerce with France, Louisiana products did provide freight for West Indian vessels, although the exports—mostly lumber—were more economically shipped on larger vessels than West Indian merchants used in the trade.

At the same time that French merchants began to reduce their economic investment in New Orleans, they attempted to cash in on opportunities arising from the outbreak of war between Spain and Great Britain and the consequent opening of Spanish colonial ports to French shipping. A certain amount of trade always existed between New Orleans and the Spanish colonies, especially the Florida posts, but the value of this trade was insignificant compared to the possibilities held out in Havana, Vera Cruz, and other major Spanish colonial cities. French merchants viewed New Orleans as a convenient advanced base in which to stock Spanish trade goods and from which to initiate ventures into the Spanish colonies. West Indian merchants made a similar use of the strategic location of Louisiana's capital to pursue an exchange with the Spanish. Vessels from Martinique and St. Domingue frequently stopped at Havana before running on to the Mississippi. At New Orleans these vessels might load up with Spanish rather than Louisiana goods and drop down to Vera Cruz before heading east to Havana. There were numerous market possibilities open to French and West Indian merchantment in the Caribbean and Gulf of Mexico, not all of which redounded to the benefit of New Orleans.

However, merchants in New Orleans were able to develop commercial contacts with other merchants throughout this vast market area and these contacts served the town well once the products of her hinterland were sizeable enough to attract large amounts of shipping to the Mississippi. Then, the products of Spanish and French colonies mingled on the quays of New Orleans with the fruits of a productive hinterland. This chapter will be concerned with the development at New Orleans of both the French West Indian and Spanish colonial trades. In addition, the slave trade—a trade that failed to respond to real demand in Louisiana—will be treated. Indeed, the failure of this trade fixed the economic value of Louisiana at such a low level relative to that of other French colonies that French and French West Indian merchants assessed the worth of the colony in terms of its location rather than its products.

Among the most damaging consequences of the cession of Louisiana to the crown in 1731 was the abrupt ending of the slave trade to the colony. Whatever the faults of the company, under its rule an effort was made to introduce slaves into the colony, a policy that was certainly not initiated with any vigor or persistence by the crown in the last three decades of French possession. The company, by its count, carried some six thousand slaves to Louisiana between 1719 and 1730 and available shipping data substantiate this estimate. This was probably more than twice the number entering the colony between 1731 and 1765. Bienville and Salmon in 1740 and 1741 wrote that few slaves had been received in Louisiana for a dozen years. After that, there is little evidence of large shipments direct from Africa but there is some indication that individual planters purchased slaves in the French West Indies.[2]

The Company of the Indies possessed the monopoly of the slave trade (first granted in 1720) until 1767. Before 1740 the company transported Negroes on its own account to the French colonies and also issued licenses to private traders to engage in the trade. After 1740 the company withdrew from the direct trade, selling the slaves to traders for shipment to the colonies and receiving a subsidy from both the crown and private traders for each Negro introduced into the colonies. Thus the company was in apparent control of the trade and, to that degree, responsible for the failure to meet Louisiana's needs. But the breakdown in the traffic did not result simply from company neglect or arbitrariness and the crown must bear a substantial portion of whatever blame is meted out in accounting for the failure. The crown wielded enough influence to guarantee an

---

[2] Frégault, *Vaudreuil et la Louisiane*, 411, estimates that there were 10,500 Negroes in Louisiana in 1749. Salmon believed the number to be about 4,000 in 1741 and there is no evidence of large imports between 1741 and 1750.

adequate supply of Negroes in Louisiana—or at least some supply—
if it had acted with diligence and with less concern for economy.

Royal apathy coincided with the most active period of the French
slave trade prior to the French Revolution. The trade was worth
some 10.5 million livres annually merely in the value of the 203,000
slaves introduced by ships of France into its colonies between 1728
and 1760. Supporting upwards of forty vessels annually with a full
complement of sailors and trade goods for the African intermediaries, the ships carried back to France hundreds of thousands of
quintals of sugar and other colonial products which were marketed
throughout Europe and which contributed substantially to the favorable balance of trade enjoyed by France during these years.
Slaving provided an essential source of wealth for the major ports,
especially Nantes and La Rochelle. Of 44,394 slaves carried to the
colonies between 1736 and 1741, Nantes furnished 26,123 and La
Rochelle 14,446. In addition, the French colonies received unknown
thousands of slaves from foreign interlopers, in spite of the frequently reiterated prohibition of that commerce.

Slaves were available and there were individuals willing to transport them to Louisiana. The Company of the Indies was not inactive
in the days following the retrocession, although it did not compete
with the British as vigorously as it might have for the live cargoes
of the Gold Coast. Nonetheless, the company submitted claims to
the Ministry of the Marine for bounties on 5,414 slaves delivered to
the colonies between May, 1730, and November, 1732. There is no
evidence that any of these reached Louisiana, but the company approached Maurepas in 1732 with a proposal to furnish Negroes to
Louisiana in partial payment of the money owed to the crown as a
result of the retrocession. But even when the company lowered its
price to the reasonable figure of 600 livres per head, nothing came
of the proposal.

There is hardly a dispatch to or from Louisiana dealing with the
general condition of the colony which fails to emphasize the importation of slaves as a condition requisite to prosperity. To Bourgine in 1735 and Rasteau in 1736, Maurepas expressed his awareness
that only the lack of Negroes kept Louisiana's agriculture from
developing rapidly and cheated French merchants out of valuable

cargoes. Maurepas assured the Rochelais merchants that he searched diligently for the means to provide them. Yet Rasteau, between 1732 and 1740, presented several concrete proposals to Maurepas, all of which were rejected.

The Rasteaus were experienced participants in the triangular trade between France, the Guinea Coast, and the Antilles. Their vessels were consistently employed in the traffic after 1725 when licenses became available from the Company of the Indies. Rasteau's interest in supplying slaves to Louisiana was expressed at the start of his correspondence with Maurepas concerning the government support available for those engaging in the recently opened trade. Maurepas' replies to several general overtures were noncommittal but he instructed Bienville and Salmon in 1733 to indicate the number of Negroes necessary, what price the colonists would pay, and how payment would be made. Proposals from several other individuals were rejected and things dragged on until a comprehensive scheme was received from Rasteau in early 1737.

Rasteau's proposal was equitable regarding prices—including payment in indigo, tobacco, or pelts—and credit. But a group of eighteen prominent Louisiana planters made a counterproposal unacceptable to Rasteau. The settlers' recalcitrance appears myopic. Maurepas recognized the equity of Rasteau's offer but refused to intervene, even though he feared that better terms would not be readily obtained and knew that the Company of the Indies was disinterested in such a venture. His motivation or lack thereof may be partially explained in a letter written to the company official, M. de Fulvy, in 1737.

Maurepas suggested several reasons that he hoped would convince the Company of the Indies to renew slave shipments to Louisiana. Need and facilities to conduct the trade were mentioned but the argument emphasized the debts which the company was trying to collect in Louisiana. Slave sales by the company would result in an increase in production and provide the colonists the means of discharging their obligations to the company. Success in indigo cultivation awaited only an adequate labor force, Maurepas explained. If, however, the company neglected this market, the colonists would purchase slaves from private merchants, incurring new obligations and retarding payments to the company. The crown had a vested interest in the solvency of the company because the latter was in the process of paying a million livres to the crown and financed these payments partially with funds collected in Louisiana. As noted earlier, these funds were employed in subsidizing merchant ventures to Louisiana.

Unimpressed with Maurepas' circuitous reasoning, the company recognized that there was little percentage in increasing the debts owed to it in Louisiana in a long-run effort to stimulate greater productivity. In effect, an acceptance of Maurepas' arguments would burden the company with a commitment to long-term capital development which was more properly the government's responsibility. Besides, the company, in the process of phasing itself out of any direct connection with the slave trade, received 33 livres per head delivered in the colonies without risking a sol and when a direct shipment was made, it sought the higher prices of the agriculturally progressive markets in the Antilles. Maurepas was not ignorant of these realities but made no move to overcome them beyond assuring Bienville and Salmon that all the offers received from merchants were onerous. He likewise hinted, without seriousness of intent, that the government might have to enter the trade in order to supply Louisiana.

The Rasteaus persevered in forwarding proposals to Maurepas in 1737, 1738, and 1739 but without success. Finally, in 1742 Rasteau, in partnership with the Rochelais merchant Vivier, struck an agreement with some Louisiana planters to bring a cargo of slaves the following year. The slaver *Triton* was captured by the British, taken to Jamaica, and condemned. But at the same time a new effort, initiated by two wealthy planters in Louisiana, was nearing fruition. Rasteau's refusal to accept the colonists' counteroffer in 1737 actually led to two colonial initiatives to obtain slaves; one by a group of merchant-planters, some of whom had earlier responded to Rasteau's offer, and the other, out of an association between Du Breuil and Dalcour, two of the wealthier Louisiana planters. The first initiative advanced no further than Bienville and Salmon, for it implied a flagrant infringement upon the company's monopoly. The Du Breuil-Dalcour proposition of 1741 met a more favorable response.

Little information is available concerning Dalcour other than his role in this single venture and his appointment to the Superior Council in 1740 or 1741, but Du Breuil has been encountered earlier in this narrative. He must have been a rare man indeed; always searching for the main chance, sensitive to the public welfare yet favored with an active entrepreneurial nature, infused with an optimism hardly in keeping with conditions in Louisiana, mechanically inventive, and greatly respected by the governors and *ordonnateurs* of Louisiana and by Comte de Maurepas. It is not surprising to record the success of this effort and the probable success of subsequent ventures had not the French intervened in the War of the Austrian Succession in 1744.

Simple enough in structure, the proposal had the merit—political rather than economic—of utilizing the services of the Company of the Indies. The partners suggested that the company send a cargo of three hundred slaves to be accepted at the Balize ten days after their arrival by Dalcour and Du Breuil at a price of 550 livres per head payable in France in three annual installments. Negotiations in 1742 and 1743 resulted in modification of this plan and brought to the surface the basic difficulties endangering the success of this endeavor. Most serious of the obstacles was the location at which the company would deliver the slaves, how quickly full payment must be made, and, unrelated to the company, providing the partners the means to remit their capital to France. Only Maurepas possessed the authority to overcome or alleviate such vexatious roadblocks.

The deteriorating monetary position of Louisiana in 1741 and 1742 served to increase the difficulties of the associates in getting funds to France to finance the operation. Always an impediment to commerce, the scarcity of exchange was doubly a burden in times of serious inflation. Maurepas extended large favors to Dalcour and Du Breuil to smooth the path somewhat. They were granted free freight on royal vessels for colonial produce exported to France for sale, the proceeds of which were earmarked for the slave trade; large sums in letters of exchange were granted and paid at sight in France; piastres were sold to the partners at less than the current rate in New Orleans; and Maurepas authorized the purchase of Du Breuil's townhouse to provide additional funds. Inflation, however, eroded the financial strength of the partners. Having no other way to get funds to France, tobacco was purchased at New Orleans for nine sols the livre weight and sold in France for five. Similar losses were taken on indigo, pitch, and tar shipments. By 1743, though, an adequate capital was accumulated in France, but only after Maurepas' intervention satisfied the company that payment would be made on time.

As might be anticipated, the Company of the Indies was not an enthusiastic recipient of the proposal. Maurepas' mediation and the partners' willingness to compromise certain points finally gained the company's acquiescence. The company would supply two hundred slaves deliverable in Guinea and assume none of the risks associated with the middle passage. Dalcour and Du Breuil were compelled to make shipping arrangements, while paying 280 livres per head instead of 550 livres. The partners offered to pay half on receipt of the Negroes and the remainder in the following July. The company hesitated to extend any credit until Maurepas offered to guarantee payment of the second installment. As the minister informed Fulvy, the Marine would pay in January, 1744, if the partners were unable to pay in July, 1743. This was acceptable to the company and 220 slaves were received by the partners, who in the meantime had obtained the services of a La Rochelle vessel, the *Sultane*, either on a lease or by taking the owner Pascaud into the partnership. The vessel arrived in New Orleans in September, 1743.

Dalcour pressed Maurepas for authority to bring in a second cargo before the first one arrived, but Maurepas refrained from committing himself until the outcome of the first venture was known. The partners ran into frustrating problems in attempting to market their slaves. Conditions in Louisiana were unfavorable to an extreme. A short tobacco crop in 1742 and poor prospects for the crop of 1743 coupled with the grave currency situation prevented many colonists from paying the 1,000 livres asked for each slave. Only twenty-three were sold as of September 24, and the partners determined to hold on to the slaves until conditions improved and the new crop was in. Dalcour and Du Breuil sold their goods only for piastres, letters of exchange, or provisions at the price in France. Most colonists wished to pay in treasury notes but the partners refused to accept the depreciated paper. Demand was great, the means of payment were not. The expense of maintaining the unsold slaves mounted and the partners were again compelled to purchase produce at inflated prices for shipment to France. In April, 1744, Maurepas tersely informed the company that the Treasury of the Marine would make immediate arrangements for the 36,000 livres balance due on the slaves.

However, the slaves were finally sold and Maurepas concluded an arrangement for a second venture with Dalcour and Du Breuil. War forced a cancellation of this project which was not, to my knowledge, revived when peace came. The shipment of Dalcour and Du Breuil appears as the first and last large-scale infusion of slave labor into Louisiana during the period of crown control. Negroes were introduced to be sure, but in small batches and, it seems, largely from St. Domingue or Martinique and generally at the order of a planter. This traffic helped increase the significance of the French islands as intermediaries in the commerce between New Orleans and France.

The slave trade to Louisiana was a patent failure and this doomed Louisiana to the same fate as a colony, at least from the perspective of the French government. Few American colonies, regardless of nationality, received as many slaves as they wished but most received some. It is remarkable that in an age when tens and tens of thousands of Negroes were stuffed like putty into every available crevice and corner of hundreds of vessels and scattered like flotsam along the beaches of North America so few reached Louisiana. It seems the more remarkable if the sheer need of Louisiana is recalled, along with the fact that Maurepas recognized this need. Much of the minister's time was consumed in discussing a trade which resulted in the introduction of 220 Negroes into Louisiana over a twelve-year period.

While the French government was willing to support private initiatives, it was not ready to subsidize them as heavily as French merchants desired. French merchants such as the Rasteaus, already engaged in the trade, were unwilling to deviate from their normal marketing patterns without the incentives of heavy subsidization as security against the inconveniences and hazards of trading at New

Orleans. Neither the private merchants nor the Company of the Indies was ready to underwrite the economic development of the colony by the sale of Negroes on long-term credit. Maurepas' role in the Dalcour and Du Breuil venture suggests that, in spite of limited funds, he was moving in the direction of applying government credit to the task of providing Louisiana with an adequate labor supply. The war interrupted this trend and Maurepas, running afoul of the Marquise de Pompadour in 1749, was ousted from the office he had held since 1723. His successors did not renew the effort before 1756 and could not thereafter. Only the English presence in West Florida in the 1760s brought some relief to the labor-starved planters of Spanish Louisiana.

Great activity in the overseas trade was a major factor in the pronounced growth experienced by the French economy following the Treaty of Utrecht. A large portion of the advance, if not the dominant portion, was contributed by the trade between France and the French West Indies. After 1713 the West Indies entered their most prosperous period, becoming the most valuable of all the possessions of France and a larger source of profits for the metropole than any of England's American colonies. A rapid rise in population, especially that of slaves, provided the labor for an impressive increase in agricultural productivity and the market for vast quantities of French goods and provisions. Several hundred French vessels were employed in carrying goods to the Antilles, primarily St. Domingue and Martinique, the latter handling the trade of Guadeloupe and the Windward Islands, and transporting sugar, coffee, cotton, and cacao to France.

By the early eighteenth century, the French islands were committed to a staple economy and thus depended upon outside sources for foodstuffs, livestock, and myriad other goods, including raw and semifinished lumber. Unable to supply all these items from their own output, France was compelled, for example, to permit French merchants to carry foreign salted meats to the colonies. Efforts to develop an exchange between Canada and the West Indies, especially in livestock and lumber, resulted in only a small trade. New England was a much more significant source of goods and services for the islanders than was Canada. French officials also turned to

Louisiana as a source of supply for the islands. The possibilities here seemed infinite, considering the proximity of the colonies and the natural resources of Louisiana. While a Louisiana-West Indian trade was established, the form in which it evolved was not anticipated and it did not replace the contraband trade with the Yankees.

In an effort to establish a coasting trade between Louisiana and the islands, the French government, from 1731 to 1737, removed various restrictions, culminating in a royal order in 1737 exempting all colonial goods passing between the colonies from tariffs for ten years. But the direct exchange of Louisiana lumber for island products was of small value as Louisiana's productive capacities were limited. Before 1740 the trade was conducted with little regularity or profit. Several ventures, originating in New Orleans, were failures. When the commerce did pick up—Bienville reported five West Indian arrivals in 1740, twelve in 1742; Vaudreuil reported twenty in 1744—it was not in addition to a direct trade with France but was rather a substitute.

The arrivals observed by both men contained wine, brandy, flour, and other French wares. It was much simpler for French merchants to dispose of their full cargoes at island ports than to continue on to New Orleans where remittances might be difficult to obtain. As noted earlier, this was a difficulty faced from the beginning of free trade with Louisiana, as merchants attempted to collect the subsidy for goods carried to Louisiana while frequently selling parts of the cargo at St. Domingue before proceeding to New Orleans. The merchants Frotin, Bourgine, Jung, and Pascaud were detected in such maneuvers at various times before 1747 and lost their bonuses as a result.

War in 1744 accelerated this tendency, fixing the pattern for the remainder of the French period. Du Breuil evaluated the West Indian trade of Louisiana as basically harmful to the mainland colony. Vessels from St. Domingue and Martinique purchased goods from French vessels and resold them in Louisiana at a 150 percent markup. West Indian vessels arrived with cargoes valued at 40,000 to 50,000 livres, according to Du Breuil, but carried away produce worth much less, taking the difference in letters of exchange payable in

France. Indies merchants then negotiated the letters with French vessels arriving in Indies ports to purchase new goods for Louisiana. Louisiana's planters were deprived of the means to ship their produce directly to France, paid higher prices for French goods and for freight while receiving low prices for their produce, and saw their money drained off to pay West Indian merchants for services more efficiently performed in France. Du Breuil recognized that a solution depended upon the guarantee of return cargoes at New Orleans and that, in turn, was impossible unless the colonists received many slaves.

Merchants at New Orleans accommodated themselves to the evolving pattern by establishing contacts in the French West Indies. Associations of varying duration were formed and merchants in both areas bought and sold for one another on commission. West Indian merchants faced the same problem of remittances that discouraged the French, with the exception that lumber was always available for a return cargo and fetched good prices in the islands. Lumber was of little value relative to its bulk, however, and the West Indians purchased myrtle wax, tobacco, rice, vegetables, tallow, and bear's oil when available. Lumber was the principal return, nevertheless, and Louisianians complained about New England competition in the French islands.

The lumber trade in New Orleans was handled by merchants, planters, and merchant-planters. De Pradel managed his own shipments of lumber to St. Domingue while the Rasteaus of St. Domingue contracted for specified types and quantities of timber with Paul Rasteau in New Orleans, Paul, in turn, contracted with planters for the desired quantity. In 1746 Rasteau purchased cypress planks and 16,000 shingles from Joseph Blanpain of Houmas. Blanpain paid the freight downstream while Rasteau picked up the landing charges. While the Rasteaus in St. Domingue sent occasional shipments of French goods on consignment to Paul at New Orleans in the late 1730s, the young Rasteau received most of his French goods direct from La Rochelle. Generally he shipped lumber on his own account or jointly with his uncles, the proceeds of which were forwarded to France in sugar and coffee, sold on his account at La Rochelle, and used to meet obligations there. But by the 1750s merchants on the islands were ordering goods specifically for Louisiana both for general sale and at the order of New Orleans businessmen.

Clemens Rondes, merchant of St. Pierre, Martinique, received merchandise from his brother in Bordeaux for shipment to New Orleans via vessels leased by Rondes for that specific purpose. In 1752 Rondes freighted the vessel *L'Élisabet*, owned by Jacques Malvezin, with goods sent by his Bordeaux correspondents. Insurance at 4.5 percent was written in Bordeaux for the trip from St. Pierre to New Orleans and return. Jean Jung had an interest in this shipment and apparently in several which preceded it. At New Orleans, Rondes operated through Thibault de Chanvalon and Pierre François Rouissillon. These two merchants provided the return cargoes of lumber and sold the incoming assortments on commission for Rondes and his associates. Chanvalon, originally from La Rochelle, received goods from that city via Rondes at Martinique and forwarded produce to La Rochelle by the same route.

This was an expensive way of doing business. The trip from Bordeaux or La Rochelle to New Orleans via Martinique was much longer than the direct route. Insurance charges from France to New Orleans, in peacetime, were the same as to Martinique or St. Domingue, thus shipments to New Orleans via the latter ports paid double insurance. The utilization of two vessels augmented freight and handling charges, required unloading and reloading at the island ports, kept the goods afloat for a longer period of time, and thus tied up the funds of New Orleans merchants for longer intervals. All of these inconveniences which raised the prices paid by consumers at New Orleans, had the effect of lowering the purchasing power of money at New Orleans. A hundredweight of tobacco purchased fewer goods when they came via the islands than when they came direct from France.

The purchasing power of New Orleans produce was further diminished when shipped to France via the islands, because all the expenses noted above would be applicable again. New Orleans planters and merchants divided the difference between prices in France and prices in Louisiana with the island middlemen. Compounding the loss to Louisiana merchants and planters was the double discount exacted on payments in money. The New Orleans merchant shipped a lower value of goods to Martinique or St. Domingue than he received, with the difference paid for in cash. After the voyage of *L'Élisabet* in 1752 Rouissillon owed Rondes 5,000 livres, the difference between Rouissillon's imports and the lumber exported. As the colonial notes issued by Michel had no currency in Martinique, Rouissillon purchased letters of exchange at the going discount of 35 percent, paying 6,750 livres colonial money for 5,000 livres in bills. The bills were then discounted by Rondes' agent, Captain Malvezin,—at what rate is unknown but perhaps 10 percent—because Rondes would probably negotiate them in Martinique at a similar discount in purchasing new goods for Louisiana. It was this second discount that added to the costs of the indirect trade. Rouissillon wound up paying 7,425 livres for goods that could be purchased at 6,750 livres if shipped directly from France. He undoubtedly passed this charge on to the consumer who, if a planter, might attempt to raise the price of his produce. But staple prices in France were not affected by those in Louisiana and thus the planter's flexibility was severely limited.

Trade with the West Indies may have grossed 200,000 livres annually for Louisiana during the early 1740s and prior to the Seven Years' War, but this was probably less than 25 percent of the cost of imports from and charges for services paid to that area. It was conducted largely in place of rather than in addition to the trade with France and developed partly in response to economic deficiencies and inconveniences implicit in direct commerce with Louisiana. It was the kind of trade likely to occur between a developed and undeveloped economy when the stronger sovereign unit felt no compulsion or was unable to invest in the strengthening of the weaker, yet was obliged to provide minimal support.

Originally, the West Indian market was viewed as a potential outlet for Louisiana goods supplemental to the French market and, because West Indian goods were not in demand in Louisiana, as a source of money for the delta colony. Possibilities of trade between Louisiana and the American colonies of Spain were regarded from a similar perspective which, however, emphasized much more sharply the benefits of exchanging goods for Spanish piastres. Although waxing and waning in response to outside pressures, the trade was established, contributing in a small way to a high policy of French governments from the sixteenth to the nineteenth centuries, which was to obtain as much Spanish silver as possible without being too fussy regarding the means.

One scholar, in summing up the prevailing attitude toward Spanish silver, describes it as one of the principal engines of commerce in the world of the seventeenth and eighteenth centuries.[3] Much of Europe's trade with the Levant, India, the East Indies, and China was financed by specie and as Spain controlled the primary source of silver, it was incumbent upon the maritime powers to divert as much Spanish silver as possible to their own treasuries.

The maritime powers competed vigorously and occasionally viciously for a share of Spain's wealth. Some was stolen but out-and-out piracy had declined by the eighteenth century except when war justified a resort to force. The interloping trade was a more efficient, more profitable, more Christian, and less sanguinary method of both fleecing the Castilian and selling manufactured goods. West Indian waters became the focus of the struggle since the contraband trade was a primary source of silver, and proximity held out advantages in plying the illicit commerce. Considerable quantities were also obtained by the maritime powers through powerful mercantile houses located in Cadiz and the Canary Islands. Spanish regulations against the export of specie from Spain were circumvented by various illegal devices made necessary because of Spain's unfavorable import-export balance.

The Dutch, Portuguese, English, and French all possessed territories in America with easy access to Spanish ports, but in terms of location, few colonies enjoyed the geographical advantages of Louisiana. As Crozat had observed, the colony bordered Spanish Florida and Texas, the latter offering possibilities for trade through the back door, perhaps even into Mexico, while the normally placid Gulf of Mexico was easily navigable to Tampico, Vera Cruz, the Spanish Main, Cuba, and Hispaniola. Crozat's expectations were disappointed and the Company of the West experienced little more

[3] Louis Dermigny, "Circuits de l'argent et milieux d'affaires au XVIII siècle," *Révue historique*, CCXII (October–December, 1954), 239.

success. A small trade with Florida, a smaller one out of Natchi-toches, and a few Spanish vessels at the Balize tell the tale of the trade into the period of crown control.

At any given period, the extent of the trade was generally con-ditioned by political events in Europe rather than by the logic of economic requirements in America. Comte de Maurepas, Bienville, Vaudreuil, Kerlérec, and the *ordonnateurs* frequently expressed their devotion to the principle of establishing solid commercial con-nections between Louisiana and her Spanish neighbors. But the solidity of the connection depended upon the seriousness of the foreign crisis confronting Spain at that particular moment. Before 1739 Spanish intractability prevented all but a marginal and danger-ous trade with the Spanish islands or New Spain. During this peri-od, products valued at from 5,000 to 6,000 piastres passed annually between New Orleans and Mobile and Florida. This was conducted under the authority of the Viceroy of New Spain and on credits furnished by the French and dischargable at Vera Cruz or Havana. Payment was obtained frequently only with difficulty. In 1736 Captain François Marin, at the order of the Viceroy, delivered two hundred muskets to Pensacola, where the Spanish commander wished to pay four piastres apiece instead of the contracted price of five. Payment at five piastres was ordered by the Spanish govern-ment only in 1740.

Such vexations, combined with a debt of 35,000 livres owed New Orleans merchants by Florida officials, prompted Vaudreuil and Salmon in 1743 to prohibit French merchants at New Orleans and Mobile from carrying goods to Florida. Designed to compel the Spanish to come to New Orleans for the goods and to pay cash, the order had the effect of concentrating the trade at New Orleans with the exception of some pitch and tar which the Spanish ob-tained at Mobile. There is no evidence that New Orleans merchants had a hand in Vaudreuil's decision. One wishes that they had, for it would form an excellent example of urban commercial imperial-ism. The overland trade through Texas was even less significant than the small commerce with Florida.

Trade was carried on most energetically between the Spanish islands, Mexico, and Louisiana. While officials of the colonial government and merchants at New Orleans preferred that the Spanish fill their needs at the Mississippi port, the bulk of the traffic was carried in French ships which wandered about the Gulf and Caribbean seeking an open Spanish port. There was little predictability in the trade for the French were never certain about the reception they would meet as they sailed into a Spanish harbor. Prior to 1739 the French contended with a rigorous execution of Spanish laws prohibiting trade with foreigners. French vessels from Louisiana and France, as well as British vessels, were seized while off the coast of Cuba and Spanish Hispaniola by the Spanish coast guard. Great Britain was particularly incensed by this for her merchants were engaged in large-scale smuggling with the Spanish colonies, some of it under the cover of the *asiento* privilege extracted from Spain at Utrecht. Anglo-Spanish enmity increased during the 1730s until the British government undertook a war of commercial despoliation in 1739. Neither belligerents nor neutrals could anticipate the merging of this war into the world conflict known as the War of the Austrian Succession.

Always jealous of British commercial success in the Spanish colonies, the French seized upon the opportunities presented by the war and their neutral status to augment greatly their trade with the Spanish. French merchants were not always assured of hospitable treatment when entering Spanish colonial ports and risked seizure by British cruisers and privateers which hovered outside Spanish ports. But as the scope of the war widened in Europe the Spanish became more tolerant and the profits of the trade overrode the risk of seizure by the British. Spain had no alternative but to turn to France as the primary source of provisions for her colonies, and it was anticipated by Maurepas that Louisiana would derive some benefits from Spain's travail.

Benefits were certainly forthcoming in terms of the general Franco-Spanish trade, but the extent to which New Orleans participated in the largesse is problematical, even when transactions were consummated in New Orleans. Let it be known at the outset that Vaudreuil estimated the annual New Orleans-Spanish trade to be worth about 150,000 piastres, or 750,000 livres, in the years 1742 to 1744 in goods carried by Spanish vessels to Florida, Campeachy,

Mexico, and Havana. Probably as much was lost in 1740 and 1741 when Spanish vessels appeared at the Balize with piastres but were compelled to depart because merchandise was lacking. Vaudreuil and his predecessor encouraged the Spanish to seek out French goods at New Orleans—the ordinance of 1743 had this intent—but at the same time several vessels were outfitted at New Orleans for Spanish colonial ports. The value of this trade is apparently not included in Vaudreuil's estimate. Although it is not possible to make more than an educated guess as to its quantitative dimensions, it is possible to comment upon its qualitative properties and perhaps in this way to draw some tentative conclusions about the usefulness of the trade to New Orleans before France became a belligerent.

Some information is available about eleven of twelve vessels which departed from New Orleans for various Spanish colonial ports between 1740 and 1744. Only one of these, owned by the merchant Gerard Pery, may be properly termed a New Orleans vessel; six were Rochelais, two from St. Malo, one from Nantes, one from Martinique, and one from an unknown port. Not all of the ships received even part of their cargoes at New Orleans but were outfitted for the Spanish trade in France, put in at New Orleans for supplies, and went on their way. One vessel, Rasteau's *Lion d'Or*, anchored at the Balize only long enough to take on biscuits and water and to unload consignments addressed to New Orleans merchants. Of those that did take on cargo at New Orleans, only one, the *St. Jean Baptiste*, Nicholas Forstall, Martinique, is known to have loaded predominantly Louisiana goods and this vessel at 60 tons was the smallest of the lot.

The value of the merchandise carried is known for two of the vessels; the *Chevaliere*, owned by one Mayeux, of La Rochelle, freighted goods worth 50,000 livres and Pery's cargo was worth 55,000 livres. All the vessels were between 100 and 150 tons except Forstall's *Themis*, 260 tons, La Rochelle, and the *Lion d'Or*, 350 tons. Full cargoes on the eleven vessels would be worth about 600,000 livres if all French goods, and proportionately less if Louisiana products were included. The cargo of the *Chevaliere* for Vera Cruz was largely liquid cheer, including 47,000 livres in wines and brandies, 3,580 livres in Louisiana pitch and tar, and 3,000 livres in beaver hats. Pery's cargo was composed largely of dry goods as was the *Lion d'Or's.* Of the eleven full cargoes, it is unlikely that over 10 percent was made up of Louisiana goods. A similar percentage is probably applicable to the goods fetched from New Orleans by the Spanish. Adding Vaudreuil's estimate for 1742 to 1744 to the total of 600,000 livres carried to the Spanish for 1740 to 1744, we obtain an annual average trade of 570,000 livres for the five-year period, of which 10 percent was Louisiana goods. An additional 25 percent of the goods was probably owned by New Orleans merchants such as Pery, which would make New Orleans' direct interest in the trade worth about 193,500 livres annually. To this must be added all charges for services rendered in New Orleans, such as handling goods and provisioning vessels, perhaps 5 percent of the difference between the figure representing New Orleans' direct interest and the annual average, or 21,800 livres. This brings the total estimate to 215,300 livres annually which New Orleans derived from the Spanish traffic and which may be entered as a credit in the port's balance of trade. This is considerably less than Vaudreuil's undifferentiated estimate of 750,000 livres annually.

The trade was not only extremely hazardous because of the unpredictability of the Spanish and the ubiquitous British cruisers but it was expensive as well. At Havana, the Spanish seized the *Themis* and *L'Harmonie* and commandered the *St. Jean Baptiste* without compensation. Pery complained that he did not make expenses partly because of heavy freight costs but primarily because of the heavy payments (bribes) extracted from him to gain permission to enter Spanish ports. Some of the confiscations resulted because of French efforts to introduce goods other than those allowed temporary entrance because of the war. But even when the most comprehensive permissions were obtained prior to a voyage, little was certain when one's ship was anchored in the roadstead of a Spanish port. The Rasteaus discovered this in 1743.

The voyage of the *Lion d'Or* was planned with the approval and overt aid of Comte de Maurepas in 1742, under licenses and contracts granted by two successive viceroys of New Spain. Under the command of Eli Rasteau, with Paul serving as first officer, the vessel left Rochefort in November, 1742. Part of the cargo contained goods for New Orleans (belonging to Rasteau and to other La Rochelle merchants) which were to be left at the Balize. The bulk of the cargo consisted of the goods ordered by the viceroy of New Spain and other trading goods demanded in Spanish ports. The *Lion d'Or* stopped at St. Domingue, escaped from the British while passing to Louisiana, and entered Vera Cruz in June, 1743.

Rasteau presented his papers to the port authorities and requested permission to unload the goods ordered by the viceroy. The papers listed the remainder of the cargo as destined for New Orleans, which it was not. The Spanish must have been suspicious, for Eli Rasteau requested that a Spanish guard be mounted on board as a testimony of his good faith. This was done, but when the unloading was completed, the governor of the city ordered the remainder of the cargo unloaded, confiscated the vessel and the cargo, and fined the Rasteaus 1,000 piastres. Rasteau immediately appealed the seizure to the viceroy and the French government. Acting swiftly, the viceroy ordered the return of the vessel and its cargo to Rasteau, but not the fine. The goods were then charged duties at full valuation and sold while clearance papers were issued to the Rasteaus in September. By early 1744 the ship was on its way back to France via Louisiana and St. Domingue. The whole affair reads like a scheme in which all parties were involved and in which the ship's papers, seizure, fine, protest, restitution, and sale served the purpose of protecting the individuals involved from any sudden decision actually to apply the letter of Spanish law against interlopers.

The *Lion d'Or* made a second voyage to Vera Cruz in late 1744–45 and was captured by the British as it sailed for Cadiz with a freight of 193,000 piastres and other goods. This was a bad time for the Rasteaus who lost four vessels to Great Britain, with the ships and cargoes worth almost 2.5 million livres. Such seizures, accelerating after 1744, prompted French merchants to deal as directly as possible with Spanish ports rather than through New Orleans.

Both Vaudreuil and Maurepas complained about the irregularities in shipments to Louisiana caused by the reinvigorated trade with the Spanish colonies in the early 1740s. Maurepas sympathized with the plight of Louisiana but favored the trade, taking the larger view of general French commercial interests into account. Vaudreuil was less stoical regarding the harm done to Louisiana's commerce by the saturation of its market with goods suitable only for the Spanish trade. The *Suedra*, La Rochelle, outfitted for Louisiana but went first to Campeachy, sold part of its cargo and took on logwood, traveled to New Orleans for a new outfit and refused either to sell or take on cargo, and left for Havana to sell the remainder of its goods. Similar conduct, Vaudreuil recounted in 1747, caused a two-year crop of tobacco to accumulate. Vessels came to New Orleans but, instead of carrying off local products, took on sugar and logwood stockpiled there by French and Spanish merchants. Even royal vessels loaded Spanish goods and left Louisiana produce on the levee.

There was the usual amount of activity at New Orleans because of this commerce, with vessels coming and going before and during the war. Observers, contemporary and modern, also note an abnormally large flow of silver into New Orleans. Silver flowed through rather than to New Orleans, which served as a way-station in the traffic and reaped rewards commensurate to its function. Those merchants such as the Leynard brothers of that port, who handled some gold shipments requiring storage and a change of vessels, earned commissions while other merchants sold provisions and supplies to and made minor repairs on the incoming vessels. But only a fraction of the gold was actually used to purchase Louisiana goods for export to France. The Leynards, in one instance, invested a large sum in the purchase of Guatemalan indigo when a considerable supply of the Louisiana variety was available. The incoming silver had a negligible effect on Louisiana's balance of trade.

After the war, the Spanish applied their exclusionist policies with more severity than ever, especially at Havana where Vaudreuil reported the confiscation of many French vessels. A small traffic in pitch, tar, and lumber was plied with the Royal Company of Havana, which held the monopoly of these and other trades but, by and large, Vaudreuil, Kerlérec, and the intendants wished to resume the favored practice of tempting Spanish vessels to the Mississippi by maintaining large and well-assorted inventories of goods. Merchants at New Orleans were no more enthusiastic about journeying to Spanish ports than the officials. A group of the former made an arrangement to supply some Mexican merchants inside the bar at the Balize from warehouses in New Orleans. At least four Spanish vessels appeared at the Balize in 1750, 1751, and 1752, while in each of the last two years, the Spanish seized two West Indian vessels on their way to Louisiana, one of which was supposedly twenty leagues off Cuba. The trade appeared to be at a stalemate when a new war threw the Bourbon powers into another uneasy alliance.

Spain succeeded in keeping the trade between her colonies and the French at a minimum, except when it was to her advantage to permit its expansion. The Spanish coast guard confiscated French and Spanish vessels engaged in this commerce or remotely suspected of intending to do so. The Spanish did not treat English vessels with such impunity because the British navy maintained an active squadron of warships in West Indian waters which was quite ready to retaliate against the Spanish. Merchants in New Orleans simply refused to run any risks in this trade. When Governor Kerlérec approached a group of them in 1752 about the possibility of sending a deputation to Mexico to regularize relations, the merchants rejected the proposal. They recognized the value of the trade but replied that experience taught that it must not be conducted on Spanish territory. They deftly used their convocation by the governor as an opportunity to criticize monetary conditions in the colony. Within a few years, the interwar prosperity was wiped out and economic life at New Orleans was stifled for the duration.

Before Vaudreuil left his post in Louisiana, he estimated the value of the commerce with the Spanish at a million livres annually. In terms of its relative value to New Orleans, the governor's calculation is subject to the same qualifications as his earlier one. The Spanish trade was encumbered with the same disadvantages to New Orleans as the West Indian commerce. Although the Spanish colonies were primary markets for lumber and its derivatives, these were not valuable products and supply was limited both by labor scarcities and unsuitable vessels. The French West Indian commerce was a poor substitute for direct trade with France while the Spanish ports were actually competing with Louisiana for French wares and provisions during the period 1739 to 1748. Spanish piastres proved an irresistible lure to French merchants who could hope for little beyond depreciated *billets* in New Orleans. Hardy's vessel the *Nereide*, La Rochelle, preferred in 1746 to sell its flour in Havana and its Indian trade goods at Pensacola for piastres rather than tie up capital in New Orleans. There was a severe shortage of flour in New Orleans at the time and the garrisons at the Tombigbee and the Alabama turned to the Choctaw for sustenance. The economic magnetism of New Orleans was not overwhelming.

New Orleans was the capital of a territory which exerted little visible influence on the economic policies of the ruling state. Its products were valuable but they were not available in quantities sufficient to attract merchantmen from France. Its lands were more fertile than the increasingly depleted soils of the French West Indies but so wretched was the reputation of Louisiana that immigration was negligible after the fall of John Law. Louisiana needed people, white and black, if its position in the colonial pecking order was to improve. People finally came but they were British or British-owned, and they came only after France relinquished the colony to her Bourbon cousins in Spain.

8

The French Regime in Review

WHEN the crown, in its instructions to Kerlérec in 1752, blamed Crozat, the Company of the West, and the Company of the Indies for the slow progress of Louisiana, it was not telling the full story. The new governor may have known differently in 1752; it is almost certain that he did a decade later as he prepared to depart from a colony soon to be headed by a new sovereign—a colony which had suffered grievously from the recent war without ever seeing an enemy soldier under arms.

Louisiana indeed was in wretched shape in 1762 and 1763. Of all the American colonies of France, the isolation of Louisiana was most complete after 1757. Crops rotted in the fields and on the levee for want of transport to a market. There was no specie money in the colony but only hundreds of thousands of livres of treasury notes which were worth less in 1762 than during the height of inflation in the early 1740s. Planters lapsed into subsistence agriculture; merchants found no one to buy from or sell to; townspeople lived under the constant threat of famine; and persistent rumors drifted at intervals into New Orleans telling of a British invasion fleet sighted off this or that coast, heading for the Mississippi. Invasion might not have been a bad experience for the colony. As it happened, recovery in Louisiana coincided with the arrival of the British to occupy West Florida.

Great Britain brought the full weight of her naval power to bear on France during the Seven Years' War, with disastrous results for the government of Louis XV. The government of Cardinal Fleury and the competent administration of Comte de Maurepas created a naval force which fought Great Britain to a standstill in the War of the Austrian Succession. Successive governments did not avail themselves of the period of peace to improve His Majesty's naval service or even to maintain the level of efficiency achieved in 1748. France was unprepared for the next test at sea and there can be little doubt that the price of naval inferiority was ejection from North America and India. The French navy, however, recovered and even won a temporary advantage over the complacent British during the American Revolution but although the United States was an obvious beneficiary, the gains for France are not so clear.

France lacked the power to wage war both against Prussia by land and Great Britain by sea. Frederick II, King of Prussia, more than held his own against the combined might of Austria, France, and Russia and, even though France enjoyed minor success in the Great Lakes region in 1757 and 1758, the naval war turned against her in 1759. In that year, the French navy was decisively beaten in the Mediterranean and the Atlantic. The French fleet no longer existed as a potent fighting force and Great Britain proceeded to exploit her advantage by seizing Guadeloupe in 1759, along with several smaller islands, and Martinique in 1762. The French colonies, completely isolated, were at the mercy of Britain. Louisburg fell in 1758, Quebec in 1759, and Montreal in 1760. There was little more for the French to lose in America save Louisiana and St. Domingue. It was all over for France by the time Spain entered the war against Great Britain in 1762, and Spain succeeded in losing Havana to a British force before peace came in 1763.

Beginning in 1755, a year prior to the formal declaration of war, the French merchant marine suffered severe losses. British privateers—pirates in 1755—cruised off Cuba intercepting French ships running to and from St. Domingue, the Spanish islands, and Louisiana. The Rasteaus lost three vessels off St. Domingue, including two slavers carrying a total of 526 slaves and three vessels off France, all before the war started. By the time the war had fairly commenced, French merchants were extraordinarily reluctant to risk their vessels in the American trade.

George II's naval units raided up and down the French coast. La Rochelle was menaced by an invasion force in 1757 and was blockaded the following year. Cherbourg was sacked; St. Malo repulsed two invasions in 1758 but lost 70 vessels to the English torch. La Rochelle lost 70 of 76 vessels sent to America; Bordeaux's fleet was diminished by 224 vessels. Of 70 ships which Le Havre outfitted for America or Guinea, 14 remained while Nantes had lost 90 ships trading in Africa or America. In 1762, the French attempted to reinforce Louisiana, sending out a squadron of eight vessels, some carrying troops. Five were captured; one, the *Medée*, reached New Orleans. It was virtually impossible to get through.

Distress in Louisiana was intense as early as 1756. It was no wonder, considering the maritime losses sustained by the French to that point. More than thirty English privateers cruised off Cap Français alone. One British warship, the *Augusta*, put into Kingston, Jamaica, with nine prizes carrying a total of 185 cannon. The French had only a few men-of-war in West Indian waters and a number of privateers, some of which were armed at New Orleans. But in 1757 the magazines were empty in New Orleans and remained empty for the duration. The best that could be hoped for was an occasional vessel from the West Indies or the arrival of a few British vessels seeking to exchange goods for indigo. This latter trade provided the best possible method for getting Louisiana goods to a market and was apparently condoned by Governor Kerlérec who intervened against the corrupt *ordonnateur* Rochemore to protect those vessels.

Merchant vessels reappeared at New Orleans with some frequency in 1763 and 1764. By then, the French residents of New Orleans and vicinity had new rulers, although they had yet to appear, as well as new neighbors who did appear, fortunately for that colony. Save for a few months in 1803, when a handful of French officials arrived to claim Louisiana for Bonaparte, the French epoch was terminated in North America.

France ceded Louisiana to Spain not because of the military debacle of the Seven Years' War but because of disinterest. The war, of course, did no service to Louisiana, and Spain did not come into legal possession of a flourishing colony in 1764. But then, when had the colony deserved to be so described? France may have lost Canada to military force and witnessed the capture of many of her lush West Indian islands by the world's premier naval power, but Louisiana was lost to apathy, and not in 1763 but in the 1730s. At the time the crown took possession of the colony, France had fully recovered from the consequences of Louis XIV's adventures. France was neither threatened by nor was a threat to any European nation. The government of Cardinal Fleury, promising peace abroad and responsible administration at home, created an atmosphere conducive to economic development both in the colonies and the mother country. There would be no better moment in the eighteenth century to assume a new colonial responsibility—a responsibility which was the less burdensome because of the accomplishments of the Company of the Indies.

By 1731 the facts necessary for an evaluation of the economic possibilities of Louisiana were available in the trials and errors of the three prior decades. The land was rich with agricultural potential and the most suitable locations were known for the major staples of tobacco, indigo, and rice. Corn grew easily in most any area; wheat did not mature in the Lower Mississippi Valley. Cotton did well but awaited a ginning machine. Sugar was a question mark. But with two valuable cash crops such as tobacco and indigo, the development of a third was not an absolute necessity. In any case, the two primary staples could be supplemented with lumber production, livestock, and rice or corn as food crops.

One serious drawback to the resource potential of the land was its unsuitability for wheat. This would have to be obtained elsewhere, preferably the Illinois country, but, if not, from France. The quantity and quality of the natural resources susceptible to exploitation by the colonists were superior to those of any of the West Indian islands.

New Orleans provided adequate facilities in 1731 for the massing of agricultural produce for shipment overseas. To be sure, the navigation of the Mississippi from the bar at the Balize to the town was hazardous and time consuming, a serious inconvenience to trade. But it was not a deterrent to commerce, for the ships would come if there were cargoes to be had at New Orleans and a market for European goods. So well situated was the town as to make it unlikely that goods from the Mississippi Valley destined for export abroad would bypass it. The artificial hinterland of New Orleans was one of waterways as well as delta lands, and all the waterways fed the Mississippi which, in turn, disgorged its goods at the last place before the sea.

The future of New Orleans was to be determined by the bounty extracted from its hinterlands. Given the prevailing technology and the availability of land, this meant that increases in agricultural productivity would be a result of extensive rather than intensive land use. Development in New Orleans could occur only with an increase of population in its hinterlands. An augmented population would provide large quantities of staples for export and more business for New Orleans as well as a larger market for imported items. Demands made upon New Orleans by an expanding population would be met by a corresponding sophistication in the services rendered by the town. Economic development in the town resulted initially from growth in the countryside.[1]

The French government did not take over a wholly undeveloped area in 1731. Underdeveloped to be sure, but the building blocks of the colony were not scattered about in their natural state awaiting a preliminary ordering. That ordering had already been done. The crown inherited an organic structure which, while functioning at a primitive level, required only proper nourishment for steady growth. Nourishment did not come in the steady draughts necessary nor was a proper balance achieved. Instead, the royal government acted energetically in some areas and not at all in others just as critical, if not more so. Its greatest effort was aimed at committing the French merchant to engage in the trade with New Orleans. On the French side of the ocean, all that could be done in this regard was done by Maurepas and the Marine officials in the ports of France. Much sup-

[1] In considering the question of economic progress, economists and economic historians distinguish between "development" and "growth." By development they mean an increase in the per capita output of goods and services; by growth, an increase in goods and services caused by a proportionate increase in population. It is assumed that development leads to an improvement in the well-being of the society due to an increase in income per capita. The economist uses this concept primarily in seeking means to induce development in today's lagging nations. Economic historians of the United States are engaged in pinpointing that time in history when "growth" became "development." However, one must be certain that the fruits of a statistically proven rise in income per capita are shared at most levels of society rather than only by the establishment. One must also guard against the assumption that "growth" suddenly stops and "development" takes over and that the latter is something which can be understood historically or achieved in fact without due regard to the total culture of a society.

port, monetary and political, was available to interested merchants and, considering the reputation of Louisiana and the conservatism of French merchants, the initial results of Maurepas' campaign can be described as a limited success.

A fully satisfactory result, however, depended upon the conditions that greeted the merchants as their vessels anchored in the roadstead at New Orleans. These conditions were as frequently discouraging to traders as not. And it was in this essential part of the trade that the French government acted, when it acted, with least effect. Maurepas understood what had to be done. His letters to Bienville, Vaudreuil, and Salmon contain well-formed opinions as to the needs and potentials of the colony. Time and again, the minister reminded officials in Louisiana to make certain that cargoes were available to French merchantmen as if those officials should go out and immediately sow crops of indigo or tobacco. How often Maurepas instructed Salmon to adopt a liberal policy in issuing letters of exchange to French merchants; and how often Salmon was criticized for a liberality which inevitably resulted in exceeding the inadequate annual quota of letters of exchange. Frequently, Maurepas' communications with French merchants and Louisianians demonstrate his awareness of the serious shortage of slaves in the colony, a shortage which negated the possibility of a colonial response to his exhortations regarding increased production.

On the two most critical issues of a labor force and colonial remittances, the crown declined to allow Maurepas the budgetary flexibility requisite to effective action. The French government had the resources during the period 1731–44 to provide Maurepas with the needed funds. But the Ministry of the Marine was a poor cousin in the competition for funds among the agencies of government. One can inveigh against the ostentation of the court of Louis XV which spent more money for fetes, balls, and masquerades in a six-month period than was alloted for the Louisiana budget annually, but the monarchy still contained much of the essence of France. The erosion of confidence in the monarchy was still to come. One can also criticize the continental orientation of France and say, with one eye on the obvious success of Great Britain, that the game of power in which western European states were engaged was to be won or lost on the seas and in the colonies. But this was not so apparent to a nation with hundreds of miles of land frontiers to defend. Nor was it really true. British and American historians naturally believe that France lost much in the Treaty of Paris of 1763. In fact, the territorial losses were confined to areas of marginal value. French power, as colonial losses during the wars of the French Revolution and Napoleon indicate, was not based upon *la France d'outre-mer*.

The budgets that Maurepas struggled with reflected the importance assigned to that agency, as did that portion of each budget earmarked for Louisiana. Both of these fiscal units were assigned low priorities within the budgetary category in which they fell. Maurepas was pressed by many more important concerns than Louisiana. Bienville, Vaudreuil, and Kerlérec officially had only one concern to press upon Maurepas' attention. Maurepas, in turn, represented but one of a host of interests competing for royal support. Neither the governors nor the minister enjoyed conspicuous success in their representations.

Louisiana suffered much from war. Although the mother country turned to account the relative peace that prevailed after Utrecht, the Natchez and Chickasaw Indians burned and scalped while the British traded and agitated along a broad frontier north and northeast of New Orleans. Occasionally raiders pushed the frontier farther south, but only at Natchez was permanent damage sustained by the agricultural hinterland of New Orleans. The loss of furs to the British was of minimal economic significance to the future of Louisiana and New Orleans. The way to prosperity was not along the trapper's path. The quicker the proportionate value of the fur trade declined relative to other trades in New Orleans, the better for the colony.

Louisiana governors, responsible for security and aware of the essential military weakness of the colony, overreacted to the Indian menace. In their incessant demands for a larger Indian budget as a means of retaining Indian support, they were the prognosticators of a doom that failed to materialize. There is little reason to believe that larger budgets would have resulted in greater security. More Frenchmen would have.

In draining the strength of the colony both physically and fiscally, the Indian wars contributed to an economic malaise made more acute by the impact of French involvement in European war. But even the financial policies implemented by Lénormant and the isolation experienced between 1744 and 1748 (and, more totally, between 1756 and 1763), did not destroy the recuperative powers of the planting society. The economy of the colony responded quickly to peace in 1748 and again in 1763. Changing patterns of trade at New Orleans with the West Indies and the Spanish colonies, partially in response to the war, were more reflective of economic weaknesses in the colony which had little to do with war but much to do with people and productivity. The filling up of more land around New Orleans would work another transformation upon the nature of the port's trade.

And then there was the colonial system. There seems little point in condemning France for seeking to derive maximum returns from her colonies with a minimum investment. There is even less justification in judging the French performance in Louisiana from the vantage point of nineteenth century laissez-faire economics. Laissez faire, like mercantilism, is an abstraction or modular device useful in generalization but less applicable as one comes closer to specific historic situations. Governments are always interventionist, the degree varying with time and place, and there has normally been a greater degree of intervention in overseas possessions than at home. The application of a laissez-faire construct to the relationship between mother country and colony is a contradiction in terms. Louisiana required not less but more state intervention and aid. Jacques Rasteau and Jean Jung would probably not have involved themselves in Louisiana at all without tangible government support. The allocation of French resources to Louisiana may well have been inadequate in some respects and almost completely missing in others, such as the slave trade, but, then, Louisiana was not highly regarded relative to other colonies.

The merchants of New Orleans did not, any more than the French, seek to revolutionize the economic structure of the empire. This now brings to the surface a difficulty or weakness inherent in all the preceding pages of this narrative. When does New Orleans become an economic unit distinguishable from Louisiana? Can this occur before those living, working, and governing in New Orleans become aware that the community possesses a set of economic interests separate from those of the metropole on the one hand and the province of Louisiana on the other? Is it justifiable to treat New Orleans as an urban entity before its citizens act as if it is? The *fact* of the city, at least in terms of economic function, seems to have antedated *recognition* in New Orleans. There is no evidence that the inhabitants of New Orleans were conscious of an urban identity or that the best interests of the urban unit were not necessarily served most effectively by subordination to France or the colony of Louisiana. The various rulers of Louisiana from Crozat to the crown did not admit to a difference between the administrative center of the colony and the colony. Bienville and his successors promoted the interests of the colony of Louisiana. Merchants in New Orleans operated within a provincial rather than urban context. There was no municipal council or municipal police. The town was subsumed in the colony. It is, then, doubtful that the conditions requisite for the emergence of an urban identity were present to any significant degree during the French period.

One of the consequences of this is the difficulty in abstracting from the general economic history of Louisiana those developments which have special relevance to the city itself. Even though one sees the functional development of New Orleans as an entrepot, one does not see any awareness on the part of the inhabitants of New Orleans that this embryonic economic specialization demanded any particular care, protection, or encouragement apart from that required by the entire colony. The citizens of New Orleans operated within the French colonial system. While they may have complained bitterly about the administration, company or crown, at a particular time, they were not attacking the system itself. It may be tentatively suggested at this point that when the people of New Orleans were forced to adapt to the totally foreign regime of the Spanish, they reflected upon the possibility that their economic needs were ill served by the new and apparently inflexible system. In defining the needs of the city, the community discovered its identity. This added a new dimension to the economic history of New Orleans.

Spanish Louisiana, 1763–1772, and English Economic Domination

A T the time Spain received Louisiana at Fontainebleau, November 3, 1762, Spanish power and prestige had recently suffered a jarring setback with the loss of Havana and Manila to Great Britain. Spain's intervention on the side of the French in the Seven Years' War was disastrous for both nations. The French had wooed the Spanish assiduously in an effort to unite their strengths against the British. The diplomatic success of the French postponed a peace for which they were ready in 1762 while the military success of Britain strengthened her hand at the bargaining table. She was prepared to receive Canada and Louisiana from France, who appeared willing to make these cessions in exchange for the restoration of Martinique and Guadeloupe. Spain agreed to exchange Florida for Cuba and the Philippines but opposed the cession of all of Louisiana to Britain. Spain was neither prepared to see the Gulf of Mexico transformed into a British lake nor willing to accept the English presence west of the Mississippi.

Louisiana thus became a major bargaining point in the negotiations leading to the Treaty of Paris in 1763. France was ready to use it in the most expedient manner: to give it all to either Britain or Spain; to divide it; or, if necessary, to retain it. Spain and Britain recognized the strategic value of Louisiana. The latter coveted lower Louisiana, and especially New Orleans, as the key to the control of the fur trade of the Upper Mississippi and Missouri river valleys and for its proximity to Spanish colonies. The Spanish, deceived by no illusions regarding the commercial value of Louisiana under their control, viewed possession as a means of insulating their other North American colonies against British penetration. In the final settlement, Great Britain received that portion of Louisiana east of the Mississippi to the Iberville River [Bayou Manchac] and a line through the three lakes to the Gulf of Mexico. Spain came into possession of the west bank, including St. Louis and the Missouri River, to the Iberville and then both banks to the Gulf. New Orleans became the capital of Spanish Louisiana.

The division of Louisiana became public knowledge with the signing of the Treaty of Paris in February, 1763, but official orders to cede the colony to Spain reached New Orleans only in September, 1764, and the Spanish did not arrive officially in the colony until March, 1766. Even then, the new sovereigns did not assume formal control but functioned through French intermediaries who served in their normal official capacities.

Spain did not control the colony politically until the arrival in New Orleans of General Alexander O'Reilly in August, 1769. During this interregnum there was great disorder in the colony stemming from the isolation experienced during the Seven Years' War and further compounded by the political confusion resulting from the liquidation of French sovereignty. Now the neighbors of Spanish Louisiana, the British, managed to turn this fluid situation to account and in so doing provided New Orleans and vicinity with the most invigorating economic stimulus experienced since the days of John Law.

Havana's capture brought fighting to an end in the Western Hemisphere, allowing the resumption of normal business activity. Great Britain, occupying Havana, Martinique, Guadeloupe, and several lesser islands, carried off thousands of cargoes of staples from and introduced large numbers of slaves into their acquisitions. France and Spain tried to pick up the pieces in their remaining possessions. At New Orleans, commercial activity resumed in late 1762 and 1763 but there are indications that the economic revival did not follow the normal or traditional course. Property transfers were numerous and many vessels changed ownership during this period. The frequency of such transactions increased between 1763 and 1765 in response to the knowledge that Spain was soon to receive New Orleans. Some men pulled out of the colony while others decided to wait out events. But the Spanish did not come. French officials remained at their posts. Rumors that France would retain possession were eagerly believed by the colonists in the face of evidence that the crown was liquidating its affairs in the colony. All of this added to the uncertainty concerning future economic prospects and arrangements.

Two problems were especially critical: there was a great shortage of food and other necessities at New Orleans in 1763–64, a scarcity dating back to 1759, and the money circulating in the colony was seriously depreciated, a condition traceable to 1759 or 1760, when the payment of letters of exchange drawn in Louisiana was suspended. Merchants in the French West Indies and France refused to involve themselves in the New Orleans trade because of the financial and political confusion. Colonists were forced to pay exorbitant prices for flour that trickled in on occasional French vessels and the planters were without the means of shipping their crops to markets. Routine business transactions were concluded only with great caution because no one knew on what terms the French government would eventually receive the million livres worth of treasury notes issued during the war. Large sums of colonial notes were simply withdrawn from circulation by their holders pending a final settlement. Credits were available only to those with property to serve as security. As acting Governor Aubry informed the Duc de Choiseul in 1765: "The lands and the Negroes have lessened [in value] by a half; the debtors no longer pay; three fourths of the debts are remitted [postponed] until the arrangements of the finances which does not take place." [1]

A final resolution of the problem of the outstanding treasury notes finally occurred in 1769. This unfortunate postponement contributed not a little to the embarrassments experienced by the first Spanish governor Antonio de Ulloa who arrived at New Orleans in March, 1766, but only partially ruled until his expulsion from the colony in 1768. By the time of Ulloa's arrival, the paper money of the colony was worth about 25 percent of face value. The total colonial debt stood at between 6 and 8 million livres. Governor

[1] Aubry to the Minister [Choiseul], February 12, 1765, in Clarence W. Alvord and Clarence E. Carter (eds.), *The Critical Period, 1763–1765, Collections of the Illinois Historical Library*, X [British Series, I] (Springfield, 1915), 435–36. Dabbadie made the same point in September, 1764, *ibid.*, 318.

Ulloa was greeted by colonial demands that the treasury notes be accepted at par value. The governor's offer to make the paper legal tender at 65 percent of par value was quite reasonable but unsatisfactory to numerous colonists who had purchased the notes on speculation. Ulloa received some funds from the Spanish government during his short tenure but they were inadequate to meet even current expenses. He reported to his superior in June, 1767, and again in July, 1768, that all payments were suspended and that the colony was in great peril.

Order came to the finances of Louisiana in two ways: by the arrival of O'Reilly, the normalization of Spanish authority, and the regularization of Spanish fiscal support; and with the promulgation of an *arrêt du conseil* in 1769 which provided for the redemption of the treasury notes. Holders of the notes then learned that Ulloa's terms were quite generous as the *arrêt* ordered the conversion of the *billets* into letters of exchange at 60 percent of face value. Even this was a liberal settlement, considering the actual value of the money. By then, provision had also been made for the payment of letters of exchange drawn on the French government through 1765. Thereafter, Spain assumed responsibility for debts contracted by the government in Louisiana.

In the meantime, the trade and commerce at New Orleans was conducted primarily by Englishmen, occasionally by French and French West Indians, and infrequently by Spaniards. During the period 1764–78, the English dominated the economic life of the colony in spite of the rigorous efforts of General O'Reilly to destroy their commerce in Louisiana between 1768 and 1772. It was fortunate for Louisiana that the English were prepared to fill the vacuum created by the cession of Louisiana and the reluctance of French merchants to venture cargoes to New Orleans. Without the English presence, conditions would have been much worse. With this activity, conditions in certain respects were better than in any prior period.

Great Britain received the right to navigate the Mississippi in the Treaty of 1763 and was thus afforded an unparalleled opportunity to introduce goods into Spanish Louisiana. No time was wasted. Flour-laden vessels appeared off New Orleans in 1763, prepared to take full advantage of food shortages in the town. For the remainder of the Spanish period, Englishmen or their American successors furnished New Orleans with the greater part of its food supplies. These supplies were indispensable at all times but especially so in 1765 with the arrival of several hundred indigent Acadian refugees.

Rare indeed were the opportunities presented to the Anglo-Saxons along the entire course of the Mississippi River to capture the Indian trade of the midcontinent and even to penetrate Spain's colonies west of Louisiana. Contact, competition, and tension existed between Spain and Great Britain at many points in the Mississippi Valley. The British occupied the Illinois settlements of Kaskaskia and Cahokia and by 1769 were trading actively with St. Louis and Ste. Genevieve in Spanish Illinois. Even the trade nominally controlled by Spanish subjects was administered by French Louisianians who were dependent upon New Orleans as a source of supply and as a market for their furs and hides. And New Orleans received much of its supply from the English. Maxent, Lacléde, and Chouteau, the three principal traders in Missouri, cooperated frequently with the English in Illinois and the Lower Valley, making the trade with the Missouri tribes and New Mexico as much British as Spanish. There was also, of course, bitter competition for the fur trade of the Upper Valley between Englishmen and the new Spanish subjects.

New Orleans was the strategic point in the competition between Great Britain and Spain throughout the entire Mississippi Valley. It was of no advantage to the English to capture a large share of the trade in the Upper Valley and with the Indians of the Southeast if that trade ultimately fell into French hands at New Orleans. Before the arrival of O'Reilly, the English established themselves in New Orleans but their permanence could not be taken for granted. Several alternatives were available to them, all of which assumed the diversion of trade from New Orleans to points within British Florida. As there were English established at New Orleans, this led to a certain amount of intra-English competition. Such competition probably preserved a portion of New Orleans' trade, for so complete was British economic ascendancy that authorities at New Orleans could do little to prevent a diversion of trade. The entrance of Spain into the War of the American Revolution finally presented the Spanish with the long-awaited opportunity to regain control of the Floridas, thus removing the Anglo-Saxon menace along with the vigor they brought to the economy of New Orleans.

Thwarted in their hopes to receive New Orleans at the conference table in 1763, the British were compelled to make do with Pensacola and Mobile on the Gulf and Baton Rouge and Natchez on the Mississippi. Britain viewed the possession of both East and West Florida as convenient points from which to carry on trade with Spain's island and mainland colonies. It was expected that Pensacola and Mobile would soon dominate the Indian trade in Chickasaw, Choctaw, and Creek country, while simultaneously diverting Cuban vessels from New Orleans by virtue of the superior goods obtainable at the Gulf ports. In both instances, trade would be diverted from New Orleans. Cuban vessels traded with Mobile and Pensacola but so did they with New Orleans, where their connections were of longer standing and where, due to the efforts of English merchants, the assortment of trade goods was superior to either of the Gulf ports. Nor does it appear that Mobile and Pensacola diverted the Indian trade from New Orleans. Englishmen supplied the goods, but largely to French traders who forwarded the furs to New Orleans.

The major British effort was to utilize the connection between the Iberville River and Lake Maurepas as a means of bypassing and isolating New Orleans. In 1764 British troops began moving past New Orleans on their way to the post at Natchez; to construct a post, known as Fort Bute, at the Iberville; and to occupy the Illinois. This latter expedition was driven back by an Indian attack after journeying upriver for a month, but the convoys to Natchez and the Iberville were successful in reaching their objectives. Through late 1764 and 1765 the British labored to deepen the channel of the Iberville between the Mississippi and Lake Maurepas and to construct Fort Bute. Governor Johnstone of West Florida reported prematurely in December, 1764, that the task was completed, but it was never completed and trade was not diverted from New Orleans.

British efforts to settle at the Iberville were beset by many difficulties. There was inadequate labor to make much impact on the river's channel and settlers and troops alike were harassed by hostile Indians. In August, 1765, about fifty Alabamas and Houmas penned up the British at Fort Bute, looting the stores, carrying off what their canoes could hold, and burning the remainder. The settlers were forced to evacuate, arriving at New Orleans in September. Aubry sent out a party to find the raiders and repossess the loot. He endeavored to protect the British from the tribes that remained loyal to the French but his efforts met with limited success and the British questioned his sincerity.[2] Through 1770 the British suffered from marauding warriors. The Choctaws struck frequently in and around the British territory across the lakes and welcomed French traders into their villages. Then, in 1770 the Choctaws pillaged the British stores and fort at Natchez. The forts at both Natchez and the Iberville were abandoned by the British but not the settlements, which continued to attract immigrants. The Natchez area grew quite rapidly through the period of the American Revolution, becoming a major source of staples for New Orleans. The settlement at Bayou Manchac flourished also for it developed into the center of the contraband trade between British Florida and Spanish Louisiana.

English merchants were firmly entrenched both at New Orleans and in their floating warehouses between New Orleans and Baton Rouge by the time Ulloa made his appearance. While Ulloa's orders were to stamp out this trade, he had neither the power nor the incentive to hew closely to his instructions. These businessmen were too necessary both as suppliers of basic necessities and as purchasers of the staple produce of Louisiana's plantations and of the pelts which the annual convoys carried to the town. Aubry, the real governor, and Ulloa both realized this as they frequently turned to the English for flour and provisions. Indeed, according to one English observer, Ulloa purchased flour and pork not only for local consumption but to transport to Havana. Traffic in flour and provisions opened up the first commerce between New Orleans and the Atlantic coast colonies of Great Britain. Evan Jones, Oliver Pollock, and William Moore all entered into the New Orleans trade in this

---

[2] Governor Dabbadie died in February, 1765, and Aubry took over his functions, although not the title. It was Aubry who finally handed Louisiana over to O'Reilly.

way. In addition to British goods, they brought with them credit, shipping, and contacts with New York, Philadelphia, and Baltimore. Perhaps more immediately critical, such traders also imported the first large numbers of Negroes since the Dalcour-Du Breuil ship-ment in 1743.[3]

It was the English rather than the French that imparted life to the commerce of the colony and the staff of life to the colonists be-tween 1763 and 1769 and then again following Alexander O'Reilly's departure. Although the French did not totally abstain from the trade with New Orleans—in 1764, eight vessels arrived from French ports and a number from the French West Indies—the number of arrivals apparently declined between 1766 and 1768, even though trade between Louisiana and the French West Indies was permitted during those years. There are no figures that tell us how many British vessels navigated the Mississippi, but they must have been numerous because the river was open to them and their services were so necessary to the colony. Only during and after the American Revolution did French merchants come close to wielding ascendant economic power in Louisiana and they were challenged by the Anglo-Americans who came to the colony as Spanish subjects. The French Revolutionary Wars destroyed this trade; in 1806–1807 of 269 foreign arrivals in New Orleans, 80 were Europeans, including 69 from Great Britain and 17 from France. France, of course, was an important market for southern staples but the trade was carried in American and British vessels.[4]

[3] For the career of Oliver Pollock, see James Alton James, *Oliver Pollock: The Life and Times of an Unknown Patriot* (New York, 1937). Evan Jones came to New Orleans in 1765 and pursued an active career in the city as partner in Evan and James Jones Company, which dealt with mercantile houses in Philadelphia. He served on the city council, as the first president of the Bank of Louisiana in 1804, and as a director of the New Orleans branch of the Bank of the United States in 1810; William Moore was the New Orleans agent of a New York firm which con-tracted to supply flour to the government at New Orleans.

[4] Pierre H. Boulle, "French Reactions to the Louisiana Revolution of 1768," in John Francis McDermott (ed.), *The French in the Mississippi Valley* (Urbana, 1965), 145, is mistaken in stating that no Spanish merchant vessels came to supply Louisiana prior to 1767. At least five Spanish vessels reached New Orleans between 1764 and 1767 and probably others as well, as it was an established port of call for vessels from Havana, Campeachy, and Vera Cruz. Neither is Boulle correct in writ-ing that "Louisiana would have been wholly abandoned had it not been for French merchants who continued to trade with New Orleans even after it became known that the colony was no longer French."

Ulloa's arrival did no damage to the position of the English merchants. Ulloa catered to the trade, contracted through Aubry with
English merchants to supply the garrison, and tried to resolve the
colony's pressing financial difficulties, but because he lacked power
and authority, his efforts were largely frustrated. Arriving in 1766
with only a small body of troops and confronted by the refusal of
the French garrison to serve Spain, Ulloa delayed his formal acceptance of the colony. Supplies were so short that both French and
Spanish troops were put on half rations while funds were unavailable
to meet even the most immediate demands. Ulloa called for Spanish
troops and money. He received no troops and only 160,000 piastres
during his unhappy tenure.

Because he was forced to rule indirectly through Aubry, there
was little possibility that Ulloa would enjoy much success in implementing the commercial system decided upon by Charles III for his
new colony. Ulloa's major tasks were to take possession of the colony and effect a reorientation of commercial patterns from France
to Spain. But Great Britain controlled the economy and the new
governor, aware of colonial needs, could not—would not—act dras-
tically toward the English merchants. He paid lip service to his
instructions by prohibiting trade with the British in 1767 and complaining to his superiors about the insolent independence demonstrated by English traders who came and went as they pleased. But
at the same time he continued to contract with such merchants for
food and other supplies for the government while allowing the
English to service the private needs of the colony.

Fortunately for the colony, the English were quite willing to
trade in kind, accepting local crops in payment for imported items
and also extending credits to the local planters. English traders were
far more accommodating in extending credits than shipowners from
the French West Indies, who were permitted in 1767 to bring certain supplies to New Orleans in exchange for lumber and hides. The
West Indians, bound to accept the current money in payment when
goods were not available, did not work this trade with great energy.
The English—legally, actually smugglers—could not be compelled to
accept the treasury notes and unpaid letters of exchange but preferred in any case to take produce, particularly indigo, tobacco,

furs, and the little cotton that was being raised. But in 1768 times were hard for everyone. Ulloa, in June, had received no funds for almost a year. Cash transactions were rare, as an English merchant in New Orleans, John Fitzpatrick, informed his correspondent at Pensacola. Then, in October, Ulloa published the Royal Decree of March 23, 1768, which intended to bring Louisiana fully within the orbit of the Spanish colonial system.

The new regulations were potentially unsettling to the commerce of the colony. In terms of the traditional system of commerce forced upon the Spanish colonies, the decree appeared as a concession, a liberalization of the system itself. It permitted commerce between New Orleans and nine Spanish peninsular ports. Exports to Louisiana were freed from duties while the import tax was lowered to 4 percent on Louisiana products which could then be reexported from any of the stipulated ports. The carrying trade was confined to Spanish vessels, which were prohibited from making unauthorized stops at any of the Spanish colonies. All intercourse was prohibited between Louisiana and the French colonies.

If there had been any basis for an advantageous exchange between Spain and Louisiana, the regulation would have been extremely favorable. But as there was no such basis and as it sought to close off the traditional markets of Louisiana, the regulation was oppressive and so regarded by many merchants and planters in Louisiana. Spain could neither supply Louisiana with goods nor market the agricultural production of the colony. If Ulloa enforced the decree literally, as the colonists feared he would, great damage would be done to the economy. But in 1768 Ulloa was in no position to enforce any regulation strictly. By expelling Ulloa, in October of that year, the colonists only hastened the arrival of the force necessary to implement the regulation. British proximity at Manchac and on the river, as well as across the lakes, would make it difficult for even the most powerful and effective force to completely ruin the normal commerce of the colony. It was not, however, the British trade which the disaffected wished to save. It was the French and French West Indian trade that they were directly interested in and which was, to a degree, competitive with the British.

The summer and early fall of 1768 were difficult months for

Louisiana. The temperature was unusually warm. There was no flour and prices were extremely high. There was no cash and many of the colonists were dissatisfied with Ulloa's propositions regarding the *billets* as well as anxious about the terms of the final settlement to be imposed by the French government. Fitzpatrick also reported that Spanish soldiers were expected shortly. Ulloa's publication of the commercial regulations apparently was the efficient cause for his expulsion by a decree of the Superior Council on October 29, 1768. The much-abused governor, who was never really governor, left for Havana on November 1 and for ten months the colony drifted along with Aubry, who opposed the expulsion, serving as the head of the colony.

The events involving the expulsion of Ulloa are generally referred to as the Revolution of 1768, which actually was more like an attempted coup for little change resulted, apart from Ulloa's absence. There is no reason to suppose either widespread support of the action or to attribute to it any more of a design than the sending of delegates to France to plead for some sort of aid, preferably the resumption of French sovereignty. There was defiance by the leadership and the voicing of basically legitimate grievances by merchants and planters against the commercial decree in their written memorial which justified the occurrences of October 29 through November 1, 1768, and attacked the commercial decree as destructive to the economy of the colony.

Maintaining that the privileges extended by the decree were poor compensation for the destruction of commerce with France and the French West Indies, the memorialists argued that the major products of Louisiana could find no market in Spain. Furs were of no value in Spain; Peru, Cuba, and Campeachy provided lumber and sugar; Guatemala produced superior indigo; and Hispaniola produced tobacco. Reexportation privileges, if ever utilized, would only increase the cost of export for the owners of the goods, the more so since Spain could not provide return cargoes to Louisiana. The decree, the memorialists charged, condemned Louisiana to a future of indolence and want.

As an argument for the resumption of trade with France and her islands, the memorial was unanswerable. But it assumed that the decree could be enforced and it ignored the presence of the English merchants, who took all of those products listed as unsuitable for the Spanish market. Fitzpatrick and others received furs from Maxent, Laclède and Company or Jacob Monsanto; tobacco from Pointe Coupée; indigo from below New Orleans; and boards and shingles. Ulloa emphasized the need to provide a market for lumber. While Governor O'Reilly endeavored to enforce the regulation, he was unable to end the British trade and recognized the need for modifications in the terms of trade for Louisiana. The action by the Louisianians was as premature as it was hastily conceived. It met with an unfavorable response in France and it elicited a quick and overwhelming response from Spain.

There was no doubt that Spain intended to maintain her sovereignty in Louisiana. General O'Reilly received command of the expedition which sailed from Havana on June 6, 1769, with twenty-one vessels and 2,056 troops. The personnel of the entire force was probably not too much smaller than the population of New Orleans. Louisianians were ignorant of these preparations. Discussion still centered around the possibility of the French repossessing the colony. From Fitzpatrick's point of view, the Spanish were preferable because cash would then circulate and debts could be collected. French residents obviously applied other criteria in voicing preference for the traditional connection with France. But this preference was not acted upon, for when the moment of truth arrived for the rebels there was no disposition to oppose O'Reilly.

O'Reilly's fleet reached the Balize on July 24, just a few days after the residents had received letters informing them that Louisiana was restored to France. On August 17, the fleet came to anchor before New Orleans. Formal ceremonies were scheduled for the next day. Nothing so impressive had ever been witnessed at New Orleans. The majesty and reality of Spanish power was fully apparent to the assembled townsfolk and country people who had flocked into New Orleans for the festivities. Line upon line of brightly uniformed Spanish soldiers disembarked from their vessels onto the levee and marched smartly down into the plaza where they formed three sides of a square with the comparatively grubby French militiamen closing it out. This maneuver took up most of the day. General O'Reilly came ashore at 5:30 P.M. and presented his credentials and orders to Aubry. Aubry placed the keys of the city at the general's feet while Spanish flags were run up all over the city, accompanied by a shattering salvo from the fleet and the troops. O'Reilly, Aubry, and other officers then entered the church for God's blessing and the chanting of a *Te Deum*.

The lowering of the *fleur-de-lis* resolved certain long-range questions, left certain others resolved in theory if not in fact, and left open certain pressing questions of an immediate and more personal nature. The fate of the leaders of the movement was resolved with the arrest of thirteen men on August 21, 1769. Six were executed, six were imprisoned, and one died before his trial. Other suspects were exiled. O'Reilly treated the remainder of the population with courtesy, liberality, and sagacity. New Orleans received its first bona fide city government when the Cabildo, composed of Creoles and endowed with considerable municipal authority, replaced the Superior Council. The Spanish also came to depend primarily upon Frenchmen for offices and militiamen.

Great uncertainty was felt in the area of commercial affairs. Would O'Reilly adhere to the letter of the decree of 1768? Would he make any compromises relative to the English trade? Did the regulation of 1768 represent the final word of the Spanish government? John Fitzpatrick was deeply concerned with these questions as were other merchants, English and French, in New Orleans. The answers involved not only O'Reilly's immediate reaction to conditions in Louisiana and measures that he might take to improve or aggravate the situation, but also the high policy of the Spanish government toward the Spanish economy in general and the colonial system in particular. Spanish policy in Louisiana during the years prior to the American Revolution must be viewed within the context of the efforts of Charles III and his government to inject new energy into the Spanish economy and to reorganize colonial commerce so that Spain might derive a major share of the profits from the trade with her colonies.

Spain did little in a coordinated way toward reversing the existing pattern prior to the Treaty of Paris. There were periods when she exercised great vigilance in preventing smuggling at various critical points in her empire. Occasionally the system was altered in detail. But this had little impact on the volume of the contraband trade which the British pursued with the most success. Utilizing the *asiento* privilege in the slave trade, enjoyed from 1713 to 1750 (excepting 1744–48), Britain penetrated the Spanish empire with ease and continued to do so after 1750.

The reforms of Charles III seem revolutionary when compared to the earlier and random changes. Success came grudgingly but perceptibly both in his domestic and colonial reforms as he steadily chipped away at the accumulated crust of centuries. For a time he led Spain down a new path that was not quite parallel to the old one and his subjects in Louisiana formed part of the entourage when the journey began.

Charles III and his advisers moved swiftly in the field of foreign and colonial commerce after 1763. Activity was concentrated in two general areas: efforts were made to loosen the hold of France and Great Britain on commerce in Cádiz where there were more than one hundred French commercial houses alone in 1770; and a secret committee was formed, charged with a review of the colonial system, and authorized to suggest concrete reforms. Various measures were taken to effect the first goal such as prohibiting the importation of cotton goods, which struck at the cotton industry of England, and the aborted effort in 1772 to prevent the export of foreign goods aboard the *flota* to the Indies. Reasonable success in this area, however, depended upon the thoroughness of the reforms advocated by the secret committee and translated into specific proposals by a second commission in 1765.

The commission listed eight major causes of decay in the colonial trade: (1) the monopoly of shipping at Cádiz; (2) restrictions on shipping by licensing and high export duties; (3) the costs of shipping both to and from the colonies; (4) collecting a duty on volume without reference to value; (5) scarcity of slaves in America and the neglect of agriculture; (6) failure to prevent practices in the colonies prejudicial to Spain, such as the trade between the Philippines and New Spain which drained the latter of silver; (7) high import duties; and (8) smuggling. In 1765, using this critique as a basis, the crown initiated its reforms by throwing open the trade of Cuba, St. Domingue, Puerto Rico, Margarita, and Trinidad to the peninsular ports of Cádiz, Seville, Alicante, Cartagena, Málaga, Barcelona, Santander, La Coruna, and Gijón under the least possible regulation. No longer were special licenses required, and numerous duties and fees were replaced by an impost of 6 or 7 percent ad valorem. These privileges were extended to Louisiana in 1768, Campeachy in 1770, Yucatan in 1776, and by 1778 to all other parts of the empire except Venezuela and Mexico, the latter receiving the privilege in 1789. Also, restrictions on intracolonial trade were removed between New Spain, New Granada, and Peru in 1774 and between Chile, Buenos Aires, and Guatemala in 1778.

The results were gratifying. Spanish merchants competed successfully with foreigners in the port cities. Between 1778 and 1788 the value of Spain's trade with Spanish America increased 700 percent and brought relative prosperity to many parts of the empire. It was within this general system—with significant amendments made at intervals—that Louisiana functioned. As we shall see, prosperity came to Louisiana as well, but so different were the problems of that colony, pressed as it was by the advance of the Anglo-American into the Mississippi Valley, that it is possible the prosperity came in spite of the system. Or, perhaps, prosperity resulted from modifications in the system forced upon Spain by the uniqueness of Louisiana's situation and the pressure of external events. In either case, one can agree with Arthur P. Whitaker that Louisiana was not a laboratory in which Spain experimented with colonial reforms which were to be applied elsewhere if successful on the Mississippi. The concessions of 1768 and 1772 were designed to assimilate Louisiana into the empire.[5] Subsequent concessions may have been reactions to foreign impingement on Louisiana and designed to strengthen the colony as a buffer against American imperialism.

O'Reilly was charged with the restoration of order in Louisiana, the establishment of civil government, and the implementation of

[5] Arthur P. Whitaker, "The Commerce of Louisiana and the Floridas at the End of the Eighteenth Century," *Hispanic American Historical Review*, VIII (1928), 195–96, and Whitaker (ed. and tr.), *Documents Relating to the Commercial Policy of Spain in the Floridas with Incidental Reference to Louisiana*, Publications of the *Florida State Historical Society*, No. 10 (Deland, 1931), xxiii.

the decree of 1768. With regard to the latter, he retained some discretionary powers and was authorized to suggest modifications in the decree which would benefit Louisiana. But until his suggestions were acted upon, the decree was to be enforced. Enforcement threatened the extinction of the English trade, that with the French West Indies, and the traffic between New Orleans and other Spanish colonies. All of these were prohibited by the ordinance of 1765 and the decree of 1768 extending the former to Louisiana. Any one of these trades was of greater value to New Orleans than all of the privileges granted in the new regulations.

The general came down hard on the English established in New Orleans. O'Reilly found them in control of the commerce of the colony with merchants scattered about among the various settlements within Spanish Louisiana. Their vessels entered the port of New Orleans and moored at any point along the Spanish shore that was convenient in terms of anchorage and trade. O'Reilly took steps in September and October, 1769, to eject the English residents of New Orleans and to prevent English vessels from taking berths along the Spanish shore. By September 2, all English merchants were under notice to depart after disposing of their present stock of goods and submitting an inventory to the general. John Fitzpatrick was forced to leave on September 22, leaving numerous debts to collect in town. He settled in Manchac, believing that he could operate as usual among the residents of Spanish Louisiana. This was the real beginning of the contraband trade at the Iberville but it was not pursued with ease, for O'Reilly made it extremely difficult for the English to collect their debts in New Orleans and elsewhere within his province.

Fitzpatrick ventured into New Orleans in February, 1770, on a debt-collecting mission for himself and other English merchants including Baynton, Wharton, and Morgan, a Philadelphia firm then heavily engaged in the Illinois trade. He was seized and jailed by local authorities and then rushed out of town under escort. Thereafter, Fitzpatrick employed an agent in New Orleans to collect debts on a 5 percent commission. He was also thwarted in his efforts to collect from Maxent by O'Reilly's order stopping payment on

Maxent's bills until that merchant's creditors in Spain were satisfied. Most of Maxent's local obligations were to English merchants at Manchac and East Florida.[6]

English vessels were denied berths along the Spanish riverbank and even prohibited from anchoring in the river within the boundaries of Spanish Louisiana. The English vessel *Sea Flower*, seriously damaged in crossing the bar at the Balize, made New Orleans leaking badly and applied to O'Reilly for permission to repair and to sell twenty-eight slaves. Both requests were refused and the ship was forced to move away from New Orleans under threat of confiscation. But at the same time that O'Reilly acted so inflexibly toward some English traders and vessels, he treated others with leniency and even favor since he was dependent upon the English for the local flour supply. By offering O'Reilly flour at a reasonable price when it was selling at thirty dollars per barrel, Oliver Pollock ingratiated himself with the governor and received the freedom to trade with Louisiana. In August and September, 1770, vessels from New York, Baltimore, and Philadelphia provided a plentiful flour supply and prices fell to six or seven dollars per barrel. Flour also came to New Orleans from English Illinois. O'Reilly was not fully successful in interdicting the trade with Britain during his term of office and his successor subjected the English to much less harassment. As a merchant of long standing in New Orleans wrote in 1771, British vessels covered the river and the English retained their undoubted superiority in commerce. O'Reilly achieved little of permanence in this regard.

Numerous merchants at New Orleans engaged in a trade with the Spanish colonies, fostered by the French government prior to 1763 and tolerated by Dabbadie, Aubry, and Ulloa between the cession and the latter's expulsion. Intracolonial trade was forbidden under Spanish law until the regulations of 1774 and subsequent years lifted the restriction, but it was only with the coming of O'Reilly that the Spanish were able to enforce the laws in Louisiana. New Orleans, French West Indian, and Cuban merchants traded actively under the

---

[6] Fitzpatrick remained at Manchac and was captured by Gálvez in 1779, becoming a Spanish subject in 1780 and complaining in that year of the difficulty of collecting debts at New Orleans because of the indulgence of the Spanish governor.

cover of the confusion dominating New Orleans between 1763 and 1769. This commerce was still of little value to the planters of Louisiana, however, for the trade involved an exchange of French and especially British manufactured goods for Campeachy wood, Guatemalan indigo, silver, and other Spanish colonial products. The silver was of no more service to Louisana than it had been in former years because it flowed increasingly into the hands of English merchants.

Several merchants at New Orleans owned vessels in association with Spanish residents of Havana, pursuing a trade that included stops at Martinique, Havana, Vera Cruz, Campeachy, and New Orleans. Jacob Monsanto of New Orleans associated with two other Havana merchants in outfitting the *St. Jean Baptiste* for trips to Vera Cruz and Campeachy while Chantalou engaged in ventures with the Cuban shipowner François Aredonda bringing logwood to New Orleans.

O'Reilly proceeded swiftly against this traffic. As he reported in October, 1769, his suspicions were aroused by the Duraldes brothers, Genevans who dealt in diamonds, watches, and other costly goods for which there was little market in New Orleans. Investigation ascertained the use of these goods in an illegal trade with Campeachy and Vera Cruz. The Duraldes confessed when confronted with the evidence. Other merchants, including Monsanto, were discovered engaged in this trade and banished from Louisiana. O'Reilly acted similarly toward merchants found involved in the contraband trade with Texas via Natchitoches and Opelousas. Monsanto was also operating in this commerce. As in the case of the British trade, once O'Reilly departed, the trade with neighboring Spanish colonies resumed. Monsanto returned, as perhaps others did, and in 1780 faced judicial proceedings for selling goods at Natchitoches purchased from the English at Manchac and destined for Texas and New Mexico.[7]

O'Reilly's policies were not confined to the stifling of illegal trade nor did he intend to dam the normal channels of trade without offering alternatives. In a report of October 17, 1769, the governor proposed for the consideration of the Spanish government that a

[7] Monsanto received furs and flour from English and Spanish Illinois and was the correspondent of several merchants of Bordeaux.

free trade be instituted between New Orleans and Havana. He pointed out that of the major products of Louisiana, timber was one of the most significant and could not possibly find a market in Spain. Havana needed wood and could supply Louisiana with manufactured goods. O'Reilly suggested that the vessels of both colonies be received at New Orleans and Havana on the same footing as Spanish vessels and that the goods of both colonies be received duty free. O'Reilly anticipated that Spanish vessels would bring supplies to New Orleans, load wood for Havana, and pick up sugar for a return cargo to Spain. Temporary permission implementing this proposal was granted in 1770 and it was formally approved in a decree of 1772.

But no sooner had O'Reilly left New Orleans and arrived at Havana in 1770 than he leveled a blow at Louisiana's commerce which far outweighed the potential benefits of a New Orleans-Havana trade. In April, 1770, he ordered Governor Unzaga to prohibit the export of Louisiana tobacco which was judged inferior and potentially damaging to the tobacco trade with Cuba. The colonists of Louisiana immediately protested this decision. Between the destruction of the tobacco trade and the prohibition of commerce with the French islands, it was argued, the inhabitants would be reduced to vagabondage and beggary. The Cabildo petitioned the king for permission to export tobacco to St. Domingue in exchange for slaves. The king rejected this proposal, informing his subjects that they would enjoy great benefits from the free trade between Havana and New Orleans.

This is a fine example of the formulation of colonial priorities by the officials of the mother country. However necessary tobacco was to Louisiana as an export crop, the welfare of the more valuable colony of Cuba took precedence. Cuban tobacco merited a certain reputation for quality both in Spain and Europe, which was threatened through the introduction of inferior leaf from Louisiana. It was the proper decision for the crown to make, although unfortunate for Louisiana. It was all the more unfortunate because the trade with Havana was not as beneficial as O'Reilly anticipated, partially due to the prohibition of tobacco exports but also because of the nature of the trade and consumption habits of long standing in Louisiana.

Louisianians had no choice but to give the Cuban trade a good try as other avenues were legally closed and the intentions of Governor Unzaga toward the illegal options were still undisclosed. New Orleans shipowners, assured of prompt service in Havana, immediately loaded vessels with Louisiana goods and dispatched them. The first ventures, mostly in lumber, discovered no market for any wood save in planks which required some restructuring of the lumber milling industry in Louisiana. These trips were generally without profit. Two voyages by Captain Lemaire netted losses of 10 percent in Cuba and 25 percent on the sale of the Cuban goods in New Orleans. Captain Bartolomé ventured twice and lost once. He included Illinois flour in the first cargo, which was confiscated by officials at Havana. In spite of these precedents, Captain Langourais loaded a brigantine with rice, indigo, and wood but could find no purchasers in Havana and was compelled to give up the cargo to the Cuban merchant Clavarie on unfavorable terms and long credit. Clavarie then gathered a cargo of wines, brandies, sugar, preserves, and other delectables valued altogether at 4,981 piastres which he freighted aboard a Catalan vessel for New Orleans. The assortment sold for 3,540 piastres, which he used to purchase oaken timbers, planks, and rice for the return trip. The freight alone for the round trip was 1,400 piastres and this was about equivalent to the loss suffered by Clavarie.

The years 1770 and 1771 were among the worst experienced in Louisiana under the Spanish and during peacetime. Cubans did not want Louisiana's products nor could they satisfy the taste of Louisianians for French and English goods. The prohibition of tobacco exports, the ending of the French West Indian trade, and the temporary cowing of the English caused commerce to languish and destroyed any incentives among the planters to improve their agriculture. The fur trade at New Orleans was depressed because of the lack of trade goods and the ability of the British to intercept the furs at Manchac. Money was in desperately short supply and the depression was accompanied by a plummeting in the value of property. Disaffection appeared general among the colonists and François Marie Reggio reported the number of emigrants to be considerable. It was truly a time for despair for workers and merchants in New Orleans, planters and farmers in the country, for rich and poor alike. Difficult times were ahead should the new governor, Luis de Unzaga y Amezaga, prove to be as stern and unrelenting in his conformity to the letter of Spanish law as his predecessor.

Historians agree in describing Unzaga as a mild, even-tempered man of good judgment and his administration as a happy period for the colony. To juxtapose this assessment with the realities of Louisiana leads to the conclusion that happiness was achieved only at the expense of Spanish law; and, further, that happiness was a commodity of British manufacture and export. In fact, the English regained their ascendancy in the economy of New Orleans and the colony during Unzaga's governorship. This was not a development satisfactory to Unzaga or his superiors, but the choice for Unzaga was either to apply the law rigidly and bring further ruin to the colony or officially to ignore the clandestine trade with the English, allowing the colonists to derive from it whatever benefits they might. What Unzaga might have done had other options been available is not known. His successsor, however, availed himself of the opportunity presented by the American Revolution to chase the English away.

In May 1774, seventy vessels were counted between New Orleans and Manchac, while another observer stated that the English always had a dozen vessels in the river while no more than six or seven came from Spain annually. Unzaga, of course, felt constrained to keep up appearances, as in March, 1774, when a merchant at Natchez, Richard Carpenter, wrote his correspondent at Newport, Rhode Island, that five or six English vessels had been seized by the governor. Carpenter learned that only one seizure had in fact occurred, but he stated that Spanish vigilance made it difficult to do business in New Orleans. The seizure was exceptional and symbolic. Carpenter, selling goods on consignment from John Collins of Rhode Island, had accounts with English merchants who resided in New Orleans. English merchants in Manchac, such as Fitzpatrick, and in the city, such as the firm Pollock, Waught, and Company, were really the only outlets the planters had for their produce and provided the only source of credit, goods, and Negroes. Pollock's firm purchased indigo from Bobé Descloseaux in 1773 for the account and risk of Mathew Mather and John Stuart of London and furnished fourteen Negroes in return.

There was a certain tentativeness or insecurity in this system, as for example in the collection of debts or the adjudication of commercial disputes, but Unzaga seems to have acted fairly toward both creditors and debtors. It is likely that even greater insecurity hounded officials in New Orleans, dependent as they were upon the illicit trade for victualing the town. In March, 1775, a flour shortage, aggravated by the failure of the previous fall's corn and rice crops, caused bread prices to soar. The Cabildo appointed commissioners to approach the several English vessels in the river to purchase flour which was then to be distributed equally among the city's bakers. In the following November, fearing another food shortage, the Cabildo convinced Governor Unzaga to prohibit the export of food until the public was provided for. Recurrent pressure on the city's food supply may have dissuaded the governor from acting more forcefully against the British.

The role of the English in the economy of the colony developed as a result of the territorial changes agreed upon in the Treaty of Paris and the confusion incident to the delay in the occupation of the colony by Spain. Temporarily dispossessed by O'Reilly, the English solidified their position during the administration of Unzaga. The far-reaching reforms of Charles III indeed revived the trade between Spain and her major possessions and contributed to the economic development of the colonies—with one exception. Louisiana did not benefit from the first reforms but instead suffered. Unprecedented though they were by Spanish standards, the concessions granted to Louisiana in 1768 and 1772 had little relevance to the colony's requirements. Louisiana, consigned by Spain to the role of buffer between the English and New Spain, found in the British the only available buffer between modest prosperity and poverty. In a sense, their presence guaranteed the fulfillment by Louisiana of her assigned role. This became evident in 1779–81 when Governor Gálvez found Louisiana sufficiently strong to support his highly successful military campaigns against West and East Florida.

The American Revolution ended the direct menace of Great Britain to Louisiana and Spain's other North American colonies. It did not end the influence of English and Scotch merchants and mercantile houses in Louisiana. Spain acted to weaken the economic position of the British prior to the former's entry into the war against Great Britain. In 1776 a decree opened up the trade between New Orleans, France, and the French West Indies. Further concessions were granted in 1778 and 1782. In 1777 Gálvez applied great pressure against the English, confiscating a number of vessels and ordering their departure from Louisiana. This effort to divert the trade of New Orleans from the English to the French was crowned with success by the conquests of Gálvez.

The French, however, did not enjoy their period of economic superiority without challenge. Great Britain was certainly less of a factor but many Anglo-Saxons remained in Louisiana as Spanish subjects, retaining their traditional connections with England and Scotland. Moreover, a new element—or perhaps an old element in new guise—in the form of an independent and commercially oriented United States of America entered into competition with the French and replaced Great Britain as a threat to the mainland colonies of Spain. American pressure against the borders of Spanish Louisiana coupled with the crises associated with the wars of the French Revolution compelled Spain to make concession after concession regarding the economic system of Louisiana and ultimately forced her to withdraw from the colony. All of this served the interests of New Orleans, especially after 1783, when she found herself in possession of a vast hinterland that held not only commercial potential but increasing numbers of people.

10

New Orleans and Its Traditional Hinterlands, 1763–1783

IN 1765 New Orleans and its three thousand residents seemed condemned to a destiny of insignificance unless the hinterlands experienced a higher rate of growth than they had in the previous half century. For the most part, growth depended upon an increase in population but it also implied the existence of some outlet for the industry of a rising population either within or without the Spanish empire. Stable in extent and productive capacity during the last three decades of French rule, the frontier areas experienced neither an energizing influx of population nor any change in the system of Indian alliances originally formulated by Bienville. Decades of marked growth in the area, population, and productivity of the hinterlands followed the first Treaty of Paris. During those years, large portions of the older areas were steadily transformed into an agricultural heartland. New settlements were also appearing in areas hitherto beyond the range of New Orleans' influence. Although for a time these newer natural hinterlands would remain remote from and of little value to the capital, they were soon brought within the purview of New Orleans by increased population, political events, and the southerly course of the Ohio and Mississippi rivers.

The rejuvenation of old and the birth of new hinterlands susceptible of a close economic relationship with New Orleans may be separated into two periods, divided by the American Revolutionary War. After the Louisiana Purchase, the process continued, of course, at an even quicker pace, but substantially along those paths charted between 1783 and 1803. The interval between 1765 and 1775 is distinct not because of a rapid expansion in the area served by New

Orleans or because of any dramatic rise in population, but rather for the introduction of a new factor—the British—into two areas of Louisiana. In the north, they possessed everything south of the Great Lakes, east of the Mississippi River, and north of the Ohio River—the old French Illinois. In the south, Englishmen came to Natchez, Baton Rouge, and scattered along the perimeter of the three lakes into the Pearl River country and on to Mobile and Pensacola.

In the north—in Illinois—the English did not come in force. Permanent settlement beyond the Appalachians was prohibited by the Proclamation of 1763 but the influence of British fur interests expanded to the Mississippi, encompassing the permanent but struggling French settlements at Vincennes, Cahokia, and Kaskaskia. The British valued the Illinois because of the fur trade both within the area and to the west, in Spanish Louisiana. English or colonial merchants moving into the area were confronted by stiff competition in this field by the former French masters whose primary commercial connections were with New Orleans. Hoping to divert the trade to the east, the English found the pull of New Orleans virtually impossible to overcome. In adapting the trade to the southerly flow of the great rivers, the English in Illinois contributed to the revival of commerce at New Orleans. Also, those traders at Illinois and others elsewhere in the Ohio River Valley struck up a traffic with the towns and posts of Spanish Louisiana.

Britain's impact in the South was more immediate and more intense, and it was frequently the difference between scarcity and sufficiency in the provisioning of New Orleans. Economic services provided by Spain's new neighbors were a major inducement to the advancement of commercial agriculture before O'Reilly's coming and virtually the only stimulus during the years following the implementation of the commercial arrangements of 1768. British shipping, credit, and merchants monopolized the economic life of New Orleans and serviced the planters, whether operating out of New Orleans, or Manchac, or merely from the river. English or American colonists moving into the planting areas along the Mississippi and south of Natchez added lasting strength to the hinterland of New Orleans, for many English planters remained to take the oath of allegiance to Spain after 1779. Although the planting country dependent upon New Orleans displayed little physical change, its population was considerably more heterogeneous after 1763.

Plantations below and in the immediate vicinity of New Orleans were firmly established during the French era, changing little in extent or agricultural pursuits until the 1790s, when sugar replaced indigo as the money crop. Until within some dozen leagues of the city, marsh, overflowed lands, and thick woods provided the scenery for travellers approaching New Orleans from the sea in 1763 as well as 1803. Then, they encountered a succession of plantations, extending along both sides of the river to the town and for twenty leagues beyond. Ownership of many of the plantations had changed since the French period. The Flamand family purchased Governor Kerlérec's plantation in the early 1760s. Jean Étienne de Boré developed a beautiful plantation below New Orleans, as did François Livaudais and Francis Duplessis. New names and new generations took their places in the colony. The daughter of the wealthy Pointe Coupée planter Benjamin Farar inherited her father's estate and married Richard Butler, owner of Ormonde Plantation on the German Coast; Oliver Pollock operated an indigo plantation in the late 1780s; and Gilbert Maxent, father-in-law of Governor Gálvez, employed 167 slaves on three plantations. The elite of the colony, as in the past, were found on the plantations at Gentilly, Cannes Brûlée, Chapitoulas, and other places around New Orleans and upriver as well.

The plantation establishment around New Orleans grew rapidly after the American Revolution. It was then that Maxent spent money lavishly on his estates and that Patrick Macnamara and the seven Saucier brothers invested large sums in their farms. It was also then that Pierre Philippe de Marigny received a large concession of land across Lake Pontchartrain, bought up plantations above the city along the river, purchased land on Bayou St. John, and became the largest landowner in the colony. There were changes upriver as well, perhaps on a less sumptuous scale, but no less significant for New Orleans.

Along both sides of the river, the land was rapidly claimed during the Spanish period and especially during the tobacco boom of the

1780s. Nearly four thousand people farmed the lands between New Orleans and Pointe Coupée in 1769, with the number perhaps doubling by 1800. In this region, including the German and Acadian coasts, Baton Rouge, and Pointe Coupée, the French residents—largely on the west bank—were engaged in general farming and lumbering. Plantations were intermixed with smaller farms, the latter producing poultry, vegetables, tobacco, some cotton, and corn, and the former, like the Julian Poydras plantation at Baton Rouge and the Farar place at Pointe Coupée, emphasizing indigo until the late 1790s. Suffering from a serious shortage of labor in the 1760s, this region obtained large numbers of slaves from the English during subsequent decades.

Above Pointe Coupée, only scattered habitations appeared along the river until the bluffs at Natchez. More or less abandoned by the French after the Natchez revolt, this area was judged by the Spanish to be of little value because of its distance from New Orleans. Some English, however, settled around the fort which the British military attempted to establish in the late 1760s. Prior to the American Revolution, Richard Carpenter, William Dunbar, and James Brown all owned plantations in the Natchez area of British West Florida. Dunbar was heavily engaged in stave making and other lumbering, readying 100,000 staves for delivery in 1771. Carpenter planted and also served as the mercantile agent of John Collins of Rhode Island. Sustained growth at Natchez commenced after 1783, at which time some two thousand people, including slaves, engaged in planting, producing crops of tobacco, cotton, vegetables, and lumber worth 150,000 to 200,000 piastres. Most of the residents were Americans and their numbers shot upward after Pinckney's treaty of 1795 established the sovereignty of the United States over the region and guaranteed access to oceangoing vessels at New Orleans. By 1803 Natchez contained a couple of hundred houses, and the district almost eight thousand people. Even more rapid growth occurred between 1800 and 1810.

West of the Mississippi and south of the Red River, the settlements at Rapides, Natchitoches, Opelousas, and Atakapas contained, according to census figures, between thirteen hundred and fifteen hundred inhabitants in 1770, about half at Natchitoches. This may be too low for Opelousas and Atakapas, as both received a large number of the Acadian refugees who arrived in the colony between 1765 and 1770. Population in the entire region probably quadrupled by 1800. Natchitoches passed 1,000 in 1776 and was said to have some 1,300 inhabitants by 1800, while a census in Atakapas in 1803 listed a population of 3,746. The region was one of general as well as livestock farming, the latter industry demonstrating notable development between 1776 and 1803. Large herds of horses, mules, cattle, and hogs raised on the grasslands of Atakapas and Opelousas supplied New Orleans with much of its meat supply. Cotton, indigo, and tobacco served as cash crops, with cotton predominating after 1790 and sugar advancing into the region early in the nineteenth century. Several combination cotton mills and tanneries were flourishing in Opelousas in 1803, vending cheap cloth in New Orleans for the outfitting of slaves.

Around Natchitoches, farmers produced relatively large quantities of tobacco even during the French period, supplemented this activity with livestock, especially horses and mules, traded with the Spanish *presidios* in Texas at Los Adaes and San Agustin del Orcoquisas, and carried on an illicit commerce with the Indians in Texas. The closing of the two *presidios* in 1772–73 caused some decline in the prosperity of Natchitoches which had been supplying them with goods from New Orleans and Manchac and also selling small quantities of wheat there. Natchitoches was the most suitable place in old French Louisiana for raising wheat but yields were generally small and cotton crowded out other cash crops after 1800. For a few years after O'Reilly prohibited the export of Louisiana tobacco, the Indian trade was almost the sole economic activity pursued in the region, with the bulk of the trade goods obtained from English merchants at Manchac.

Most of the country west of the river received groups of additional colonists at various times as did some of the more heavily settled areas along the river. Spanish authorities were alive to the need to strengthen the colony through immigration. Ulloa corresponded with Roman Catholics in Maryland in 1767 about the possibility of moving to Louisiana and in 1774 a group arrived and were settled below Manchac. More than a thousand Acadians reached

New Orleans in 1765 and 1766, settling both sides of the Mississippi as high as Pointe Coupée. Other groups of Acadians arrived thereafter and were located in the Opelousas and Atakapas regions. They were joined in 1788 by an immigrant group of fifteen hundred Canary Islanders, transported to Louisiana at the king's expense and located at Terre aux Boeufs, on the east bank of the river, twelve miles below New Orleans; at Bayou Lafourche; above New Orleans at a town called Valenzuela, at the mouth of the Amite River; and at a settlement—New Iberia—on Bayou Teche. Probably more than three thousand immigrants were placed on lands between 1765 and 1780. Another fifteen hundred Acadians reached Louisiana directly from France in 1786, half settling at Bayou Lafourche.

Land laws formulated by the Spanish between 1770 and 1799 were generous in their provisions for granting lands to incoming settlers. Even squatters were recognized as possessing certain rights to crown lands and if they had been on the land for ten or more years they were not dispossessed. The regulations were intended to get the land into use and to prevent the engrossment of large tracts by speculators. Incoming settlers also received very essential material support from the Spanish. The fifteen hundred Canary Islanders were transported to their lands and furnished supplies. Those who settled at New Iberia under the direction of Nicholas Forstall received a total of 73,936 reales in supplies and food. Each family received two mares, ten cows, two hogs, a shovel, a cart, and one hoe per man, in addition to lesser tools. Similar treatment was experienced by the Acadians. The crown bore this expense in the sure knowledge that lack of support would imperil efforts to populate the colony.

By 1781 five new settlements were established: Galveztown, on the south side of the junction of the Amite and Iberville rivers, which housed a number of refugees from the American Revolution; Valenzuela, on the left bank of Bayou Lafourche; Barataria; Concepcion or Terre aux Boeufs; and New Iberia. None were flourishing but neither were the settlers in desperate straits. The towns were less important than the farms springing up around them which not only contributed to the provisioning of New Orleans but developed into rich staple plantations, with sugar coming to dominate in the south and cotton vying with sugar as the Red River was approached.

Immigrants like the Canary Islanders or the Acadians presented few problems for the authorities in the sense of threatening the political power of the colony. They were nonpolitical and content to live out their lives on the land. While the Acadians retained a sense of community and cultural homogeneity, they were not disruptive to the primarily French culture and Spanish political structure. The same cannot be said of the English and Americans who migrated to Louisiana during the Spanish regime. They were potentially disruptive and although valued by the Spanish authorities for their talents as pioneer farmers, they were distrusted and feared as the vanguard of a people determined to sweep the Spanish from North America. Politically unsettling, the Anglo-Saxons nonetheless established plantations and farms which, in conjunction with the Creole plantations, formed New Orleans' principal domestic market and provided the town with the staples that sustained the overseas trade.

Indigo was the most valuable of the staple crops during the last years of the French period and most of the Spanish era. Even though the Louisiana product was considered by some inferior to that grown in the West Indies and by all inferior to the Guatemalan plant in the quality of the dye produced, a large market was assured in Germany, Russia, Sweden, and other European countries. While it was hoped in 1770 and 1771 that the Spanish would receive the Louisiana products, these hopes were disappointed because the Spanish preferred the Guatemalan product. As during the French period, indigo plantations were located from below New Orleans to Baton Rouge on both sides of the Mississippi. The methods of cultivation and production remained unchanged. High production costs prevented most settlers from undertaking the culture. It was confined to the largest and wealthiest planters such as Maxent, Mccarty, Maurice Conway, and Bobé Descloseaux who owned large slave gangs. An increasing availability of slaves made large-scale production practical, but even though the labor situation was not as critical as in the earlier periods, planters still cried for more hands.

Prices and production remained high through the 1780s. A normal crop ran between 400,000 and 600,000 pounds and prices varied from five to seven livres per pound. But in the 1790s the crop suffered a series of setbacks from which the industry did not recover. Crop failures caused by adverse weather occurred from 1791 to 1793. Lack of rain one season and flooding the next thinned out the fields and frost finished the job. Dampness seems to have been the most serious problem because indigo requires a fairly dry climate. With the dampness came a worm which ferociously attacked the fields in 1793 and 1794, destroying the roots and leaving only naked stems standing. Most planters, discouraged by successive crop failures, declined to make a new start and switched instead to sugarcane or cotton, or utilized their labor force in lumbering while deciding what steps to take. Although a few planters continued to raise the crop, its significance to Louisiana was at an end. The crop of 1801 was only about 80,000 pounds.

If indigo was the most valuable staple per pound, tobacco was the most widely grown and could be cultivated with less dependence on the supply of slave labor. Thus, it served as a cash crop for both large and small planters, and because of its general culture throughout the colony, the demand for it in Europe was a matter of great concern for all Louisianans. Under the French, the relationship between the national government and the tax farms determined that the tobacco trade be highly regulated as to prices and quality. The connection between the state's revenue and the tobacco trade and the tax farm's preference for the British colonial leaf, along with a shortage of slaves and shipping problems, retarded the progress of tobacco cultivation in Louisiana.

Spain, no less than France and Great Britain, recognized the tobacco trade as an important source of revenue for the state. After 1614 the crown controlled the trade either through a royal monopoly, through contracts with individuals enjoying the exclusive right to exploit the traffic, or through the Havana Company, founded in 1740. The company monopolized the trade between 1740 and 1760 when the monopoly was returned to the crown. From the mid-eighteenth century to 1790, tobacco was the most important Cuban export, shipments reaching a peak of five million pounds in 1789. Spain sought to protect this trade between Cuba, the mother country, and Europe and simultaneously supply the tobacco requirements of its other possessions. Because the crown monopolized the manufacture and sale of tobacco products throughout the empire, this was a significant source of revenue. This fact held out both dangers and opportunities for Louisiana when it came under the Spanish flag.

Until O'Reilly assumed control of Louisiana, the Spanish could do nothing to control the tobacco trade at New Orleans. Some leaf found its way to Cuba in 1763 and apparently the practice continued after England returned Havana to Spain. It is unlikely that Louisiana tobacco was manufactured as such but Cuban merchants probably mixed it in with their own leaf before selling to the royal factories. In any event there was a problem because, as we have seen, in prohibiting the export of Louisiana tobacco in 1770, O'Reilly sought especially to prevent its entry into Cuba. At the same time, the prohibition of trade between New Orleans and France and the French West Indies coupled with O'Reilly's serious effort to dry up the trade with the English, virtually destroyed the value of tobacco as a cash crop. The post commander at Natchitoches wrote that the new regulations greatly discouraged the planters. Unzaga assured his disconsolate subordinate that God would provide them the means for selling their tobacco. God moved slowly and planters at Natchitoches and Pointe Coupée cut back production sharply.

The direction from which relief would come was presaged in 1771 in a small order from Vera Cruz for twelve hundred pounds of Louisiana tobacco. But five years elapsed and tobacco production languished before the impact of this initial shipment provided any benefit for Louisiana. Then, in 1776 arrangements were worked out whereby Louisiana became the sole supplier of tobacco manufactured for consumption in Mexico. Royal factories in Mexico agreed to purchase 800,000 piastres worth of tobacco annually at a price decided upon through negotiations between Governor Gálvez and a group of planters. Regulations were published in June, 1777, to control quality and packaging. This good news was received in Louisiana shortly after the trade between New Orleans and French ports was reopened. Tobacco production immediately rose and 29,448 rolls of tobacco were exported to Mexico in 1778, although this was not as large an export as anticipated. War intervened to prevent further growth in the trade, postponing the tobacco boom until the 1780s, when its impact extended north beyond Natchez to the American settlements in the Kentucky and Tennessee regions.

Tobacco crops in Louisiana during the 1780s were the largest produced in the colony to that time. With the exception of the small crop in 1782–83, production seems to have exceeded 2 million pounds annually through 1789. One estimate puts exports at 3 million pounds for the account of the crown, in addition to a contraband trade with the French West Indies. In 1786 and 1787 Martin Navarro, Intendant of Louisiana, placed exports in both years at about 1.5 million pounds. This was the equivalent of 5,000 tercios of 300 pounds each, or some 1,800 hogsheads of 800 pounds each.

Natchitoches and the district of Natchez, the latter under Spanish dominion but claimed by the United States, produced the bulk of the crop. Estimates for Natchitoches place exports at 2 million pounds annually during the middle 1780s and the crop at Natchez in 1789 was reported to surpass a million pounds. If the production of Atakapas and Opelousas is included in the figure representing production at Natchitoches, the estimate is believable. For Natchez, available figures include the number of tobacco planters and the size of each crop. A million-pound crop is a minimal figure. There were 263 tobacco planters in the Natchez district, an overwhelming majority Anglo-Saxon with a few French sprinkled in. One hundred and sixty-four, or 62 percent of the planters, produced crops of less than 5,000 pounds, or about 22 percent of the total crop. Eighty-five planters, or 32 percent, produced 54 percent of the total crop. Sixteen planters reported crops in excess of 15,000 pounds, with two reporting yields of 45,000 to 50,000 pounds. These sixteen planters contributed 24 percent of the crop.

A vague idea of the acreage and labor force involved in producing the Natchez tobacco crop is projected in Table IV, based upon estimates of yields of tobacco per acre and per hand developed for the Cheseapeake Bay area and North Carolina. The size of each family unit is impossible to determine, as is the extent to which each planter committed acreage and labor to purposes other than tobacco. If the figures are taken at face value and if it is assumed that the full labor force was devoted to tobacco, it seems likely that 62 percent of the planters owned no slaves and that only about 5 percent can be con-

TABLE IV

Tobacco Planters at Natchez and Estimates of Crop per Planter,
Acreage, and Labor Force Required per Planter, 1789*

Number of Planters	Crop per Planter (pounds)	Tobacco Acreage per Planter	Hands Required per Planter
26..............	500	.8	1
91..............	2,000	3.2	1–2
47..............	4,000	6.1	3
38..............	6,500	10.0	5
18.............	9,000	14.0	7
29.............	12,500	17.7	8+
9.............	17,500	27.0	13+
3.............	30,000	46.0	23
2.............	47,500	73.0	36+

* Sources: Carlos de Grand-Pre to Miro, March 2, 1790, in Lawrence Kinnaird
(ed.), *Spain in the Mississippi Valley, 1765–1794,* Vols. II and III of the *Annual
Report of the American Historical Association* (4 vols.; Washington, 1945–49),
part 2, 306–11; Lewis Cecil Gray, *History of Agriculture in the Southern United
States to 1860* (2 vols.; Washington [reprinted 1958]), I, 530–33; Joseph Clarke
Robert, *The Tobacco Kingdom: Plantation, Market, and Factory in Virginia and
North Carolina, 1800–1860* (Durham, 1938, Appendix D, 249–50. Robert estimates
that an acre produced between 650 and 750 pounds and that one hand could culti-
vate two acres. The lower yield was used in this table.

sidered plantation owners. This breakdown is compatible with most
analyses of the distribution of slave ownership during the antebellum period in the tobacco producing regions. Landholdings would
increase in size as cotton replaced tobacco in the early nineteenth
century.

The boom reached its climax in the late 1780s when the crown
agreed to purchase the entire tobacco production of Louisiana. Tobacco planters responded by expanding the acreage under cultivation and purchasing additional slaves. But in 1790–91, the crown,
advised by Mexican officials that the market was seriously oversup-
plied, cut back its purchases to 40,000 pounds and terminated the
trade completely in 1792. Planters were caught with large quantities
of unmarketable leaf, seriously in debt for land and slaves, and ignorant of remedial steps. A limited market was available in France

and the French West Indies but the outbreak of the first war against republican France in 1793 ruled out this alternative. At the same time, increasing quantities of American tobacco reached New Orleans and won the preference of merchants and manufacturers. Tobacco production declined in Louisiana, especially in the area between New Orleans and Natchez, until it lost its position as a major crop by the turn of the century. The tobacco trade retained its importance at New Orleans but it was based upon the production of the Upper Mississippi Valley. Southern planters turned then to cotton.

Observers of the economic life of Louisiana concurred in their assessment of the importance of the lumber industry to the colony. Travelers on the river who were fortunate enough to find a publisher for their observations normally devoted some space to a description of this industry. It had changed little since the French period. Masts, casks, staves, construction lumber, sheeting and shingles, pitch, tar, and turpentine were among the many commodities extracted from the forests. Travelers also noted the location of sawmills, the seasonal nature of the industry (resulting from both the depth of the rivers and staple crop seasons), and the markets available to lumber producers. Pitch, tar, and turpentine were still concentrated across Lake Pontchartrain although there was some manufacturing of them above New Orleans.

The West Indies remained the best market but the prohibition of trade with the French islands damaged the commerce between 1768 and 1776. Trading privileges with Havana were meager compensation. Between 1783 and 1793 the value of the trade rose from about 800,000 livres annually to one million. As many as 100,000 sugar casks, costing 3 livres each to produce, were shipped to the Antilles for sale at 6 livres, while cypress planks 10′ x 1′ x 1″, costing 1 livre, sold for 5 livres in Martinique and St. Domingo. By the 1790s Cuban demand was quite extensive also. Valued at 1.4 million livres in 1803, the traffic remained an important source of income for planters well into the American period, and supported thirty sawmills in the neighborhood of New Orleans. Americans provided most of the shipping between 1793 and 1801 and Britain drove France from the seas and turned on Spain after the Treaty of Basel of 1795.

Commerce in furs and skins is the last of the traditional staple trades of Louisiana that requires treatment. This involves events and developments along a broad front beginning at Natchitoches— along the Louisiana-Texas frontier; passing through Arkansas; including both the Spanish and English Illinois, or the Missouri, Upper Mississippi, and Ohio River valleys; and sweeping south into the old warring grounds in Creek, Choctaw, and Chickasaw country. It involves competition between Frenchmen, Spaniards, and Anglo-Saxons, scattered from Texas and Louisiana to the Spanish and English Illinois (later American) and it involves Indian tribes— from the Lupan Apache to the Osage and from the Sioux and Shawnee to the Creek nation. Forts and trading posts were established which developed into towns and, eventually, cities. Indian wars were fought, treaties negotiated and broken, settlers murdered, and Indians betrayed as nations with imperial and commercial ambitions sought to consolidate their hegemony over huge portions of the interior of North America. To do all of this justice, even in the form of a bare outline, would involve an expenditure of space and time disproportionate to the value of the trade to New Orleans. So an injustice will be committed in the matter of this particular topic. Emphasis will be placed on the Illinois country because information is more readily available and because most furs that arrived at New Orleans originated in the Upper Mississippi Valley.

During the period 1763–1803 the Illinois country was divided between Spain, Great Britain, and then, after 1783, the United States. English influence was dominant, however, until the negotiation of Jay's treaty, and although many furs passed through St. Louis and New Orleans before export to Europe, English traders and merchants supplied the French trappers while British and American shipping carried a large part of the product to market.[1] The French establishment in Illinois as of 1763 centered east of the Mississippi in Kaskaskia and Cahokia, both defended by Fort Chartres. A small settlement existed at Vincennes. West of the river, Ste. Genevieve, opposite the mouth of the Kaskaskia River, was the only

---

[1] In the following discussion reference will be made primarily to the French and English who operated out of both English and Spanish Illinois. There were few Spaniards involved.

organized community in the Missouri country until 1763, when Maxent, Laclède, and Company established the St. Louis post in an effort to control the fur trade of areas to the northwest. These western establishments passed to Spain in 1763, along with the post at the Arkansas. From the beginning of British and Spanish occupation both parties feared the incursions of the other into their domain, and in both cases the intruders were, at least in the beginning, primarily Frenchmen who felt no loyalty to either government and traded wherever they liked.

Both governments placed great weight on the potential value of the fur trade, and estimates of its actual value in the 1760s go as high as £100,000 sterling. However magnified this figure may be, and it is probably three times the actual value, it was the estimate that moved the English in Illinois to search for the means to divert the trade from New Orleans. General Sir Thomas Gage asserted in 1767 to Sir William Johnson, the crown's Commissioner of Indian Affairs, that very little benefit would accrue to Great Britain from the fur trade of the Illinois "so long as the Skins and Furrs have a high price at New Orleans." They will, he said, "never be brought to a British market . . . [but] . . . always go with the Stream." [2] Efforts to bypass New Orleans, as we have seen, failed at the Iberville River and traders in English Illinois complained bitterly that the market was preempted by French traders stocking goods from New Orleans. George Morgan, of the Philadelphia firm Baynton, Wharton, and Morgan, wrote that the French engrossed the trade on both sides of the river because of their long-standing influence with the Indians and preferred to ship their skins through New Orleans where credit and trade goods were available.

Just as the English in the South failed to isolate New Orleans, the English in the Illinois were unsuccessful in their bid to take over the fur trade and ship directly east to Philadelphia and New York. However, English merchants in the Lower Valley shared the trade with French merchants. By 1768 Morgan was sending furs to and receiving trade goods from New Orleans, which route, in spite of

---

[2] Gage to Johnson, January 25, 1767, in Clarence W. Alvord and Clarence E. Carter (eds.), *The New Regime, 1765–1767, Collections of the Illinois State Historical Library*, XI [British Series, II] (Springfield, 1916), 499.

high freight rates on the journey upstream, was both quicker and cheaper than the overland trip from Philadelphia to Fort Pitt and then to Fort Chartres via water. Oliver Pollock, John Fitzpatrick, and others outfitted as many as five hundred traders, who ascended the river in batteaux carrying eighteen to twenty men and forty tons of goods. In May and June, 1769, Fitzpatrick received furs from Maxent, Laclède, and Company and Jacob Monsanto while Morgan utilized Pollock as his New Orleans correspondent. This overt relationship between British and Spanish subjects was, as we know, temporarily interrupted by O'Reilly. English merchants were back in business by late 1771, taking off most of the pelts coming to New Orleans.

British officials in the colonies and at home, disgruntled at their inability to effect a total monopoly of the fur trade of Illinois prior to 1776, tended to undervalue if not ignore the dominant position English merchants had attained in New Orleans. The view that the country above New Orleans would never be of value unless Britain occupied the city was not wholly accurate. Although French traders dealt directly with the Indians, to the detriment of English traders, the judgment overlooked the fact that the furs of Maxent, Laclède, and Company were obtained with English goods and that a good share of the pelts passed into the hands of English merchants. Such a view, as applied to Illinois, reflected the assumption that whoever handed the goods to the Indians thereby won their allegiance. Englishmen were convinced that French traders conspired to turn the Indians against them. Such apprehension is understandable in the light of Pontiac's destruction of seven British posts in May and June, 1761. Nonetheless it does appear that the British retained, until the mid-1790s, the largest share of the fur trade in the Upper Mississippi Valley even after they relinquished sovereignty to the United States.

Spanish efforts to counter the British in the Southeast ran into the same difficulties confronted in the competition for trade in the Illinois; namely, the inability of Spain to provide the trade goods, lack of sufficient capital at New Orleans to extend credits, and the closing of the French West Indian trade between 1768 and 1776. This left only the British as a source of supply for trade goods before the

American Revolution. Thus, even though various individuals, including Maxent, Laclède, and Company, and Louis Rançon, received exclusive trading privileges, recourse to the English was necessary and reluctantly allowed even by Governor Gálvez. Conditions in East and West Florida were similar to those in the Illinois in another regard. The British occupied the region and wished to deny the fur or skin trade to French trappers in an effort to channel the trade through Mobile. This was not accomplished because the French roamed at will through their old trading grounds, penetrating Chickasaw, Choctaw, and Creek country with goods and carrying skins to New Orleans. As in the Illinois, most of the goods were of British manufacture and many of the skins were handled by English merchants.

The American Revolutionary War undid the territorial settlement of the Seven Years' War. Spain regained both Floridas while the United States seized English Illinois and both powers laid claim to Transappalachia between Florida and the Ohio River. The precipitation of America as a sovereign and expansive power onto the scene presented Spain with grave problems since the Americans wished not only to possess but occupy these lands. Spain experimented with several tactics to defend Louisiana against American encroachment. One traditional method was to consolidate Spanish control over the Indians, separating the two contestants by monopolizing the Indian trade and thereby, theoretically, securing the allegiance of the tribes and gaining the use of their military power. In order to achieve this goal, the Spanish granted monopolistic privileges to several individuals, operating out of New Orleans, to supply Indian trade goods.

Governor Gálvez initiated the policy by first appointing Gilbert Maxent, his father-in-law, as Commissioner of Indian Affairs and Lieutenant Governor of West Florida in 1780. This appointment was connected with Maxent's proposal to guarantee an adequate supply of Indian trade goods for the Choctaw and for the Missouri nations. Maxent, in association with the New Orleans merchant Michel Fortier negotiated a contract with the crown in March, 1782, whereby the associates agreed to ship 380,000 pesos worth of French and Spanish goods to New Orleans at a cost 10 percent less than that charged by the major previous supplier. Maxent agreed to furnish a security of 200,000 pesos when the war ended to guarantee compliance and to maintain at all times a stock of at least 80,000 pesos worth of merchandise. Other merchants, believing that Maxent controlled the entire trade, began to withdraw from it. Governor Miro sought to assure them that Maxent's privileges were confined to supply, but this had little effect as Maxent obtained goods from his store at cost while selling to other merchants at wholesale.

In addition, Maxent, Laclède, and Company retained their control at St. Louis. The Indian trade of the Upper Valley became more exclusive during the last fifteen years of Spanish control. When Maxent and Laclède passed from the scene, Auguste Choteau, son of Pierre Laclède, succeeded them as the dominant trader in Missouri. In 1793 the Spanish gave the monopoly of the Missouri trade to a group of twenty-eight merchants, twenty-five from St. Louis, alloting the entire trade among this group. The bypassed merchants complained that the monopoly caused a drop in the value of goods imported at St. Louis from New Orleans from 150,000 to 180,000 piastres annually to 40,000 piastres. Lieutenant Governor Zenon Trudeau of Spanish Illinois (Missouri) confirmed a yearly decrease in the value of trade, putting it in 1798 at 80,000 piastres. Trudeau had substantial evidence behind him when he charged that the monopolists dealt extensively with the English operating from the American Northwest Territory. General Georges Henri Victor Collot, travelling through the Upper Valley, buttressed Trudeau's assessment with the observation that many furs from Spanish Louisiana passed into American territory and thence by way of the Great Lakes to Canada. He added that "the profits of the merchants under the Spanish Government settled at St. Louis, and who deal in furs, are nothing in comparison with those of the English merchants . . . ." [3]

Similar exclusive privileges were resorted to by the Spanish to obstruct American influence in the Southeast. In this area the Spanish were less concerned with deriving profit from the trade than in keeping the Indian nations dependent upon the Spanish for the satisfaction of their wants, thus forestalling American efforts to win

[3] Georges Henri Victor Collot, *A Journey in North America* . . . (2 vols.; Paris, 1826), II, 183.

their allegiance and dependence, preliminary to negotiating the Indians out of their tribal domain. Recognizing her inability to furnish the necessary goods and the Indian's preference for English goods, Spain turned to English merchants in New Orleans and Florida to accomplish their purpose.

Spanish officials in Louisiana such as Martin Navarro, Intendant, and Governors Gálvez and Miro counseled the use of English goods to retain Indian loyalties. A Florida official also emphasized the importance of the English, in recommending that an English firm, Panton Leslie and Company of West Florida, be employed by Spain to extend Spanish influence among the Indians. It would be dangerous, he warned, to expel the firm because of its connections with Alexander McGillivray, half-breed leader of the Creek nation until his death in 1793. McGillivray was an advocate of a confederation of southern tribes and the implacable foe of Georgia's efforts to relieve the Creeks of their domain. Acting on such advice, the Spanish negotiated an agreement with James Mather, an Englishman settled in Feliciana, and Arthur Strother to bring two boatloads of Indian goods from London to Mobile and Pensacola.[4] Mather and Strother agreed to conduct the trade under the Spanish flag and to take colonial produce rather than silver in exchange for their goods.

Although patently illegal according to the regulations issued in 1782, the contract was justified by Miro on several counts. The urgency of the situation in Creek country demanded that goods be obtained with speed. Mather's friendship with McGillivray and his superior credit standing in London made him an obvious choice. While trade was permissible with France according to the recent *cédula*, low prices and quality goods were better obtained in England where manufacturers specialized in producing the proper goods. Of the most vital importance, argued Miro, was preventing the Americans from entering the Indian trade. As a further measure to prevent this, Miro appointed McGillivray commissioner of the Creek nation, a salaried position, under the authority of the governor of Florida. Under the contract, Mather and Strother, in association

---

[4] Mather was a partner of George Morgan between 1776 and 1783, a director of the Orleans Navigation Company from 1808 to 1810, and Mayor of New Orleans from 1807 to 1811.

with Panton, Leslie and Company, were involved to the sum of 500,000 piastres; and Strother negotiated a contract allowing him to bring a cargo of Indian goods for the Mississippi trade, in addition to the two annual vessels for Pensacola and Mobile. Creek raids against settlements in Georgia, not altogether desired by the Spanish, attested to the success of the Spanish program.

The policy of controlling the southern tribes through the Indian trade was weakened in 1787 by an edict stipulating that Indian goods be ordered in Spain rather than London. This threw the trade into confusion and, while Miro did his best to salvage the time-proven policy, McGillivray moved toward a reconciliation with the United States in the Treaty of New York, 1790. McGillivray, suspicious of the ability or willingness of the Spanish to protect the Creeks, apparently sought to use the United States as a counterforce against the aggression of Georgia.

The Creeks, after McGillivray's death in 1793, and the Spanish alike were to lose out in this contest. The commercial policy lapsed into disuse, replaced by the efforts of Governor Francisco Louis Hector, Baron de Carondelet, appointed governor and intendant of Louisiana in 1791, to resurrect McGillivray's earlier dream of a confederation between the Cherokee, Chickasaw, Choctaw, and Creek nations.[5]

An organized Indian trade under Spanish auspices collapsed in the Southeast during the 1790s. It fell victim to the above-mentioned decision of 1787, the more militant policies of Carondelet, the repercussions of the French Revolutionary wars in North America, the push of American frontiersmen-land speculators, and the success of American diplomacy. A trade continued but it was no longer a major instrument in Spanish policy because most of the tribes came within the American sphere of influence as a result of Pinckney's treaty. Moreover, the days of the trapper in the Southeast were numbered as the cotton planter pushed steadily westward from the

[5] Carondelet succeeded, on paper, in creating a confederation of the four tribes, protected by Spain, in the Treaty of Nogales, October, 1793. Pinckney's Treaty of 1795 destroyed this agreement. For the panicky response of Carondelet to the wildest of rumors portending the imminent invasion of Louisiana by thousands of western Americans, see Abraham P. Nasatir, *Spanish War Vessels on the Mississippi, 1792–1796* (New Haven, 1968).

leading edge of the southern Appalachians and as cotton and slaves moved eastward from bases on the Mississippi River. It was of little economic moment that this trade should come to an end, although implicit in its demise are the recorded and unrecorded tragedies experienced by American Indians and Negroes. As De Villars, French Commissioner of Trade at New Orleans, reflected in 1778, European brandy, wine, smallpox, intertribal wars and wars caused by the European had so decimated and enfeebled the tribes that the once powerful Choctaw could field no more than two hundred warriors. Only the statistic is arguable.

One last Indian fur frontier requires brief notice not because of its intrinsic economic value, which was minimal, but because it illustrates the wide-ranging nature of the fur trade, involves tensions between the Spanish establishments in Louisiana and Texas, and demonstrates the pervasive influence of the British. One of O'Reilly's projects was the prevention of a trade with Mexico through Natchitoches and Opelousas, pursued on a small but regular basis during the French period and invigorated by the availability of English goods after 1763. The drying up of this trade was also a purpose of Governors Unzaga, Gálvez, Miro, and Carondelet which, in each individual case, is testimony to the success of the previous governor. English or American goods were central to the trade during the entire period and obtainable at both ends of the Mississippi River. In 1774 De Mézières informed Unzaga that English merchants resided in Opelousas and operated along the Gulf Coast with trade goods purchased at Manchac and New Orleans. That same year, Jacob Monsanto was seized at Natchitoches with contraband bought at Manchac. In 1792 Governor Carondelet received word from Natchitoches that Osage war parties, armed and supplied with American goods purchased at St. Louis, terrorized the district and also traded with neighboring Indians, a complaint voiced in 1770 as well, but about English weapons and goods.

Officials in Texas complained of the intrusion of Louisiana traders into their colony. Texas blamed traders at Natchitoches for encumbering the Texan tribes with large debts, causing them to commit robberies to gain the means to make payment and obtain other goods. Arms obtained in Louisiana, it was further charged, filtered into the hands of the Apaches and were used against Mexican out-posts. At the same time, traders from the Arkansas caused con-sternation at Natchitoches by selling arms to the Osage and even penetrating to the Red River Valley in search of horses, mules, and skins. Traders from St. Louis and the Arkansas received pelts while Spaniards to the south suffered harassment from Indians supplied in the North. The Osage appeared especially adroit in robbing Pedro to pay Paul. In 1791 Natchitoches reported a desperate shortage of tongues, skins, bear's oil, salted buffalo meat, and tallow as a result of Osage raids on Indians that normally supplied those goods.

Exports from New Orleans in the major staples of the late eight-eenth century probably approached 6.5 million livres, or in the other currencies 330,000 pounds sterling, 1,485,000 piastres, or $1,485,000. Such a figure, applicable to the period between 1783 and 1793, that is, during the tobacco boom and prior to the disasters suffered in indigo culture, included 3 million livres in indigo, 1.4 million livres in lumber, one million livres in tobacco, 600,000 livres in furs, and 500,000 livres in cotton, waxberry, rice, tallow, and other goods. This represents an increase of 300 percent over the highest exports during the French period while the population probably doubled.

The 1790s were years of remarkable economic change in Louisi-ana, partially reflected in the declining importance of the traditional staples indigo and tobacco and their replacement by cotton and sugar. Further modification of the old trade network came with the decreasing importance of furs as an export staple from New Or-leans. Finally, and most significantly, upriver developments trig-gered by the American Revolution and the pressures on Spain generated by the wars of the French Revolution accelerated the evolution of new commercial patterns in New Orleans and elicited fresh economic responses from the merchants who flocked to the city.

New Orleans was losing one hinterland, the fur and Indian fron-tier, and gaining another, the farming frontier of the Upper Valley, which was of infinitely more value than the other. The fruits of this development poured into the port of New Orleans in unprece-dented volume during the last decade of the eighteenth century.

11

The Hinterlands' Changing Nature 1783–1803

N the two decades following Spain's declaration of war against Great Britain on May 18, 1779, New Orleans assumed roles and developed relationships with its hinterlands which were to characterize the port for the subsequent half century. The economic regime of these areas changed radically during this period as immigrants from the newly formed United States of America swarmed into both the Upper and Lower Mississippi valleys. In the Upper Valley, farming encroached steadily upon the fur industry, dominant since the coming of the Europeans, ultimately transforming the area into one of small grain and livestock farms dependent upon the waterways for access to a market and the sea at New Orleans. In the Lower Valley, an influx of farmers and planters pressed against the Mississippi from Natchez to the south. Englishmen from the Atlantic colonies settled in West Florida, mixing with the prior French residents, becoming subjects of the king of Spain in 1779, and, if above the 31st parallel, United States citizens as a consequence of Pinckney's treaty of 1795. At about the same time, cotton replaced tobacco as the major staple north of Baton Rouge while sugarcane replaced indigo from Baton Rouge to the south.

These developments occurred within the context of a world turned upside down politically by revolutions and wars and economically by unprecedented advances in industrial technology. The American Revolution gave birth to a power which claimed dominion over half a continent in 1783 and exercised sovereignty beyond the Mississippi River by 1803. The conflict also presented Spain with the greatly relished opportunity of dispossessing Britain of her Florida lands, thereby setting up a territorial confrontation between republican America and monarchical Spain. The French Revolution plunged Europe into a series of wars which sapped the strength of Spain in Europe and weakened her powers of resistance to American penetration in Louisiana. New Orleans was forced into the American sphere of economic influence, thus greatly extending the field in which the United States could operate effectively in diplomacy and commerce.

There was a concomitant revolution on a different level. It began in 1705 with Newcomen's steam engine, progressed through the inventions of John Kay, James Hargreaves, and Samuel Crompton to the power loom of Edmund Cartwright in 1787 and the harnessing of James Watt's steam engines to the looms in the 1790s. These achievements so reduced the costs of cotton clothing and so greatly increased the demand for cotton that the invention of an efficient cotton gin was almost inevitable. Dozens of men, including Du Breuil, had worked on the problem before Eli Whitney was successful in 1793. By the turn of the century, cotton was the dominant cash crop in both the recently created Mississippi Territory and in large areas of Spanish Louisiana. Even though Louisiana's commitment to sugar was not the product of the Industrial Revolution nor, properly speaking, of the stresses and strains of wars, the damage suffered by West Indian sugar cultivation during the long period of international chaos eased somewhat the competitive situation for Louisiana sugar in world markets.

The role played in the American Revolution by the Spanish in Louisiana was basically a dual one: providing financial and material assistance to American agents stationed at New Orleans for the support of American military operations in the Upper Mississippi Valley between 1776 and 1781; and the initiation by Governor Gálvez of military campaigns against the British in West and East Florida from 1779 to 1781. Spanish assistance began with Governor Unzaga's sale of gunpowder in August, 1776, to an agent from the revolutionary government of Pennsylvania who journeyed to New Orleans and there obtained the aid of Oliver Pollock. Throughout the entire war, Pollock assumed critical responsibilities among the Spanish for the revolutionary government of the United States and the state of Virginia. Pollock gathered supplies for George Rogers

Clark's conquest of Illinois, purchased with money loaned to the Americans by Governor Gálvez, and for which sums Pollock assumed personal responsibility. Pollock served as the commercial agent of the new government, assuming consular duties in interceding with the Spanish authorities on behalf of increasing numbers of Americans who found their way to New Orleans.

This last development was one of the most important results of the war for the economic future of New Orleans. American merchants from eastern seaboard cities received their first comprehensive introduction to the trade possibilities of the river port. Some, like Reed and Forde, merchants of Philadelphia, attempted to establish a trade with New Orleans from a base at Pittsburgh, but this route was less satisfactory than the direct coastal route and was used only because of the presence of British war vessels along the Atlantic coast. Merchants such as James Mather, associated with Benjamin Morgan, and Daniel Clark, Jr., nephew of the Baton Rouge planter Daniel Clarke, cooperated with Pollock in handling shipments on account of the Continental Congress while trading, when conditions permitted, with contacts in Philadelphia and New York.[1] These preliminary contacts of the colonial and revolutionary periods burst into full flood following the war when dozens of American merchants and men-on-the-make sought to establish themselves in New Orleans. With Americans located in New Orleans and in the upcountry, it would be difficult for the Spanish to isolate the capital from the economic influence of the United States. This was impossible, as it turned out, but the Spanish made a good try.

The appointment of Bernardo de Gálvez as Governor of Louisiana eased the task of Americans in New Orleans. Gálvez, more aggressive than Unzaga, was sympathetic to the American cause and hostile to the British position on the Mississippi. He protected American vessels from seizure by the British who cruised the lakes, the Gulf, and the river; harbored American privateers and allowed them to sell their prizes in New Orleans; advanced tens of thousands

[1] The planter Daniel Clarke turned over his personal fortune of $40,000 to Pollock to meet expenses, allowing Pollock to exchange specie for the continental currency circulating in New Orleans and giving the latter value for a time. Later, Daniel Clark, Jr., presented Pollock's claims before the Congress of the United States.

of dollars to Pollock for supplies needed in the Illinois; authorized American convoys on the Mississippi to utilize Spain's river facilities; and succored James Willing's expedition down the Mississippi which temporarily captured Natchez, pillaged and burned Loyalist plantations, and auctioned off the loot in New Orleans. The aid received from Gálvez and his seizures of English vessels in 1777 and 1778 isolated West Florida and thwarted English plans for a great Indian offensive against American settlements in western Virginia and Kentucky. Gálvez anticipated a Spanish declaration of war against Great Britain, and when official word reached New Orleans of Spain's entry, the governor was prepared to strike immediately.

He acted none too quickly, for the British military in Florida received orders in June, 1779, to attack New Orleans. But Gálvez, recognizing the indefensibility of New Orleans, took the offensive before the British could gather their forces at Pensacola. Between August, 1779, and May, 1781, Gálvez attacked and captured Manchac, Baton Rouge and Natchez, Mobile and Pensacola, while Spanish forces in the Upper Valley scored other successes.

William Dunbar, who journeyed to New Orleans in August, 1779, with a load of staves, was arrested and detained until the capitulation of Baton Rouge, returned to his home to find it plundered by the Indians. He reported that tranquility was restored by January, 1780, and decided to put a new field into tobacco. John Fitzpatrick, captured at Manchac, enrolled in the Spanish militia for the march to Baton Rouge. By September, 1780, apparently mustered out of service, he was busily engaged in enlisting the aid of Morgan and Mather to collect debts from an American firm, Williams and Foley, recently launched in New Orleans. Loyalties appeared fluid as most Englishmen resident in West Florida remained on their lands, the subjects of His Most Catholic Majesty, Charles III of Spain, while other American colonists, to whom recent events were distasteful, joined them on the Mississippi.

Spain, successful in war, was soon confronted with the peacetime problem of foreign infiltration of her conquests and possessions. As John Hancock, Governor of Massachusetts, informed Gálvez in a letter introducing one Edward Church, merchant of Boston, the latter "goes to New Orleans to inform himself whether a Commercial Intercourse may not be Establish'd between the Two Countries to reciprocal Advantage." [2] The dilemma facing the Spanish and the needs of western Americans were nicely explained in a letter from Governor Thomas Jefferson to Gálvez:

> Our vicinity to the State over which you immediately preside, the direct channel of commerce by the river Mississippi, the nature of those commodities with which we can reciprocally furnish each other, point out the advantages which may result from a close connection . . . . Our people . . . are lately beginning to extend their Settlements rapidly on the waters of the Mississippi and . . . there will in the course of another year be such a number of Settlers as to render their Commerce an object worth your notice . . . .[3]

Spain did indeed notice the activity of Americans in the Upper Valley, but instead of responding to the opportunities cited by Jefferson, closed the Mississippi in 1784 to all but her own vessels. Spain's intention was to deny the Americans any share in the economic benefits of her military victories. This policy did not succeed, meeting as it did persistent opposition from the United States and being repeatedly subject to qualifications forced upon the Spanish by the commercial needs of Louisiana. The expulsion of the British from the Floridas, for instance, made it necessary in 1782 that the Spanish formalize and extend the commercial privileges granted to France in 1776.[4] No less immediate were the fears engendered in the minds of Spanish officials in Louisiana by the movement of Americans toward the Mississippi. Spanish policy toward this threat was twofold: on the one hand, Spain tried to mobilize Indian opposition to American expansion; on the other hand, Spain saw in a populous colony the best defense against American encroachment. This involved, eventually, a contradiction in means and ends. In 1780 Intendant Navarro anticipated harmful consequences from American proximity unless Louisiana was sheltered behind a nu-

---

[2] John Hancock to Gálvez, August 15, 1781, in Kinnaird (ed.), *Spain in the Mississippi Valley, 1765–1794*, part 1, p. 434. Gálvez had received similar letters from Patrick Henry, *ibid.*, 272.

[3] Jefferson to Gálvez, November 8, 1779, *ibid.*, 362.

[4] These concessions, other commercial regulations relevant to Louisiana and the overseas trade in general will be treated in Chapter XII.

merous population capable of restraining the Americans. But where was this multitude of loyal Spanish subjects to come from? Navarro suggested, as did Governor Gálvez, that Spain employ countercolonization to check the Americans and that she draw American settlers into Louisiana through liberal immigration and land grant policies. As part of this plan, Spanish officials in Louisiana were instructed to work to separate dissident Americans from their new political affiliations by using the right to navigate the Mississippi as a lever to pry them away.[5]

The Spanish attempted to implement these policies at various times and, insofar as they succeeded, doomed to failure their larger plan to erect a strong buffer against the United States. Liberal immigration requirements attracted large numbers of Americans into both upper and lower Louisiana. Lands were granted free in proportion to the number of hands available to farm the tracts. Religious freedom at the private level and permission to trade at New Orleans and other posts under the same terms as prior residents were guaranteed. This generous program proved extremely inviting to many Americans. These would-be settlers, for some time, had been resentful of the relatively high price of public lands (raised from $1 to $2 an acre by the 1796 Land Act). They were equally disturbed by the inability of the United States to guarantee security in the Ohio River Valley or to gain the right to navigate the Mississippi. A prime motivating force in the search for new agricultural land was the tobacco boom in the 1780s. Arthur St. Clair, President of Congress, was informed in 1787 that Americans were moving into Spanish Illinois and the Lower Valley, where land was free and their tobacco marketable in New Orleans at from $7 to $10 a hundredweight.

Some Spanish officials opposed as suicidal the policy of multiplying the enemies of Spain within its own borders. It was in the not-so-long run. Wherever Americans appeared, they also took over. Zenon Trudeau, Commander of Spanish Illinois, testified to their industry, maintaining that the Americans were far more industrious and productive than the original French inhabitants and tended to

[5] Nasatir, *Spanish War Vessels on the Mississippi*, 13-15, uses the term "counter colonization."

dominate the local economy. This was the case throughout the length and breadth of Louisiana, including New Orleans. The danger was compounded for Spain because behind these immigrant Americans, nominally subjects of Spain, were 150,000 other western Americans in 1790 and 400,000 in 1800, all clamoring for and dependent upon the use of the Mississippi to get their goods to market. As one visitor to the Transappalachian country in 1795–96 correctly observed: "I had scarcely crossed the Alleghanies, before I heard the borderers of the great Kanhaway and the Ohio give in their turn the name of Back Country to the Atlantic Coast; which shows, that their geographical situation has given their views and interests a new direction, conformable to that of the waters, which afford them means of conveyance toward the Gulf of Mexico, the chief focus of the speculative ambition of all the Americans." [6]

The sheer number of these borderers induced fear and trepidation in the hearts of Louisiana's rulers. Spanish spies roamed through the American settlements, especially south of the Ohio River, sending alarming reports to New Orleans of projected barbarian incursions—American frontiersmen readied a force of two thousand or ten thousand to march on St. Louis, to occupy Chickasaw Bluffs, to seize Natchez! The Spanish would be swept out of New Orleans! The Americans planned to invade Mexico and conquer the world! The appearance of one flatboat at Natchez in 1785 owned by Richard Breachen of Kentucky loaded with fifty-four barrels of flour was given as much attention as the approach of an armada. At the same time, unprincipled men like General James Wilkinson played on Spanish fears of invasion while advocating that Spain exploit western dissatisfaction by fomenting and supporting financially the separatist schemes of the plotters.

The Spanish were catholic in their acceptance of and experimentation with proposed solutions. As noted in the previous chapter, the Indians were vigorously courted and almost won over by Governor Carondelet until Pinckney's treaty undid his work. A settlement— New Madrid—was initiated on the west bank of the Mississippi, ten

---

[6] C. F. Volney, *View of the Climate and Soil of the United States of America: to Which are Annexed Some Accounts of Florida, the French Colony on the Scioto, Certain Canadian Colonies, and the Savages or Natives* (London, 1804), 21.

miles below the mouth of the Ohio, to obstruct the invasion route of the Americans. But it was the creation of an American, George Morgan, and peopled, at first, with Americans. Fort Nogales was constructed in 1790 to keep Americans away from the mouth of the Yazoo River while Fort San Fernando, built in 1795 at the Memphis Bluffs, was a counter to the erection by the Americans of Fort Massac at the mouth of the Ohio River. The years 1793 to 1795 were filled with activity in New Orleans and throughout the colony as the Spanish reacted to the Genêt conspiracy and the expected invasion of George Rogers Clark and his mercenaries. In 1793 Carondelet prepared colonial defenses against an anticipated two-pronged attack by the French fleet from the sea and Clark from the north. Carondelet established a fresh-water navy which scurried up and down the river to meet and vanquish a dozen rumors of impending invasion. His navy met and communicated with dozens, hundreds, of ungainly and peaceful flatboats carrying flour, meat, millstones, butter, tobacco, tallow, candles, and saddles without recognizing them as the true enemy to Spanish hegemony in Louisiana.

By 1795 it was too late for Spain to take effective steps against the Americans. Perhaps it had been too late since the combination of the American Revolution and Spanish foreign policy led to the opening of New Orleans to both French and American commerce. Once the Americans developed the habit of trading with New Orleans both by river and sea approaches, it was difficult to deny them after the war. Beginning in 1784 the river was closed to American shipping, but for only three years and this stoppage did not totally eliminate either river or ocean commerce with the United States. Opening the river to Americans in 1787 upon the payment of duties for cargoes unloaded at New Orleans neither stilled American demands for free access to the sea nor furthered the separatist cause— if such really existed—in the western territories. It did, however, attract more Americans to New Orleans, thus augmenting their already sizeable economic influence in Louisiana.

The French Revolution and the wars of the First Coalition against France propelled Spain into a desperate situation. Seeking peace with France, Spain sought to guard against the retaliation of her former ally Great Britain by placating the United States, thus pre-cluding an Anglo-American descent upon Louisiana. In Pinckney's treaty or the Treaty of San Lorenzo of 1795, Spain recognized the 31st parallel as the southern boundary of the United States and allowed Americans the free navigation of the Mississippi and the privilege to deposit their goods and reexport them, duty free, in the vicinity of New Orleans. A great influx of Americans followed in 1796 and 1797. Only in 1798 and thereafter did Spain finally act to restrict American penetration by prohibiting the granting of land to Americans. By then it was too late.

New Orleans would have experienced great hardship if American trade had ended in 1784 for it was dependent upon continuous contact with the United States via sea or river as surely as the western Americans were captives of the river route to New Orleans. The Cabildo recognized this in 1787 when it protested against the seizure of American flour at a time when flour stocks were low. Admitting the illegality of the trade, the Cabildo nonetheless informed the governor that without American flour absolute want would prevail. Governor Miro was not ignorant of this fact, having explained to José de Gálvez that American flats were permitted to bring flour because of the difficulty and expense of obtaining it through legal channels. Although it was still hoped that Spanish Louisiana could supply the necessary foodstuffs for the Lower Valley, the Missouri district was an uncertain source of supply in spite of its growth between 1775 and 1803.

By 1798 the settlements in Spanish Illinois included St. Louis; its outlying Missouri River communities St. Charles, Florissant, and Carondelet, some seven miles below St. Louis; San Fernando, fifteen miles west of the latter hamlet; Ste. Genevieve, fifty miles below St. Louis; and scattered settlements along the Mississippi River beween Ste. Genevieve and Cape Girardeau, fifty miles farther to the south. New Madrid was forty-five miles directly south of Cape Girardeau. From there to Natchez, the Spanish occupied only the Arkansas post during their entire tenure in Louisiana. Most of the Missouri towns had some Americans and none could be described as flourishing, with the possible exception of St. Louis. In 1795, General Collot considered commerce almost extinct in upper Louisiana while Trudeau believed it commensurate with the population.

Population in Spanish Illinois increased slowly, at less than 2.5 percent annually, between 1765 and 1800, reaching some 7,000 by the beginning of the new century. Most of the growth occurred between 1794 and 1800 when the population rose from 2,665 to around 7,000. In 1800 St. Louis had some 1,200 people, Cape Girardeau and Ste. Genevieve were each approaching 1,000, and New Madrid about 600. An effort was made in the 1790s to attract the French settlers in the Northwest Territory to New Madrid and other Spanish communities. Carondelet hoped that French farmers brought in from the Scioto River settlement of Gallipolis and from Vincennes would turn to the production of foodstuffs for the Lower Valley. To further this, Carondelet advanced funds for the construction of flour mills. Augmented production did occur in Spanish Illinois but it was not sufficient to feed both upper and lower Louisiana.

From 1765 to 1775 annual exports from the Spanish Illinois to New Orleans included between 1,200 and 2,500 barrels of flour, a diminishing quantity of lead that did not exceed 60 tons in any given year, between 1,000 and 3,000 packs of furs, and some tobacco and salt. From 1771 to 1775 the settlers exported as flour approximately 30 percent of the wheat harvested, with enough consistency to indicate that the remainder was retained for consumption since there were no other markets. The local market included not only the producers but soldiers and itinerants such as traders and trappers who outfitted in these communities for ventures further west. In the Lower Valley, there were at least ten thousand inhabitants in 1771, counting the English in West Florida, so that at a barrel of flour per person per year, flour imports from the Spanish Illinois left a considerable deficiency, filled largely by imports from the English cities along the Atlantic coast.

In the 1790s wheat production in the Missouri country was fairly stable at 38,000 to 45,000 bushels, except in 1799 when a harvest of 92,000 bushels was reported. Using the lower figures and translating them into flour at five bushels per barrel would result in a production of 7,600 to 9,000 barrels of flour, perhaps half of which reached New Orleans. By this time there were between thirty-five and forty thousand people in the Spanish possessions in the Lower Valley, including more than eight thousand in New Orleans, plus eight thousand Americans in the Mississippi Territory. The production of Spanish Illinois was inadequate to provision New Orleans, let alone all of Louisiana. Of the other commodities, lead exports increased to about 200 tons and salt to some 3,500 barrels in 1800, while no more than 50 hogsheads of Missouri tobacco were recorded as reaching New Orleans prior to 1800. The fur trade was valued at about $80,000.

The produce and provisions trade of New Orleans obviously derived from sources substantially more productive than the Spanish Illinois. These sources were largely the American settlements in the Kentucky country but, increasingly, the Northwest Territory as the eighteenth century came to a close. Kentuckians and Tennesseeans numbered 109,000 in 1790 and 326,000 a decade later while the population in western Virginia and the Northwest Territory reached 130,000 by 1800. It may be, as a recent study of the West suggests, that the need of an open river to New Orleans was "vastly exaggerated" in the West and that the "river was never actually closed ... to those who were actually in a position to utilize it." [7] Smuggling certainly existed and Spanish officials such as Governor Miro allowed Americans to bring down flour. But flats and cargoes also were confiscated and heavily taxed and crews were subjected to frequent harassment. What is allowed may be quickly disallowed and there was little security in a trade already too sensitive to the vagaries of weather and market conditions. Western Americans depended upon agriculture for their livelihood. The nature of their production and freight rates precluded the possibility of a large overland trade with the East Coast and there was no local market as most settlers produced the same commodities. Farmers east of Pittsburgh found it cheaper to ship their produce to market via New Orleans than to forward it to Philadelphia. It is not an exaggeration to state that without a market in New Orleans westerners would not have advanced much beyond subsistence agriculture.

It is impossible to determine the volume of the trade flowing from the Ohio Valley to New Orleans. It was much less in the years prior

[7] Francis S. Philbrick, *The Rise of the West, 1754–1830* (New York, 1966), 173–74.

to the establishment of the deposit in New Orleans in 1798 than in subsequent years. But the quantity was much more than Arthur Whitaker supposes when, in summarizing American arrivals at New Orleans as listed in the port records, he concludes that fifteen American flatboats arrived between 1782 and 1790 carrying tobacco and 2,640 barrels of flour.[8] Oliver Pollock received a greater quantity in the single year 1782 and again in 1783, and George Rogers Clark shipped 1,500 barrels of flour to New Orleans in 1786. James Wilkinson, who received permission in 1787 to ship a quantity of goods to New Orleans, sent at least twelve flats with more than 400,000 pounds of tobacco and contracted with a western miller to obtain flour for New Orleans. And to repeat, Governor Miro permitted flour-laden flatboats to sell their cargoes at New Orleans. Unfortunately, there is no way of quantifying these odd bits of information. Even if the consumption needs of the Lower Mississippi Valley were precisely known, along with receipts from Spanish Illinois, there would still be receipts via sea from Atlantic Coast ports and an unknown quantity brought in from French sources. Traffic was greater than Whitaker suggested but smaller than in ensuing years.

In 1788 the crown permitted all Americans to use the Mississippi as far south as New Orleans. Goods were assessed at 15 percent ad valorem when landed—reduced to 6 percent in 1793—and another 6 percent if reexported. The pace of the trade increased with this stimulus. According to Whitaker, only forty-six flatboats reached New Orleans from 1790 to 1794, carrying 319 barrels of flour in 1790, 786 in 1791, 846 in 1792, 3,200 in 1793, and 5,400 in 1794.[9] Again, the trade was significantly greater than these figures reflect. Carlos de Grand-Pré, commandant at Natchez, summarized the river traffic for Governor Miro. His reports indicate that between February and July, 1790, forty-one flatboats stopped at Natchez on route to New Orleans carrying 4,904 barrels of flour, 586 casks and 330 hogsheads of tobacco, 261 barrels and 34,000 pounds of meat, 47 barrels and 100 gallons of whiskey plus seven stills, 35 barrels and

[8] Arthur P. Whitaker, *The Spanish-American Frontier, 1783–1795: The Westward Movement and the Spanish Retreat in the Mississippi Valley* (Boston, 1927), 95.

[9] *Ibid.*; and Whitaker, *The Mississippi Question, 1795–1803: A Study in Trade, Politics, and Diplomacy* (New York, 1934), 83–84.

500 pounds of butter, 11 tons of iron, seven tons of hemp, 32 Negroes in one flat, and a host of other items. In later years at New Orleans 80 percent of the flour arrived between November and June. Grand-Pré's observations may have included some 75 percent of the receipts at New Orleans for the calendar year, or in terms of flour, a total of more than 6,000 barrels. Receipts rose steadily through 1797, precipitately after the establishment of the deposit in 1798 and the opening of New Orleans to neutral shipping in the same year.

Flour receipts at New Orleans exceeded 90,000 barrels in 1801 and reached 80,000 in both 1802 and 1803, and the total upriver trade was valued in excess of a million dollars in 1799 and at $2.6 million in 1802. These were the peak years in the flour trade of New Orleans until after the War of 1812. Most of the flour and other produce originated in the settlements along the Monongahela River in western Virginia and western Pennsylvania, Kentucky, and Tennessee, with the volume from Ohio increasing during the 1800s. Grand-Pré identified twenty flats as Pennsylvanian and twenty-one as Kentuckian. Many observers noted the vast increase in the traffic from the western settlements. Governor W. C. C. Claiborne of Mississippi Territory and William E. Hulings, merchant of New Orleans and unrecognized vice-consul of the United States, counted hundreds of flatboats with flour, whiskey, and other articles headed for New Orleans and spoke of a large number of American vessels in port awaiting cargoes.

The market was buoyant in 1801, between the time of public confirmation of the retrocession of Louisiana to France in March, 1801, and the suspension of the American deposit in October, 1802. Peace between France and Great Britain had not yet affected the commerce of the United States. While Americans were restless over the thought that France would soon return to the Mississippi River, they came to New Orleans with and without cargoes in increasing numbers. William Johnson, with two boatloads of flour from Pittsburgh, arrived in New Orleans on April 15, 1801, sold his goods on the following day, and noted that many arrivals on April 21 drove down the price of that commodity. Others experienced greater difficulties, frequently at the hands of Spanish officials.

Evan Jones, acting Vice-Consul of the United States in 1801, charged Spanish customshouse authorities with willfully obstructing the trade with the American West. Duties were charged even though the goods were destined for the deposit. Flatboats were boarded and the cargoes and crews molested by Spanish guards, and all kinds of permissions, each involving a fee, were required. Another vice-consul, Daniel Clark, Jr., confirmed Jones's charges in detail and added others. The most harmful practice, according to Clark, was the requiring of a security on the importation of produce from the Upper Valley intended for the deposit. This security was given by two resident merchants of New Orleans, who were then answerable for the tariff if the goods were sold in New Orleans. Boatmen were compelled, said Clark, to consign their property to their bondsmen who then exacted a commission. The transaction involved fees to notaries and customshouse officials plus storage even though the goods were never meant for sale in the colony. Once the flour or other items touched Spanish soil, outside of the deposit, they were chargeable with import taxes, and if then loaded on an American vessel, taxed for export.

Spanish harassment of American trade climaxed on October 16, 1802, when Intendant Juan Ventura Morales closed the American deposit. The United States government believed France responsible and ordered James Monroe to France to negotiate for the sale of New Orleans. The French Prefect Laussat, in New Orleans to receive the colony from Spain and reestablish French rule, blamed Governor Juan Manuel de Salcedo. Suspension of the deposit caused grave but temporary inconvenience to the trade. For one thing, Morales, in January, 1803, allowed the importation of flour and provisions from the United States but on payment of a duty of 6 percent, as it had been prior to the establishment of the deposit, and exportable only on Spanish vessels. While the river remained open, foreign vessels were prohibited from trading with New Orleans—a standing order but now enforced—and Claiborne believed that few American vessels would enter the river because the possibility of advantageous exchange was checked by the closing of the deposit.

The uproar over the revocation of the deposit was quieted when Morales restored the treaty right on April 19, 1803, and the fear of future French control of the mouth of the Mississippi was dissipated by the purchase of Louisiana by the United States. France received control of the colony on November 30, 1803, and turned it over to the new sovereigns on December 20. Prefect Laussat made light of the alleged threat of militant American westerners during these tense months. That the West was upset, he acknowledged; that they were arming, he denied, saying that reports from boats descending from upriver indicated quiet: "Not a squad is being organized there; . . . they are much more concerned there with the bad harvests of the year and the best means of selling what they have." In New Orleans, Laussat went on, the suspension was supported by those merchants dealing mainly with France and Spain and opposed by those merchants, primarily American, dealing with the upriver traffic.[10] This division between merchants with divergent economic interests was intensified with the imposition of American political control in Louisiana. The competitive economic interests of the two groups were compounded by latent ethnic hostilities and created a charged atmosphere which led to several incidents, considerable dissension, and factional political strife in the years following the purchase. This last ingredient was to be a permanent legacy of the American occupation, reaching the zenith of absurdity in 1836 with the division of New Orleans into three largely autonomous municipalities.

By December, 1803, the flour, grain, and provisions trade between New Orleans and the Upper Valley was a primary component of the economic life of the city. It became one of the most important single sectors of the port's trade within the first American decade, retaining its ascendant position until the early 1840s, when the total value of the foodstuffs trade declined relative to the total value of the trade in southern staples—cotton, sugar, tobacco, and molasses. In 1803 Laussat witnessed the arrival from Pittsburgh of a schooner and frigate loaded with flour which was exchanged for sugar consigned to Philadelphia. Sugar and cotton were making great progress in the Lower Valley by the end of the eighteenth century and were already significant components of New Orleans receipts and exports.

10 Henri Delville de Sinclair (tr.), *Memoirs and Correspondence of Pierre Clement de Laussat* (n.p., 1940), 32–33, 36.

Both staples had been experimented with at various times during the French period but encountered difficulties which eluded solution. Cotton was easy enough to cultivate and some was grown from the 1730s on, but the great labor entailed in separating the fiber from the seed retarded the further development of the crop. In the 1770s the residents of the Acadian and German coasts grew cotton and manufactured some cloth for domestic sale, and the settlers around Natchez produced small quantities during the same decade, some of which was exported to Bordeaux. But it was only in the middle 1790s, with the spread of efficient ginning techniques, that large-scale commercial production became feasible. The cotton gin and large numbers of American planters and slaves reached the Mississippi River simultaneously.

In 1796 cotton production in the Natchez area was placed at 3,000 bales of 250 pounds each, all of which had no exit to market except New Orleans. Production increased and, according to Governor Claiborne, in 1801 the value of the crop was estimated at $700,000, the equivalent of some 10,000 bales of 300 pounds each, to which must be added an unknown quantity grown in Louisiana. In the following crop year, shipments from New Orleans totaled 18,000 bales of cotton between October 19, 1801, and May 23, 1802. If these figures are compared with estimates of total cotton production in the United States for 1796, 1800, and 1801, it appears that New Orleans' cotton receipts were the equivalent of 14 percent, 13 percent, and 19 percent of the total production in those three years. The value of the crop of 1801 at New Orleans prices probably surpassed $800,000.

Sugar was quickly accepted as a staple crop once the major difficulties that had earlier plagued Du Breuil were circumvented. Circumstances unrelated to the cultivation of sugarcane accelerated its development. Indigo, as noted earlier, suffered a succession of failures in the mid-1790s so severe that the crop was abandoned by most planters. At the same time, chaotic conditions caused by war and revolution disrupted sugar production in the West Indies and also induced a number of experienced sugar planters to emigrate to Louisiana. With the production of West Indian sugar temporarily diminished, times were propitious for Louisiana to enter into competition for overseas markets.[11]

After Du Breuil's and Father Beaubois' experiments, interest in sugar lagged in Louisiana. Some planters attempted to introduce the crop in the 1760s and erected mills to process the cane, but yields were low even when frost did not kill the cane in the ground. The cane was not sufficiently hardy and did not mature early enough to beat the frost. The effort was given up before the American Revolution and not revived until 1795. The first successful plantation was started in 1795 by Jean Étienne de Boré, who worked some thirty to forty Negroes on a plantation about twelve miles below New Orleans. Ignoring the skeptics and naysayers, de Boré plunged into the cultivation with cane brought in from Brazil and with the aid of an experienced sugarmaker imported from St. Domingue. His first crop, cut in nine months, was successful and reputedly netted him a profit of $12,000 which more than paid for the cost of constructing his sugar factory. Within the year, sugar replaced indigo as a great staple of the Lower Valley and Collot, journeying down the river in 1796, admired the extensive sugar plantations of the "great colonial capitalists." [12]

While it is unlikely that de Boré's profits from one crop were so large, his success was sufficient to stimulate that concentration on sugar that marked the agriculture of the lands between Baton Rouge and the English Turn.[13] De Boré and other planters continued to test new varieties of cane and methods of distillation. De Boré tried new varieties from the West Indies in 1801 or 1802 while his brother-in-law, Jean Noel Destrehan, "the most industrious and intelligent planter in the whole colony" according to Laussat, was

---

[11] Silvio Zavala, *The Colonial Period in the History of the New World*, abridgement in English by Max Savelle (Mexico, D.F., 1962), 124, discussing the interrelatedness of regions in America producing sugar, writes that "the vicissitudes which affected production in some of them were likely to affect the market of the others. There was competition in the world market between the sugar products of Brazil, the French . . . and the British West Indies."

[12] Collot, *A Journey in North America*, 93. De Boré was appointed Mayor of New Orleans by Laussat in 1803 and resigned in 1804. He left an estate of at least $300,000 when he died.

[13] De Boré's largest crop (1802) yielded 80,000 pounds. If his first crop was equal to this, which is unlikely, sugar prices would have been 15c per pound, which is 3c per pound higher than any prices I have uncovered for the Spanish period and was only surpassed once, in May, 1816, at 16c per pound, between 1812 and 1860.

the first to utilize bagasse for fuel in the distilling process and also as a cover for cane caught in the fields by frost after it was cut.[14] The cane sugar industry by 1800 provided an outstanding example of the rewards to be gained through the application of science and technology to agriculture.

By the time of the Louisiana Purchase, New Orleans was surrounded by a complex of sugar plantations, many in the process of constructing their own distilleries. From a point about fifteen miles above New Orleans to the English Turn, there were between sixty and seventy sugar plantations along the river on both banks. Estimates of the average production per plantation run from 65,000 to 75,000 pounds or a total production between 4.5 and 6.2 million pounds. Prices fluctuated between 9 and 10 cents per pound in 1802, which, at the higher figure, places the value of the crop between $650,000 and $750,000.

Using Sitterson's estimate that a good sugar plantation of 100 arpents (*ca.* 100 acres) of cane and 40 Negroes produced 120,000 pounds of sugar, it is possible to derive a statistical picture of the average sugar plantation. For this purpose, it is assumed that 65 plantations produced 5.3 million pounds of sugar. The yield per acre was 1,200 pounds and the yield per Negro 3,000 pounds, which means that the typical plantation employed 27 Negroes on 63 acres of sugar cane, or that the total crop utilized 4,500 acres and a labor force of 1,800 Negroes. De Boré's plantation and the neighboring estate of Livaudais both employed some 60 Negroes and both plantations produced around 80,000 pounds of sugar in 1802, a yield not wholly incompatible with these projections.[15]

The development during the 1790s of the upriver trade in flour, tobacco, provisions, and the two major staples, cotton and sugar, created the nucleus of an export trade for New Orleans almost four times greater than that existing between 1783 and 1793. During the earlier period the export potential of New Orleans was estimated at about $1.5 million. By 1803 the new trades and staples contributed

[14] J. Carlyle Sitterson, *Sugar Country: The Cane Sugar Industry in the South, 1753–1950* (Lexington, 1953), 9–10, note 10, describes bagasse as "the remainder of the cane stalk after it has been crushed in the rollers of the mill."

[15] *Ibid.*, 11. The estimates as to yield per Negro or hand do not vary much from those of a later period cited in Gray, *The History of Agriculture in the Southern United States to 1860*, II, 743.

an export potential of approximately $4.1 million to which must be added about $900,000 representing the value of the traditional trades in lumber, furs, rice, and other items, making a total of $5 million.[16]

This remarkable expansion in the export base of the city represents a real plunge into the future, or, to employ current jargon, which hardly does justice to what was happening, the initiation of a period of sustained growth. When de Boré ignored his critics and planted his cane, he performed an innovative—if not desperate—act in search of a substitute cash crop for indigo. Hardly less can be said of the dozens of planters who imitated him within a year or two. Less dramatic but still risky was the commitment to cotton, accelerated by the uncertainties of the tobacco market and made practical on a large scale by the spread of the cotton gin. Thousands of individuals poured into the Natchez district, cleared the land, and planted cotton. Other thousands far to the north ventured their goods and persons on the flimsiest of craft for a thousand-mile journey to the unpredictable market at New Orleans.

No less venturesome were the merchants at New Orleans who, if they did not barricade their persons behind salt pans and flour barrels for the trip downstream, still laid their capital on the line with each commercial exchange in which they engaged. Merchants were no more knowledgeable of what awaited them in Havana, Cap Français, New York, or Bordeaux than the flatboatmen were of the state of the market at New Orleans. The entire process from sowing to selling and shipping was a gigantic speculation, the more so in a period of extreme fluidity in international affairs. Revolutions and wars in Europe and elsewhere created opportunities for trade by opening new markets, restricted trade by closing off others, and, in general, added to the risks facing the ordinary merchant or shipowner seeking external markets. What was a legitimate trade one day became smuggling the next. It was only good sense for ships captains to carry as many sets of papers as they could obtain and to be prepared at all times to show a different set of colors.

---

16 Indigo was excluded in these calculations and tobacco is included in the new upriver trade. It is likely that the trade in lumber increased while receipts of furs decreased as did receipts of rice and waxberry, thus reducing the value of the miscellaneous category.

12

The Overseas Trade, 1783–1803

SPAIN failed to integrate the colony of Louisiana into the re-
formed and more viable colonial system which evolved in the
1760s. Louisiana's great staples—indigo and tobacco or cotton
and sugar—competitive with the products of other Spanish colonies,
were not marketable in Spain. Total integration was unlikely and,
from the viewpoint of Louisiana, undesirable. Spain had neither the
time nor the inclination to enforce an integration that must have
been ruinous to the colony. Yet New Orleans prospered and its importance as a seaport grew. This prosperity, measured in terms of
staple exports, was grounded in the capacity of the plantation and
farm hinterlands to produce valuable crops in quantities sufficient to
attract the commerce of the maritime powers.

The absence of opportunity was probably the critical factor in
limiting integration. External pressures not only obstructed assimilation but pried concessions from the sovereign, each of which made
assimilation more difficult. Spain reluctantly allowed Louisiana to
operate almost entirely outside of the system. This might reflect the
minor position which Louisiana held in the Spanish empire as well as
the disinclination to do the colony permanent damage. Louisiana
was a newcomer in a colonial structure more than 250 years old.
Few Spaniards developed an interest in the region sufficient to
prompt resistance to flexibility in dealing with its peculair problems.

Spain possessed Louisiana for forty years but was fully in control
for only thirty-five years, for effective occupation commenced in
1768. Of those thirty-five years, Spain and Louisiana enjoyed only
two somewhat lengthy periods of peace during which time Spain
was relatively free to work her will in the colony. Even during

peacetime, 1768 to 1775 and 1783 to 1793, it was only during the former period that Spain was genuinely free to attempt the integration of the colony into the reforming empire. This effort culminated in the regulations of 1768 and 1772 which opened up trade between an enlarged number of Spanish ports and New Orleans and allowed a direct trade between Havana and New Orleans. At the same time, General O'Reilly attempted to eliminate English trade and to substitute Spain for both France and Great Britain as the primary supplier and market for New Orleans. None of these policies brought permanent advantages to the colony, and fortunately, events prevented the infliction of any severe damage upon it.

Gálvez clearly discerned the ineffectiveness of the privileges and reported that there existed no natural basis for a commercial relationship between Spain and New Orleans. The only available remedy was the reopening of the trade between New Orleans and France and the French West Indies, which Gálvez believed would bring prosperity to Louisiana and provide Spanish shipowners with new opportunities. The colonists demanded English and French goods but could hardly afford to purchase them in Spain at a cost of 40 percent above the normal retail price of the merchandise. A report of 1779 cited the example of a Spanish firm's losing 15,000 pesos in shipping Spanish claret to New Orleans because the consumers preferred French claret. It pointed out, too, that the many natural advantages of Louisiana could not be exploited by a strict adherence to the regulations of 1768 and 1772 and that they were not susceptible of further development by insisting upon a direct Spanish-Louisiana connection.

The process of accommodation to the legitimate requirements of Louisiana began in 1776 with an agreement between France and Spain granting limited trading privileges to the French West Indies for commerce with specified ports in Spain's colonies, including New Orleans. French commissioners were appointed to reside in New Orleans to administer the trade, duties were lowered, and the importation of Negroes from the French islands was permitted as a means of paying for the products purchased by the French in Louisiana. Governor Gálvez interpreted these provisions with great liberality, even permitting direct imports from France. According to the French commissioners de Villars and Favre d'Aunoy, within forty-eight hours of publication of the regulations, property values, rents, and the prices of colonial produce rose so dramatically that the commissioners complained they were reduced to poverty because of their inadequate salaries.

The agreement of 1776 was further extended when Gálvez in April, 1778, directed, in accordance with instructions from Spain, that colonial produce might be exported to any port in France or Spain which enjoyed the privilege of trade with the Spanish colonies. In the same month, similar privileges permitted trade with all ports of the United States. Theoretically, the carrying trade was restricted to Spanish vessels but this requirement was overlooked by colonial officials because Spanish shipping was generally inadequate to meet demand, especially after Spain entered the war against England in 1779.

The War of the American Revolution was the catalyst for these modifications in the economic system of Louisiana. Although forced to accept the English presence by the failure of the regulations of 1768 and 1772 to stimulate economic growth in Louisiana, Spain had never accepted the commercial superiority of the English in the Lower Valley as a fixed and final condition. Spain was moving toward the reopening of trade between Louisiana and the French islands and the war hastened the implementation of this decision. French and then Spanish belligerency prompted the enactment of further reforms in the commercial system.

Between 1776 and 1778 the French gradually replaced the English as the dominant element in the economy of New Orleans. By 1778 English shipping no longer monopolized the carrying trade of the colony and after 1779 it disappeared entirely from the Mississippi River. Although the French were restricted according to the regulations of 1776, to the sending of vessels in ballast or with Negroes to New Orleans, French merchants sent goods to New Orleans. Both La Fitte and Pedesclaux of Bordeaux managed to introduce goods into Louisiana by routing their vessels via St. Domingue and carrying papers attesting to Spanish ownership of the vessels. Generally, a correspondent in New Orleans acted as the alleged resident owner of the ship engaged in the trade or the French consigned their cargoes to correspondents in Havana, who then reexported the goods to Louisiana. Vessels arriving at New Orleans carried off tobacco, indigo, and furs, frequently paying for these goods with Negroes. The system worked well enough until France entered the war against Great Britain and suffered the inevitable losses at sea from British cruisers and privateers stationed in the Caribbean and Gulf of Mexico. It was at that point that American vessels were allowed to navigate the Mississippi to New Orleans.

The apparent success of the reforms convinced Spain of the necessity of continuing the French connection after the war was over. If Spain could derive no direct commercial benefits from Louisiana, at least the colony could be strengthened in its role as a buffer by diverting its commerce to the ally of Spain. If France did not get the trade, it was certain that either Great Britain or the United States would step into the vacuum and this was unacceptable to the Spanish. The Spanish government accepted these facts. It admitted the failure of O'Reilly's efforts to stimulate a trade between Cuba and New Orleans that would replace the traditional traffic between the latter and the French islands and published in 1782 a further extension of trade privileges for Louisiana that was operative until the outbreak of the War of the First Coalition against France in 1793.

A royal *cédula* of 1782 legalized for a period of ten years a trade in Spanish vessels between New Orleans and any French port where a Spanish consul resided. This covered all goods of French or colonial production. The exportation of specie was prohibited (except when remitted for the purchase of Negroes and then the specie paid a tax of 6 percent). Under certain conditions, to be determined by the governor of Louisiana, trade was permitted between New Orleans and the French West Indies. Possibilities for trade with other Spanish colonies were widened by the permission to reexport Spanish goods, received duty free, from New Orleans to any Spanish colonial port, paying only the normal export duty exacted in Spain. Other duties were also lightened or voided, of most importance on the importation of slaves from friendly powers. All exports from New Orleans were subject to a tariff of 6 percent. The same privileges were extended by this *cédula* to Pensacola. News of the *cédula* reached New Orleans in April, 1782, and a jubilant Cabildo ordered a day of rejoicing on April 14, complete with parades, illuminations, and thunderous salutes from the decorated vessels in the harbor.

Adhering quite closely to the advice of Gálvez, the *cédula* was a logical formalization of the regulations of 1776 and 1778. It also allowed Gilberto Maxent to pursue his scheme for organizing the fur trade of the Missouri country. Maxent, supported by his son-in-law Gálvez, petitioned the Spanish government in 1781 to allow direct trade between New Orleans and France or St. Domingue in order to insure a market for his furs and a source of trade goods. He further suggested that merchants be allowed to reexport Spanish goods for which there was no sale in Louisiana to other Spanish ports and also that Negroes be admitted free of duty. Much of this was obtained in the *cédula* of 1782 which applied the privileges granted to Maxent in a private contract to the colony as a whole. This caused some muttering among less advantaged merchants in New Orleans who feared that Maxent and his associates would use the new privileges in conjunction with the contract to create a monopoly of Louisiana's trade. Governor Miro's assurances to the merchants that nothing devious was intended were borne out in his liberal administration of the new regulations.

The *cédula* went into effect with the signing of the Treaty of Paris and, coupled with the closing of the Mississippi River to vessels of foreign nations, appeared to place Louisiana within the French commercial orbit. New Orleans merchants could trade legally in Spanish vessels with France and Spain, the Spanish colonies, and in cases of emergency with the French West Indies. Slaves could be purchased in any friendly port. The Spanish government guaranteed the purchase of the Louisiana tobacco crop, most of which went to Vera Cruz or, if the price was advantageous, to St. Domingue or France. While the *cédula* did not operate entirely according to plan, it provided a stimulus to trade in New Orleans and strengthened the interest and influence of France in the economic life of the colony. It did not eliminate the Americans or the English from the commerce of New Orleans. The American presence was experienced physically, while English goods found their way into Louisiana and the Floridas during the entire time of the *cédula*'s operation.

The pattern of trade that evolved between 1783 and 1793 deviated markedly in several particulars from the requirements of the *cédula*. Although the decree was not designed to advance the direct commerce between Spain and Louisiana (not surprisingly, this trade did not develop), it was intended to secure the carrying trade for the Spanish merchant marine which increased from below 500 vessels in 1778 to more than 900 by 1801, the latter figure being probably considerably lower than the number engaged in trade prior to the French Revolutionary wars. At the same time, Spain's share in the trade with her colonies rose sharply. At the end of the seventeenth century, about 12 percent of the goods shipped from Spain to America was of Spanish origin, whereas by 1788 the Spanish share amounted to more than 50 percent. In the decade 1778–88, the Spanish colonial trade rose by 700 percent, much of which was directly profitable to Spanish merchants. In 1788 Spain exported 300 million reales to the Indies and imported 804 million reales worth of colonial products. Louisiana contributed virtually nothing to this growth. The commerce of Louisiana grew but the share of Spain was negligible, both in the value of the goods moved and in the number of vessels engaged. Frenchmen were the earliest beneficiaries but were replaced by Americans in the period after 1793.

France assigned a high value to the concessions granted by the *cédula* of 1782, even though the French commissioner De Villars criticized the law for permitting only an occasional trade with the French West Indies. Still, the French realized that Spain might have opened up the trade to other European ports instead of confining it to France. They hoped that the decree would promote a large beaver trade, make available large amounts of tobacco, and give France the opportunity to engage in the valuable contraband trade with Mexico. For these reasons, France agreed to treat Spanish vessels going to and coming from Louisiana as French vessels when in French ports and to admit Louisiana goods into France on the same basis as goods from the French colonies. As the trade developed, however, it assumed a different form than that anticipated either in the *cédula* or by the French.

During the later French period, it will be recalled, direct trade between Louisiana and France declined in favor of an indirect commerce via the French islands which performed a middleman's role in the exchange. This trade, while not as advantageous to New Orleans as direct exchange, assumed considerable importance, providing as it did a market for the lumber products of Louisiana. Spain interdicted this traffic in 1768 but was compelled to permit it in 1776, after which time it resumed its traditional function as a major trade of New Orleans. The *cédula* of 1782 was intended to weaken this commerce in favor of the direct New Orleans-France connection. It did not succeed for the island trade was too firmly entrenched. French merchants preferred to avoid direct passage of their goods to New Orleans; and, as a new factor, much trade between the United States and New Orleans was conducted through St. Domingue while both Americans and Spanish subjects were permitted to trade in the French islands.

In 1783 De Villars reported that in the previous year, of 37 French vessels entering the port at New Orleans, 36 were of French West Indian registry and one was from Marseilles. At the time the report was written, De Villars counted 15 French vessels at anchor, 11 from the islands and four from France. In 1786, as Table V below indicates, of the 72 French vessels entering the port, 58 originated in the French islands, all but five voyaging from St. Domingue. This was the persistent pattern of the decade 1783–93 and countenanced by Spanish officials in New Orleans. In 1786 Governor Miro tested the attitude of his superiors relative to this trade by seizing the island vessel *Saint Vincent-de-Paul*, venturing to New Orleans for lumber and making no effort to assume Spanish colors. The vessel and cargo were ordered returned to the owners. This was Miro's last gambit against this trade. Everyone recognized that the trade would stagnate if the requirements regarding Spanish ownership and Spanish crews were strictly enforced.

Although the merchandise which arrived at New Orleans was normally transshipped from St. Domingue in West Indian vessels, French merchants were heavily involved in the trade. Ships of Spanish registry were utilized when available to carry cargoes of indigo directly to France, and when not available, West Indian vessels carried the goods to St. Domingue for reexport to France. Several French mercantile houses established branches at New Orleans to

TABLE V

Origin of Arrivals at New Orleans, 1786, 1801, 1802, 1808, 1815–17*

	1786	1801	5 mos. Aug.– Dec. 31, 1802	1808	1815	1816	1817
New York		26	25	35	–	–	–
Philadelphia	1	23	18	28	–	–	–
Baltimore		10	9	15	–	–	–
Boston		7	8	13	–	–	–
Charleston		2	7	11	–	–	–
Other U. S.		12	9	11	–	–	–
Total U. S.	1	80	76	113	198	191	238
England		6	14	7	31	35	43
British West Indies . .	8	43	18	18	25	21	29
France	14	2	14	8	15	36	42
French West Indies . .	58	4	8	2	–	12	17
ªOther Europe . .		2	4	4	11	24	31
Havana	16	15	22	7	–	–	–
Spanish Mainland Colonies	27	29	16	39	–	–	–
Total Spanish Colonies	43	44	38	46	68	75	142
Total	124	181	172	198	348	394	542

ª Figures for 1815–17 include arrivals from Danish and Swedish colonies.
* Sources: Financial Report, Francisco Blache, City Treasury, New Orleans, January 1–December 31, 1786, in New Orleans Municipal Papers, 1770–1858 (Louisiana State University Department of Archives); Anchorage Fees, Report 1801, *ibid.*; New Orleans *Moniteur de la Louisiane*, August, 1802–December 31, 1802; New Orleans *Louisiana Gazette and New Orleans Advertiser*, 1808; État des bâtiments entrée à la Nouvelle Orleans et de ceux qui en ont été expédier l'année de terminans au 1 octobre (Louisiana State University Department of Archives).

facilitate this traffic. As Miro explained in 1788: "The inhabitants of . . . [New Orleans] . . . get their shipments of merchandise from France and her islands . . . and . . . the French are . . . the interested parties in these shipments. If it were not for this merchandise, the province would be entirely unprovided . . . ." [1]

French merchants operated in association with New Orleans merchants to maintain a semblance of legality in the trade. The establishment of an agency in New Orleans provided some cover, as did the joint ownership of vessels by French traders and New Orleans residents. Bertrand and Jean Gravier, Bordelais merchants, operated in association with the New Orleans firm of Reaud and Fortier until Jean was sent to New Orleans to act as agent for the Bordeaux firm and, as it happened, to amass a considerable fortune. Michel Fortier, François Louis Delayroue, and Jean Carrière, all New Orleans merchants, obtained individual permissions to purchase vessels and cargoes for New Orleans in France under the authority of the *cédula* of 1782. The requirement that two-thirds of the crew must be Spanish was waived in each case. Generally, if a Spanish consul signed the ship's papers in France, the vessel experienced no difficulty in New Orleans. Such a signature, however, was not available in all French ports. An order of 1785 prohibited vice-consuls from authorizing voyages to Louisiana. The order named Bordeaux, St. Malo, and Rouen as the habilitated ports in France to which Le Havre was later added and St. Malo deleted.

There had been some trade with other European ports prior to 1782. Even before the formal signing of the Treaty of Paris, the New Orleans merchant Jerome Lachiappella routed his vessel from New Orleans directly to London, carrying goods on account of several merchants in New Orleans. The ship wrecked on the return voyage only two leagues off the Balize and insurance claims were presented to the London underwriters who held the policy. A vessel also arrived at New Orleans in 1782 from Ostend. The Spanish occasionally complained that many of the vessels, nominally originating in French ports and supposedly coming directly to Louisi-

---

[1] Estevan Miro to Don Joseph de Ezpeleta, March 1, 1788, in Dispatches of the Spanish Governors of Louisiana, 1776-1794, Book 3, Vols. XI–XV, 1780–88 (Tulane University Library, Manuscript Division).

ana, actually began their voyages or made stops at London or other English ports. Because the goods for the Indian trade were almost entirely of English manufacture, it was considered the lesser of two evils to have them conveyed to New Orleans or Pensacola in French vessels. British shipowners tested the clause in the Anglo-American treaty of peace in 1783, which recognized the right of Great Britain to navigate the Mississippi River. But two English slave vessels which entered the river were confiscated by Governor Miro, who refused to recognize a right not mentioned in the peace treaty between Great Britain and Spain.

Trade with the French, Spanish, and British West Indies was central to the economy of New Orleans during the decade 1783–93. A glance at Table V shows that, of 119 registered arrivals at New Orleans in 1786, 82 came from the Indies. In later years, the Spanish West Indies retained their significant position while the importance of the French and English trade declined. In the period after the War of 1812 the arrivals listed in Table V do not reflect accurately the actual ownership of the vessels, as many of those listed as originating in England, France, and the Indies were of United States registry. In the pre-Louisiana Purchase period it appears that most of the vessels listed as arriving from West Indian ports were of West Indian registry or ownership.

The methods and commodities of the West Indian trade were basically unchanged from those in the French period. The islands served as a general warehouse for manufactured articles and as an entrepot for goods exported from New Orleans. European vessels that ran directly to New Orleans frequently plied the coasting trade while awaiting the gathering of a cargo in New Orleans by an agent of the shipowner or ship's master. Since the *cédula* of 1782 allowed the French West Indian-New Orleans trade only in cases of emergency in Louisiana, shipowners adopted various tactics to gain entrance to the river port while awaiting the formulation of a policy toward the trade. Dumas and Grieumard, merchants at Cap Français instructed the master of their vessel bound for New Orleans to draw up an affidavit to the effect that contrary winds forced him to steer for New Orleans. Part of the cargo consisted of Negroes, which it was hoped would insure a friendly reception for the vessel. The captain was instructed to take deerskin, tobacco, indigo, or piastres in payment and to exercise caution in extending credits. Most vessels from the French islands carried large quantities of wines and liquors, which Navarro estimated composed a third of the total imports of Louisiana. Manufactured goods, frequently English, flour from Philadelphia or other American ports, and Negroes, often from the British Indies, filled out the remainder of receipts from the islands.

Virtually all of New Orleans' exports went to the islands but most were destined for other markets. The lumber trade was, as in the past, the major staple in the direct exchange with the islands. Construction materials, sugar casks, boxes of all types, and pitch and tar were exported to numerous ports in the Caribbean and Gulf of Mexico. In 1793 the Cabildo, in objecting to the wartime commercial regulations promulgated in 1793, estimated that 3,000 workers were employed in lumbering and milling in about 40 mills located on the Mississippi River. The lumber trade required the continuous employment of some 30 vessels each year and the annual value was generously set at 560,000 pesos. Considerable quantities of wood products were shipped on the king's account to Havana, some went to Jamaica as a remittance for slaves, with the balance paid in piastres, but the largest quantity went to the French islands where the best prices were obtained and where the proceeds were applied against exports to New Orleans. In addition, naval stores were exported from New Orleans directly to Vera Cruz and Cartagena.

The lumber trade to Spanish mainland ports and to the British and the French islands not only met a great demand for such products but also supplied the opportunity to introduce contraband goods, especially in the Spanish ports. Lumber and all kinds of English and French goods were sold in Vera Cruz for piastres used to balance out the foreign trade deficit experienced by New Orleans. The tobacco trade of the 1780s, which contributed so greatly to the agricultural prosperity of Louisiana, afforded other opportunities for shippers to introduce contraband into Vera Cruz and the tobacco itself became contraband when New Orleans merchants, seeking higher prices, exported it to Europe. Louisiana tobacco and piastres furnished an illegal means of paying for contraband American flour in St. Domingue. Mather and Strother employed lumber, tobacco, and piastres in paying for the Indian trade goods which the Spanish authorized them to bring into Louisiana and the Floridas.

A matter of some dispute among Spaniards was the incidence of smuggling between New Orleans and the other Spanish colonies. Merchants in Spain, in the belief that the *cédula* of 1782 promoted an enormous contraband traffic throughout Spanish America, attacked the decree in the late 1780s and advocated the promotion of Spanish commerce in the borderland colonies of Louisiana and the Floridas. Don Diego de Gardoqui, Spanish minister to the United States, accepted the existence of smuggling at Louisiana as quite a natural enterprise at New Orleans and unconnected with the *cédula*. Governor Miro and Navarro categorically denied the existence of smuggling between Mexico, Cuba, and Louisiana, unlike the period of French dominion when such trade was rife. Miro maintained that the goods reaching New Orleans were all consumed in the colony. Such opinions were to be expected as neither the intendant nor the governor could readily admit to the existence of a contraband trade.

Gardoqui was quite correct. There was so much smuggling pursued in New Orleans that it was part of the economic landscape. Julien Poydras, a wealthy planter, renounced the practice of smuggling after an unprofitable shipment of indigo to the English. He was indignant at being duped by the English, complained of the heavy insurance premiums exacted, and bemoaned the lack of security in such ventures. The captain of the frigate *Matilde*, out of Havana in 1785 and charged in the Court of the Intendant at New Orleans with running to Philadelphia before coming to New Orleans, protested formally "for the first, second, and third time against the sea" and winds which forced him off course. Contrary seas and winds served New Orleans well by compelling vessels to make port where markets and services were available for the city's merchants. This was especially true relative to the contraband trade between New Orleans and the United States. Gardoqui, in New York, reported the presence of several ships from New Orleans, with clearance papers for St. Domingue, that entered under the pretext of a forced call.

Further expansion of the trade between New Orleans and ports of the United States was perhaps the most significant, if unwanted, consequence of the *cédula* of 1782. The New Orleans-American trade, whether direct or via St. Domingue, was of critical importance to Louisiana, providing as it did a major portion of the flour and provisions consumed in the colony. Patently illegal in any of its various forms, the trade was so essential that it could not be prohibited.

Trade with the English communities along the Atlantic Coast was not unknown during the French period but was first pursued with regularity between 1763 and 1768 and before the American Revolution. Spain's benevolent attitude toward the American rebels and her eventual belligerency allowed the trade to continue during the war. The commerce entered its most active period at the end of the war, in spite of the closing of the Mississippi to foreign shipping. Spanish officials recognized the necessity of the trade in providing foodstuffs and provisions. When a new round of wars began in 1793, Louisiana was cast into an almost absolute dependence upon American provisions and shipping.

Natural and man-made disasters striking at New Orleans—from the devastating hurricanes in 1779 to the fire in 1788 which turned New Orleans into an ash heap—provided a pragmatic justification for the trade with the United States. But even without these incidents, the trade would have developed at just as rapid a rate for the colony could not feed itself. Flour was obtained in the French and Spanish islands and occasionally at Vera Cruz, but these sources could not be depended upon. Until the farming hinterland of the Upper Valley assumed the role, the only other sources were such coastal cities as New York, Philadelphia, and Baltimore, all located in the wheat growing states of the East Coast. Spanish authorities in reluctantly sanctioning this illegal trade arrived at a much more satisfactory solution to the provisioning problem than the French who consigned Louisiana to a permanent state of want rather than allow foreigners to feed the colony.[2]

[2] C. Richard Arena, "Philadelphia-Spanish New Orleans Trade in the 1790s," *Louisiana History*, III (1961), 429–45; and Minter Wood, "Life in New Orleans in the Spanish Period," *Louisiana Historical Quarterly*, XXII (1939), 642–709, both assume that trade with the United States was basically through Philadelphia and that it originated in the late 1780s. Neither assumption is correct. A better treatment is found in Whitaker, "Reed and Forde: Merchant Adventurers of Philadelphia," *Pennsylvania Magazine of History and Biography*, LXI (July, 1937), 237–62.

The trade was conducted in two ways. Both New Orleans and the United States enjoyed the privilege of entering the French West Indies during the decade 1783–93. It was simple enough for a Spanish vessel from New Orleans to load American goods at Cap Français or for a West Indian vessel bound for New Orleans to do the same. There was always great demand at New Orleans for foodstuffs and English manufactures, and most vessels were permitted to discharge their goods without penalty. Many Americans in Philadelphia, New York, and other cities established contacts at New Orleans to provide some cover for the clandestine traffic. A direct trade was also possible and was carried on with sufficient persistence to belie the notion that the entire trade was conducted through the French islands. Here, too, Americans operated through Spanish nationals resident at New Orleans. Frequently ships from New Orleans with papers attesting to a St. Domingue voyage turned up in the United States. It was also possible to obtain licenses for the direct trade. Minister Gardoqui observed one Captain Wooster selling such licenses through public advertisements, with fees dependent upon the vessel's tonnage. However it was accomplished, Thomas Hutchins observed in 1784 that Philadelphia and New York received great quantities of pelts and piastres in return for flour and dry goods.

During the 1780s merchants in New Orleans developed extensive contacts with their counterparts in the United States. Daniel Coxe of Philadelphia, brother of Assistant Secretary of the Treasury Tench Coxe, entered into partnership with Daniel Clark, Jr., of New Orleans in the early 1790s. Clark was previously employed as the correspondent of the Philadelphia firm Reed and Forde. Evan Jones of New Orleans served as the agent of Thomas and John Cliffords of Philadelphia. Nicholas Low and Company of New York dispatched Michael O'Connor to New Orleans as their agent and then engaged in some ventures with J. B. Macarty, merchant of New Orleans. The latter served as an agent and associate of Thomas McIntire of Philadelphia and as a partner in several ventures with William Smith of Baltimore. Michel Fortier corresponded frequently with Stephen Girard of Philadelphia, trying to interest Girard in the New Orleans trade.

A number of inducements prompted Americans to engage in this commerce in spite of its illegality and the risks of Gulf and river navigation. Specie was the real lure, even though its exportation from New Orleans was against the law except in payment for slaves. Americans counted on their cargoes of flour to gain them access to the port where specie and staples were received in payment; but those who dispatched vessels on their own account without the services of an established New Orleans merchant frequently encountered difficulties in marketing their goods. Nicholas Low and Company of New York directed the *Richmond* to New Orleans with flour in 1783. The company's agent O'Connor, recently established in the city, described his troubles in disposing of the cargo. Sales should have been good, he wrote, for there was little flour in the town. He refused sales at $10 per barrel, hoping for an advance in price. The intendant then ordered him to sell within twenty-four hours or leave the port. "Thus . . . you see," O'Connor explained, "the impossibility of doing business in a place where there is neither money or produce, nor even liberty allowed a man to dispose of his property as he pleases." He charged collusion between the government and influential merchants, enabling them to "purchase any Cargo that may be in demand, and . . . of course yield an advantage on their own terms." [3]

At this time the Low firm was attempting to gain a contract with the Spanish government to provide the colony with flour and approached J. B. Macarty about the possibilities. Others were similarly interested and also in touch with Macarty, whose ability to cut through the red tape of Spanish commercial laws was highly appreciated. Daniel Clark, Jr., Evan Jones, and Oliver Pollock were much sought after for the same reasons. At this time, Macarty was heavily committed in a number of ventures with Americans. Thus while he replied to Low's queries negatively, he wrote to William Smith suggesting a joint venture in flour. In his response to Low, Macarty pointed out that a contract was not essential because American flour was always in demand. To Smith he pointed out the desirability of a contract which was obtained with no little difficulty—but obtained

[3] Michael O'Connor to Nicholas Low and Company, October 31 and November 24, 1783, in Robert Smith and Nicholas Low Papers, 1782–1811, 1857 (Tulane University Library, Manuscript Division).

nonetheless. To his agent Thomas McIntire, then in Philadelphia to invest $12,000 of Macarty's capital in trade goods, he advised the purchase of Negroes rather than flour.

Macarty approached trade from as many angles as possible in order to diminish risk. Still he suffered occasional heavy losses in the American trade. He lost $5,000 invested in a partnership with William Smith's son Robert in 1782, in a venture to bring Baltimore flour to Louisiana or Havana, depending upon prices. Smith failed to insure Macarty's share of the vessel and cargo and the ship was lost at sea. In 1784 Macarty was engaged in a suit against Smith for failing to carry out written instructions regarding insurance. In the same year, Macarty was trying to recover the $12,000 placed in McIntyre's hands. Throughout this period, he corresponded fully with Nicholas Low, advising him as to conditions at New Orleans, how to beat the Spanish commercial regulations, and how to circumvent possible losses in New Orleans caused by the monetary crisis facing the colony. Such advice was indispensable for Low who could hardly have operated successfully in New Orleans without such information.

A year before the Spanish closed the Mississippi to foreign vessels, Macarty advised Low to put under Spanish colors any vessels sent to New Orleans. A vessel, fitted out in Macarty's name, would have no difficulty in gaining entrance to New Orleans or in refitting there for a voyage to Vera Cruz or Havana. Low, however, was dubious about venturing goods to New Orleans during a time when greatly depreciated paper money served as the only medium of exchange at that port. Macarty had remedies to suggest in this regard. Flour and Negroes were the items to send because anything else would be confiscated. Macarty maintained that flour would bring at least $15 to $20 a barrel and good Negroes $450 to $500 each. The price was double if paid in paper but, Macarty contended, there was no reason to accept paper. Instead, Macarty would receive payment only in bills of exchange from the treasury of the colony drawn on the treasury at Vera Cruz, where they were punctually paid. The trip to Vera Cruz would be legal and there was the chance that items could be obtained there for sale elsewhere.

Macarty never minimized or ignored the obstacles but instead sought methods to overcome them. In one joint venture with Low in 1784, the brig *Hercules* carried sugar cases to Havana for sale, loaded a cargo of coffee, sugar, and cocoa which Low sold in Philadelphia, and returned to New Orleans with a full cargo of superfine flour. Low advanced funds in Philadelphia for needed repairs on the *Hercules* and handled the insurance. Remittances from Macarty to Low were frequently made in piastres from Havana. The value of Macarty's services were driven home to Low in 1785 when he sent the schooner *Navarro* to the Mississippi without Macarty's knowledge. Entrance to the river was denied the vessel, which then foundered and sank in attempting to put to sea.

Similar services to American merchants were provided by other New Orleans residents. By 1791 Reed and Forde had five vessels engaged in the New Orleans trade. Opening of the river to the navigation of the Upper Valley provided additional quantities of goods for the merchants to remit in American shipping. Reed and Forde opened a store in Natchez and undertook to organize a trade between the Upper Valley and New Orleans. In the early 1790s Oliver Pollock obtained a license for the firm to trade at New Orleans and by 1794 the Philadelphians were working closely with Daniel Coxe and Daniel Clark, Jr., who had earlier helped Reed and Forde pick their way over the shoals of Spanish regulations. A gratuity to certain officials was the best guarantee of admittance to the New Orleans market. Fortier advised Girard that good profits were possible from the French goods that Girard's vessels brought in from Marseilles. These should come via St. Domingue, Fortier warned, rather than directly to New Orleans as was possible with flour.

An expanding trade with the Ohio River Valley increased the attractiveness of the New Orleans trade to Americans without changing its formal nature. However necessary, it was still contraband and as such a fit target for occasional harassment by Spanish officials in New Orleans. Gardoqui's criticisms of the illicit trade in 1787 had repercussions in New Orleans, where a number of American vessels were seized and condemned, but this did not become policy and the trade continued as in the past until Spain's entrance into the war of the monarchs against republican France.

Spain entered this war in a much stronger economic position than she enjoyed prior to her other eighteenth century conflicts. But the progress made following the Seven Years' War could only be maintained with continued peace. The war against France did not do mortal damage to the Spanish economy and, although it retarded growth in certain domestic industries, it did not destroy the colonies. It was the next war with England that proved the ruin of Spain, followed as it was in the nineteenth century by a decade of internal revolution, foreign invasion, and consequent widespread devastation. The decade 1793 to 1803 initiated Spain's undoing in Europe and generated forces in the American colonies that resulted in the utter collapse of her empire—a result quite acceptable to a generation of Americans who derived tangible benefits from the agonies of Spain.

The outbreak of war in 1793 forced Spain to place a hopefully temporary stamp of approval on the American trade with New Orleans. France, once the faithful ally, was now both a military and ideological menace to the traditional values of Bourbon Spain. The *cédula* of 1782, sanctioning trade between France and her islands and Louisiana, was automatically voided by the declarations of war, leaving the United States—suddenly emergent as the world's major neutral carrier—as the only available source of supply for Louisiana. Even before the war, Minister Gardoqui had proposed opening the trade of the North American colonies to all nations with whom Spain had a commercial treaty. This would exclude the United States and act as a lever to pry from the United States a renunciation of its extravagant territorial claims and its incessant demands regarding navigation on the Mississippi. The war gave Gardoqui's project additional merit except that it was no longer feasible to exclude the United States which was the only maritime power with the capability and experience to service the borderland colonies. Within a decade, the United States absorbed the larger portion of Louisiana's trade and then absorbed Louisiana itself.

The royal order of 1793 granted permission to all friendly and allied nations to trade with Louisiana and the Floridas upon the payment of a 15 percent duty for imports and 6 percent for exports. It stipulated that vessels must stop at one of two designated Spanish ports before proceeding to New Orleans. Commerce between Spain and these colonies was freed from all duties and goods reexported from Spain to foreign countries were taxed at 3 percent. Article 19 prohibited trade between either New Orleans or the Florida ports and the Spanish-American colonies. This latter point elicited an immediate protest from the New Orleans Cabildo, which pointed out the importance of Havana as a market for the lumber products of New Orleans and went on to criticize the order for increasing the tariffs, especially on products or money exported for the purchase of Negroes.

The war and the regulations increased the chances for profit as well as adding to the risks of the New Orleans-American trade. American vessels were not admitted with any greater regularity than in the past. However, more of them undertook the New Orleans trade using the precaution of sailing with two sets of papers and two flags. While on the high seas, they displayed the American flag, but this banner was replaced by the Spanish pennant when the approach to the river was made. Governor Carondelet was fully aware of this stratagem but considered the commerce too vital to treat with great severity. Michel Fortier sensed this attitude in 1793 when writing to Girard that Franco-Spanish hostilities would assure a good market at New Orleans for goods such as flour and pork. Officials in Louisiana did not investigate the true ownership of vessels with any vigor, generally accepting the declaration of the consignee that he was the actual owner of the vessel. Nonetheless, the trade continued in a kind of limbo—it was illegal but allowed.

War created opportunities for some such as Reed and Forde who, in anticipation of higher prices at New Orleans, committed additional vessels to the run; and Daniel Coxe and Daniel Clark, Jr., who handled some of Reed and Forde's ventures in addition to working on their own account. But the struggle also destroyed the ancient connections with France and her islands. Julien Poydras claimed that the suspension of commerce with France involved him in the loss of 100,000 piastres. When the Franco-Spanish war came to an end, Poydras pessimistically refused to risk anything without a virtually absolute guarantee of success. He did, however, journey to Philadelphia where he left 36,000 piastres in various mercantile houses for profitable investment. He did not elaborate on the kind of investment but probably it involved the flour trade with New Orleans.

Others also took advantage of that brief period between Spain's wise decision to pull out of the English-subsidized coalition against France and the insane act which plunged her into war with Great Britain, to renew old connections and exploit the privileges extended in the regulations of 1793. Anthony P. Walsh, planter at Bayou Sara in West Feliciana Parish, shipowner and merchant, and captain in the colonial militia, sought and received permission from Carondelet to venture a cargo to Vera Cruz. In addition, Intendant Juan Ventura Morales sanctioned ventures to any port in Europe where there resided a Spanish consul.

Brief though it was, the interlude of peace was of great moment—not so much because of the volume of commerce undertaken during the period, as for the sudden shift in the foreign policy of Spain. Peace with France implied the possibility of war with Great Britain. War with Great Britain held the threat of an Anglo-American alliance and a joint assault on Spain's North American possessions. To alleviate this danger, Spain made great concessions to the United States in Pinckney's treaty, including permission to the United States to navigate the Mississippi River from source to mouth and to establish a place of deposit in the vicinity of New Orleans. American penetration of the commercial life of New Orleans was almost complete, and from the point of view of New Orleans, it came none too soon.

In 1796 Spain went to war against Great Britain. Trade between Spain and her colonies, cultivated with such success since the 1760s, soon passed into the hands of other powers. War on the high seas turned rapidly against Spain; a large squadron was lost in February 1797 while her coastal cities were blockaded and her possessions thrown on their own resources. Recognizing the inevitable, the Spanish government, in November, 1797, authorized neutral vessels to carry all goods, with certain minor exceptions, to Spanish-American ports and to load all colonial goods but specie. Intendant Morales, in June, 1798, informed Daniel Clark, Jr., acting Vice-Consul of the United States, of the crown's decision, noting that it actually applied solely to the United States as the single neutral capable of carrying on the trade.

Although the deposit went into effect only in 1798, American vessels appeared before New Orleans in increasing numbers after 1796, and Americans from the Upper Mississippi Valley forwarded mounting quantities of western produce to the port. At the same time, Louisiana planters shifted from indigo and tobacco to cotton and sugar, and large numbers of American immigrants moved into the territory recently recognized as part of the United States by Pinckney's treaty. Louisiana and its remote areas were finally in the process of being peopled. Products were available for export and a consumer market of considerable size developed in New Orleans and its plantation hinterland. But the opportunities now presented were attended by great risk. Hostilities between Great Britain and Spain preceded by a year the deterioration in relations between France and the United States which finally resulted in the undeclared naval war of 1798–99. These two conflicts caused American shipping to be preyed upon by both British and French warships and privateers. The run to New Orleans was especially dangerous after both France and Great Britain launched swarms of privateers into the Caribbean and Gulf from their West Indian bases.

In 1797 the Cabildo complained that war with Great Britain made maritime operations virtually impossible. Information from incoming vessels indicated that at least nine English privateers operated between New Orleans and Vera Cruz while others lay in wait of shipping approaching New Orleans through the Florida Keys. The isolation of New Orleans from other Spanish ports greatly worsened the critical monetary situation of the city. The colony was without funds and could not expect any for some time. Spain lacked the naval power to protect its West Indian sea lanes and her ally France viewed the shipping of the United States, the dominant carrier for Louisiana's products, as fair game. Daniel Coxe and Daniel Clark lost vessels in the Philadelphia-New Orleans run as did Reed and Forde.

Still, American shippers, attracted by the profits of the New Orleans trade, braved the privateers and cruisers to make the run. Daniel

Clark, Jr., who acted in consular capacity in New Orleans in 1795 and 1796 and in later years, pointed to the hazards facing American shipping departing the port even with proper documents attesting to the neutral character of the vessel.[4] Establishment of the deposit in April, 1798, eased the situation slightly. When Spain, in June, opened New Orleans to neutral shipping for the duration of the war and also extended permission to trade with Havana and other Spanish colonial ports, the attractiveness of the trade was further enhanced.

Implementation of the territorial and commercial clauses of Pinckney's treaty and the exigencies of war tightened the dependence of New Orleans upon the United States. Settlers on the east bank of the Mississippi and north of the 31st parallel, largely Anglo-Saxon, were now American citizens. American ships were admitted legally to the river and could dispose of goods and obtain cargoes at the deposit without the payment of any duties; or they could trade directly with merchants in New Orleans as a result of the neutral shipping regulations with duties assessed under prior regulations. Far more than 50 percent of the vessels entering the port of New Orleans carried the American flag while other vessels, under Spanish registry, were owned by Americans. Spain did not accept the rapidity of American penetration of Louisiana's economic life with the best of grace. The Spanish government, in 1799 and again in 1800, in attempting to rescind the privileges of 1797 throwing New Orleans open to all neutral shipping, encountered intense opposition in the city from the colonial officials, the Cabildo, Daniel Clark, Jr., and Evan Jones, acting in the interests of the United States as well as for the mercantile community of the port.

The privileges applicable to the United States were expanded in 1798, largely through the exertions of Clark. The tariff schedule called for the payment of duties of 21 percent ad valorem on goods of Louisiana exported in American vessels and duties of 12 percent

4 Governor Carondelet, without recognizing Clark's official title, allowed him to act in a consular capacity. Governor Gayoso, Carondelet's successor, recognized Clark as the vice-consul of the United States but was compelled to renounce this recognition. Thereafter, Evan Jones and William E. Hulings, who were appointed full consuls by the United States government, had to be content with the tacit recognition of their duties by the colonial governors. They were never recognized officially.

on goods in the deposit exported in vessels of Spanish registry. Clark requested of Intendant Morales that the duties be lowered. Governor Gayoso and the merchants of the port favored the reduction. So, too, did the planters in American territory, who had to either deposit their goods or pay the 12 percent duty. This disturbed them because under Spanish jurisdiction their goods were exported duty free and generally without the delay which transshipment from the deposit entailed. The regulations were partially circumvented, Clark explained, by a confidential title given by the American owner of the vessel to a New Orleans resident so that the vessel appeared in the customhouse books as a Spanish vessel. Then, however, goods in the American deposit could not be shipped free of duty upon such naturalized vessels but paid duties amounting to 12 percent. Clark maintained that unnaturalized American vessels could not afford to operate in New Orleans. This was an exaggeration even though it was expensive for these vessels. In June, 1798, Clark informed Secretary of State Timothy Pickering of notable concessions granted to American shipping by Morales.

Morales permitted the exportation of Louisiana products in American vessels on payment of a six percent duty with the same rate applicable for goods of American origin imported at New Orleans. He also exempted from duty all exports from New Orleans to the American settlements along the river. Prior duties amounted to as much as 26 percent on liquors. All in all, these were significant advantages. American vessels could now carry out whatever was available in the deposit or load lumber and other goods for voyages to Havana. However, orders received from the Spanish government suspended not only those favors but also the regulations of 1797. Trade with New Orleans was again restricted to vessels of Spanish ownership. Although the operation of the deposit was unaffected, the intention of the new regulations was to restrict American commerce in Louisiana to that authorized in Pinckney's treaty. Evan Jones informed Pickering of the new orders, adding that several American vessels then before New Orleans were prohibited from selling their cargoes.

Seconded by Clark, Jones, and the merchant community, the Cabildo immediately protested the implementation of the new orders.

The councilmen, through a report of Attorney-general Arnaud, maintained that the regulations of 1797 saved the colony from great hardships by allowing neutrals to trade freely in New Orleans and that the impact of the new orders would be more severe than all the natural disasters recently experienced. Arnaud believed that the new orders would greatly increase American smuggling, to the detriment of the government's revenues, and affect agriculture adversely by increasing the costs of shipment and narrowing market opportunities. The new regulations, the official concluded casuistically, were so completely opposed to prior policies that it was impossible to believe them applicable to Louisiana and therefore they must be inapplicable. Morales, for his own reasons, acknowledged the weight of this reasoning and suspended the implementation of the regulations. He also continued to allow American shipping those privileges earlier granted at Clark's request.[5] This was the last major crisis until Morales suspended the operation of the deposit in 1802. Even though the peace of 1801 theoretically rescinded the wartime measures, they remained operative in New Orleans.

While American vessels were treated as Spanish at New Orleans, the trade was still hazardous and always attended by sundry inconveniences. During the quasi-war with France, French privateers infested the Gulf approaches to New Orleans, seizing a number of American ships which were carried to New Orleans for sale, supposedly as lawful prizes. Daniel Clark, Jr., endeavored to secure the release of prizes brought to New Orleans as well as to prevent the arming of privateers by New Orleans residents for use against American shipping. In 1794 a New Orleans vessel with forged letters of marque captured four American ships, three of which were escorted to New Orleans for sale. Two of the prizes were, at Clark's insistence, returned to their legitimate owners while an armed vessel, owned by Clark and Coxe, sought for and recaptured a third. Local Spanish officials acted with great caution in such matters, being

---

[5] Such decisions on the part of colonial officers, while perhaps exceptional, partially qualify the criticism that these officials, operating with limited decision-making powers, were unable to handle problems requiring immediate action. Only rarely had officials in New Orleans enforced the letter of Spanish commercial law and frequently went far beyond their powers in attempting to guarantee adequate supplies, shipping, and markets for Louisiana.

unwilling to offend the French, their allies, or the Americans, their impatient neighbors. If Clark protested with vigor, the Spanish acted to prevent the outfitting of privateers or the sale of prizes in New Orleans. Otherwise, they closed their eyes to the practice and allowed vessels to slip down the river to make war on American shipping.

Both Evan Jones and Daniel Clark complained of the inefficiency and negligence of the pilots at the entrance to the river. Several American ships were lost in navigating the passes and both acting consuls believed that Americans should be allowed to bring in and take out their own vessels. One American merchant was imprisoned for attempting to sound the channel in order to take his vessel out. The consuls also relayed the irritation of merchants whose vessels were constantly boarded and searched by Spanish officials. Vessels were guarded while loading and searched before sailing. The Spanish, according to Clark, also proclaimed frequent embargoes on all shipping, detaining vessels in the river under various pretexts. A British privateer sighted off the mouth of the river or the anticipated arrival of a Spanish vessel served as an excuse for preventing departures from New Orleans, and even when a departure pass was obtained, further delay was often encountered at the mouth. The consuls, as best they could, protested against such arbitrary treatment of American merchants and shipping.

Suspension of the deposit, coming as it did during the Peace of Amiens and while the United States fretted over rumors (soon confirmed) that France was to assume sovereignty over Louisiana, had a greater political than economic impact. Revocation of the privilege had only a temporary economic effect and was but the last of a series of acts in which the Spanish sought to weaken the commercial position of the United States in New Orleans.

Daniel Clark reported, in June, 1802, the intention of Morales to close the port to all but Spanish shipping as soon as the definitive treaty of peace was promulgated. This was aimed at goods bound both to and from Louisiana in American bottoms. Morales, according to Clark, wished to force American settlers along the river to utilize the deposit or pay import-export duties on the produce landed at New Orleans. Then, in March, 1802, Morales instituted a tax of

3 percent on all cash brought into New Orleans in American vessels, either from the sea or from upriver, and whether for use through the deposit or in New Orleans. This was followed in October by the publication by Morales of the revocation of the deposit and the closing of New Orleans to all foreign shipping.[6]

The announcement of suspension coincided with the arrival of the cotton crop and foodstuffs from the Upper Valley. Vice-Consul Hulings predicted that Americans would experience great difficulties and incur serious losses from Morales' arbitrary act. American vessels could enter the river but cargoes could not touch Spanish soil and had to be loaded or unloaded while anchored in the river. Suspension was so rigorously enforced at first, as Claiborne wrote, that it was difficult to get permission to bring to the levee the soaked cargo of a cotton boat which capsized in the river before New Orleans. The rigor relaxed a bit toward the end of the suspension. Protesting that suspension caused a great scarcity of flour and provisions in New Orleans, the Cabildo obtained a decree in February, 1803, from Morales permitting the entry of American foodstuffs from upriver sources. Shippers with less necessary commodities frequently found it possible to land their goods by the payment of a *douceur* (a tip or an extralegal fee) to the proper officials. When this device failed, shippers were forced to sell at any price. Without markets or shipping, produce prices declined. As Clark informed James Madison, cotton did not sell for more than 14 cents per pound during suspension and rose to 18 cents when the deposit was restored. Suspension also harmed flour prices and, by discouraging shippers from freighting their vessels to New Orleans, forced freight rates up. These inconveniences were but temporary, however, for the deposit was restored to its formed footing in April, 1803.

The impact of suspension on the economic life of the port was minimal and transitory. A month prior to restoration, Hulings counted upwards of 120 vessels in the river and the port, about one-half American. Prefect Pierre Laussat, commenting in 1803 on the increasing numbers of French vessels in port, many coming with

[6] During this same period, Morales sought to interdict the free navigation by the United States of the Mobile River. Morales sought to charge tariffs on United States government supplies passing through Spanish territory to Fort Stoddard on the upper Mobile River.

passengers, also perceived that Anglo-American vessels outnumbered those of France and Spain. But at precisely the same time that Laussat, busily engaged in preparing for the anticipated arrival of a French army of occupation, reported large numbers of vessels in the port, others commented on the stagnant trade at New Orleans caused by the recent Spanish actions against American shipping and the uncertainties of retrocession. The hopes of merchant Stephen Zacharie that the arrival of the prefect would settle conditions and still unfounded rumors were blasted by new rumors that France had sold Louisiana to the United States.

Confusion ran wild in New Orleans. To prepare for the arrival of General Victor and 4,500 troops, Laussat and the Cabildo let contracts for flour, provisions, and other supplies and also saw to plans for the construction of barracks and other buildings. This flurry of activity and demand artificially inflated prices for some goods, while the rumors of American occupation and the known disasters suffered by the French army in St. Domingue depressed the prices of other goods. Imported goods found no purchasers while available shipping went unemployed until staple prices declined so that cotton could be purchased for $13 per hundredweight in New Orleans and sold for $45 in France. Prices fluctuated wildly and some shrewd operators bought up unsold French dry goods for reexport to France where they sold at a profit. Laussat scurried around town drumming up support for France while Daniel Clark, Jr., who had no good use for Laussat, accused the prefect of committing acts prejudicial to the United States. Clark specifically charged Laussat with cooperating in the arming of a privateer to cruise against American commerce. Then came word in July that the troops were not coming, followed by official notification of the sale of Louisiana to the United States. Contracts were cancelled, prices gyrated dizzily, and Laussat, according to Clark, stirred up trouble by denying the possibility of such an event.

Laussat received official word of the transfer on August 18, 1803. Disappointed though he was, the ex-prefect attributed the event to the persistence of Americans in pushing their settlements westward and their skill in exploiting the deposit to the greatest advantage, thereby monopolizing the economic life of Louisiana. Laussat and other observers recognized that the great number of American vessels at the port adequately symbolized the fact that the city functioned within the American economic sphere of influence and that the Louisiana Purchase, in a sense, merely added political legitimacy to economic facts operative for over a decade. Of 33,700 tons of shipping entering the river in 1802, some 21,300 tons were American and other vessels of Spanish registry were also American. Table V provides an idea of the extent of American domination in 1801 and 1802 but the official port records did not make entries for the American vessels which worked the deposit. Thus, for 1802, of 256 vessels entering the river, 170 were American, a considerably higher number than cited in the table for a part of the year 1802.

The United States came into possession of Louisiana at a most propitious time. Amazing increases in the production of sugar and cotton which, as Morales noted, almost balanced the imports of the colony, provided a cargo vendable for cash in both the United States and Europe. Demand for cotton rose steadily in the United States, Great Britain, and France during the next decades. Sugar, running into stiff competition from the Havana-refined product, was aided by the tariff policies of the United States. Sugar and cotton provided a strong foundation for agricultural prosperity in Louisiana and thus commercial prosperity for New Orleans. Commercial advances were similarly induced by the rapid settlement of the Upper Mississippi Valley. Western farmers not only provided the necessary foodstuffs for the plantation-slave economy but also furnished large quantities of exports and, in combination with the southern staples, provided cargoes sufficient to attract hundreds of vessels to New Orleans each year.

And this was but the beginning. Development of the steamboat in the period 1810–20 added a new dimension to the commerce of New Orleans by creating a viable two-way trade between the upper country and the Lower Valley. This traffic, vastly augmented in volume and frequency over the old convoy system, lessened the direct dependence of both the up-country and New Orleans on the Atlantic Coast by providing transportation economies which stimulated agriculture throughout the valley and manufacturing along the Ohio River. Moreover, the political unification of the Mississippi

Valley, excepting Spanish West Florida, welded this region to the largest free trade area in the world and generated an atmosphere in New Orleans conducive to economic innovation and growth.

The foundation for this was basically a development of the Spanish period. New Orleans exuded a new dynamism during the last decade of the eighteenth century. Agriculture assumed its nineteenth century form. Not all of this was wanted or anticipated by the Spanish. Much was the result of pressures exerted on the Spanish in other parts of the world. But the Spanish did not react to these pressures with the inflexibility often attributed to them. In Louisiana, they bent with the wind and moved with the tide in seeking a tenable accommodation to a revolutionary world for their border colony. Even so, they adapted themselves unwillingly, changed with reluctance, compromised only when forced to, procrastinated and hedged in meeting commitments and needs when possible. And when the home government proved obdurate or ignorant of conditions, a series of competent governors from Unzaga through Carondelet, aided by Intendants Navarro and Morales, were willing to circumvent whatever was static in the system, if conditions in Louisiana warranted unilateral and largely unofficial action. They recognized the futility of stemming American economic penetration and refrained from applying measures which might have done severe injury to the colony. The strength and value of America's inheritance would be fully demonstrated once Europe succeeded in defeating Napoleon and after the United States had its fling against Great Britain.

13

Economic Life Before the Louisiana Purchase

WHEN Will and Sam Johnson arrived at New Orleans in April, 1801, with a boatload of flour from Pittsburgh, they found a host of opportunities for dealing profitably. Their flour was sold advantageously just prior to the arrival of large quantities from Baltimore and Philadelphia and on large numbers of flats riding the spring flood to New Orleans from the Upper Valley. Flour prices dropped rapidly, making it possible for the Johnsons to purchase at a much cheaper price than they sold, with the aim of taking it to Havana. An agreement was struck for the freighting of the flour aboard the ship *Ocean*, but when the time came to load, the ship was nearly full and a portion of the Johnson's flour remained on shore. The arrival of seven vessels on May 1, seeking cargoes of flour, stimulated a rise in flour prices, and the Johnsons bartered their remaining supply for cotton, securing space aboard the *Neptune* bound for New York. Will traveled with the latter vessel while his brother went to Havana where he sold the flour and purchased sugar for New York—where the two men were reunited.

This business venture reflects not only flexibility, ingenuity, and risk taking by the Johnsons but reveals also the notably augmented choices available to entrepreneurs operating out of New Orleans. For the most part, the days were over when vessels arrived at New Orleans and departed in ballast or when produce rotted on the levees for want of shipping to overseas markets. An established port of call for the vessels of a number of nations, particularly the United States, France, and Great Britain, the city was hardly less prepared to provide the necessary services for planter, merchant, and shipowner than were older ports such as New York or Philadelphia. The agglomeration of people in the place called New Orleans became residents of a genuine city sometime during the Spanish period. A municipal government was established which assumed responsibilities and provided services hitherto within the purview of the provincial government, adding new functions as necessity demanded. In this process, the city gained an identity of self—absent during the French period—which was manifested in the Cabildo's persistent efforts to improve the economic position of the municipality as well as to raise its own standing vis-a-vis the colonial government of Louisiana.

During the last years of Spanish rule, New Orleans was hardly the backwater village it had been even as recently as Kerlérec's administration. The Cabildo, growing increasingly sensitive to any incidents that remotely slighted or diminished its institutional dignity and prerogatives, engaged in 1802 in a stout defense of its right to a larger box in the *Casa de Comedias*. Charging that the Cabildo box was suddenly and arbitrarily divided so that the space was inadequate, the councilmen demanded that Governor Salcedo rectify this insult. The governor told the Cabildo to stop wasting its time on such trivia, whereupon the indignant council hired a lawyer to protect its prerogatives and criticized the governor for flouting its rights. Calling upon precedent, the group pointed out that in Havana the Cabildo occupied a spacious box in the very center of the theater. Salcedo, unimpressed with the facts of history, suspended and arrested four Cabildo members for pursuing this unseemly argument. And in the best tradition, the shows went on in spite of the discomfort of the offended city fathers. Even before this dramatic confrontation, the theater had become as inseparable a part of the cultural landscape as the Cabildo, with both institutions providing the community with a degree of autonomy normally associated with cities.

By 1803 the population of New Orleans stood at some 8,000, although some estimates go as high as 11,000. Another 3,000 people were located below the city. These figures reflect some growth since the census of 1777 placed the population of the city and surrounding areas at 3,000. Most of the increase resulted from immigration, although the Creoles of Louisiana reported that drinking water of the Mississippi stimulated the propogation of the race. It may have been true that Louisiana women became pregnant more easily than others, but it was also true that the general unhealthiness of New Orleans contributed to an appalling infant mortality rate. A small-pox epidemic in 1802 snuffed out the lives of 1,500 children; yellow fever took others, and measles and other childhood diseases still more. More than prolific parents were needed to build a thriving city.

Like most cities, New Orleans offered a variety of the innocent and not-so-innocent of life's diversions. Indeed, to certain ascetic visitors to the city, New Orleans represented almost the epitome of human vice. Visitors of the Protestant persuasion were especially shocked at the looseness in manners and morals displayed in New Orleans. The moral fibre of the strict Presbyterian might well feel assaulted when witnessing gay, colorful throngs disporting in the streets with religious relics and statuary. Others might inveigh against the abundance of tippling houses located at every cross street, crowded and riotous places of intoxication whose taps were eternally going. The apparent spread of luxury and ostentation supplied another source of inspiration for the moralist. High living was the rule among the smart set, the well-to-do who distinguished themselves by the expensiveness of their apparel, vehicles, home furnishings, and other visible symbols of wealth. One perceptive visitor, however, penetrating the facade of luxury, warned travelers not to be fooled by the beautiful houses along the Mississippi into thinking that New Orleans enjoyed a well-distributed affluence. After walking the streets of the city, Paul Alliot observed homes "whose construction and roofs show a depth of poverty which is surprising." [1]

There were rich and poor in New Orleans as in any other city in the world. Also, as one might expect in a city still in a frontier stage, the streets were in wretched condition, unlighted during most of the period and filled with mud or chuckholes depending upon the season. When floodwaters topped or penetrated the levees in front of the town, the waters spilled into the streets. When they receded, tons of fish were left to decay along with other garbage, providing a

1 Paul Alliot, "Historical and Political Reflections on Louisiana," in James A. Robertson (tr. and ed.), *Louisiana under the Rule of Spain, France, and the United States, 1785–1807: Social, Economic, and Political Conditions of the Territory Represented in the Louisiana Purchase* (2 vols.; Cleveland, 1911), I, 65–67.

proper environment for the microscopic and macroscopic carriers of contagion that abound in a city, as well as contributing a variety of smells to offend the sensitive nostrils of visitors. The Cabildo devoted considerable energy and substantial portions of a limited budget to dealing with such problems with but qualified success. The same was true with fire prevention, crime, and other hazards of urban dwelling.

For all the natural and man-made calamities that disrupted and occasionally destroyed life in New Orleans, life went on as usual within the confines of the stockade and five gates that separated town from country. For one down from Pittsburgh on a flatboat in 1801, the fact that New Orleans could not boast a college or public library did not diminish the image of a large and beautiful town with some houses of elegant construction. By this time the town had been almost totally rebuilt following the major fires in 1788 and 1794. As in the French period, the town formed a square, now somewhat larger, extending from the crescent of the river north toward Lake Pontchartrain and containing in 1800 some 1,600 houses, mostly of brick or stone covered with tile and plaster. The suburbs were already forming around the city, one in particular, St. Mary, noted by Alliot at the time of the transfer as the residence of many wealthy planters and merchants and also as a center of a considerable illicit trade. The extensive plantations of de Boré, Livaudais, and others delighted the view of visitors who approached the city from the sea and may well have ill-prepared the seaborne travelers for the great stench that emanated from New Orleans.

As for the residents of the town, there was probably enough going on to take their minds off the local odors and other inconveniences of eighteenth century urban living. Many of the more common diversions were open to the people of all classes and of all races seven days a week, with Sunday being no less a day than any other for business as well as fun and games. Gambling, although illegal and the object of much legislation and occasional raids, was indulged in openly by all ranks and colors with cash in their hands. Dancing was legal and easily the most popular recreation in the city. By 1805, there were some fifteen public ballrooms, with an ordinary ball attracting some five hundred people. Sunday was a big day for dancing, the theater, and opera—the latter introduced during the 1790s.

Of concern to the authorities was the availability of most of these pleasures to slaves as well as whites. Frequent efforts were made to eliminate such activities among the slaves who wandered freely about the city. The regulations were repeated and strengthened frequently enough to indicate their general ineffectiveness. Slaves were forbidden to sell or purchase liquor, to assemble at night, to gamble, to dance the tango before evening services, to possess firearms, to duel, or to be in town without the written permisson of their masters. The reputation of the quadroon women was notorious enough by 1786 to prompt Governor Miro to attack the hair styles of these unfortunates, ordering them to comb it flat or provide a cover if combed high. Slave revolts in the 1790s in St. Domingue caused great uneasiness in Louisiana, where there were abortive slave uprisings which resulted in even more stringent slave laws in New Orleans.

The population of New Orleans consisted mostly of Europeans, Americans, and Negroes. There were but few Indians remaining in the area by 1800, so not too much should be made of the reputation of New Orleans for a polyglot population or as America's first melting pot. As a seaport, it naturally attracted a variety of peoples but no more so than New York and probably much less so than a cosmopolitan center such as Marseilles. Basically, the French Creole, the Anglo-Saxon, and the Negro jostled for living space, with the Anglo-Saxon and the Negro numerically preponderant after the Louisiana Purchase. In its class structure New Orleans was not much different than any other established American city. High society began with the governor and intendant, both Spanish and transient, and included an indigenous aristocracy composed of members of the Cabildo, officers in the occupation force and the local militia, wealthy planters, and successful merchants, many of whom served in official capacities.

Francisco Bouligny, who accompanied O'Reilly to Louisiana in 1769, served in the military, pursued commerce, was lieutenant governor in 1777, and senior official in the colony when Governor Gayoso died in 1799. Nicholas Forstall, one of the Cabildo members arrested in 1802, served earlier as commandant at Atakapas and was an important merchant in New Orleans. Denis de la Ronde, also arrested in 1802, served in the militia and was a businessman. Evan Jones, a militia officer and Spanish subject, was almost arrested when appointed Vice-Consul for the United States at New Orleans in 1801. B. Gravier and Étienne de Boré, both mayors of New Orleans before the Louisiana Purchase, were successful planters. These men in official capacities and other influential and wealthy individuals such as Gilbert Maxent, Daniel Clark, Jr., Michel Fortier, Oliver Pollock, and Pierre Philippe de Marigny de Mandeville were among the aristocracy of the city.

For the most part such individuals arrived at their exalted social status through success in business or planting. Many individuals pursued both occupations concurrently, although the tendency was to advance from the counting house to the plantation veranda. The class system was not entirely closed to newcomers, as there was apparently considerable opportunity for upward social mobility based upon prior economic success. Nor were conditions during the last decades of Spanish rule favorable to the establishment of a caste system. Hurricanes and floods wiped out planters; fires burned out merchants in 1788 and 1794; and epidemics carried off people of all classes. Opportunities and risks assured the existence of an upper crust but also guaranteed changes in personnel.[2] Manners and morals among the elite were, however, fairly stable, being the creation of the French Creole, who attempted with some success to maintain a cultural enclave in the face of an increasing influx of Anglo-Saxons.

In 1779 Governor Gálvez explained to his uncle that "persons of distinction" resisted service in the militia where they were compelled to stand in rank next to their shoemakers and barbers. Gálvez, sympathizing with the plight of the elite, created a cavalry troop for this class. The *caribiniers* would now ride while the common sort walked. Urban growth called for a large number of petty trades-

[2] Wood, "Life in New Orleans in the Spanish Period," 675, speaks of the prosperity of the later Spanish period as the monopoly of a few merchants, planters, and officials. This exaggerates the intensity of class domination of the economic resources of the city. Some were obviously wealthier than others but many made an adequate living without gaining entrance into the elite. Moreover, there was little stability in the membership of the elite. It may be that class domination was more complete during the first American years than during the Spanish regime. Chapter 16 below will treat this problem in more detail.

men to service the needs of each other and other citizens. Including tailors, carpenters, butchers, bakers, and candlestick makers, and a variety of other occupations and skills, the class of *petit bourgeois* probably accounted for the vast majority of the town's white population. This group, including a number of free men of color who could own property and pursue a trade, ran the gamut from the wealthy if socially unacceptable bartender or cabaret owner to the peddler wandering about the town or set up in temporary headquarters upon the levees. This class of trader tailed off into the marginal economic groups, primarily city slaves engaged in selling the surplus of their gardens and loot from nocturnal activities, or Indians peddling vegetables, fish, blankets, and trinkets. With the expansion of the port and market at New Orleans, transients such as sailors and upriver boatmen composed an increasing number of the more lively if temporary inhabitants of the town.

In this diverse community, the Cabildo functioned as the institution responsible for the maintenance of law and order. The difficulties experienced by this reasonably efficient organ of government were frequently monumental. Wars and their consequences periodically stymied progress in the city, cut off food supplies, and threatened the populace with economic and nutritional starvation. Floodwaters at intervals devastated farm lands and inundated New Orleans. Three great hurricanes swept through the colony in August, September, and October, 1794, ruining crops and destroying buildings and shipping. Immense destruction, estimated in excess of $3 million, was caused by the fire of 1788 which reduced to ashes more than eight hundred houses and buildings. Coming, as Governor Miro mourned, just after the colony had recovered from two hurricanes, the fire wiped out the stock of every merchant in town as well as the residences of the most aristocratic families. Rebuilding began, much of it destined for burning in the lesser fire of December 8, 1794, which destroyed most of the structures remaining from the French period, as well as the city's flour reserve.

New Orleans always mended rapidly after these shocks, partially through the exertions of the Cabildo and the willingness of the Spanish government to provide necessary relief, and because of the inherent powers of recovery found in a growing town. Established by Governor O'Reilly conformably to the Spanish tradition of local self-government, the Cabildo exercised a direct and increasing influence upon the daily economic life of the town. Provided with a permanent revenue based on a tax base which the Cabildo constantly sought to widen, the governing body exercised responsibility in a variety of areas that expanded as the city grew. Repair and construction of roads, bridges, and levees; regulation of the port; establishment of city lighting, sanitation, police and fire prevention services; regulation of the local food market—all of these and other matters— were properly within the cognizance of the Cabildo. Of these duties, none was more difficult or more pressing than the regulation of the market place.

The root of the problem in this area was to guarantee an adequate and edible food supply at a price equitable to producer, manufacturer, and consumer. Acting fully within the tradition of paternalistic municipal government, the Cabildo intervened directly to set prices, inspect for quality, assure the use of standard weights and measures, and prevent recurrent food shortages from benefiting monopolists and forestallers at the expense of the public welfare. Private interests, on the other hand, employed various tactics to circumvent the regulatory authority of the public agency. Conflict between the public welfare and private interests continued into the American period, fought out with much the same results as in other parts of the United States. Deterioration in effective regulation by the municipal government and ultimate weakening of its power to intervene came about as the Cabildo voluntarily surrendered some unenforceable authority or had some of its authority stripped away by the action of a more powerful sovereign body.

In Louisiana, the tradition of regulation in the public welfare endured longer than in many parts of the United States and during the Spanish period regulatory powers were persistently utilized by the city with some success. Simultaneously, the Cabildo came to view the city as possessing interests separate from both the colony and the Spanish empire.

The local government did not solve the problem of food supply, which was eventually taken care of by the movement of farmers into the Upper Mississippi Valley. Time and again, as in the French period, the city suffered serious food shortages. In 1772, 1779, and 1781, the Cabildo used city funds to purchase foodstuffs from a variety of sources. Both Governor Miro and the Cabildo acted quickly to alleviate pressures on the food supply following the great conflagration in 1788. Miro cooperated with Oliver Pollock to obtain flour, medicines, and other items from Philadelphia. In 1794 the war, fire, and hurricanes brought new misery to the colony, prompting the Cabildo to authorize agents to purchase foodstuffs. In 1796 the Cabildo contracted with Daniel Clark, Jr., to supply rice which the city then sold. The Cabildo also requisitioned flour from merchants who had any in stock, distributed it to the city's bakers, and then administered the sale of bread to the populace.

Conditions were so serious in 1796 that the Cabildo requested supplies from Havana and Vera Cruz, chartering a boat from John McDonough to carry them; invited merchants in the United States to forward flour to New Orleans; contracted with Clark and others for corn; and purchased rice as a hedge against further scarcity. In an effort to stretch existing supplies of flour and rice Cabildo members almost donned the baker's caps and aprons in supervising experiments in which various mixtures of rice and flour were baked into bread to achieve an edible combination. In both 1800 and 1803 the Cabildo, fearing further shortages, formally and successfully requested that the intendant prevent rice exports.

The Cabildo needed to guarantee the availability of about six hundred barrels of flour monthly which would provide each citizen of the city with something under a pound of bread daily. City authorities tried to ascertain the precise quantity of flour baked into bread for the bakers paid a tax on each barrel. This revenue, along with a tax on the butchers, supported the street lighting system. At the same time, the Cabildo regulated the price, weight, and quality of the bread offered to the public at retail, just as it regulated through similar measures the vending of meat in the city. In both instances, the regulations sought to protect the public as well as to provide an annual revenue to the city for the support of necessary public services. There was an obvious need for such regulation.

Before John Fitzpatrick was thrown out of New Orleans by O'Reilly, he confided with obvious satisfaction to some associates that he had managed by a strategem to conceal some "excessively rotten" flour from the Cabildo which was searching for spoiled flour and throwing it into the river. Frequently, thereafter, the Cabildo complained that in spite of regulations and inspection, bakers obtained rancid flour which they mixed with good flour, selling the product as fresh bread. Moreover, retailers of bread were repeatedly accused of using fraudulent weights. In times of shortage, the problem was especially critical because merchants met flour-laden vessels on the river, purchased the stock, and held it for high prices. Bread prices were fixed in 1769 by the use of a sliding scale hitched to the price of flour, and the Cabildo posted official prices each week throughout the Spanish period and into the American. Regulations were passed protecting the right of the public to buy in small lots ahead of the retailers by prohibiting retailers from purchasing provisions and supplies in large units in order to resell. In 1773 a gauger was appointed to protect against abuses in the weighing and measuring of foodstuffs and liquors. In 1793 he became the inspector of weights and measures and, armed with official weights, confiscated large numbers of inexact weights.

Periodically, subcommittees of the Cabildo stormed through the warehouses seeking out and destroying spoiled flour or, if pressures on the food supply existed, as in 1779 when many new families arrived, authorizing the expenditures of city funds for the purchase of food to be stored for distribution when required. The Cabildo was also active in its efforts to secure a regular meat supply for the city.

When Louisiana was ceded to Spain, the meat supply of the city was obtained largely by hunting parties operating in the wilderness to the northeast and northwest of Natchez and through imports of salt beef from stocks in the French West Indies which originated in the English colonies, Ireland, and other places. To regularize the supply and stimulate the development of domestic herds, the Cabildo in 1770 or 1771 granted a monopoly of the meat market to an individual after competitive bidding. Those interested in obtaining the contract bid a particular sum and suggested the details of the agreement, such as quantities, prices, and the location of the slaughter sheds. The primary contractor, acting as lessee of the butcher shops located in the central meat market, let subcontracts to other individuals who were the actual suppliers of meat.

This system did not solve the problem of supply as only an increase in population and thus in the demand for meat would induce individuals to enter the livestock industry. By the 1780s, however, significant beginnings had been made in the Atakapas and Opelousas districts as well as at Pointe Coupée and the German Coast. In 1781 the Cabildo amended the system of contracting by drawing up its own requirements with which the highest bidder must comply. Contractors, nevertheless, experienced difficulties in meeting their obligations, some stemming from disagreement with the subcontractors and others from the severe inflation existing during the 1780s when large sums of paper money circulated at a great discount in the colony. In 1789 the Cabildo decided to end the contract system and establish a free meat market by allowing livestock raisers to transport and sell their herds on their own terms to the butchers of the city. At the same time, the Cabildo retained a tax of three reales per head of cattle sold in the city and fixed the retail price of meat.[3]

Within those limits the meat market remained free, as was the wish of interested parties in New Orleans, Atakapas, and Opelousas. The Cabildo set the retail price of beef and pork, responding to shortages in supply by authorizing price increases; supervised and policed the operation of the central meat market in which the butchers rented stalls from the city; and tried to keep the pens and slaughter sheds outside of the city limits. In general, these activities seem to have assured the city an adequate supply of meat at moderate prices as well as guaranteeing it a revenue of more than 4,000 piastres annually, which increased in 1799 when the butchers' tax was raised. The Cabildo acted shrewdly in this particular matter for it was seeking a revenue to support the street lights and the residents of the city had refused to pay a chimney tax for such purposes. Nor were the

---

[3] Hilario Bontet, the prime contractor in 1781–84, complained that the subcontractors in Atakapas and Opelousas would sell only salted meats rather than drive their herds to New Orleans as the contract called for. Bontet was also caught in the inflationary squeeze. When he made the contract, the paper currency had only lost 15 percent but in 1784 the paper was only worth 40 percent of face value. The cattle owners increased the price of cattle to compensate for depreciation while Bontet could sell to the butchers only at a fixed price. The Cabildo authorized an increase in the price of meat.

butchers happy about the new tax rates. But at that moment an association in Atakapas proposed to pay for the street lights if they were granted the monopoly of the meat supply of New Orleans. Informed of this, the butchers willingly agreed to an increase in the tax without a price hike with the understanding that no monopoly would be granted.

Responsive to public needs in the critical area of food supply, the Cabildo exercised its authority with discretion. Although composed of prominent merchants and planters, the public body acted energetically to prevent forestalling and price fixing, to maintain quality control, and otherwise protect the consumer without damaging the wholesaler and retailer. In 1798 the Cabildo listened sympathetically to vegetable retailers protesting the imposition of a weekly tax on their stands. The council frequently acted against itinerant peddlers who sold spoiled foods of unknown derivation and who littered the levees with their refuse. Municipal authority was exercised in other areas as well. Apothecaries were regulated by a price tariff. And in 1801 the Cabildo granted the monopoly of the firewood supply to a single contractor in order to thwart the efforts of wood retailers to make excessive profits during the winter season.

No brief is presented for the total success of such measures. When the Americans took over, bakers were still mixing bad flour with good to sell at the established prices; peddlers moved their shops from spot to spot on the levee, prompting fifty New Orleans merchants to petition the Cabildo for the removal of these competitors; and tavern owners were in collusion to fix the price of wines purchased at public sales. Nonetheless, the city government recognized the existence of such practices and sought to eliminate or control them through the application of methods derived from the medieval city. Such concepts as fair price, reasonable profit, consumer access to the market place, purity in products, accuracy and standardization of weights and measures, and prohibitions against engrossment and forestalling were all applied in the name of the public welfare. Climaxing during the Spanish period, the role of the city government in these matters then declined in the face of contradictory concepts of the market place introduced by Americans and current in other cities throughout the United States. The city government, in any event, had quite enough to do in providing other less controversial but basic services for the growing population.[4]

The maintenance, improvement, and construction of public works were among the pressing responsibilities of the Cabildo, which, unlike the regulation of the market, involved the outlay of considerable sums of public monies. As in most cities, budgetary considerations compelled the city government to formulate projects on a somewhat smaller scale and perhaps less rapidly than the legitimate needs of the city demanded. Inadequate revenues plagued New Orleans no less than other urban areas around the world making it likely that a performance gap would always exist between the quality and variety of services offered to and the services demanded by the public. Thus, visitors and residents alike complained about the disrepair of the streets and levees, the lack of street lights, inefficient drainage and sanitation systems, inadequate police and fire protection, and other similar deficiencies.

O'Reilly's political settlement assured the city government an annual revenue of about $2,000 by allocating the revenue of specific taxes to the Cabildo. An anchorage tax on vessels, initiated by the French, was retained for the upkeep of levees and harbor. Similarly earmarked was a tax of one piastre, later raised to two, on each barrel of tafia imported at New Orleans. Taxes were also levied on taverns, billiard halls, rooming houses, butchers, and bakers. At intervals thereafter, licenses were required for the operation of dancehalls, vegetable and fish stands, and for auctioneers, river pilots, and other professions. The public gauger, port warden, and other officers charged fees, the bulk of which went for the salaries of the civil servants. By 1776 the revenue from cabaret owners alone surpassed the total city budget of 1770. No wonder, since there were three

---

[4] New York City abandoned many similar activities prior to 1803, giving up, for example, the fixing of bread prices in 1802. See Sidney I. Pomerantz, *New York, An American City, 1783–1803: A Study of Urban Life, Columbia University Studies in History, Economics, and Public Law,* CDXLII (New York, 1938), 170–77. For an excellent discussion of the market-regulating role of colonial American cities, see Carl Bridenbaugh, *Cities in the Wilderness: Urban Life in America, 1625–1742* (New York, 1964) and Bridenbaugh, *Cities in Revolt: Urban Life in America, 1743–1776* (New York, 1964). For the western cities, see Richard C. Wade, *The Urban Frontier: Pioneer Life in Early Pittsburgh, Cincinnati, Lexington, Louisville, and St. Louis* (Chicago, 1964), 81–83, 280–282.

times more cabaret owners paying taxes, to say nothing of the enterprising individuals selling unlicensed hooch from mobile shops.

Spain was reasonably liberal in committing funds from its own sources to finance public improvements in New Orleans while Spanish colonial officials were permissive in allowing the city to broaden its tax base. In 1772 the crown sanctioned the leasing of royal lands by the city to prospective storeowners, with the revenue accruing to the Cabildo, and in 1801 the crown donated land for sale to help the city defray the expenses of the lighting system. Spain was also willing to lend funds to the city on a six year repayment plan. Still, in 1790 the Cabildo, faced with the danger of a break in the levee along some abandoned lands, was constrained to increase the debt of the treasury. Moreover, since the public spirit of the citizenry disintegrated when confronted by the tax collector, the city lost unknown sums when the bakers reported the use of less flour than actually consumed, tafia importers tampered with invoices, or bootleggers and peddlers failed to apply for licenses before vending their goods. The city, constantly in financial trouble, was thus slow rather than lax in paving streets, erecting street lights, and establishing police and fire departments.

The fire of 1788 not only emptied the city treasury, necessitating the raising of funds by voluntary subscriptions to meet the threat of floods which followed the fire, but resulted in the appointment of Oliver Pollock by the Cabildo to purchase fire fighting equipment in Philadelphia. Mounting violence on city streets and banditry in and around New Orleans after dark motivated the Cabildo to establish a municipal lighting system in the 1790s. The street lights, eighty-six in number, arrived from Philadelphia in 1794, bids were let for their placement, and means were sought to finance their operation. Rejecting a frontage tax on city lots, the Cabildo decided upon a chimney tax which the citizens refused to pay, and finally, as noted above, allocated the butcher's tax to support the service. At the same time, the Cabildo and Governor Carondelet established the night watch or patrol to service the lamps and patrol the streets. The N.O.P.D. was in being. Major disbursements from city funds were made each year to repair levees and bridges, to pave the streets, and to drain and fill low areas in the city.

Governor Gálvez impugned the loyalty of the Cabildo in 1779, charging that its members "maintain a spirit of rebellion and hatred for the Spanish nation, which they cannot hide . . . ." [5] The Cabildo, for its part, acclaimed its loyalty, pointing out that it executed royal orders with precision even if harm resulted to the colony. The issue was not one of loyalty—this confused the issue—but of interest and identity. By 1779 the Cabildo identified with and represented the interests of the municipality. Achieving self-identity, the Cabildo, as most political bodies, sought to aggrandize its powers at the expense of competing bodies. The dispute between governor and Cabildo (or executive and, to stretch a point, legislature) that occurred in Louisiana was a faint mirror image of disputes that had occurred in the English colonies of America from their founding.

Although somewhat comic, the controversy between Governor Salcedo and the Cabildo regarding a theater box symbolized this sense of interest and identity. So, too, did the vigorous criticism directed by the Cabildo at the commercial regulations of 1793 in which the city fathers defended the interests of the colony vis-a-vis the Spanish empire. A more positive indication of the Cabildo's concern with the interests of the colony occurred in 1797. News that nine English privateers operating in the Gulf threatened to intercept the payroll boat due at New Orleans from Havana induced Governor Carondelet to propose that local merchants contribute to the outfitting of an armed vessel to escort the treasure ship into port. The merchants refused. The Cabildo contributed a thousand piastres from a sorely strained treasury. One suspects that the Cabildo, in tendering this support, thought first of New Orleans, then of Louisiana, and finally, perhaps vaguely, of the empire.

The budget of the Cabildo and business in general at New Orleans suffered from serious inflationary pressures during most of the Spanish period. The root of the problem then, as in the French period, lay in the paper money which circulated in Louisiana between 1779 and 1790 and again at the turn of the century. It was somewhat ironic that Louisiana, highly regarded by both French, English, and American business interests as a source of specie, should suffer longs years of specie shortages and, for a medium of exchange,

[5] Gálvez to Don José de Gálvez, March 2, 1779, in *Confidential Dispatches of Gálvez*, 60.

rely upon a paper issue which experienced as severe a depreciation as any issued during the French period. The war with England between 1779 and 1783 compelled the first issues of paper not only in Louisiana but in Spain as well. In Spain, the paper depreciated rapidly during the war but then recovered its value and remained stable until the outbreak of the French Revolutionary wars. But in Louisiana the paper enjoyed no such stability.

Governor Gálvez had recourse to the issue of credit certificates in 1779 to alleviate the shortage of specie and finance his campaigns against the English. In 1782 Intendant Navarro authorized the issue of *billetes*, to provide further relief from a shortage of coin presumed to be temporary. Within a year, Navarro suspended all payments in specie and the colony functioned entirely on a paper system. As in the French period, confidence in the paper eroded rapidly, forcing a slow rise in prices and causing numerous disputes regarding payments. Debtors wished to pay in paper; creditors demanded specie. When a contract stipulated payment in specie, as was the case in James Mather's suit against Francisco Marmillon, the court adhered to the original terms. However, when there was no prior stipulation as to the kind of money to be received, paper was favored. Navarro, for instance, tried in 1783 to shore up the value of the paper by ordering a Bordeaux merchant to accept paper in payment of a bill of exchange.

Rapid depreciation occurred during the postwar period in spite of the tobacco boom and the annual shipment of large sums of money to meet the rising expenses of the colonial establishment. The value of imports surpassed the value of exports, with the gap increasing during the decade and with the Spanish government unable to rectify the situation with specie. The insufficiency of colonial remittances assured a deficit in the trade balance of Louisiana. Unforeseen costs of war exaggerated the deficit and forced the issue of paper which drove prices up. As Evan and James Jones informed Nicholas Low: "This circumstance has raised the prices of Indigo, Furs & Skins ... so exorbitantly high that they would in no degree answer as a remittance to any part of the Continent." [6]

The financial situation deteriorated further. J. B. Macarty re-

[6] Evan and James Jones to Nicholas Low, April 9, 1784, in Robert Smith and Nicholas Low Papers.

ported colonial money at a discount of 25 to 30 percent in April, 1784, which was manageable if depreciation had ended there. Confidence in the paper collapsed, however, and by October, the paper was discounted at 50 percent. Thereafter, the discount on colonial paper fluctuated between 60 and 70 percent, depending upon the availability of exports at New Orleans. James Mather explained to a planter correspondent that the current exchange was 160 paper dollars for 100 hard but it was probable that this would decline when the tobacco came down. Both the Cabildo and Governor Miro were insistent in their demands that the paper be withdrawn and the currency of the colony returned to a specie base. The fire of 1788 dramatized the validity of these demands.

Governor Miro, in 1786, observed that New Orleans contained strong mercantile houses fully capable of handling the commerce of the colony, if unhampered by a lack of capital caused largely by the depreciated paper. He expressed his surprise that so much commercial activity existed in the colony. New Orleans merchants were forced by the absence of specie to purchase the crops of the colony at high prices in paper and sell the produce at prices current in Europe. According to Miro, many merchants sustained large losses in these transactions, with a consequent weakening of the economic foundations of the colony. The situation facing the Cabildo was no more enviable because its revenues were fixed. It received two piastres per barrel of imported tafia, regardless of the price of tafia or the market value of the currency. But the city government paid for goods and services at the inflated prices. Both the governor and the Cabildo applied to the crown for a remedy. The fire of 1788 occurred first.

The degree of destruction—involving nearly eight hundred homes and businesses and the city's food supplies—demanded a massive infusion of public funds not only to clear away the debris and begin rebuilding but to alleviate the distress of the homeless and prevent the outbreak of epidemic disease. But the colonial treasury was so strapped for funds that Miro, instead of expanding his welfare program, was compelled to discontinue the daily rations of rice previously issued to two hundred families. In the months after the fire, Miro coupled pleas for increased assistance with appeals for the immediate withdrawal of the paper currency. Instead, however, the Intendant General of Havana decided to retain 100,000 piastres budgeted for Louisiana. Before the crown was able to order the restoration of this sum, Miro and Navarro issued another 100,000 piastres of paper to meet urgent needs. The sum of paper outstanding as of August, 1788, totaled 839,000 piastres. Only then did the crown respond to Miro's pleas, authorizing the shipment of specie from Vera Cruz for the retirement of the paper. By 1791 the Cabildo noted that the colony had returned to a specie base and that the small amount of paper in circulation was received at face value.

Unfortunately, this stability was disrupted by the French Revolutionary wars which threw the monetary system of both mother country and colony into another inflationary spiral. From 1790 to 1795 or 1796, New Orleans conducted its business with an adequate supply of specie money. This was fortunate because the colony received a severe jolt when the crown ceased purchasing Louisiana tobacco for its Mexican factories. This left Louisiana with one staple product, indigo—the days of which were numbered—and two potential staples, cotton and sugar, both still in the developmental stage. New Orleans, however, received at this time its first substantial imports from the American West, which soon combined with sugar and cotton to more than compensate for the demise of tobacco and indigo as staple crops of the Lower Valley. Political tensions flowing from the French Revolution and republican enthusiasts in the United States, notably the Genêt and Clark plot against Louisiana, induced many a nervous flutter in the stomachs of Louisiana's resident officials. But there is no substantial evidence that rumors of impending invasion blighted business prospects.

Specie scarcity and inflationary pressure caught up with the Cabildo in 1795. Yielding to necessity, the Cabildo reversed a hitherto consistent position and rented places on the levee to the small merchants and peddlers that the city normally chased away. War with Great Britain and the destruction of the indigo crops came in 1796. As the Cabildo sadly noted the following year, British sea power not only reduced the maritime activity of the port, it also reduced the city's revenue. The treasury was penniless and the paper had already depreciated as much as 90 percent. Trade with the Americans provided a source of coin but in adding to the attractions of contraband trade it further reduced revenues. Property values were tumbling, Nicholas Forstall complained when he was forced to sell property in order to pay a debt. There was to be no relief. Paper money was discounted 100 percent in 1801. To advance credit was risky, becoming more so when successive rumors and final confirmation of two cessions swept through the colony. But tight money made credits more necessary than ever. It was either advance credit or forego sales.

It is difficult to ascertain with any assurance the impact of monetary stringency, wars, quasi-war, and threats of war, hurricanes, floods, human and plant diseases, and the rumors and realities of successive cessions upon the economic life of New Orleans and its people. Ninety-nine percent of the people lived inarticulately, in either wealth, comfort, pinchedness, or squalor. The other one percent has left some written remembrance of themselves—but unfortunately they were of the elite and better buffered against adversity than most folk. Julien Poydras might complain about hard times but still manage to live in a style sufficient to entertain the Duc d'Orleans, future king of France, when he and his two brothers visited New Orleans in 1798. But what of the less affluent? What of Antonio Caperdoni, porter of the Cabildo in 1795, earning an annual wage of 240 pesos, or Juan Percetto, guardian of the prison, salaried at 150 pesos yearly? Inflation certainly must have hit hard at such individuals.

Take Juan Percetto, for example. It is not known whether he had a family but his salary is known, as are meat and bread prices. In 1797 the daily consumption of a pound of bread and a pound of meat for a year required 31 percent of his income; in 1798, 40 percent. In addition, there would be clothing, drink, and rent. According to one observer, house rents were so excessively high in New Orleans that they would equal the purchase price in five years. If Percetto had a family, they were on the verge of indigence. The cost of living was more oppressive in 1803 when 50 percent of the daily wage of a laborer or artisan-helper was spent to purchase a loaf of bread and a pound of meat. A master carpenter expended 25 percent. And in all cases, the annual proportion spent on food would be higher if there were periods of unemployment. Wages may well have been high, but prices were higher and it is difficult to accept Laussat's judgment that workers were well to do. Paul Alliot believed that few were able to live in comfort. For many residents, if not most, New Orleans remained a city with an economy of scarcity.

Opportunities for employment in New Orleans for the unskilled or semiskilled free worker were restricted by the lack of an industrial base and by the presence of slavery. The city government and its contractors employed slaves on construction jobs. Slaves were hired out as coachmen, cooks, gardeners, maids, and so on. Stevedores, teamsters and draymen, and garbage collectors frequently were Negroes. Quadroon and darker prostitutes competed with the white professionals, ignoring Governor Miro's order that black women abstain from a licentious life. In spite of local ordinances, Negroes hawked a variety of goods from the levee or at street corners. Slaves were also employed by their owners or as hired hands in the few manufacturing establishments located in or near the city.

At the time of the Louisiana Purchase, a number of sawmills and distilleries formed practically the entire industrial plant of the city. At least two cordage factories were operating, one owned by Elisa Winter and the other by Daniel Clark. The latter was located across the end of Royal Street and obstructed the right of way, causing a dispute between Clark and the city government. This plant burned to the ground in 1806 when the tar in storage caught fire. In the suburbs of the city, two cotton mills and a sugar refinery were established, along with a small rice mill. The historian François-Xavier Martin also lists plants manufacturing hair powder, vermicelli, and small shot. Facilities for the construction and repair of ships were available, but the town never progressed far in the construction of either oceangoing or larger river craft.

Vessels were occasionally built in New Orleans. The French commissioner de Villars recorded the construction of three vessels all under 300 tons by Beauregard in 1772 and 1773. From 1781 to 1800 none of the fifty-five vessels enrolled and registered at New Orleans was constructed in the city. Firms such as Lieutaud and Company specialized in structural repair and furnished lumber and workers such as ships' carpenters and caulkers. Other firms supplied pitch and tar while the cordage works provided the rigging, and individual blacksmiths or ironmongers hired themselves out to make special repairs.

The economic hub of New Orleans remained the harbor and port facilities. Most employment, from the dock worker to the merchant, concentrated on the single task of moving goods to market and selling goods in the local market. The form of business had not changed much from the days of the Rasteaus, Jung, and Chantalou, even though market possibilities for exports had widened significantly and the quantities involved were many times larger than in the French period. During the Spanish period the products themselves had changed and the points of origin expanded to include many new areas within the Mississippi River Valley. But whether it was indigo from the Farar plantation, cotton from John Bisland at Natchez, distilled sugar from George Mather above New Orleans, or flour and tobacco from farms in the Ohio River Valley, many essential services were only available in New Orleans. Planter and merchant remained the two principals in the mercantile world.

Uncovering the subjective relationship between these two interests is difficult. One can accept Captain Philip Pittman's evaluation of the French and early Spanish period that planters were treated with great indulgence in economic matters without totally rejecting Paul Alliot's charge, in 1803, that the merchant fixed staple prices and through credits extended to the planter "forces the settler to deliver . . . his products at a price much lower than the current price." [7] The strictures of Berquin-Duvallon and Prefect Laussat, who both condemned the absorption of the townspeople in material acquisition, represent an accurate observation and an irrelevant value judgment. The observation should also be extended to the planter. Julien Poydras or Étienne de Boré were no less acquisitive than Daniel Clark, Jr., or James Mather. The issue is further confused by those who would distinguish between the planter-aristocrat and the bourgeois-merchant. There were wealthy planters to be sure and they attempted to emulate the aristocratic life. But their wealth was gained through the application of bourgeois-capitalist standards, ideals, and methods of operation. This truth became more pro-

[7] Alliot, "Reflections on Louisiana," 69.

nounced following the cession of Louisiana to the United States. The new century, in New Orleans as well as New York and Liverpool, was the century of the bourgeoisie.

There is some evidence, however, that planter interest diverged from mercantile interests on certain matters of policy. Following the 1788 fire the merchants, many of whom suffered total losses, requested the privilege of going to any European port to obtain goods for Louisiana. Planters opposed this because they were fearful that such a privilege would allow the most powerful merchants to monopolize commerce and fix crop prices. The planters suggested opening up the trade of New Orleans to all foreign ships. Miro supported their position, recognizing however, that they asked too much. The French Revolutionary wars and Pinckney's treaty forced Spain to concede tacitly most of the planters' demands. It was the planters' object to assure the greatest competition possible among merchants and shippers for the crops of the colony. Established merchants in New Orleans would willingly sacrifice such competition.

Conflicts of interest between merchants and planters became more overt and intense during the American period when new institutions such as banks were established in and controlled by merchants of New Orleans. Then the planters resorted to the territorial and state legislature in an effort to lessen the economic dominance of the city merchants. Conflict was also latent in the increasing number of merchants in New Orleans who engaged in the commission business and served as agents in New Orleans of overseas purchasers and suppliers.

One individual spoke of the transient nature of merchants who extracted what wealth they could from New Orleans and then left with their fortunes. Others, however, noted the ambition of merchants to amass a fortune for investment in a plantation. Merchants who came and went are less significant than those who remained permanently but whose interests were not identifiable with the community. The appearance of this latter type becomes more marked in the American period as scores of agents of English and American merchants and manufacturers flowed into New Orleans to purchase cotton, sugar, and western produce and sell manufactured wares to the agrarians.

Many individuals about whom something can be learned from ex-

tant documents fit all categories so that blanket and inflexible cate-
gorizations are untenable. Daniel Clark, Jr., for instance, came to
New Orleans as the partner-agent of Daniel Coxe of Philadelphia
and was soon one of the first merchants in the city. He served as
consular agent, owned a cordage factory, purchased a plantation at
Natchez in 1787 and a 208,000-acre tract on the Ouachita River in
1803. He served as a director of at least two banks after 1803 and as
territorial delegate to Congress in 1806. A similar pattern was followed by Evan Jones, although he may not have owned any land or
worked a plantation. Evan and James Jones were agents of Nicholas
Low of New York as well as of William and James Walton and
Company of Philadelphia. They purchased crops for the account of
these firms and for their own account as well as handling, on commission, the crops of planters. Insofar as they operated on their own
account or for Low, it behooved them to purchase at a low price.
When acting as commission agents for planters, the object was sale
at the highest possible price.

There was room for a conflict of interest in these operations. J. B.
Macarty, merchant and owner of a sawmill, purchased American
goods on commission for Louisiana planters. In 1783 Macarty instructed Nicholas Low to place an advertisement in the newspapers
that "J. B. Macarty, merchant of New Orleans informs the merchts
of the United States that he will receive new flour on commission,"
promising the most careful attention to their interests. But in purchasing flour on commission for the planters, Macarty was obligated
to buy at the lowest possible price. Other merchants, Morgan and
Mather, Chew and Relf, Joseph McNeil, to name a few, engaged in
the same variety of business operations and were undoubtedly faced
with the same dilemma. If the planters were resentful about inequi-
ties in their relations with the merchants, they remained unexpressed
until self-government came to Louisiana and until rural communities
discovered identities which they were able to articulate in the legislature and news media.

Specialization in business was rare in New Orleans through the
Spanish period and into the early American years. The volume of
business in the city was not large enough nor the hazards of trade
sufficiently tempered to support the business specialist. Moreover,
brokerage, banking, and insurance services among others were un-

known in New Orleans until the transfer to the United States.[8] Insurance was obtained elsewhere. Credit was extended from one firm or individual to another as a personal service and on the basis of the borrower's reputation for business integrity, rather than on any objective measurement of his assets. Investment opportunities outside of the traditional sectors of trade and land were almost nonexistent. Times and conditions would change, especially after the War of 1812 and the integration of New Orleans and its hinterland into the American system. But until then, nonspecialists dominated business circles in New Orleans and many of the most successful eventually invested part of their profits in land and slaves.

Beverly Chew and Richard Relf, associated as Chew and Relf at least by 1801, pursued as wide a variety of business activities as possible in New Orleans. They purchased from and sold goods to Reed and Forde of Philadelphia; provisioned, freighted, and leased vessels to St. Domingue, Bordeaux, and London; received English goods on consignment; and bought and sold staples and groceries on their own account. With the American occupation, their interests and occupations proliferated even more. The firm of Morgan and Mather provided many services: collecting debts for and from planters; handling the crops of John Bisland of Natchez; forwarding slop buckets, millinery, and other articles to George Mather's store in St. James Parish; and handling the sales from the sugar factory of George Mather and Company.

The services offered by New Orleans merchants to the plantation economy were so necessary—to say nothing of their convenience and reasonable cost—that it was all but impossible for even the largest planter to bypass them. John Bisland of Cross Creek near Natchez, a store owner and proprietor of a plantation with thirty-six slaves at the turn of the century, grew and purchased staples from others for sale on his own account in the 1780s and later years. Bisland bought from and sold directly to merchants in Scotland whenever possible. In 1802 he accompanied a shipment of 208 bales of cotton, insured for $17,000, aboard the ship *Neptune* for Greenock. Two other New Orleans merchants, James Ewing and James Johnson, accompanied personal consignments of cotton with the full cargo

8 The impact of the new institutions and the role of the business community in their direction will be treated more fully below in chapters 14 and 16.

totaling 777 bales. A part of Bisland's cotton was purchased from other planters and some was sold to William Kenner of New Orleans. The expenses of freight, storage, drayage, and loading in New Orleans came to $640, the details of which Kenner handled. Total freight charges came to $2,638, about $12 per bale, the arrangements negotiated by Kenner. Bisland instructed a correspondent in Glasgow to take out insurance. The *Neptune* struck sandbanks off Ireland in September, 1802, and much of Bisland's cotton was ruined, but the insurance claim was settled by the following year.

From start to finish, Bisland and other planters depended upon the services and labor of a number of firms and individuals located in New Orleans. The dependence, of course, was reciprocal, with each party courting the good opinion of the other through the efficient consummation of their business. So long as most merchants in New Orleans acted primarily on their own account and largely as the agents of the planters, the possibility of contention was minimized. When the merchants learned that their bread was buttered more thickly by the overseas interests, or when the merchants in association in a banking venture utilized their position to serve only their own welfare, or practiced discrimination in the extension of loans, then a form of city-country strife was all but inevitable.

The matter was never quite so clear cut, of course. Ethnic animosities, the organization of political parties, and competing regional interests tended to blur urban and rural divisions—but never to wholly efface them. Besides, it was virtually impossible for planters and farmers in the Mississippi Valley to ship any other way than through New Orleans until the construction of the great canal and railroad systems between the Northeast and the Old Northwest. Merchants in New Orleans became fully aware of their strategic position in the early nineteenth century. The exploitation of all of these advantages by the business community of that city resulted in a perceptible shift in the urban-rural balance of power favorable to the urban interests. While the city might eternally bemoan the existence of a rurally dominated legislature, New Orleans slowly but surely achieved economic ascendance over the country. New steps in this direction were taken in the decade following the Louisiana Purchase.

14

The Problems of a Free Economy
1803–1812

N organizing the Territories of Louisiana and Orleans in 1805, the United States government incorporated a land mass of some 828,000 square miles stretching from the Mississippi to the Rocky Mountains. Although sparsely inhabited, with the white population clustered in small settlements south of the Missouri River and in the Lower Valley, the acquisition added a major urban center to the nation. In 1800 no more than half a dozen cities in the country were larger than New Orleans. By 1810 New Orleans was the largest city south of Baltimore and, with a population of 24,522, the fifth most populous city in the nation. In 1810 more than 25 percent of the population of the annexed area resided in the immediate vicinity of New Orleans. By 1820 30 percent of the population of the state resided in New Orleans and below the town.

At the time of the purchase, the population of Louisiana's capital was, in order of numerical importance, French Creole, Negro, and Anglo-American; and during the first decade of American control, the French and free Negro populations both experienced a greater accretion than did the American. Governor William C. C. Claiborne, as early as 1804, worried over the influx of French West Indians, their slaves, and free Negroes who were fleeing the disasters wrought in the islands by war, revolution, and bloody racial strife. Noting the arrival and anticipated arrival of several hundred West Indian emigrée families, Claiborne doubted if they were suitable settlers for Louisiana. A couple of thousand emigrées trickled in over the next few years until 1809 when the influx reached flood stage.

The era of revolution caught up with those French West Indians who had sought a Cuban sanctuary from its blows. Fleeing the chaos

that was descending upon the Spanish empire in America, thousands
of French exiles sought refuge in Louisiana. From May 12 to May
22, 1809, at least ten vessels arrived with emigrées and their slaves.
Claiborne, in early May, anticipated the arrival of 2,000 people from
Cuba within ten days and 6,000 within the month. Altogether some
5,700 arrived in the spring of 1809. The resources of the city were
sorely strained by the inflow. Rents and food prices rose quickly,
exhausting the finances of the newcomers in short order and augmenting the usual number of poor and distressed persons in town.
Although the city council established a welfare committee to aid
the refugees, to which the public donated funds, there was much
suffering before the homeless were finally settled.

This last injection of strength into the French population of Louisiana did little to assuage the occasionally tense relationship between
Americans and French Creoles, which erupted periodically in rioting between the two groups. The new government and especially
the private persons who flocked into the city were anxious to Amer-
icanize the community just as the Creoles were prepared to and did
resist these efforts fairly successfully. While some strident American
voices demanded that the English language and American practices
replace the French in the conduct of business, other voices complained that the new authorities terrorized the populace and depressed business. Governor Claiborne, as ranking official of the new
regime, was roundly criticized by both factions.

Ex-Prefect Laussat condemned American authorities for introducing their laws so rapidly and displaying definite partiality toward
the American residents in the administration of the law. Others commented on the enmity existing between the Creoles and the Americans which resulted in several fights and challenges and at one point
the closing of the public ballrooms. Opposition to Claiborne's administration continued among the Creole population during his
tenure in office as governor of both the territory and state of Louisiana. However, not all of the opposition originated in ethnocultural
differences. Many of Claiborne's opponents were Americans and not
all of these had been residents during the Spanish regime. Daniel
Clark, Jr., with whom the governor fought a duel in 1807, was one
of Claiborne's major antagonists. But relative newcomers like James

Brown, federal district attorney, and Edward Livingston also lined up against Claiborne. Brown criticized Claiborne for being so "true to the Republican maxim of Government by a Majority that he submits to it where foreigners compose that majority and . . . act in opposition to the most sacred principle of good policy and of the Constitution." [1]

Claiborne, damned by residents old and new, by French and Americans, acted with great forbearance and tolerance in presiding over Louisiana. As Secretary of the Treasury Albert Gallatin instructed the Collector of Customs at New Orleans to conciliate the minds of the inhabitants of Louisiana, so Claiborne attempted to win over the most influential of the older residents and soften the cultural shock of the transfer by administering the laws with moderation. Even though Claiborne occasionally expressed apprehension concerning the tranquility of the city, he tried to avoid engendering "that fearful and *Sullen Calm* which despotism produces . . . ." [2] Claiborne's earliest intentions of pursuing a nonpartisan approach to government were frustrated by his opponents and in 1812 he ran for governor and won as a factional leader. He had not avoided factions but their formation cut across ethnic lines or longevity of residence, a trend further promoted when organized parties came to Louisiana.

Nor did Claiborne guarantee tranquility—a term never quite descriptive of New Orleans, least of all during the first decade of

[1] James Brown to Henry Clay, February 26, 1810, in James A Padgett (ed.), "Letters of James Brown to Henry Clay, 1804–1835," *Louisiana Historical Quarterly*, XXIV (1941), 93. Brown was a United States Senator from Louisiana from 1813 to 1817 and 1819 to 1823 and served as Minister to France between 1823 and 1829. Livingston arrived in New Orleans from New York in 1804, became a prominent lawyer, the owner of two plantations, and United States Senator from Louisiana between 1829 and 1832.

[2] Claiborne to Madison, February 4, 1804, in Dunbar Rowland (ed.), *Official Letter Books of W. C. C. Claiborne, 1801–1816* (6 vols.; Jackson, Miss., 1917), I, 358–59. William B. Hatcher, *Edward Livingston: Jeffersonian Republican and Jacksonian Democrat* (Baton Rouge, 1940), 191–93, speaks erroneously of Claiborne's defeating the French faction of "ancient Louisianians" in 1812. Julien Poydras, who arrived in Louisiana in 1768, was a Claiborne supporter, as were Bernard Marigny, Étienne de Boré, and J. B. Thiery, editor of the *Louisiana Courier*. Livingston was the chief anti-Claiborne leader and, incidentally, far less of a Jeffersonian in principle than Claiborne. Interestingly, Marigny, wealthy planter, land speculator, local and state politician, and Democrat in the 1830s, became a Native American leader in the 1850s.

American control. Excitement, uproar, flux, boom and bust, disasters, disappointments, and achievements are the lyrics of New Orleans—from that heady day in December, 1803, when Claiborne and Wilkinson received Louisiana from a dejected Laussat to the organized riot between the Americans and English on Chantilly Field in 1815. The city could hardly expect calm with eight newspapers vying for the attention of the public in 1809, each promoting its own pet interest, supporting its friends, and villifying its enemies. The city council reacted indignantly to the opposition of the *Louisiana Gazette* and *Le Télégraphe* by denying them the public printing business. While the latter sheet extolled Louisiana's extent, climate, and products, and praised New Orleans for its location, transportation facilities, health, and economic opportunities, Claiborne complained of the spread of "disorderly houses" and the city council petitioned the territorial legislature for effective antigambling legislation. Every boat from the western country and the Atlantic states brought adventurers and settlers to New Orleans. S. Phillips, however, wished in 1808 that he were out of town for yellow fever was raging; and John Palfrey was reluctant to send his sons to New Orleans as trainees in a counting house because the city harbored such depravity that he was fearful their morals would be corrupted.

Human life, while not necessarily cheap in New Orleans, was frequently difficult to preserve from the violence of men and nature. Affairs of honor, chance encounters between testy armed men, and criminal elements produced numerous corpses. A Forstall might kill one man in a fight at Tremoulet's Coffee House in December, 1811, but thousands died in yellow fever epidemics in 1804, 1807, 1808, 1811, and 1813. In some of the epidemics, people died faster than they could be buried. Burial for many consisted of an unceremonious dumping into the Mississippi River while the church bells, intoning the occasion of a funeral, rang with such maddening and monotonous frequency that the city council passed an ordinance prohibiting the ringing of funeral bells between July 1 and December 31 of each year. Those deceased interred in the above-ground vaults were more than likely to suffer immersion when floodwaters poured into town following high water, as in 1811 and 1813, or during the devastating hurricane which struck on August 19 and 20,

1812. This great storm left bodies strewn along the levees, driftwood littering the public square, and the hulks of half-sunk vessels blocking the port.

All types of men came to New Orleans. A boatload of German artisans from Hamburg debarked in 1806. Irish-born Maunsel White, councilman, merchant, banker, railroad promoter, and proprietor of Deer Range Plantation in Plaquemines Parish, came to the city from Louisville, Kentucky. Samuel J. Peters, Connecticut-born son of a Massachusetts Loyalist left his mark as a local politician, bank president, and advocate of a public school system in New Orleans. Men of desperate fortunes likewise were drawn to the city. Among the latter, Aaron Burr and his projected expedition kept the town in a tizzy for several months in late 1806 and 1807 until his arrest at Natchez. During this crisis when no one knew Burr's intentions, when General Wilkinson—another man of questionable morality— and Governor Claiborne mobilized the armed forces of the territory to meet the invasion, an embargo was proclaimed on all commerce. Wilkinson arbitrarily arrested a number of men for opposing his unreasonable reaction to the Burr threat, and the business of the city ground to a halt. A year later, the troops were again parading in New Orleans, this time because hostilities with Spain were believed imminent. It was at just this moment that the West Indian refugees began to arrive.

The tongues at Fry's Coffee House never ceased wagging as one excitement followed another. A two-night battle on the levee occurred between American and foreign sailors in August, 1808; William Brown, successor in 1804 to yellow fever victim H. B. Trist as Collector of the Customs, married a La Branche in March, 1809, ran off with $150,000 in customs receipts in November, was captured and returned to New Orleans for trial in December, 1810. Whatever philosophic reflections on the state of matrimony this incident might have stimulated must have ceased abruptly a month later as news spread of a slave insurrection in St. John the Baptist Parish. Terrified planters fled to the city and drums rolled as federal troops and the entire city militia were mobilized against the several hundred insurgents. The troops repulsed the ragged band of Negroes some twenty-five miles above New Orleans. Those captured were summarily tried and executed in the Place d'Armes and their heads displayed on poles for the edification of the remainder of the servile population. The first decade of American rule closed with English cruisers hovering off the mouth of the Mississippi and the locals ever fearful of an English invasion.

Insofar as these occurrences impinged on the city of New Orleans, to that degree the city council assumed responsibility for formulating municipal policy toward them. Probably no other political institution in Louisiana received a greater buffeting during the first decade of American control than that body. Other than Governor Claiborne, who inherited all the powers of the Spanish governor and intendant when he assumed office, the city council was the only historic political body in the territory. Inheriting all the powers and responsibilities of the Cabildo, the council's duties were further defined by "An Act to Incorporate the City of New Orleans," passed by the legislative council in February, 1805. This act provided for the election of fourteen aldermen presided over by the recorder and a mayor, appointed by Governor Claiborne, who held a limited veto over council enactments.

The basic functions of the city council, while not radically different from those of the Cabildo, were complicated by the need to define relationships with other political bodies exercising some degree of authority in New Orleans. Chief among these, of course, was the government of the United States, but hardly less significant were the territorial and parish governments. These four political bodies, the United States government, the government of Orleans Territory (the state of Louisiana in 1812), the governing body of Orleans Parish, and the city council (the least autonomous of the four bodies) shared jurisdiction in New Orleans. Concurrently, the city fathers were confronted with the need to formulate relationships with private or quasi-public corporations operating in the city under charters granted by the territorial or state government. These aggregates of private capital occasionally acted with disregard for the public welfare of New Orleans, precipitating a clash with the guardian of the public welfare, the city council.

Critical to the evolution of the city council were the economically liberating promises and consequences of American sovereignty.

While the Spanish had acted leniently toward Louisiana in formulating economic policy, the regulation of economic and political affairs in New Orleans was a fact of life. Practically every legitimate commercial transaction fell under some regulation. Relative to the past, American sovereignty meant a free economy in New Orleans and the territory, making possible not only the chartering of private corporations but stimulating bakers, butchers, and others to attack the regulatory powers traditionally exercised by the city government. Buffeted by assaults by the butchers, the parish, the state, and the federal government, the city council was an institution in a state of seige during its first decade of existence.

As with the Cabildo, the economic impact of the council upon the city was basic and sustained. With the exception of the one improvement company which operated in the pre-1815 period, the city government was the only economic unit devoted to the creation of social overhead capital in the form of bridges, roads, port improvements, public market buildings, and the like. As the economy matured, other economic units shared this role but without diminishing the intrinsic significance of the capital inputs authorized and administered by the city government. Service demands upon the city government intensified as the population and territorial limits of the city expanded.[3] The ability of the city government to honor its obligations necessitated an equivalent increase in its annual revenue. Various groups, for different reasons, not only resisted the efforts of the city to expand its revenue base but also attacked the authority of the city to tax traditional sources of revenue. Involved in this campaign was the desire of special interests to escape taxation and circumvent the regulation implicit in certain revenue measures.

No sooner were the laws of the United States declared in force in New Orleans and the territorial government organized, than the municipal government was forced into a defensive stance relative to traditional revenues. The federal government possessed the sole authority to tax imports and to otherwise legislate regarding the trade and navigation of foreign nations with the United States. The Con-

[3] The Bernard Marigny plantation was subdivided and sold by Marigny in 1805 and, as the Faubourg Marigny, was added to New Orleans as the Eighth District in 1810. During the same year, the city of New Orleans purchased the Trémé plantation for purposes of subdivision and public sale.

stitution further prohibited the taxation of goods or shipping passing between the several states. Major sources of city revenue were threatened by these injunctions during a decade in which the revenue requirements of the city more than doubled. In 1811 the police department budget equaled the total city budget of 1804. The city imposed an anchorage tax, inherited from the French and Spanish governments, upon all vessels utilizing the port of New Orleans, with the income designated for the upkeep of the levees. Although this tax was validated by the city charter enacted in 1805, the Congress of the United States on at least two occasions, in 1811 and 1813, questioned its legality and the city council in both instances responded with long memorials justifying the impost. That crucial source of revenue was retained by the municipality and collected in spite of the frequent efforts of shipowners to evade payment. The city was less fortunate in its efforts to retain a tax on imported rum and tafia, also used for the maintenance of the levees and also inherited from the Cabildo.

Two dollars was assessed for each container of rum or tafia imported into the city and, in addition, the city collected taxes on mahogany, logwood, and other lumber unloaded on—and frequently causing damage to—the levees. Various interests in New Orleans, including tavern owners and importers of these goods, opposed the assessment as unconstitutional. The city attempted to lessen the opposition in 1807 by exempting rum and tafia manufactured in the United States. In 1808 Rezin D. Shepherd challenged the tax and was sustained by the courts which declared it unconstitutional. A portion of the lost revenue was recovered by amending the anchorage tax so as to impose an additional fee on vessels remaining in the harbor over two months, later changed to three months.

In initially prohibiting the council from taxing butchers, bakers, or the owners of public vehicles, the city charter itself contained the most immediate threat to the tax powers of the municipality. This decision was appealed in a petition to the legislative council pointing out that its effect would be to diminish the annual revenue of the city by $15,000 to $18,000. Taxation of the meat markets alone netted the city $10,300. An amendment to the charter in 1805 sanctioned the continued collection of these taxes and extended the authority again in 1806. This marked the beginning of a controversy between the city council and the bakers and butchers which lasted until 1816, involving not only the question of taxation but the power of the council to regulate the price and quality of bread and meat.

Defending its taxing powers by appealing both to the precedents of the Cabildo and its fiscal requirements, the city emphasized the public welfare in its plea for the authority to regulate the price, weight, and quality of meat. Not only were consumers charged exorbitant prices for meats of inferior quality but, the council argued, the "principle of liberty of commerce . . . sanctioned by this law seems in this instance to favor the greed of some individuals and to be prejudicial to the citizens . . . ." [4] With this power restored to the city, the butchers joined the bakers in an endeavor to abolish both the taxing and regulatory powers of the council over meat and bread.

The city waged a losing battle against the principle of free enterprise. Wily bakers failed to report all of the flour that they used, mixed good flour with bad, and utilized fraudulent weights in vending their products. According to the bakers' consumption reports, they were using no more flour in 1812 than in 1804. Frequently selling salted meats fit only for the river, the butchers at times acted in collusion to falsify the price paid for livestock which was the determining factor in fixing meat prices. City officials strove diligently to cope with the entrepreneurs but lacked the manpower to police the food market effectively. Spoiled goods were seized intermittently along with bread short of the standard weight, but the days of the fair price and regulated market place were numbered.

In 1813 the state legislature repealed the amendments to the city charter authorizing the tax on flour and ordered that, in regulating the assize of bread, the city allow a profit of $3.50, raised to $5 in 1814, on each barrel of flour baked. James Grymes, the city attorney, protested this action, maintaining that the charter was a contract susceptible to change only with the consent of the city. Unimpressed by such Jeffersonian logic, the legislature moved the whole way in

[4] City Council Session, June 26, 1805. [New Orleans] City Council, *Proceedings of Council Meetings, 1803–1814*, 5 vols. in French and English, I, No. 2, p. 60 (New Orleans Public Library).

1816 when it prohibited the city from fixing the sale price of any goods whatsoever. Although the city could still establish the market place for perishables and determine the method of inspection for all foodstuffs sold publicly, the basic powers to tax and regulate prices were lost and the fiscal condition of the city so precarious that proper inspection was all but impossible.

Even though the city council was composed mostly of local businessmen, it was not this source that threatened the powers of the city. One might assume that merchant-aldermen would faithfully represent the interests of the merchants of the community. If this is correct, it appears that the merchant community demonstrated a certain sensitivity for the public welfare in electing to the city council men who supported anchorage taxes and the like. If merchants turned aldermen suddenly discovered a public responsibility that ran counter to the private interests of their constituency, one would expect that such councilmen would be turned out in favor of men of different predilections. This did not happen. While the council drew its members from among the elite of the city, there is no evidence to warrant a charge that on such basic matters as the regulation of the food market the councilmen subordinated the public welfare to private interests.[5]

In their efforts to provide a revenue for the city, the merchant-councilmen were not averse to taxing themselves. A carriage tax for private vehicles was passed in 1805 supplementing previous taxes levied on commercial vehicles. A tax, affecting most merchants at one time or another, was placed on all goods stored on the levee or other public property. Taxes were instituted on slaves and real estate throughout the city. The tax on slaves was repealed in early 1812 and reinstituted in the same year as a result of the decline in revenue caused by the war, as well as by the expenses incurred in repairing the damage done by the August hurricane. Other sources were also tapped: a lottery was tried in 1805; the public markets were leased out; garbage collection was farmed out, as was the reve-

---

5 The merchant-aldermen represented the "establishment" and in petitioning the legislature to raise residency and property requirements for voters, indicated their desire to continue doing so. This reflects no intention to disregard the welfare of the community but rather a commitment to the concept of leadership by the elite— by those with a measurably significant economic stake in society.

nue from the tax on vessels using Bayou St. John; and all kinds of licenses were required to pursue various trades in the city. Few stones were left unturned in the quest to stabilize the fiscal condition of the municipality. But, as in the case of the bakers and butchers, the city ran into the obstruction of various interests. The tavernkeepers, in 1809, prompted by the antitax campaign of the bakers and butchers, petitioned the state legislature to obtain the reimbursement of taxes paid since 1805 and attempted unsuccessfully to obtain a court injunction to stop the collection of taxes. Some councilmen believed that a general conspiracy existed to disorganize and impoverish the municipal government.

It did appear that a subversive league between man and the elements would batter the city into insolvency. The city went to court against the tavern owners, R. D. Shepherd, and those, including Edward Livingston and Bertrand Gravier, who sought to establish their title to the batture fronting Faubourg St. Mary. This controversy, initiated in 1805, effectively tied up most of the batture in litigation until the 1850s and stripped the city of a valuable source of revenue. The Orleans Parish police jury joined in the "conspiracy" too. In 1807 that body informed the city that it considered the tax on rum and tafia as oppressive and unconstitutional. Between 1807 and 1814 the parish levied a tax on slaves living in New Orleans and attempted to restrict the boundary of New Orleans to the city proper and the faubourgs St. Mary, Marigny, and Trémé. Responsibility for the operation of the ferry service across the river was in dispute between the two bodies. In 1814 the city and the parish were engaged in a court fight over the ferry service and taxation.

These challenges to the city's tax powers combined with occasional floods, pestilence, and hurricanes to weaken the financial structure of the municipality. In June, 1811, the council was forced to retrench by laying off city employees of various kinds and reducing the salaries of others. New reductions in salaries and staff were ordered in January, 1813, as the war further reduced city revenues. By February the city treasury was empty—a condition lasting for the duration—and the city had recourse to a $4,000 loan from Alderman J. Lanna.

Challenges to the city's authority originated largely from rural interests ensconced in the parish and state governments. One facet of the conflict revolved around state revenue measures. In 1807 the apportionment of the lower house of the Louisiana legislature resulted in New Orleans receiving six seats of thirty-one, or 19 percent, while the city's tax share was set at 44 percent. In debates over the revenue bill of 1813, the Louisiana House of Representatives sought to shift a larger portion of the burden to personal property while the city's representatives wished to base taxes on land and slaves. The contest was, as one observor remarked, "fairly . . . between the City and the Country." [6] The rift widened in the years subsequent to the War of 1812.

The city council set itself firmly against dirt, pernicious odors, nasty habits, disease, noise, lawlessness, and other disturbing aspects of city life. Cockfights were prohibited, as was the beating of drums before and during an auction. General Wilkinson's troops were forbidden to use the levee as a latrine. Efforts were launched to inspect arriving vessels for contagious disease. Within the limits of a restrictive budget, the police force was continued, street lighting extended, a new building code passed, new fire fighting equipment obtained, roads and bridges passably maintained, and a new meat market constructed. When the St. Philip Street Theater, in 1808, presented a theatrical piece which Mayor James Mather considered obscene and damaging to public morality, the council passed an ordinance, extended in 1816, requiring theater managers to submit all plays to the mayor for approbation.

Few phases of community life escaped the intervention of the city government. Perhaps excessively paternalistic, the council legislated in some areas normally impervious to legislative control and in others without the staff or facilities to assure effective enforcement. While it was quite proper for the council to concern itself with the lessening of congestion along the levee or to prevent the storage of dangerous combustibles in wooden shacks within the city limits, it was perhaps improper to interfere with the religious ritual of a funeral or to use the mayor as a literary censor. But in all cases, enactment was one thing and enforcement quite another. Revenue was the problem.

[6] John D. Smith to John Minor, March 21, 1813, in William J. Minor and Family Papers, 1779–1830 (Louisiana State University Department of Archives).

In certain areas within the legitimate bailiwick of the council, the city availed itself of the presence of the new corporations to provide services for the community which the council was unable to finance. In doing so, the city authorities sought to establish a viable balance between the public welfare and the profit motive of the corporations. In essence, the city council came to view itself as the arbiter between public and private interests. The evolution of this role was complicated by the newness of the relationship and by the fact that the corporations owed their legal existence to the state legislature. But perhaps an even more crucial complication was the composition of the city council during the formative period of the relationship.

Between 1804 and 1812 eight chartered corporations operated in New Orleans, including the New Orleans branch of the First Bank of the United States. There were three other banks—the Bank of Louisiana, chartered in 1804; the Bank of Orleans, 1811; and the Louisiana Planter's Bank, 1811. The remaining corporations were the New Orleans Insurance Company, 1805; the New Orleans Navigation Company, 1805; the New Orleans Water Company, 1811; and the Mississippi Steamboat Navigation Company, 1812. Of these corporations, each important to the business life of the community, the navigation company and the water company were of particular importance to the corporation of New Orleans. Because of the public nature of their proposed services, close cooperation was essential between them and the city.

An analysis of 77 councilmen who served at least one year on the council between 1805 and 1814 inclusive reveals that 28 held directorships in one or more of the private corporations during those years. Of those 28, 23 held those positions while serving on the city council. The number of directorships held during the period by each of the 23 in addition to membership on the city council is shown in Table VI.[7] Service on all boards was legally impossible because the charter of the Bank of the United States prohibited its directors from serving concurrently as the director of another bank. Nonetheless, several of the aldermen managed to do almost as well. Samuel Win-

---

[7] I believe that the figure 77 includes most, if not all, of the aldermen who served during this period. The steamboat company and the water company are not included in this survey.

TABLE VI

List of Individuals Serving Concurrently for at Least One Year as a Councilman and Director and the Number of Such Positions Held from 1804 to 1814

	1804	1805	1806	1807	1808	1809	1810	1811	1812	1813	1814
Evan Jones	3										
James Carrick	1	2	1-	1-	1-						
Samuel Winter	1	2	3	4	3	1-	1-	1-			
James Pitot	1	3	2-	2-	3-	3-	3-	2-	2-	2-	
John Watkins	2	2	2	2							
Joseph Faurie		1	2	3							
Francis Duplessis		2	2		2	2	2	2-	2-	2-	1-
Col. Bellechaise		1						1-	1	1-	
Thomas Harmon		3					3	1			
John McDonogh		2	1-	2	1-						
Louis Blanc		1	2	2							
James Mather	1-	1-	1	1	2	2	2	1	1-	1-	
Benjamin Morgan	1-	3-	4	4	4	4	3	3	1-	1-	
J. F. Livaudais			1-	1-	1-	1-	2	1-	1-	1-	
J. Blanque							2	3	3	2	1
L. S. Fontaine								2			
Richard Relf			1-	2-	3-	3-	4	2	1-	1-	1-
Joseph Soulé		1-	1-	2-	1-	1-	2	2	1-	1-	1-
P. F. DuBourg		1-	1-	1-	1-	1-	3	1-	1-	1-	2
Paul Lanusse	1-	2-	3-	3-	2-	2-	2-	1-	2	2	2
Joseph McNeil		1-	2-	2-	2-	2-	2-	2-	3	3	3
Nicholas Girod					2-	2-	2-	2-	3	3	3
J. Bte. Dejan, Jr.				1-	2-	2-	1-	1-	2	2	1-

Key: The figure followed by a dash indicates service only as a director during that year.

TABLE VII

Number of Councilmen Serving Concurrently as Directors of Various Corporations in New Orleans, 1804–15

Corporation	1804	1805	1806	1807	1808	1809	1810	1811	1812	1813	1814	1815
Bank of Louisiana	1	5	2	3	2	2	5	3	4	4	2	2
New Orleans Navigation Company			5	5	3	2	5	–[a]	–	–	–	–
New Orleans Insurance Company		3	2	2	1	1	4	0	1	1	1	1
First Bank of the United States, New Orleans Branch		0	1	1	1	1	1	1	Charter expired			
Bank of Orleans								1	1	1	–	–
Louisiana Planter's Bank								0	0	0	–	–

[a] No information available

ter, a merchant of New Orleans at the time of the transfer, was a member of the city council from 1804 to 1808 and in 1807 on the board of directors of the Louisiana Bank, the New Orleans Navigation Company, and the New Orleans Insurance Company. In addition, he served in the state Senate and as an anti-Claiborne delegate to the Constitutional Convention in 1812. Winter died in 1813. Richard Relf served on the same boards as Winter from 1808 to 1810, as well as belonging to the council. He died in 1857 at 82 years of age. Benjamin Morgan was a third business activist. A long-time resident of Louisiana, Morgan was appointed by Claiborne to the legislative council in 1804, was an alderman from 1806 to 1811, and from 1806 to 1809 served as a director of the navigation company, the insurance company, and the branch Bank of the United States. Morgan presided over the liquidation of the branch bank in 1811 and returned as president of the New Orleans branch of the Second Bank of the United States in 1816. He died in 1826.

Almost 30 percent of the councilmen serving between 1805 and 1814 were simultaneously the directors of one or more corporations. This high coincidence of political and corporate service is accentuated if stated in another way. A total of 122 directors guided the six corporations during the ten-year period. These 122 positions were filled by 74 individuals. Of the 74 men holding directorates, 23, or 31 percent, were concurrently city councilmen. The number of councilmen filling directorate positions between 1805 and 1815 is indicated in Table VII. This should make apparent the potential influence which the corporations enjoyed in the city government. Three of the corporations were in an especially favorable position to exert influence in the municipal government: the Bank of Louisiana, the navigation company, and the insurance company.

Between 1805 and 1817, 31 men served as directors of the Bank of Louisiana for at least one year. During that interval, 17 directors were city councilmen for at least one year of whom 14 served concurrently. During the same period, 21 men served as directors of the New Orleans Insurance Company with 10 sitting at least one year on the city council, while 7 men held both positions concurrently. Between 1806 and 1810, 21 men served on the board of the New Orleans Navigation Company, of whom 13 served at least one year on the council, with 12 serving concurrently as directors and aldermen. The three corporations were guided by 63 directors during the five years 1806 to 1810, the positions being filled by 39 men. Of the latter, 21, or 54 percent, were councilmen.

Although the incidence of concurrent service is sufficiently high to justify speaking of potential influence and potential conflicts of interest, the actual import of the correlation is conjectural. Many councilmen were directors of the Bank of Louisiana and the bank loaned money to the city council on at least one occasion—$10,000 in 1808. But it was the only "home-owned" bank in Louisiana at the time. It was not until 1811, after a destructive fire the previous year, that the council decided to move city funds from the frame house of the treasurer to one of the city's banks. There is no evidence that the Bank of Louisiana, through its director-councilmen, exerted any pressure on the city government in favor of this or that policy. In 1815 the poverty of the treasury prompted the council to initiate negotiations with both the Bank of Orleans and the Louisiana Planter's Bank relative to a loan to the municipality. Potential influence was also possessed by the New Orleans Insurance Company, but there is no evidence of its use.

The relationship between the navigation company and the city was direct, long lasting, and frequently less than amicable. The corporation was chartered in 1805 for the purpose of providing a system of navigable waters from Atakapas and Opelousas to the Mississippi and to open up water communication between Lake Pontchartrain and the Mississippi. Cost factors quickly determined that the latter objective become the sole concern of the company and the state legislature restricted the company to its privileges in New Orleans in laws passed in 1809 and 1814.

In New Orleans, the company was committed to the improvement of navigation in Bayou St. John, restoration of the Carondelet Canal to navigation, and linkage of this system to the Mississippi River. Governor Carondelet began construction of the canal and basin in 1794, but it was not maintained after his departure. By 1803 the canal, useless except for very small craft, was an open sewer running the width of the city. Beginning its work in 1806 with the letting of contracts for clearing the mouth of Bayou St. John, the company constructed dikes at the mouth and then moved slowly up the bayou to the Carondelet Canal. The war interrupted construction, but by 1816 navigation was opened between the basin and Lake Pontchartrain and plans were ready to extend the canal to the Mississippi.

Throughout most of the prewar period, the company was harassed by the state legislature for ignoring its charter obligations along Bayous Plaquemines and Lafourche.[8] Moreover, the city of New Orleans and the navigation company engaged in a lengthy dispute over a number of matters which retarded construction and damaged the interests of both corporations. Although the city was a major stockholder in the company—as was the Bank of Louisiana—it had no official representative on the company's board of directors. Nonetheless, as a glance at Table VII indicates, the company and the city were well represented, unofficially, in each other's councils. Table VIII marks the precise years in which the various directors of the company served and their terms, if any, on the city council.[9]

Although strife seemed to typify the relationship between the two institutions, cooperation was not altogether absent. The city recognized the usefulness of the company's projects and in 1807 willingly ceded free of charge as much of its commons as the company required to lengthen the Carondelet Canal from the basin to the Mississippi. A joint committee of the city council and the company agreed upon the proposed route. But accord between the two soon evaporated in disputes that stemmed from the juxtaposition of certain city prerogatives with the charter privileges of the company. On the one hand, work on Bayou St. John and the Carondelet Canal interfered with the city sewerage system and, on the other, the historic right of the city to collect certain tolls on the bayou was threatened.

Company work stopped up the sewerage system—open ditches

---

[8] The company defended itself against charges of negligence in an "Exposition on the Conduct of the Board of Directors of the Orleans Navigation Company," in New Orleans *Louisiana Gazette*, March 24, 1809.

[9] The Bank of Louisiana owned 100 shares in the navigation company. Of indeterminate importance, then, is the fact that four men, Joseph Faurie, Richard Relf, Samuel Winter, and James Pitot, were simultaneously members of the board of the bank and the navigation company, as well as being aldermen. Pitot was Mayor of New Orleans in 1805 and president of the navigation company.

TABLE VIII

Directors of the New Orleans Navigation Company and Their Years of Service, Terms on the City Council, and Service on Any Other Board of Directors, 1805–14

	1805	1806	1807	1808	1809	1810	1811	1812	1813
Louis Blanc	C	CD	CD						
Joseph Faurie	C	CD	CDX						
W. H. Montgomery		D							
William Kenner	X	DX	DX	DX	DX	DX	X	X	X
Paul Lanusse	X	DX	DX	DX	DX	DX	X	C X	C X
Joseph McNeil	X	DX	DX	DX	DX	DX	X	C X	C X
Benjamin Morgan	X	CDX	CDX	CDX	CDX	C X	C X	X	X
Richard Relf		D	DX	DX	DX	CDX	C X	X	X
Thos. Urquhart	X	DX	DX	DX	DX	DX	X	X	X
John Watkins	C	CD	CD						
Samuel Winter	C X	CDX	CDX	CDX	X	X			
Stephen Zacharie	X	DX	X						
James Pitot	CDX	DX	DX	DX	DX	DX	DX	X	X
Rene de la Rue				D	D	D			
P. Madan				D					
James Mather		C	C	CD	CD	CD	C		
George Pollock				DX					
Joseph Tricou	X	X	X	DX	DX	DX	X		
P. F. DuBourg	X	X	X	DX	X	CDX	X		
Thomas Harmon	C X	X				CDX	C	X	X
L. S. Fontaine						CD	CD		

Key: C ... City Council
D ... Board of Directors, New Orleans Navigation Company
X ... Service on any other board of directors

draining into the canal—in 1806 and intermittently through 1810, at which time James Pitot, president of the navigation company, informed the council that work on the Carondelet Canal required a change in the drainage ditches of the city. A company offer to construct new ditches at its expense was rejected as inadequate by the council, which then lectured the company for its use of specious pretexts for delaying the work. A resolution to that effect was passed 8 to 1, the lone dissenter being Benjamin Morgan, one of the two navigation company directors on the city council after the election of 1809. Several months later, in December, 1810, the company proposed the appointment of a joint committee to iron out difficulties, naming Thomas Urquhart, then Speaker of the Louisiana House of Representatives, Paul Lanusse, and Richard Relf to meet with the council. This proposal followed a city election in which P. F. Du Bourg, Richard Relf, Thomas Harmon, and L. S. Fontaine—all directors of the company—won seats on the city council. These four joined with Morgan to vote 5 to 4 in favor of a conference committee. This decision was tested in May, 1811, and confirmed. Again the councilmen-directors supported the committee. An agreement was worked out in the same month.

In this instance, the company packed the council and steamrollered through a favorable settlement. Moreover, while the city council was lecturing in 1810, the company initiated a court suit—not for the first time—to prevent the city from removing obstructions to the drainage ditches. Following a decision in the Superior Court of Louisiana in 1812 favorable to the company, the city approached the corporation to form another conference committee only to find that the company had raised its terms. Whereas the company had offered to replace the drainage ditches at its expense, it now informed the city fathers that New Orleans must pay half of the expenses for digging and bear the whole cost of maintenance. The court decision compelled city acquiescence. Private interests were victorious over the public welfare.

City authority sustained still another setback, more immediately critical because it involved the revenue of the municipality. The charter of the company made provision for a company-levied toll on vessels using Bayou St. John when a connection between the lake and river was completed. But in October, 1809, long before the junction was made, the company announced the levying of a toll on every vessel entering the bayou from the lake. A city toll, levied since 1797 on each vessel entering the bayou and farmed out between 1803 and 1809, supported the roads paralleling and the four bridges crossing the bayou and basin. In 1808 the legislature authorized the city to construct a new toll bridge over the bayou but the company moved to prevent the construction of the bridge.

A court injunction was obtained by the company in 1809 stopping work on the drawbridge. Six months later, in January, 1810, the injunction remained in force and it was lifted only in February, allowing the resumption of work on the bridge which was completed within a few months. The issue of the toll now came to the fore as the city charged a fee for vessels requiring the raising of the bridge. In association with the navigators of the bayou, the navigation company went to court again in 1810 and a series of decisions adverse to the city culminated in an order of the Louisiana Supreme Court, in 1814, forbidding the imposition of the tax and ordering the refund of all tolls. Small compensation was gained by the city through the levying of a toll on horses and wagons crossing the bridge.

Earlier in the controversy, a partisan of the navigation company attacked the city government in the press for its neglect of the Carondelet Canal, "that unwholesome morass" from which poisonous air emanated to endanger the public health. Charging the city with untenable obstructionism, the writer condemned the city's position as rooted in selfish personal interests. That personal interests were involved is likely, but one wonders which master they served. The company was well equipped to protect its interests within the council chamber. In disputes between the private and public interest, the courts of the era, not only in New Orleans but elsewhere in the United States, frequently handed down decisions favorable to the interests of private capital. Certainly this was the case in New Orleans.

Once challenged in the courts, the city was generally unsuccessful in defending its traditional prerogatives. In contests over taxation, regulatory powers, rights of way, and municipal properties, the city suffered a series of judicial defeats which produced a crisis in the fiscal affairs of the municipality. In the conflict with Daniel Clark—originating in the Spanish period—over his rope walk which, lying astride Chartres and Royal streets, obstructed the extension of those streets into the Faubourg St. Mary, the city was virtually blackmailed by Clark. He demanded a $20,000-indemnity for permission to open the streets through his property. The city went to court. The court fixed the compensation for the lots at $20,000. Nor was the city notably successful in seeking to enforce its building code in the courts even when the case involved obvious fire hazards.

Both the courts and the state legislature were hostile toward the municipality more often than not and the parish was a constant irritant. Butchers, bakers, tavernkeepers, flatboat owners, the navigation company, Daniel Clark, and Edward Livingston kept city attorneys like James Grymes constantly at work on legal briefs defending the authority of the city. These confrontations were not entirely without benefit to the city. The corporation learned from these experiences, especially those involving the navigation company, the expediency of an explicit protection of its interests in negotiating contracts with improvement corporations.

In 1806 Mayor John Watkins initiated an effort to secure a permanent and adequate water supply for New Orleans. Mayor Watkins wrote Julien Poydras, serving as territorial delegate to the United States House of Representatives, asking him to contact B. H. Latrobe on the matter. Latrobe, then a federal surveyor, had completed a water supply system for Philadelphia in 1799. He presented the outline of a charter to the city council in 1810 which he intended to submit to the state legislature. A charter organizing the New Orleans Water Company was granted in 1811. Negotiations between the city and the water company continued through 1812.

The agreement between the two parties granted the water company the exclusive privilege of furnishing the city and suburbs with water for fifteen years. Everything possible of definition was spelled out in the contract. When Latrobe suggested that the city subscribe to shares in the company, the council agreed on the condition that the mayor of New Orleans serve as one of the company's directors so long as the city retained ownership of any stock. Latrobe agreed to this stipulation. Areas of possible altercation between the contracting parties were narrowed as much as possible and the city secured official representation on the company board.

According to one boomer, the age ushered in by American possession heralded the transformation of New Orleans into "the new Alexandria of America." [10] For the municipality, the experience was unsettling. The Louisiana Purchase placed New Orleans and its hinterlands under one sovereignty and yet several sovereign bodies exercised and pretended to exercise authority in the community. The lowering and removal of economic barriers; the establishment of representative, not to be confused with democratic, government; the application of United States laws and procedures such as the appellate court system and jury trials; the arrival of the fourth estate in force—all these developments fostered the birth of a host of interests and provided forums from which they struck out on their own behalf. The New Orleans Typographical Society enjoyed a good brew at the Eagle Tavern while promoting its interests. New Orleans mechanics lashed out at the Louisiana Senate for its failure to pass an act incorporating a mechanic's benevolent society. Shipbuilders in front of the meat market ignored a series of orders to move. Saloon owners and food handlers hired lawyers to dispute city authority. The navigation company blocked the sewers and packed the council. The United States compelled the city to move its ferry. Confusion and dissension penetrated the city hall when the city council petitioned Governor Claiborne to remove Mayor James Mather from his office. Among other faults, Mather had prudently fled during an epidemic.

The city government of New Orleans experienced great frustration in searching for its proper role and sphere of authority. [11] Events

[10] New Orleans *Louisiana Gazette and New Orleans Advertiser*, January 26, 1813.
[11] Sam Bass Warner, Jr., *The Private City: Philadelphia in Three Periods of Its Growth* (Philadelphia, 1968), which has recently come to my attention, describes the American city as a community of private moneymakers and its dominant ideology as privatism. As privatism was manifested in Philadelphia in the late eighteenth century, it assumed a happy compatibility between private goals and the public welfare. Yet, as Warner demonstrates, privatism prevented the city from taking necessary steps to protect the public welfare against food shortages and inflation in 1778–79. The municipality was unable to reallocate scarce resources among the most needy groups. "The popular goal of Philadelphia was the individual race for wealth," untempered by a communitarian tradition. The ideology

leading to American belligerency and the War of 1812 only worsened an already precarious position. Political and economic freedom and the expansion of opportunity created difficulties as well as benefits. The Spanish government could solve problems arbitrarily, without recourse to public opinion. While the Spanish governors were generally sensitive to the commercial and financial needs of the city, they did not have to be. Local Spanish officials could take independent action knowing that a reprimand was months away. The corporation of New Orleans enjoyed no such luxury. Larger sovereignties pressed against the city at all times while smaller interests resisted its authority and rural groups resented its economic power. New Orleans, serving an ever-expanding hinterland and fragmented into a random collection of organized and unorganized vested interests, learned in the first decade of American rule that it could not unilaterally define its ecomonic role. The community had still to learn the secret of binding into a stable whole its diverse and swirling atomistic parts. Such an alchemy still remained undiscovered when Louisiana left the Union in January, 1861.

---

of privatism, as this chapter points out, came to New Orleans along with the American flag and confronted and vanquished a communitarian and paternalistic urban tradition. Perhaps the most remarkable aspect of this struggle was the ease with which privatism became ascendant.

15

New Orleans As an Entrepot

NEW ORLEANS' role as a staple port, defined by the French who were unable to exploit its potential, evolved slowly under Spain until after the War of American Independence. Settlement then spread into those natural hinterlands of New Orleans hitherto inhabited only by Indians and fur traders. By 1803 villages and outlying farms dotted the valleys of rivers emptying into both banks of the Ohio River, providing New Orleans with increasingly significant portions of her staple exports and a beckoning market for imported products. East and west of the Mississippi and south of Natchez, the old artificial hinterland received a steady influx of settlers and slaves, with movement into this area gaining momentum as a result of Pinckney's treaty and the organization of Mississippi Territory.

The impact upon New Orleans of these developments, coinciding with a revolution in agriculture in which sugar and cotton replaced indigo and tobacco as the cash crops of the lower valley, was magnified by the belligerent status of Spain after 1793. Spanish participation in the wars against France thwarted the gradual assimilation of Louisiana into the Spanish Empire. To prevent the ruin of the colony, Spain permitted and occasionally legally sanctioned a commerce which drew New Orleans and its hinterlands irreversibly into the orbit of American economic control. The Louisiana Purchase completed this process.

In New Orleans, the United States received a farm town—larger than most in the nation—geared to the service of a back country sprawling north as far as Pittsburgh; a town whose primary function was to receive and ship the produce of farm and plantation. James

Sterrett, merchant and former captain in the United States Army, expressed this relationship in 1809, writing to a friend that "the fact is cotton is the sinews of bussiness [*sic*] here, and its relaxed situation is felt in all kinds of bussiness." [1] Even at this early date, cotton was basic to the prosperity of New Orleans, its importance shared by western staples and to a lesser degree by sugar.

Sterrett, in linking the prosperity of the river city with its agricultural hinterland, was more perceptive than the city's boomers who assumed that the geographical position of New Orleans guaranteed a commercial preeminence based upon the growth of upriver dependencies. In any event, prosperity did not come easily to New Orleans during the first decade of American rule, for a host of malevolent outside forces threatened the vaulting commercial ambitions of the town.

A year after Nathaniel Coxe came to New Orleans from Kentucky to survey the prospects for establishing a business, he informed his Kentucky partner that "we are doing . . . as well as our most sanguine hope could wish both in the commission business and at the Rope Walk." He anticipated, in June, 1807, a net profit of some $9,000 from both enterprises. In the following month, news of the *Chesapeake-Leopard* Affair shocked the city and at the beginning of the new year news of a total embargo on overseas shipping reached the town. Coxe's business, as well as many others, went into a spin. In September, 1809, a downcast Coxe summed up the misfortunes of many in a letter back to Kentucky. "If there had been no failures in N. O. no frays with the Chesapeake—no Embargo no non-intercourse no Burr, no Wilkerson [*sic*] no Proclamations," he wrote ruefully, "and in short if the usual commercial arrangements had been continued between the United States and Europe my calculations might in some measure [have] been reallized [*sic*]." [2]

Although the calculations of many a New Orleans businessman were thrown askew by uncontrollable political events, the role of the city in moving the staple crops experienced a further refinement

[1] James Sterrett to Nathaniel Evans, July 22, 1809, in Nathaniel Evans and Family Papers, 1791–1932 (Louisiana State University Department of Archives).

[2] Letters of Nathaniel Coxe to Gabriel Lewis, November 23, 1806, June 15, 1807, September 15, 1809, in Coxe-Lewis Letters (Typescript in Tulane University Library, Manuscript Division).

during the decade and the total business conducted at the port rose sharply over the peak years of the late Spanish period. More goods, services, shipping, consumers, capital—more of everything necessary to handle the commerce of the lush Mississippi Valley—appeared in New Orleans between 1803 and 1812. The one desideratum absent was security from the aggression of the warring European powers. American neturality went unrespected by the naval forces of the belligerents, while the policies of neutrality pursued by successive administrations distressed many merchants almost as sorely as the martime depredations of the belligerents. The decade, then, was not without the confusion, uncertainty, and danger normally attending a world at war. Before it was all over, the danger pressed against the very gates of New Orleans.

In the midst of political crises and international tensions, the forms of business at New Orleans were partially Americanized both in legal structure and rules of conduct. Courts were established by Governor Claiborne to handle disputes arising from commercial transactions. Between 1805 and 1808 legislation concerning debtors was enacted which tightened up procedures in favor of the creditors. Acts were passed dealing with letters of exchange returned unpaid and formally protested. Auctioneers were closely regulated by territorial laws. Banks, an insurance company, and an internal improvements company were chartered. Merchants in New Orleans organized a Chamber of Commerce which adopted a tariff of commercial charges, set storage rates, established the tare to be allowed for various goods, and took other actions which further standardized routine business procedures. The city of New Orleans, as we have seen, also acted to accommodate itself to increased business activity and to define its proper sphere of influence. Growth necessitated these and other efforts to introduce minimal conformity into the business life of the town.

Growth derived in part from the Upper Valley which sent a constantly increasing quantity of flour, provisions, and other farm products downriver to New Orleans. Precise measurement of this traffic is impossible before 1815–20, but various estimates as to quantity and value have been made and figures are available for the period 1814–15 to 1816–17. The value of receipts from the Upper Valley increased from about $1.5 million annually between 1801 and 1803 to $3 million in 1807, and $5 million in 1816. Flour was the most important single item in this trade, followed by corn and its derivatives—pork and pork products, lard, tallow, and whiskey. Flour receipts, averaging some 40,000 to 50,000 barrels annually between 1803 and 1807, declined between 1808 and 1814 but then rose to 75,000 barrels in 1815 and 98,000 in 1816. Receipts of provisions also rose rapidly during the first years of peace.

Western Pennsylvania, southeastern Ohio, and Kentucky supplied most of the western goods while communities situated on the Ohio served as forwarding points in the upriver trade of New Orleans. Pittsburgh was preeminent in the early years of the nineteenth century but lost her position to Cincinnati and Louisville after 1815. Merchants in New Orleans cultivated close associations with their upriver counterparts. Indeed, some—John Clay, Nathaniel Coxe, and Maunsel White—came down from the West to establish themselves in the front rank of those dealing in western produce.

Travelers on the Mississippi invariably mentioned—if they did not count—the heavy downstream river traffic. Hundreds and eventually thousands of flats, barges, and keels rode the current each season to New Orleans. There is no question that the produce arrived on these river craft, but there is some problem as to the mechanics of the trade. Did the producers bring their own goods to New Orleans on their own craft or on a craft leased by them with the goods in the hands of the owner acting as the producer's agent? Or did producers generally sell their crops to local merchants who then assumed responsiblity for transporting the goods to New Orleans for sale or shipment? Did the western merchants who purchased locally maintain responsibility for the ultimate disposition of the goods, or did they generally sell the goods to merchants in New Orleans who then handled final sales and shipments? And, last, what arrangements did merchants in New Orleans make in bringing the trade to its conclusion?

All of the above procedures were followed to some extent. Facilities existed for western farmers to sell or barter their crops to produce and general merchants in the first stages of settlement. It was obviously more convenient for the farmer to sell locally than to spend three or four months personally marketing his crop in Natchez or New Orleans. Thus, while many farmers accompanied their crops to market, many others exchanged their produce for supplies with local country merchants who then marketed the produce elsewhere. It appears, moreover, that the barter business of country merchants evolved into the forwarding and commission merchant business at an earlier date than generally believed and that firm connections were quickly established with produce merchants in New Orleans.[3]

In New Orleans, Shepherd, Brown, and Company, Maunsel White and Company, Kenner and Henderson, and Bartlett and Coxe were among the firms that engaged heavily in the western trade. Shepherd, Brown, and Company, sold on commission for firms in Mayslick, Lexington, Pittsburgh, and Cincinnati. J. and M. Nimmo of Cincinnati, in 1804, contracted for pork and wheat with farmers in the Miami River Valley and forwarded these goods on contract to Shepherd, Brown, and Company. In this case, the Cincinnati merchants received a price for the shipment agreed upon before the goods were obtained. In most cases, the Nimmos gathered produce in Ohio and forwarded the cargoes on consignment to Shepherd, Brown, and Company, which then sold the goods for cash if possible but on as long a credit as three months if necessary, remitting the proceeds to houses in Baltimore and Philadelphia to whom the Nimmos were obligated. Other produce merchants in New Orleans followed this general pattern in their transactions with the Upper Valley.

The flow of goods was overwhelmingly from north to south in the period prior to the advent of regular upriver steamboat traffic. Some students estimate the value of the export trade of New Orleans to the Upper Mississippi Valley to be worth no more than 10 percent of New Orleans receipts from that region. This is probably accurate before 1803, but between 1803 and 1815 the proportionate value of the upriver trade to the total interior trade of New Orleans probably increased. Louisville reported receipts from New Orleans

[3] John G. Clark, *The Grain Trade in the Old Northwest* (Urbana, 1966), 41–43, speaks incorrectly of these developments as advancing through clearly defined stages from the simple to the more complex. Actually, there are elements of all stages present in the early 1800s.

between April 18 and July 18, 1814, valued at $266,000. While the source of most of these goods remained the Atlantic coast, the route changed and New Orleans became a major forwarding center in the shipment of manufactured goods from the East to the West. In this early period, the preponderant flow of goods from north to south and from east to west determined that sources of domestic credit for the movement of the goods would originate in the Northeast, passing through the Northwest to New Orleans.

While Shepherd, Brown, and Company only infrequently advanced credits to merchants in the Upper Valley or allowed them to draw letters of exchange in advance of sales at New Orleans, upriver merchants frequently sold their goods on credit to merchants of New Orleans and purchased manufactured goods on credit from eastern firms. Morrison, Boswells, and Sutton of Lexington, Kentucky, utilized Tabor and Field of St. Francisville and Bartlett and Coxe of New Orleans to make collections for goods sold on credit to planters and merchants in the Lower Valley. Bartlett and Coxe handled all the remittances, but they were made through Philadelphia in cotton or notes rather than being sent upriver in goods purchased at New Orleans. The absence or inadequacy of an upriver flow of credit worked to the ultimate disadvantage of New Orleans. Although the costs of available transportation in the precanal and prerailroad eras compelled westerners to ship via New Orleans, traditional patterns of credit determined that a competition between eastern cities and New Orleans for the produce of the Old Northwest would be decided in favor of the East.

The procedures described above used in moving western commodities underwent little change until major improvements occurred in the transportation system of the nation. Relationships between upriver and New Orleans merchants involved mostly a north–south flow of goods and credits. The risks of river and overseas shipment were shouldered largely by upriver or eastern commercial houses. Various commissions for services rendered accrued to merchants in New Orleans but the profits from sales were pocketed elsewhere. More complex were the procedures designed to move southern staples into and out of New Orleans.

Staple exports from New Orleans, reflecting production increases in the Lower Valley, rose from 18,000 bales of cotton and more than 5,000 hogsheads of sugar in 1802 to nearly 42,000 bales of cotton and 10,000 hogsheads of sugar (plus molasses and tafia) in 1810. In the three years 1815–17 cotton exports reached an annual average of 63,000 bales while sugar exports advanced from 12,000 hogsheads in 1815 to 20,000 in 1817. Staple exports in 1810 approached $3 million and with the extremely high prices of the immediate postwar period exceeded $7.5 million in 1817.

Connections between the merchants in New Orleans who moved the thousands of tons of staples and the producers were necessarily closer than that developed in the western trade. Planters were normally supplied from New Orleans and tapped the credit resources of the city both for moving the crops and operating capital. Merchants performed a wide variety of services for the planters and with increasing frequency took over the entire process of marketing the crops and provisioning the plantation. George Morgan probably went beyond the norm in his relationship with David Rees, a planter in Atakapas. Morgan not only handled Rees's crops but the latter's mistress as well, intervening in one lovers' quarrel to prevent the angry woman from bringing suit against Rees. Morgan advised Rees to "negotiate better" in these matters. Charges for such services were not listed in the Chamber of Commerce tariff.[4]

Most planters preferred to sell their staples as close to the point of production as possible. John Bisland informed two Scottish merchants soliciting his cotton that he thought it advisable to dispose of his crops in Natchez or New Orleans for cash, thus avoiding the risks of shipping on consignment. But few planters, including Bisland, were consistently able to sell locally in the pre-Ghent period because the overseas cotton manufacturers and merchants were not yet in the habit of making direct purchases in the New Orleans market. A few overseas firms did, however, maintain agents in New Orleans. James and Alexander Denistoun of Glasgow retained T. and D. Urquhart, a New Orleans house; Green and Wainwright of Liverpool retained Chew and Relf; and Chandler Price of Philadelphia worked through Shepherd, Brown, and Company. Agents in New Orleans functioned largely to keep accounts straight between

4 David Rees Papers, 1804–1965 (Tulane University Library, Manuscript Division).

the overseas firm and the planter and to expedite the shipment of staples to the former and manufactured goods to the latter. Bisland's cotton reached A. and J. Denistoun via the Urquhart firm, which also received money payments from Bisland to be credited to his account in Glasgow.

It was not necessary, of course, for the planter to ship his crops through the agent of the overseas customer. Planters chose their own agents in New Orleans just as did the overseas firms. Merchants in the city received staples from and forwarded supplies to any number of planters, and planters frequently divided their crop among several mercantile houses. It was more convenient, however, for planters to commit their crops to the care of a single firm and for that firm to maintain especially close contact with a particular firm or two in the ports that received the staples. The longevity of the relationships was determined by the mutual satisfaction of one party with the performance of the other.

Staple merchants in New Orleans sold goods for planters; made remittances from such sales in cash, bills, or goods; shipped goods on consignment; provided storage, drayage, additional packaging services; and procured shipping for the staples. These were the normal services for which planters paid a commission to the merchant. Similar charges were made for similar services rendered in handling incoming goods ordered by the planters. In addition, merchants made insurance, recovered losses, collected debts, drew, endorsed, and negotiated bills of exchange, and provided credits. Many merchants also operated general stores in New Orleans, buying and selling staples and merchandise on their own account, with some exporting and importing in their own vessels. So the business connections of merchants reached in every conceivable direction: to the farmer, to the shipper, to other merchants in New Orleans and overseas, and to the manufacturer.

In the typical transaction, the planter shipped his cotton to a New Orleans firm—David Weeks to Flower and Faulkner, Abram Ellis to K. Laverty, Stephen Minor to Kenner and Henderson. The merchant then sold the cotton, paying any charges incident to sale and exacting a commission for each individual service, all of which the merchant subtracted from the gross proceeds in presenting the final accounting to the planter. The merchants all received between 9 and 10 percent of the gross proceeds. In addition, they filled orders for plantation goods, purchasing them from other merchants, seeing to their transportation, and taking the charges for those services out of the proceeds of staple sales. If the cotton was not sold in New Orleans but consigned to a house in Liverpool, Philadelphia, or elsewhere, the merchant made the necessary arrangements to obtain shipping, load the cargo, take out insurance, and notify the consignee of the shipment. All charges for those services were borne by the consignor: .5 percent of the premium for making insurance, 2.5 percent of the invoice value of the goods for obtaining shipping, and so on. For any money which the merchant laid out for the planter, a flat fee of 2.5 percent of the sum was levied.

Staple merchants in New Orleans received large quantities of cotton from upriver merchants such as Tabor and Fields in St. Francisville and the Nathaniel Evans-Abijah Hunt stores in and around Natchez. Flower and Faulkner, Kenner and Henderson, Samuel Paxton, and Martin Gordon and Company were among the New Orleans houses closely associated with such establishments. The Tabor and Evans firms supplied local planters with their needs, receiving cotton in payment and shipping it to New Orleans in payment for goods purchased there at wholesale. In these cases, the New Orleans firms came into possession of the staple and either sold it locally or shipped it on consignment to merchants in other ports. Hudson Tabor originally operated the store in St. Francisville for Flower and Faulkner and at their suggestion bought them out, with the New Orleans firm obligating itself to take cotton sent by Tabor at prearranged prices. Tabor in return maintained his inventory through Flower and Faulkner. Very little money changed hands in these transactions because remittances were normally in the form of goods and services credited to a current account. Theoretically, staple sales balanced out the planters' accounts with the merchant and provided operating capital for the next crop year. This actually occurred very rarely.

Planters required money or credit all year long but could provide staples only after each year's harvest. Merchants in New Orleans extended credits to the planters in anticipation of their crops. As

Flower and Faulkner described the system to John Pintard, merchants in New Orleans did not normally extend advances to planters in the form of goods until October or November of each year. Writing in August, Flower and Faulkner explained that: "We consider advances made to Cotton planters at this time as money we shall lay out of for five or six months as but little cotton comes to market before the months of January or February. Our Country friends usually order their Fall Supplies in the months of October or November, at which time we shall be happy to furnish you with the articles you may want on anticipation of the consignment of your Cotton . . . ." [5] A poor crop year or depressed prices threw the whole system out of kilter and compelled merchants to carry planters over from year to year or risk losing the entire amount.

Business relations between John Palfrey and several New Orleans merchants during Palfrey's time of troubles show just how long some merchants would carry a planter. Palfrey, arriving in New Orleans from Baltimore in 1804, entered into a partnership with Rezin D. Shepherd as Palfrey, Shepherd, and Company. The firm failed in 1807. Palfrey's share of the loss amounted to $10,500 and, disabused concerning the delights of a mercantile life, he made a start as a planter. [6]

From the beginning, Palfrey ran into a series of difficulties including the embargo, poor crops in 1810, and the loss of cargoes on board two vessels which were seized by the English in the same year. He lost his plantation in 1810 after failing to meet his mortgage payments. Encumbered by this time with debts additional to the original $10,500, he obtained sufficient credit in New Orleans to purchase nine hundred acres of cotton land in Atakapas which he began to work in 1811. Undaunted by past failures, Palfrey obtained twenty Negroes from Chew and Relf for $7,750, paying $4,000 down with the balance due within one year; the company held the mortgage to Palfrey's estate as security.

[5] Flower and Faulkner to John M. Pintard, August 26, 1809, in John M. Pintard Papers, 1796–1825 (Louisiana State University Department of Archives). Pintard received a similar response in P. D. Foley to Pintard, February 12, 1809, in *ibid.*

[6] Shepherd at the same time operated with John McDonogh and Shepherd Brown as Shepherd, Brown, and Company. The common link in the two firms was the connection with William Taylor, merchant of Baltimore who had referred Palfrey to McDonogh in the first place.

In 1812, recognizing Palfrey's inability to pay his debt, the firm extended the time for repayment, committing Palfrey to ship his cotton to them. The War of 1812 intervened, forcing Chew and Relf to suffer a further delay in the collection of this debt. Fearful that his creditors would institute a suit against him, Palfrey shipped everything he could lay his hands on to his creditors, including some of his slaves. After several more extensions, Chew and Relf were finally paid off in April, 1816. Palfrey also paid debts of long standing to Thomas Harmon and John McDonogh during the flush years immediately after the War of 1812, but in 1818 Palfrey still owed the original $10,500, the note for which was now held by his ex-partner R. D. Shepherd.

Palfrey was treated with great consideration by several merchants in the city. Not all planters were so fortunate, nor could all merchants afford such indulgence as could Chew and Relf. Bartlet and Company importuned David Rees to settle a large and long-standing account, stating that payment was necessary for the company to carry on its business. This is the other side of the story. Credit extended by the merchants allowed the planters to weather a crisis but also put pressure on the capital resources of the merchants, who could hardly afford to allow large sums to remain due them for long periods of time. Such ledger credits amounted to idle capital even when the debtor planter obligated his crop to wipe out a particular debt, for the merchant receiving the crop still had to sell it before obtaining funds to meet his own obligations.

Prior to 1815 the cotton and sugar in the city generally belonged to a planter who placed it in the care of his commission merchant for disposal or in the hands of a staple merchant who owned the crop and disposed of it on his own account. Final disposal meant export and further credits. If the staples were sent to New York, Philadelphia, Boston, or Baltimore for sale, it was customary to sell at a four to six months credit. Shorter credit than four months was difficult to arrange. A planter who shipped his crop through New Orleans to an overseas destination might have to wait six months or longer for payment, while the merchant carrying the planter had to wait just as long. Merchants who operated both on commission and on their own account extended credits in two directions—to the planter and to the overseas purchaser. If sales were slow or prices suddenly fell, pressures were generated all along the line.

The largest merchants in New Orleans, such as A. and D. Hunt, Shepherd, Brown, and Company, Kenner and Henderson, or Chew and Relf, were able to overcome some of these difficulties through advances received from overseas merchants. Some of the largest planters, William Dunbar and John Bisland, for instance, enjoyed the same advantage. Overseas merchants such as Chandler Price in Philadelphia and Green and Wainwright of Liverpool, competing for the staples, found it expedient to make advances on goods consigned to them for sale. Such firms, upon receipt of bills of lading and instructions regarding insurance, advanced from two-thirds to three-fourths of the probable net proceeds. When William Dunbar shipped an estimated $12,000 worth of cotton to his correspondent in London, the correspondent honored Dunbar's drafts up to two-thirds of that amount or $8,000. Shepherd, Brown received a similar accommodation from Chandler Price and A. M. Buckley, also of Philadelphia.

The privilege of advances was not without cost. In England, the commission charged for sales on consignment without an advance was 2.5 percent and with an advance, 6 percent. In Philadelphia, and presumably elsewhere in the United States, the charge with an advance was 5 percent. Shepherd, Brown questioned the justice of the additional fee charged by Buckley and Price. Buckley believed that the additional 2.5 percent was "hardly adequate compensation for the risk which there must be in all extensive sales . . . ."[7] Both Buckley and Price argued that the extension of advances was the equivalent of a guarantee of sale for the consignor's crop. Pressures were shifted from the consignor to the consignee who had not only to effect the sales but to honor the drafts drawn by the consignor. This was especially troublesome when the shipper drew before the cargo reached the consignee. A. M. Buckley outlined the risks assumed by his house if Shepherd, Brown, and Company drew heavily before the arrival of the cargo. Admitting that premature drawing was convenient to the shipper, he pointed out that "the Vessels have

---

[7] A. M. Buckley to Shepherd, Brown, and Company, July 20, 1805, in John McDonogh Papers, 1802–50 (Tulane University Library, Manuscript Division).

a long passage are ultimately missing or even lost, funds cannot be obtained for the shipment for a length of time after acceptances become due." He suggested that because of the uncertainty of punctual arrivals owing to the naval activity of the belligerents, no drafts be drawn until the goods arrived.[8]

During this period most of the credit, whether in the form of drafts on advances or promissory notes, was extended by mercantile houses to one another and to the planters. Such business paper was negotiable, passing from hand to hand at a discount and subject to interest if not paid when due. The development of banking in New Orleans after 1803 added a new source of credit for both planter and merchant.[9] As offices of discount and deposit, the banks were authorized to negotiate drafts, issue letters of exchange at stipulated times during the business week, and discount notes drawn by planters and local merchants.

In 1812 the estate of William Dunbar negotiated a note for £3,000 sterling on Green and Wainwright at the Bank of Mississippi which in turn negotiated the note at the Liverpool firm's bank in Philadelphia. The Bank of Pennsylvania sold the note and placed the proceeds to the credit of the Bank of Mississippi which then wrote a check on the Pennsylvania institution. The estate also negotiated a draft on Chew and Relf through the Bank of Mississippi which then forwarded it to William Kenner, the bank's agent in New Orleans, for collection.

That the discounting function of the banks assumed a high degree of importance prior to 1812 is substantiated by Martin Gordon's assessment of banking policy in 1806. At this time there were only two banks in New Orleans, the Bank of Louisiana and the branch Bank of the United States. Gordon wrote that the banks were cur-

[8] A. M. Buckley to Shepherd, Brown, and Company, October 26, 1805, in *ibid.*

[9] Detailed information on the role of banks in New Orleans between 1803 and the War of 1812 is difficult to obtain, and the sources investigated for this study were disappointing in this regard. Much more is available for the postwar period. Professor George Green of the University of Minnesota is awaiting publication of his comprehensive history of banking in antebellum Louisiana. Professor Irene Neu of the University of Indiana is writing a biography of Edmond J. Forstall, who was probably the most prominent banker in the city as well as a most perceptive student of banking practice. These studies will do much to advance our knowledge of antebellum banking in general.

tailing their discounts to the degree "that it has created great alarm in those who have received large accomodations–The Banking sistem [*sic*] in this place will most unquestionably blow some of our merchants up . . . Accommodation Paper has been reduced one fourth & every two months will be continued at the same rate, until liquidated. This will have a very serious effect on us." [10] Whenever discounting was curtailed, the impact was most severe on those merchants in advance to planters. Merchants, as Gordon implied, obtained promissory notes from planters which the merchant endorsed and negotiated at a bank. As endorser, the merchant, in effect, received a loan from the bank to compensate for the capital tied up in advances. This accommodation paper was guaranteed by little more than the merchant's reputation for solvency. If the bank demanded payment before the merchant concluded his sales, the latter was hard put to come up with the necessary cash. Failure might result even though the merchant's assets were greater than his liabilities. Merchants, then, were justifiably wary of making large advances, especially during uncertain times.

There is no particular evidence during this period that planters felt hemmed in by an oppressive system of crop marketing. Planters complained about the services of particular merchants or about the "times" but apparently not about the system. In later years, considerable criticism erupted in the South about the system of marketing. Planters charged that merchants in New Orleans and elsewhere held them in thralldom by means of the credit devices utilized to move the crops. Planters then believed that they derived less economic benefit from their staple agriculture than was their due. But the dispute over the division of profits produced by the staple economy was not raised with any vigor in the period before the War of 1812. Other issues and obstacles were of more relevance to planters and merchants in an era when getting the crops to a market involved such extraordinary risk.

The activities of virtually all commercial farmers from the English Turn to Pittsburgh and most merchants in town converged at least once a year at the port of New Orleans, the nerve center of the city.

---

[10] Martin Gordon and Co. to Nathaniel Evans, September 12, 1806, in Nathaniel Evans and Family Papers.

Flour, tobacco, and provisions from thousands of Ohio Valley farms, cotton from hundreds of plantations, sugar from several score of factories poured into the port along with other agricultural commodities, all representing the labor of a season as well as the economic aspirations of tens of thousands of farmers and planters. In 1809, 1,100 flats, barges, keels, and other river vessels carried the goods downstream, a number probably surpassed in 1810 when 618 reached New Orleans in the first four months of the year. In 1817 upriver arrivals exceeded 2,000. By this time, steamboats were adding to the congestion at the levee fronting the city. Arrivals from the Upper Valley were greatest in the late fall when the rivers began to rise and again when the spring thaw began.

Most of the cotton and flour reached New Orleans between late November and early April and the sugar crop arrived between late February and spring. The busy season of the port corresponded with the arrival of the staples, stretching from November to April or May. During a normal year, and there were few of these prior to 1815, oceangoing vessels began arriving in force in November in anticipation of cotton arrivals. Shipping tonnage in the port probably peaked in March, April, and May when most of the staples had arrived. In the period November, 1817, to September, 1818, 57 percent of total cotton exports and 41 percent of tobacco exports were shipped between February and May, and the proportion is probably higher since this includes only exports to foreign ports. At this season it was not unusual to witness three or four tiers of large vessels lined up before the city, extending from near the center of town to a quarter mile or more below, flanked on both sides by hundreds of river craft.

Exports from New Orleans required an estimated 40,000 tons of shipping in 1806. By 1815 more than 66,000 tons carried the products away and in 1817, 98,000 tons were needed. Some 60 percent of this tonnage was of United States registry. Tables V and IX show the origin of the shipping arriving at New Orleans. Arrivals from the United States and the Spanish colonies were probably greater as they do not include an estimated 10,000 tons arriving via the lakes and Bayou St. John. The tables indicate that, while most of the shipping originated in American ports, a significantly smaller

TABLE IX

Origin and Destination of Vessels Arriving
at New Orleans, 1815–17, in Percentages*

	1815		1816		1817	
	Origin	Desti-nation	Origin	Desti-nation	Origin	Desti-nation
United States	55	36	49	31	44	30
Great Britain	9	29	9	17	8	18
France	4	12	9	11	8	9
French and British Colonies	7	4	8	6	9	8
Spanish Colonies	19	13	19	32	25	26
Other Europe	3	5	4	7	5	6

* Sources: Augmentation du Commerce de la Nouvelle Orleans . . . [1815–17], in New Orleans Municipal Records, Louisiana State University, Department of Archives.

proportion departed for American ports. A large number of vessels carried goods to the Louisiana port and loaded staples for Europe. William Taylor forwarded dry goods via the *Carlisle* from Baltimore to McDonogh in New Orleans along with instructions to obtain sugar for a voyage to Liverpool. Other incoming vessels loaded flour and provisions for Havana or other West Indian markets. Departures for American ports were fewer than those to the Spanish colonies, Great Britain, and France because the goods available at New Orleans were consumed in smaller quantities in the United States than elsewhere. Shipments to the United States were frequently reexported to Europe.

Responsibility for the efficient organization of the port was shared by the Commissioner of Customs of the United States and the city council. The municipality of New Orleans implemented its powers in regulations issued in 1803, 1806, and 1808. The regulations attempted to establish procedures that would expedite the loading and unloading of cargoes on the levees, protect the levee from damage, and control the freight traffic between stores and warehouses in town and the levee. A harbor master was authorized to enforce all laws of the city and the territory applicable to the port and levee.

The laws spelled out procedures for the anchoring of vessels prior to the assignment of berths, designated precise areas in the port for oceangoing vessels and river craft (later including steamboats), provided special space for the unloading of lumber and perishables, required the registration of all passenger lists at the mayor's office, established cartage rates, and regulated the employment of slave labor on the levee.

Little trouble was experienced in implementing the regulations relative to the larger vessels but the "Kentuckians," as the council called all flatboatmen, caused all kinds of difficulties by their refusal to follow regulations. They put in wherever space was available, whether within or without their assigned area. Their flats with livestock and perishables, consigned to an area above Poydras Street or below the shipyards, squeezed in between moored vessels in the heart of the roadstead. They carried their salted goods into the city for repacking although this was expressly prohibited. "Kentuckians" dumped their goods all over the levee, constructed shanties to provide some protection, and abandoned their craft after sales were made instead of breaking them up in the area designated for that purpose. The "Kentuckians" were the perfect ones on which to fasten blame for everything from riots to endangering the salubrity of the air.

City authorities performed adequately in maintaining order in the port notwithstanding the "Kentuckians" and an undermanned harbor staff. Similarly understaffed was the office of the Commissioner of Customs of the United States. Customs officials protected the interests of the United States by administering the tariff, navigation, tonnage, and other commercial laws applicable to the Territory of Orleans and guarding against illicit trade. Federal officials, including Claiborne, had their hands full in this period of partial and total embargoes, slave smuggling, Baratarian pirates, and war. Stationed at New Orleans, and cooperating with the customs officers, was a federal naval force (which included a squadron of fifty gunboats by 1809) and the public vessels which intermittently cruised in the Gulf of Mexico.

By 1804 Spanish law had been replaced by federal legislation authorizing the collection of duties and taxes on foreign goods and shipping. The new laws erased the export duties levied by Spain, as well as the various exemptions to them. Special rules were established relative to the trade of West Florida, claimed by the United States as part of the territory purchased in 1803. Articles of West Florida production were admitted duty free at New Orleans or Bayou St. John, and tonnage taxes at New Orleans were waived on local river and lake vessels if under 50 tons. Spanish vessels were allowed to pass New Orleans to Baton Rouge but customs officials were instructed to inspect these vessels for illegal goods, particularly slaves. By 1805 the mechanics of collecting duties, posting bonds on imports, applying for drawbacks on imported items destined for reexport to a foreign port, and similar details were well worked out.

Difficulties such as smuggling, particularly of slaves, were virtually insolvable problems in a region criss-crossed with innumerable bayous and creeks, many providing easy and undetectable access to the interior. Collector Trist believed the cost of rooting out smuggling was prohibitive. Bayou Teche, for example, the scene of a considerable illicit trade under Spain, afforded the inhabitants of Opelousas and Atakapas a route for the importation of tafia, coffee, and other goods directly from Havana without payment of duties. With the passage of the Embargo Act, federal officers lost control of the situation. French privateers operating out of Guadeloupe raised havoc in West Indian and Gulf waters. Forced out of Guadeloupe, which was captured by the English in 1810, the privateersmen set up shop on Barataria Bay where they plied a lucrative and illegal trade with merchants and planters in Louisiana.

French privateers (pirates according to the *Louisiana Gazette*) were undiscriminating in their choice of vessels to plunder—English, American, French, Spanish—they all were prey for these adventurers. Frequently outfitted in Charleston and Savannah as well as New Orleans, these vessels cruised southern waters for prizes and then put into New Orleans to dispose of their wares. *L'Intrepide*, *L'Épine*, and the *Guilliaume* all entered New Orleans with slavers as prizes in 1810 and, in spite of the watchfulness of customs officers, left without their cargoes, which were grabbed up immediately by slave traders and planters. With so much territory to patrol, federal officials rarely caught up with the smugglers, even when naval forces cooperated with the few revenue cutters which the collector had at his disposal.

The privateersmen were firmly established in a self-proclaimed Republic of Barataria by 1811. Operating openly, the pirates frequented New Orleans, hobnobbing with Edward Livingston, Abner L. Duncan, John K. West, and other prominent residents, selling goods to merchants and slaves to planters, and ignoring Claiborne's proclamations against them. Claiborne, unable to gain the cooperation of either the state or city in his campaign against the Baratarians, finally secured the cooperation of federal forces. A successful raid against the pirates in September, 1814, destroyed the camp and the Baratarian Republic but did not stamp out smuggling or piratical privateering. The independence movement in Spain's American colonies opened up new opportunities in both fields of endeavor.

There was more to the problem of smuggling than the wish of merchants and planters to avoid the payment of duties. Smuggling served a basic need in Louisiana by secreting into the territory large numbers of slaves which were always in short supply. A clandestine traffic and labor shortages had broken down efforts made during the Spanish period to prevent the introduction of "undesirable" slaves from colonial areas troubled by slave insurrection. In 1803 the city council prohibited Chew and Relf from landing a cargo of West Indian slaves, which that firm then sent up Bayou Lafourche for sale. The council, in denying Chew and Relf and in later discussions of the issue, emphasized their fear of slave insurrection. Claiborne, who considered the trade barbarous, hindered the traffic whenever possible and was pleased when the federal government prohibited the foreign slave trade in Louisiana in 1804, a prohibition applied nationally in 1808. Many Louisianians, however, did not share Claiborne's moral attitude.

Public opinion overwhelmingly favored restoration of the trade. A public meeting called to protest the action was well attended and resulted in the drafting of a petition to Congress criticizing the prohibition. Prominent merchants were profitably engaged in the trade. In 1804 George Pollock advertised the sale of "fresh mulatto wenches"; Paul Lanusse offered 34 new Gold Coast Negroes for sale; Chew and Relf marketed 108 slaves for notes or cotton; M.

Fortier announced the arrival of 80 choice Negroes for sale; and John McDonogh managed to bring in 200 Africans and advertise their arrival after the federal law went into effect. With little or no local support for the law, Claiborne and federal officials fought a losing battle to seal off Louisiana from the foreign slave trade. The legislature of the territory and state ignored Claiborne's appeals for conformity to federal law. The legislators were planters. Collector Williams informed Gallatin that slaves seized in 1810 from one individual were returned to him by a special act of the legislature.

A legal slave trade developed along with the illegal commerce. While some planters purchased slaves smuggled in via Mobile, Barataria Bay, or some other route, John Clay, Kenner and Henderson, Henry Molier and Company, Patton and Mossy, Chew and Relf, and other firms began to import Negroes from the other slave states. In one transaction, Evan Jones contracted in February, 1806, with Samuel Ker, John W. Leonard, and George T. Phillips for the purchase of 50 Negroes at $400 each. Jones paid $7,000 in advance to Ker who went off to Maryland to obtain the slaves. William Dunbar forwarded £3,000 sterling in notes on London, endorsed by Chew and Relf, to a Charleston slave trader. This sum was the equivalent of paying half in advance and Dunbar obtained credit for six months on the balance. Chew and Relf managed the details of the transaction. Other planters and merchants obtained slaves in New Orleans at the public auctions. Patton and Mossy, public auctioneers, sold for endorsed paper at six and twelve months credit. Merchants in other southern ports sent slaves to New Orleans on consignment, generally attempting to get their cargoes on the market before planting or harvest time. Merchants serving as brokers in the slave trade received a commission of 1.5 percent of the purchase price from both seller and buyer.

The slave trade, as well as other branches of the overseas trade of New Orleans, was still largely in the hands of generalists such as Chew and Relf and George T. Phillips. Phillips acted as the New Orleans correspondent of merchants in Boston, Jamaica, and elsewhere, shipped cotton to Bordeaux, leased space from shipowners, and leased his own vessels to merchants for voyages to Laguna, Brazil, Havana, Vera Cruz, and Antwerp. He shipped large quantities of logwood and Guatemalan tobacco to Baltimore. Locally, he engaged in real estate speculation in West Florida properties, and just prior to his bankruptcy and death in 1808, invested $30,000 in a tract of land near Baton Rouge upon which he constructed a steam-operated sawmill.

A few mercantile houses dealt more exclusively in the staples and perhaps with a particular commercial house or houses in each of a few ports. Shepherd, Brown, and Company was heavily committed to the sugar and cotton trade to Baltimore and Philadelphia, receiving a wide assortment of goods on consignment from those ports for sale in New Orleans. The earliest connections—1803—were with William Taylor and Company of Baltimore. By 1805 Shepherd, Brown dealt with at least six other Baltimore firms, had firm ties with two Philadelphia merchants, Chandler Price and A. M. Buckley, and had an arrangement with two or three houses in Liverpool.

This New Orleans firm exported cotton and sugar to England and the eastern seaboard on its own account and at the risk of merchants in those places. The firm does not appear to have pursued the commission business with planters. Both John M. Minor and Company and Mayor and Brantz of Baltimore forwarded assortments of dry goods to New Orleans, instructing Shepherd, Brown to remit for them in cotton to Liverpool or sugar to Baltimore. This latter firm also purchased sugar and cotton from commission merchants in New Orleans, exporting these goods to Baltimore, Philadelphia, and Liverpool for sale on consignment. Receiving advances on such shipments in effect augmented the working capital of the New Orleans firm by permitting it to make larger purchases at New Orleans during a crop season than would have been possible if forced to wait for final sales to replenish operating capital. In these shipments, Shepherd, Brown supplied advance notice to their correspondents who then obtained insurance on the goods at the port of arrival. Of the two staples, cotton and sugar, shipments of the latter seem to have involved the most uncertainty.

The timing of the shipment was all important. William Taylor in March, 1804, and Chandler Price in March, 1805, pressed the New Orleans house for the immediate shipment of sugar in order to beat the arrival of the West Indian crop and the resultant decline in

prices. In the spring of 1805 sugar imports were heavy in Phila-
delphia and both Price and Buckley postponed the sale of some
Shepherd, Brown sugar until fall, hoping for a better price. But as
Price informed his correspondents in November, sugar imports from
Jamaica, St. Croix, and other West Indian islands were abnormally high and prices remained low. To an extent, a similar competitive situation faced American cotton in the period prior to 1815.
Rathbone, Hughes, and Duncan of Liverpool, informing Shepherd,
Brown, and Company in September, 1805, of a good demand for
cotton, hoped that their shipment would reach England before the
crop from the Leeward Islands.

Quality and packaging were factors that influenced the price obtained for the sugar and the quickness of the sale. Buckley in Philadelphia frequently complained about the poor quality of the sugars
consigned to him, forcing him to accept prices as much as $4 per
hundredweight below the going price for good sugars. The weight
of the hogshead was also a problem. Both Price and Buckley warned
Shepherd, Brown that grocers in Baltimore and Philadelphia were
annoyed at the excess tare in New Orleans sugars. Planters passed
their casks at 10 percent of the gross weight when the casks frequently equaled 15 to 20 percent. In seven emptied casks the tare
averaged out at 31 pounds more than listed, which meant that purchasers paid for 217 pounds more sugar than they actually received.
Buckley and Price were concerned that the grocers in both cities
would combine to force a larger tare allowance. Buckley was so
irritated by the poor quality and fraudulent weights of the sugars received from New Orleans that he instructed Shepherd, Brown in
November, 1805, to cease drawing on him until he had rid himself
of the sugar on his hands.

A much lamented fact was the inferior quality and poor packaging of New Orleans cotton. John Bisland observed in Glasgow
that New Orleans cotton was so dirty it brought from six to seven
cents less per pound than clean cotton. So poor was the product in
1802—many parcels containing large quantities of leaves and dirt and
some of the cotton permanently stained—that manufacturers in England were reluctant to utilize it. Martin Gordon believed that the
poor quality of ginning would damage the reputation of New Or-

leans cotton and lower prices offered for it. The merchants blamed the planters who ginned their own cotton or had it done by a neighbor. William Dunbar, admitting that planters were negligent in ginning their crops, added, however, that the negligence was the fault of "our merchants who do not make due distinction, giving the same price for the bad as for the good." [11] Grading procedures for cotton, sugar, and tobacco were utilized with greater consistency in later years.

European wars compounded tenfold the normal problems incident to both the staple trade with the eastern seaboard and Europe and the flour, provisions, and lumber trade with the West Indies and Spanish Main. Proving the neutrality of the cargo became necessary especially after the *Essex* decision of 1805 in which the British admiralty reversed a prior policy allowing American vessels to carry belligerent goods to the United States for reexport to a belligerent port. According to the *Essex* decision such goods were now subject to seizure unless the shipper could prove that an American port was the final destination. This reversal was intended to prevent American vessels from engaging in the carrying trade between England's enemies and their colonies. Shippers from New Orleans carried various paper proofs of the American origin and ownership of the cargo. Seizures of American ships rose rapidly after the decision and by January, 1806, British vessels were permanently stationed off the mouth of the Mississippi for the purpose of inspecting the cargoes of American vessels.

Between 1805 and 1808 the naval activity of England and the other belligerents affected the staple trade only indirectly through higher freight rates, higher insurance premiums, and the like. An occasional blockade of French ports by the British navy hampered direct shipments from New Orleans to France, but indirect shipments via England circumvented the blockades. American vessels in the New Orleans-Liverpool-New Orleans run encountered some danger on the return trip from privateers operating out of Havana. William Dunbar reported the loss to privateers of cargoes in two

[11] William Dunbar to Green and Wainwright, July 17, 1809, in Dunbar Letter Book, 1805–12, William Dunbar Papers (Mississippi Department of Archives and History).

vessels returning from Liverpool via the southern coast of Cuba. Vessels passing through the Bahama channel avoided the privateers. In November, 1805, Cuban officials discouraged this activity by ordering the release, with heavy payments for damages, of an American schooner captured on the Liverpool-New Orleans run.

British warships and privateers caused serious difficulties in the trade routed south from New Orleans. New Orleans merchants sending cargoes to and receiving cargoes from St. Domingue, Cuba, Vera Cruz, Campeachy, and other colonial ports suffered severe losses from British seizures. But prices for foodstuffs and European goods were so high in those ports that a successful voyage more than compensated for the losses suffered by a seizure or two. J. B. Labutat, John Merricult, Chew and Relf, John McDonogh, George T. Phillips, and other merchants pursued the colonial trade vigorously during the period, absorbing losses, employing various stratagems to avoid seizure, and apparently making profits. Subordinate to the trade to the island colonies and the Spanish Main was the coasting trade to the Floridas, monopolized by New Orleans, and which became domestic trade following the revolution in West Florida in 1810 and the addition of that area to Louisiana in 1812.

New Orleans was a source of foodstuffs for French and Spanish possessions in and along the Caribbean. Between 1804 and 1814 about 64 percent of all New Orleans flour exports—some 15,000 barrels of flour annually—went to Cuba, St. Domingue, Martinique, and Central America. During the same eleven years, the Spanish West Indies and Florida imported an average of 120,000 barrels of flour annually. These colonies were major markets for New Orleans but New Orleans had yet—as has been suggested—to replace New York, Philadelphia, and Baltimore as the primary supplier of those markets.[12] Trade with Cuba and St. Domingue involved not only risks of capture at sea but detention, harassment, and possible seizure in port. Grant Forbes and Company of New York warned John

12 W. Freeman Galpin, "The Grain Trade of New Orleans, 1804–1814," *Mississippi Valley Historical Review*, XIV (1928), 501–502. Flour exports from New Orleans during the 11 years, 1804–14, averaged about 23,000 barrels annually, compared to an average annual export from the United States of over 900,000 in the 10 years, 1805–14.

McDonogh to be on the lookout for the ship *Polly* from St. Domingue. The vessel had been detained by local authorities, part of its
cargo confiscated, the proceeds from sales temporarily sequestered,
and the ship's register tampered with. McDonogh received instructions to do all within his power to avoid the payment of duties on
a cargo of coffee the vessel was bringing to New Orleans.

The flour, provisions, and lumber trade to Cuba and other Spanish ports was potentially lucrative but uncertain of success. Ships
captains never knew whether they would be admitted or, if admitted, under what conditions. Flour and provisions were generally
received but not always, as the list of prohibited goods changed frequently and without warning. Astute masters of vessels normally
managed to smuggle the prohibited goods in, although at great expense. Duties on legal items were extremely high, as were the gratifications paid to local officials. In one shipment of 339 barrels of
flour to Havana the freight ran $3 per barrel, duties at $8 per barrel,
and gratifications to customs officials $2 per barrel. Flour and pro-
visions from New Orleans suffered from a poor reputation because
they spoiled quickly, and Cuban inspectors occasionally and without
inspection marked whole cargoes as unfit for consumption, thus necessitating either additional bribes or sales at greatly reduced prices.

If the trader managed to surmount these obstacles, there still remained the trip home. The ship *Hornet*, returning from Vera Cruz,
was intercepted outside the bar by the British frigate *Fortune*. Real-
izing that he could not avoid inspection, the *Hornet*'s owner placed
all his specie on board the pilot vessel which came out to meet him.
The pilot boat made it to the block-house while the British boarded
the *Hornet*. The experience of J. B. Labutat was especially discouraging. His schooner *Felicity*, returning from Campeachy, was taken
by a British privateer at the mouth of the river in 1806, immediately
retaken by the American revenue cutter *Louisiana* and restored to
Labutat. Upon its return from another voyage, the *Felicity* was
libeled and seized on the suit of the captain and crew of the *Louisiana* who demanded salvage on the vessel and its cargo. The courts
upheld the libel and Labutat was compelled to pay $1,757. Labutat,
in high dudgeon, wrote in the *Louisiana Gazette* "that privateers are

not what we ought most to dread, the protection of our own people is worse . . . than British vexations." [13]

In 1806 and 1807 the war proved increasingly bothersome to the normal conduct of business at New Orleans. Both sugar and cotton moved so slowly that Shepherd, Brown, and Company turned their attention from staples to the slave trade. Part of the problem stemmed from bumper crops and it was hoped that improvement would occur by the fall of 1806. When fall arrived, however, the United States government implemented an act passed in April which prohibited the importation from Great Britain of certain articles which could be obtained elsewhere. This first nonimportation act was a measure of American irritation over British maritime practices and, although operative for only a month, it precluded any improvement in the cotton trade between the two nations. The market remained dull into 1807 when a new series of events, domestic and foreign, destroyed business confidence, closed markets, and brought the United States to the brink of war with Great Britain.

A number of New Orleans merchants turned from the English cotton market to the French in 1806 in an effort to find a more secure sale. But the British proclamation in May, Napoleon's Berlin Decree in December, and countermeasures taken by the belligerents in 1807 combined to interdict all neutral trade with Great Britain, the ports of France, and European ports controlled by France. As the major neutral carrier, the United States was most severely injured by these policies. Commercial prospects were further dimmed when negotiations with Great Britain collapsed with President Jefferson's rejection of the Monroe-Pinkney treaty in May, 1807.

New Orleans, already in a state of shock over the Burr conspiracy and the belligerent postures struck by the United States and Spain toward one another, received the news of British and French blockades with dismay. Neutral commerce was threatened with annihilation. Even greater alarm was excited when news of the *Chesapeake-Leopard* Affair reached New Orleans in July 1807. John McDonogh believed that war with both Britain and Spain might result. Merchants postponed shipments pending official American reaction to the flagrant breach of American sovereignty. Shepherd, Brown, and

[13] New Orleans *Louisiana Gazette*, April 22, 1806.

Company was advised by Chandler Price to make no ventures in articles depending on foreign sale. Business took a holiday in New Orleans while the cotton was harvested upriver and Jefferson's administration pondered its response to the attack on the *Chesapeake*.

When news of Napoleon's victory at Friedland in June and the subsequent Treaties of Tilsit (July 7–9, 1807) reached France, the threat of a continental and maritime peace greatly depressed the prices of American produce. In New Orleans, the *Chesapeake* Affair brought with it the dread of a general war or at least naval retaliation against Great Britain. Quoted prices for staples were but nominal as little produce moved. In January of the following year rumors reached New Orleans that the United States had enacted a general embargo law. The news, as yet unofficial, stimulated a flurry of commercial activity. The collector of customs, who had still not seen a copy of the law by January 28, reported the greatest confusion in his office as shippers hurried to clear their vessels from the port. In the two weeks after January 11, forty-two vessels departed. All the flour in the city was bought up and shipped to the West Indies and cotton stocks were totally depleted. A merchant in Havana wrote to his partners in New Orleans that the unusual number of arrivals from the United States, especially New Orleans, "almost convinced the Spanish that the Embargo was a *hum* . . . ." [14]

The embargo, however, was no "hum." Becoming law on December 22, 1807, it prohibited United States vessels from departing for foreign ports and interdicted land commerce to foreign ports as well. Coasting between American ports was allowed under a heavy bond. Foreign vessels were allowed to enter with goods but could not carry goods from American ports. Collector William Brown received official news of the law in February and dispatched vessels to the Balize to prevent the departure of vessels. Gunboats were stationed at the mouths of Bayou St. John and the river. Governor Claiborne was less than candid when he informed the Secretary of State that most influential men approved the measure.

Complaints were numerous. The *Louisiana Gazette* viewed the

14 [?] Williamson to [?] Meeker, Williamson and Company, January 30, 1808, in Meeker, Williamson, and Patton Correspondence, 1807–1808 (Louisiana State University Department of Archives).

embargo as an act of cowardice. One individual condemned the draconic nature of the act and was incensed at the severity of enforcement practiced by the gunboats cruising the Mississippi River. Evasion of the law by merchants and shippers was quite common. Smuggling, of course, continued along Louisiana's bayous. Shippers posted bond, amounting to double the value of the ship and cargo, that their destination was some other American port. They then made for the best market available—Havana, Vera Cruz, St. Domingue. The owners of such vessels, at the conclusion of the voyage, sued in federal courts with frequent success for recovery of their bonds, producing evidence that the wind, waves, and weather forced them into foreign ports. Many shipped goods in worthless vessels and were willing to lose the ships because sales were higher than the bonds. Others shipped cotton and flour clandestinely across the lakes to Mobile and Pensacola and from there to England or the West Indies in English shipping.

Although the embargo was hardly air tight at New Orleans or elsewhere in the nation, it caused considerable economic distress. Staples piled up in New Orleans while cotton prices were low and sales few. Merchants in Baltimore and Philadelphia suspended the practice of advances until the English market was again accessible. Merchants along the eastern seaboard such as William Machette of Boston, accustomed to receiving remittances in cotton for shipments to the Louisiana port, demanded cash or negotiable notes. Cash was in extremely short supply, notes expensive, and discounts high. Uncertainty as to the progress of negotiations between England and the United States caused producers to hold back their crops and purchasers to refrain from buying. William W. Montgomery grasped at straws in writing excitedly that a Baltimore vessel reported a French declaration of war on the United States. War, Montgomery told Nathaniel Evans, would bring better times.

Good times were not on the horizon as the year of the embargo ended. Believing that the law would be repealed and normal conditions restored, William Machette in February, 1809, ordered his correspondent in New Orleans to purchase cotton. But in March the embargo was replaced with the Non-Intercourse Act, which maintained a prohibition on trade with France and England while permitting trade with other nations. A year later, Machette suspended shipments to New Orleans because of prior misfortunes in trading with the port. Non-intercourse, lasting until May, 1810, kept the cotton market dull in New Orleans, as did the worsening relations between the United States and Great Britain following the Erskine Agreement fiasco in April–August 1809. The scarcity of cash, great quantities of cotton—the crop of two years—in the market, and very few vessels to carry it off combined to depress cotton prices below those of 1808. Few merchants were willing to trust goods on long-term notes, which almost entirely stopped the staple trade in New Orleans.

The expiration of the Non-Intercourse Act and the substitution of the useless Macon's Bill Number 2 in May, 1810, brought temporary relief until the reapplication of the Non-Intercourse Act against Great Britain in March, 1811, again sealed off that primary market and source of credits. During the brief period in which commerce again flowed freely—subject, of course, to the continued harassment of England, France, and assorted privateers—large quantities of staples left New Orleans. American cotton glutted an English market weakened by the expenses and losses of seventeen years of war and by extensive speculation in South America. Many failures were reported all over the realm. Credit was unavailable while an excess of paper circulated as a result of the suspension of specie payments by the Bank of England. In New Orleans, a rash of failures, including those of John Clay and James Sterrett, occurred in 1809. "Commercial regularity and confidence," wrote one merchant in 1809, "is almost at an end." [15]

Gloom persisted in New Orleans throughout 1811. The words *distress, trouble, scarcity, failure* are pervasive in the correspondence of the last two years of peace. A series of heavy failures jolted the community in early 1811, paralyzing commerce by destroying confidence. John Wolf and Company; Townsend and Company; Martin Farrand; Frette, *fils* and Company; William Foelkel; Meeker, Williamson and Patton all defaulted and declared bankruptcy. Failures blighted the confidence of one merchant in the solvency of

[15] O. H. Spencer to Nathaniel Evans, February 26, 1809, in Nathaniel Evans and Family Papers.

another and without this confidence there could be no credit. Men were forced to use their capital to meet present engagements whereas normally credit and confidence substituted for capital. Operating capital was tied up in unsaleable staples or in advances to other merchants and planters.

Permanent relief could come only if the United States and Great Britain succeeded in negotiating a settlement of outstanding issues. A vast though temporary market in the Iberian Peninsula brought relief to some American ports between 1809 and 1813. Although a few New Orleans merchants found markets in Spain and Portugal during those years, the impact of this trade upon New Orleans was negligible and the city contributed only a minor portion of the goods that followed British armies into the war-torn area. There was to be no relief. Great Britain stepped up the impressment of American sailors, and in May, 1811, the United States ship *President* disabled the British warship *Little Belt*. The 12th Congress debated the constitutionality of preparing for war in 1811 and 1812 and passed a 90-day embargo on April 4, 1812. Great Britain made major concessions while President Madison drafted his war message of June 1, 1812. On June 19 the President proclaimed the existence of a state of war between the United States and Great Britain. Shortly thereafter British warships appeared off the mouth of the Mississippi and Governor Claiborne reported that privateers were outfitting in New Orleans.

The war slowed down New Orleans' pursuit of an unexampled future. War closed the major foreign markets and agriculture languished. Many enterprises were postponed. Latrobe was forced to curtail construction of the water works. The New Orleans Navigation Company sat out the war. The brightness of the future heralded by the arrival of the steamboat *New Orleans* on January 10, 1812, lost its luster by July. Other hopes were dimmed. Vincent Nolte, agent in New Orleans in 1806 and 1807 for the European capitalists who transferred millions of dollars of Spanish-American treasure to Spain, set out in 1811 to return to New Orleans to establish a business. Having obtained substantial financial aid from Hope and Company of Amsterdam and the Barings in England, Nolte crossed the Alleghanies by horseback, riding part of the way to Pittsburgh with

John James Audubon. In Pittsburgh, Nolte purchased flatboats and flour for the trip to New Orleans. He was in New Madrid when the earthquake of February 6, 1812, destroyed the town. Arriving in New Orleans in March, Nolte had no sooner settled in than the declaration of war cut him off from his financial resources in Europe. This was not the time to make a beginning.

16

The Business Community
1803–1815

BEVERLY Chew and Richard Relf, partners in the New Orleans firm Chew and Relf, were two of the more prominent members of a business elite which controlled the economic and political development of New Orleans during the decade following the Louisiana Purchase. The men established a business in 1801 which weathered successfully the tumultuous years prior to the War of 1812, rode the war years out without damage, survived the postwar boom, bust, and recession, and was still operating in the 1830s. Both men were intimately involved in the organization and operation of the new forms of capitalistic enterprise which were chartered after 1803.[1]

Few men played a more significant role in the initiation of the insurance business in New Orleans. Relf was one of the founders of the New Orleans Insurance Company, chartered in 1805; Chew and Relf were among the original subscribers to company stock; and the partners served at different times on the company's board of directors. While this insurance company was organizing, the two announced their appointment as the exclusive agents of the Phoenix Fire Assurance Company of London, holding this agency until at least 1818. There was no conflict here since the London firm insured only real property while the New Orleans firm insured vessels, car-

---

[1] Many of the individuals encountered in chapter 14 as members of the city council will be discussed in this chapter as a part of the business elite. Instead of referring the reader to the earlier chapter for essential information relative to these men, certain facts pertinent to their careers will be repeated. Unless otherwise indicated, the corporations dealt with include the Bank of Louisiana, New Orleans branch of the First Bank of the United States, Bank of Orleans, Louisiana Planter's Bank, New Orleans Navigation Company, and New Orleans Insurance Company.

goes, and money in port and in transit. After the war, the New Orleans firm was reorganized as the Louisiana Insurance Company, with Relf serving as one of the directors.

Banking also opened up new opportunities for the two men. The firm subscribed to stock in the Bank of Louisiana and Relf sat on the board from 1807 to 1813. From 1818 to 1847 Relf was the cashier of the Louisiana State Bank. Chew was appointed to the board of directors of the New Orleans branch of the first Bank of the United States in 1805, serving until the charter expired in 1811, and again as a director for the local branch of the second Bank of the United States between 1817 and the time of his resignation as president in 1831. In 1831 Chew was appointed cashier of the Canal and Banking Company and was elected president in 1832. Among the other positions held by the partners, Relf was a director of the New Orleans Navigation Company from 1806 and 1810 and Chew received the appointment as Collector of Customs at New Orleans in 1816, serving until his dismissal in 1829.

This brief resume of the careers of Chew and Relf reflects a deep and durable involvement in the economic life of New Orleans. They were neither average—typical—businessmen nor completely atypical. Rather, they belonged to the business "establishment" of the community, having achieved this position by the rapid success of their mercantile house and their leadership in other areas of the community's economic life. Their acquired reputations paid immediate dividends. In 1804 Collector H. B. Trist suggested fifteen individuals to Secretary of the Treasury Gallatin as possible directors of the branch Bank of the United States. Chew's name was on the list. His partner, one of the half-dozen founders of the local Chamber of Commerce in 1806, was elected to the city council in 1810. A few years later, Relf contributed to the organization of the Thespian Benevolent Society. In 1810 Chew was a founding father and among the first elected as vestryman of the new Episcopal Church. The other vestrymen, the men recommended by Trist, the chamber organizers and the Thespians, were with few exceptions as much a part of the business elite of the town as Chew and Relf.

It is easy enough to say that a business elite functioned in New Orleans prior to the Peace of Ghent, but it is quite another matter to define its functions and characteristics or to catalog its members. In terms of American urban development, New Orleans was a unique city as of 1803, combining as it did the attributes of many American cities both new and old. Like New York, Philadelphia, or Baltimore, New Orleans was a seaport located on a river. Unlike those towns, New Orleans' river system penetrated almost every crop region in the United States, making the city an entrepot for virtually every staple, northern or southern. New Orleans was as much a river city as a coastal city and new as well as old. It was newer to the United States than Cincinnati, Louisville, or other western river cities, but it was older than Savannah in chronological age. To the casual observer, society in New Orleans appeared as fluid as in other western communities, yet operating beneath the flux was a solidly entrenched establishment. This inner core of individuals ran the town politically, set the social tone, and controlled its economic development through a virtual monopoly of corporate enterprise in the city.

As might be expected in a preindustrial and commercial city, merchants contributed an overwhelming majority of members to the elite group. Entry to the commercial class in the city was open at all levels to those caring to take the risk. Men with a few dollars could easily buy goods and commence a career of hawking and peddling. Many obviously did, for the city council, at the insistence of the solid burghers of the town, passed ordinances regulating and taxing street peddlers. But entry on a shoestring did not guarantee the wherewithal to purchase the shoes. Nor were the new merchants, arriving with capital or credit and goods, who initiated more solid ventures, likely to advance into the ranks of the elite before 1815. This was especially true of those arriving after 1808 and to a certain extent even after 1803.

At least some information is available relative to the careers of 149 businessmen operating in New Orleans between 1803 and 1815.[2] Although many more than 149 pursued trade and commerce during

[2] The number of firms involved is less than the number of individuals. Both are fluctuating numbers because of deaths, changes in partnership, failures, retirement, and the like. More data are available regarding some men than others. It is hoped that those who are ultimately identified as "elite" will not be done so merely because they left behind a full business record.

those years, this group provides as satisfactory a cross-section of the business community as extant data allow. This group will later be divided and subdivided according to certain objective criteria in an effort to identify with some precision the most prominent members of the business elite in New Orleans. At this point, however, some basic facts concerning the entire group will be discussed; these then can be contrasted with data relative to the subgroups.

The general period in which these individuals established their businesses is known. Of the 149, 19 percent were operating prior to 1800; 22 percent opened their establishments between 1800 and 1803; and the remaining 59 percent thereafter. Sixty-two, or 41 percent, owned going concerns before the Louisiana Purchase. Of the total, at least 31 percent continued their businesses into the postwar decades while no fewer than six of the group outlived John C. Calhoun and at least two, William W. Montgomery and Rezin D. Shepherd, witnessed secession and civil war. Both of the latter retired to plantations with large fortunes. Montgomery was said to own a large portion of northwestern Louisiana. Within the group, 20 men owned plantations prior to 1815, while after 1815, 34 pursued planting and business simultaneously or retired to plantations. The lure of the plantation continued to attract many of the most prominent businessmen in later years, making it difficult to generalize concerning the urban commitment of the community's leadership.

Again from the total group, 36 held either elective or appointive positions in the city or state government prior to 1815 while 56 held one or more directorships in one or more of the corporations established after 1804. After the war, at least 46, including Chew and Relf, continued to serve on the board of directors of an increasing number of corporate enterprises. James Freret served in the 1830s as a director of the New Orleans and Carrollton Railroad and the Union Bank of Louisiana. Samuel Packwood and Maunsel White were among the organizers of the Plaquemines Railroad Company in 1835; John McDonogh and Martin Gordon served as directors of the New Orleans and Nashville Railroad Company in 1836 and 1837. Benjamin Levy, who began his career as a stationer in 1811, was a founder of the Orleans Insurance Company in 1835 and invested heavily in land, railroads, and banks. Of these entrepreneurs, all but McDonogh belong more properly to the postwar elite of New Orleans.

For purposes of analysis, the original list of 149 individuals was divided into two groups. Active participation as a member of either the city council or the board of directors of one of the corporations was assumed to reflect a capacity for leadership; proven influence with the voting public of the city or the stockholders of the corporation; and, as only stockholders could be directors, the possession of and the willingness to invest funds in institutions that served as vehicles for economic growth in the city as well as potential sources of profit. Group one, therefore, was composed of all those serving as directors or city councilmen, totaling 64 individuals. Group two originally included 69 firms or 84 men, but so little information was available regarding a number of them that the list was reduced to 40 firms, or 56 merchants. A comparison between the two groups uncovered differences additional to and perhaps explanatory of the initial distinction utilized in constructing the lists.

The merchants in group one established their businesses in New Orleans considerably earlier than those in group two.[3] The average EBR for group one was 2.25; for group two, 3.25. More specifically, 55 percent, or 33 merchants, in group one were operating in New Orleans before 1803 compared with 25 percent, or 10 merchants, from group two. Twenty-five percent of the individuals in group two arrived in New Orleans after 1809, compared to 3 percent of group one. Merchants in group one were more likely to be in on the organization of the corporations as original investors and to retain their positions of leadership at least through 1815. Moreover, the merchants in group one seem to include the largest business establishments in the city.

There is no way of knowing the annual dollar volume of any of the firms involved here. Instead, it was tentatively assumed that size could be determined by focusing attention on the number of business services rendered and the kinds of ventures engaged in.[4] The

[3] A simple Establishment in Business Rating (EBR) was constructed according to the following scale: merchants established before 1800 were rated as 1; between 1800–1803, as 2; 1804–1808, as 3; sometime between 1804–12, as 4; and 1809–12, as 5.

[4] A Size of Business Rating (SBR) was constructed, based upon the performance of the following six functions: storeowner, shipowner, export-import on commis-

SBR for the firms included in group one was 3.75; for group two, 2.50. None of the firms in the latter group engaged in all of the functions rated, only two engaged in five functions, and only one in four. Fourteen of the firms were exclusively commission houses according to their circulars and advertisements. One of these houses was established by John James Audubon, who came from Lexington, Kentucky, shortly after his encounter with Vincent Nolte. The business failed shortly after its inception. Related to the larger proportion of strictly commission merchants in group two is the fact that 43 percent of them operated as agents for overseas firms compared to 33 percent in group one. Some merchants in group two, such as William McCormick, Cochran and Rhea, and Francis Wells, apparently served no other purpose than to purchase staples for and sell the goods of various merchants along the East Coast of the United States. Of the firms in group one, Chew and Relf, Kenner and Henderson, Shepherd, Brown, and Company, T. & D. Urquhart, and Samuel Winter engaged in all six functions while 11 other firms engaged in at least four. Forty-five percent of those in group one were shipowners compared to 25 percent in group two. This explains at least partially the much larger proportion of group one—76 percent—than group two—53 percent—engaged in the export-import business on their own account. Merchants in group one were less specialized in their functions than those in group two.

Operating as they did across a wider spectrum of business activities, the houses represented in group one were in touch with more areas for potentially profitable enterprise than the more specialized and smaller businessmen in group two. Profits derived from such enterprise enabled the older and larger merchants to invest heavily in corporations as well as land and slaves. For instance, the merchants in group one subscribed 58 percent of the original stock issue of the New Orleans Insurance Company in 1805 and still controlled 44 percent of the stock in 1816. Less than 20 percent of the shares

---

sion, export-import on own account, negotiation of notes and letters of exchange, and agent for one or more overseas firms. This rating is more tentative than the EBR because it is likely that some merchants of both groups engaged in activities included above that I am unaware of. Hopefully, the factor of ignorance is equally relevant to both groups.

were in the hands of the merchants in group two during this period. Nicholas Girod, the largest stockholder, owned 30 shares in 1809 worth $30,000 at par value and 16 shares in 1816. Thomas Callendar owned 12 shares in 1816; Benjamin Morgan, 10; and Paul Lanusse, 7. All of the above group one merchants owned stock in one or more of the other corporations, as did all other individuals in the group, some of whom also invested heavily in other enterprises. Morgan in partnership with William Kenner (group one) purchased a sugar plantation several miles above New Orleans for $90,000. In 1806 Chew and Relf in association with George T. Phillips engaged in townsite speculation and promotion three miles above Baton Rouge; John McDonogh and William W. Montgomery advertised in 1818 the subdivision of Shepherd Brown's estate directly across the river from New Orleans. Within the city, Kenner and Henderson and Maunsel White purchased a number of lots at the corner of Chartres and Royal Streets. Of the 20 merchants known to have owned and operated plantations—frequently through overseers—before 1815, 75 percent were included in group one. These men were concurrently members of both the urban and country elite.

Table X offers a composite view of the merchants in the two groups and provides a reasonable cross-section of the mercantile community of New Orleans in terms of establishment and function. Four of every ten merchants were in business prior to the Louisiana Purchase. Most of those established prior to 1800 were French, such as Antoine Cavalier, Jr., Francis Duplessis, Michel Fortier, Nicholas Girod, Paul Lanusse, and James Pitot. There were, however, some Americans, notably Daniel Clark, Jr., Evan Jones, Joseph McNeil, James Mather, and George and Oliver Pollock. Only two Spaniards, Fernando Alzar and Gerome Lechiapella, were uncovered. The influx between 1801 and 1803 was largely American. Thomas and David Urquhart, Scots, were exceptions. Beverly Chew had a prior career in New York and Philadelphia and in 1810 married the daughter of the late William Duer of New York; John McDonogh arrived with backing in Baltimore, as did John Palfrey; and Maunsel White came down from Louisville. The preponderance of Americans increased in later years, leavened however by a number of Europeans such as Vincent Nolte, born in Leghorn; A. and J. Denistoun from

TABLE X

Date Established in Business and Functions Engaged
in by 104 Merchants in New Orleans
before 1812, in Percentages[a]

Date Established in Business	%	Functions Engaged in	%
Before 1800	25	Storeowner	34
1801–03	16	Shipowner	36
1804–08	38	Export-Import on Commission	69
1804–12[b]	10	Export-Import on Own Account	67
1809–12	11	Negotiate notes, etc.	15
		Agent	37

[a] Excluded from the calculations relative to function were four auctioneers and two newspaper owners whose functions were somewhat different from those of the typical merchant.
[b] More precise information was lacking relative to the date of establishment for these ten. Rather than exclude them, a catchall category was utilized.

Glasgow; and Manuel J. de Lizardi, representing Lizardi and Company, a prominent house in Paris and London.

One of every three merchants managed a store, generally combining retail and wholesale services, or owned a ship. One of every five owned both a store and shipping. This combination made it likely that the merchant would engage in all the other functions listed, except perhaps the negotiation of money. The latter service was, of course, a concern of all merchants, but only 15 percent seems to have made a business of buying and selling exchange on various parts of the world. Most merchants probably utilized the discounting and exchange services offered by the local banks.

Available data indicate that between 30 and 40 percent of the combined groups traded with the United States, Europe, and an area including Central and South America and the Caribbean. As far as can be determined, there was no direct trade from New Orleans with North or West Africa, the British North American colonies, the Pacific Coast of North America, or Asia. Trade with South

America was largely confined to Atlantic ports from Laguna, Brazil, to the north. Trade in southern waters was pursued by both American and French firms. The latter enjoyed superior contacts in the French and Spanish possessions which were more significant to New Orleans than the English islands. Michel Fortier and Company developed out of Reaud and Fortier, a firm engaged in the Indian and West Indian trade in the early 1780s. The Duplantier, Duplessis, and Olivier firms followed similar business traditions. Armand Duplantier, Jr., succeeded to a business established in 1783 by his father, who retired in Baton Rouge before 1803. The Olivier firm probably antedated the American Revolution.

French firms, as might be anticipated, controlled most of the French trade but there was no absolute division whereby the French traded exclusively with France while the Anglo-Saxons dealt entirely with England. Fortier traded in the three areas noted above and Gerome Lechiapella served as an agent of Low and Wallace of New York in the 1780s. Anglo-Saxon merchants controlled most of the English trade and a growing proportion of the upriver trade with the Old Northwest, as well as the coasting trade to the eastern United States. Distinctions in geographic focus, however, were as much a factor of the time of establishment as ethnic group. Merchants in group one, older, larger, and more intimately involved in the economic life of the community, were more likely to trade in all three areas than merchants in group two. At least 16, or 25 percent, of the former are known to have done so, compared to three or four—less than 10 percent—of the latter. The trade in southern waters attracted the active attention of at least 25 merchants in group one, or 40 percent, compared to less than 15 percent of group two. Merchants in group two were the most specialized in geographic focus as well as business functions. They arrived later, took fewer risks, probably made less money, and were less involved in extra-curricular economic and political activities. The nucleus of an elite does not exist in group two. It does in group one.

More than half of the merchants in group one were established prior to 1803 while slightly less than half of the firms represented engaged in four or more of the business functions listed in Table X.

Thirteen of the merchants served only on the city council for at least one year, while 51 served at some time as a director. Sixteen served in both capacities. Thirteen men held state, territorial, or federal positions. Seven men served in all three capacities. For the purpose of defining an elite, membership on a board of directors was regarded as the most critical area of service, with a high frequency of service assumed to reflect an equivalent degree of wealth and prominence.[5]

Four corporations were established in 1805 and two more in 1811. The following discussion is confined to the period 1805–11 because the membership of each board of directors is known for each year and because 1811 represents the first year in which new administrative and investment opportunities were available to men who reached New Orleans after 1805. While each corporation was guided by ten directors, deaths and resignations meant that more than 40 positions were filled annually through 1810; on the average, 47 positions were filled annually. Taking the average for the six years, positions for as many as 282 individuals were available if each corporation in each year chose different men; in other words, with no person serving more than once or on the board of more than one company. In fact, 52 men filled all the positions for an average of 5.2 directorships per man.[6] In 1811 two new banks were chartered, creating positions for 24 new directors. Seventeen men who had no previous board experience plus seven previous directors were elected to those positions. Sixty-nine men, then, filled 351 positions during the seven years 1805–11 for an average of five positions per man.[7] The number of

[5] References are now exclusively to those firms and men included in group one. Twelve other individuals also served in both capacities but they are not included in group one. A few were nonmerchants, such as Colonel Bellechaise, a planter; John Watkins, M.D.; and L. S. Fontaine, editor of the *Moniteur de la Louisiane*. For others, such as Louis Blanc and J. Blanque, no information was discovered other than their terms as directors or councilmen. Their vocations are unknown.

[6] This could mean one directorship in each of five different years or some other combination.

[7] Not all of the directors were included in group one. Some of the directors, notably Julien Poydras, William Donaldson, and Richard Butler, were planters maintaining residences in New Orleans. At least one director, Abner L. Duncan, was an attorney, and information was lacking regarding a few others, particularly those elected as directors in 1811.

men serving and positions to be filled annually for each of seven years is noted below:

	1805	1806	1807	1808	1809	1810	1811
Men	31	35	31	34	30	34	49
Positions	37	47	47	52	46	53	69

The business elite of New Orleans derived from this group if, indeed, it was not this group.

Table XI represents an effort further to refine the membership of the elite by identifying those individuals who by available criteria were among the most prestigious in the city. Inclusion in the table was confined to those men holding six or more directorships during the seven years 1805–11. The list, while not presuming to identify *the* elite, is an objective and representative selection of men who incontestably belonged *to* the elite. Several men come to mind who, holding fewer than the required number of directorships, belonged to the establishment as surely as those listed. Edward Livingston and Abner L. Duncan, both attornies; John McDonogh and Julien Poydras, two of the wealthiest men in Louisiana; James Mather, appointed to the legislative council in 1804 and Mayor of New Orleans from 1807 to 1811; and Thomas L. Harmon and Daniel Clark, Jr., two of the most successful merchants in town, are a few examples of the elite group not included in Table XI.

The individuals included in Table XI composed 30 percent of all those serving as directors from 1805 to 1811. They filled 68 percent of the positions, averaging over ten per man. The EBR for this list is 1.82, compared with 2.25 for group one and 3.25 for group two. Of those in the table, 76 percent were established prior to the Louisiana Purchase and of those, half antedated 1800. While the SBR for group one was 3.75 compared to a rating of 3.25 for group two, the rating for those in the table is 4.16. Those individuals engaged in the six activities utilized in Table X are all included in Table XI. Many of those in the table were planters and all but five are known to have pursued active careers after 1815.

By taking certain partnerships into account, the degree to which corporate enterprise in New Orleans was controlled by relatively few individuals is accentuated. Chew and Relf, for example, filled 6 percent of all available corporate positions, as did William Nott

TABLE XI

Directors Holding Six or More Directorships, 1805–11, and Other Data

	No. of Director-ships	No. of Yrs. as Director	Director-ships after 1815[a]	No. of Yrs. on City Council	E.B.R.	S.B.R.	Planters[b]
Thomas Urquhart	20	7	B	0	2	6	—
Benjamin Morgan	19	7	B	6	2	2	BA
James Pitot	17	7	?	2	1	a	—
Paul Lanusse	16	7	B	0[c]	1	2	—
Richard Relf	14	6	B,I	2	2	6	—
William Kenner	13	7	B	0	2	6	BA
J. B. Labutat	13	7	B,I,O	0	3	6	—
Joseph McNeil	13	7	B	2	1	4	—
William Nott	12	7	B,I	0	3	3	A
Rezin D. Shepherd	12	7	B,I	0	3	6	A
Thomas Callendar	10	7	?	0	3	3	A
Samuel Winter	10	6	d.1813	5	2	6	BA
John Soulé	9	7	B,I,O	2	2	6	—
Joseph Tricou	9	6	?	0	3	?	—
Nicholas Girod	9	5	B	3	1	2	A
Beverly Chew	8	7	B	0	2	6	—
P. F. DuBourg	8	7	?	1	2	3	—
A. Cavalier, Jr.	7	7	?	0	1	?	—
Francis Duplessis	7	6	B	5	1	2	BA
Michel Fortier	7	7	B	0	1	5	BA
J. F. Livaudais	6	6	?	2	1	?	BA

[a] B = bank; I = insurance; O = other
[b] B = before 1815; A = after 1815
[c] Councilman, 1814–15
[d] Auctioneer

and Thomas Callendar of Amory, Callendar and Company. Benjamin Morgan, an inactive partner of Kenner and Henderson, and William Kenner, of the same firm, controlled 32 positions between them, to which might be added the directorship held by Stephen Henderson in 1811. Shepherd, Brown, and Company filled 12 positions through Rezin D. Shepherd, four through John McDonogh, and one through Shepherd Brown. The firm [Samuel] Winter and [Thomas L.] Harmon controlled 15 positions. These five houses held 31 percent of the directorships available. If the positions held by Thomas Urquhart, James Pitot, Paul Lanusse, J. B. Labutat, and Joseph McNeil are added, partners in or owners of ten firms occupied 54 percent of all the directorships between 1805 and 1811.

The degree of involvement of the ten firms in the new corporations is shown in Table XII. In 1809 those houses filled 61 percent of all the directorships available, averaging 58 percent for the six years 1805–10. This proportion declined in 1811 as none of the individuals associated with those firms was involved in the Louisiana Planter's Bank. Chew and Relf was represented on the boards of all four corporations in 1808, 1809, and 1810, while Kenner and Henderson held two positions on two corporations in five of the seven years. Over the seven years, the firms controlled a majority of each board 79 percent of the time. The Bank of Orleans, chartered in 1811, appears to be a replacement for the liquidating branch Bank of the United States. Five directors of the branch bank from the ten firms shifted to the nine-man board of the new bank in 1811. This led to accusations that the Bank of Orleans was the "American" bank *vis-a-vis* the Bank of Louisiana and the new Louisiana Planter's Bank which were supposedly the "Creole" institutions. With regard to the Bank of Louisiana, such a distinction is untenable. Three of the firms in Table XII—Amory, Callendar and Company, Chew and Relf, and Shepherd, Brown, and Company—had representatives after 1811 on both the Bank of Orleans and the Bank of Louisiana concurrently. The position of the Louisiana Planter's Bank is less clear.

There were more planters on the board of the Louisiana Planter's Bank than on the boards of the other corporations but merchants composed the majority. The merchants sitting on the board, while

TABLE XII

Directorships Held by Ten Mercantile Houses in Six
Corporations in New Orleans for the Seven Years, 1805–11

	1805				1806				1807				1808				1809				1810				1811					
	1	2	3	4	1	2	3	4	1	2	3	4	1	2	3	4	1	2	3	4	1	2	3	4	1	2	3	4	5	6
Amory, Callendar and Co.	2	1			2	1			1	1			1	2			1	2			1	2			1	1	1			
Chew and Relf		1				1	1			1	1		1	1	1	1	1	1	1	1	1	1	2	1	1	1				
Kenner and Henderson	1	2			2	1	2		2	1	2		2	1	2		2	1	2		1	1	2		1	2	2			
Shepherd, Brown and Co.	1	1			1	1			1	1			1	1			1	1			1	1			1	1	1			
Winter and Harmon	2				1	1	1		1	1	1		1	1			1	1	1		1	1	1							
J. B. Labutat	1				1	1			1	1			1				1				1	1			1	1				
Paul Lanusse	1				1	1	1		1	1	1		1	1			1	1			1	1			1	1	1			
Joseph McNeil						1				1	1			1				1		1		1		1		1	1			
James Pitot	1	1			1	1			1	1			1	1			1	1	1		1	1	1		1	1				
Thomas Urquhart	1	1			1	1	1		1	1	1		1	1	1		1	1	1		1	1	1		1	1	1			
Total	5	1	9	6	6	8	8	5	6	8	8	5	7	8	7	7	7	7	7	7	7	7	9	7	5	6	3	6	5	0

Key:
1 ... Bank of Louisiana
2 ... New Orleans Navigation Co.
3 ... New Orleans Insurance Co.
4 ... Branch Bank of the United States
5 ... Bank of Orleans
6 ... Louisiana Planter's Bank

not included in Table XI (with the exception of Francis Duplessis), were from solidly established firms. Solomon Hillen, Jr., was the partner of an ex-director of the branch bank, as was Nathaniel Coxe. Two of the directors in 1811, Richard Butler and William W. Montgomery, were appointed directors of the branch of the Second Bank of the United States in 1816 while Samuel Packwood moved to the board of the Bank of Orleans in 1817. Francis Duplessis, Jr., took over his father's position on the board of the Bank of Louisiana in 1812 so that the senior Duplessis could serve on the board of the Planter's bank. The banks were in competition, of course, but there is no overt evidence pointing to any kind of political tension between the Bank of Orleans and the Louisiana Planter's Bank.

There was nothing in the charter of the Louisiana Planter's Bank which discriminated against other groups in favor of planters or compelled the bank to serve planters in any special way. However, the act of incorporation of the Louisiana State Bank in 1818 established branches at Donaldsonville, Baton Rouge, St. Francisville, Alexandria, and St. Martinville.[8] A proportion of the total capital stock was reserved for those branches in an effort to augment sources of credit for the planters. The charters of the Bank of Orleans, the Louisiana Planter's Bank, and the Louisiana State Bank reflected an awareness by the legislators of the degree of control which a few men exercised over the corporations organized prior to 1811. All three charters prohibited election as a director of more than one partner from any commercial firm or any director of another bank. The charter of the Bank of Orleans, in addition, denied election to the partner of any person serving as a director of any other bank. When Kenner and Henderson, in 1811, divided their operations between two firms, William Kenner and Company and Stephen Henderson and Company, Benjamin Morgan retained an interest in the latter firm, thus circumventing the intent of the charter of the Bank of Orleans and allowing both Kenner and Morgan to serve on the board.

The investment commitment of the individuals and firms included in Tables XI and XII is known only in the case of the New Orleans

[8] The governor appointed six of the eighteen directors of the Louisiana State Bank.

Insurance Company. Individuals associated with the firms cited in Tables XI and XII owned 55 percent of the stock in 1809. Nicholas Girod, with 30 shares, Benjamin Morgan, with 16, and Thomas Callendar, with 10, controlled 28 percent of the total issue, representing an investment of $56,000. Those businessmen included in Table XI invested a total of $109,000 in the company. A very tentative and minimal investment projection for the 21 merchants in Table XI can be made, as it is known that directors of the Bank of Louisiana, Louisiana Planter's Bank, and the Bank of Orleans were required to own at least ten shares of stock. Assuming this to be the case for the New Orleans Navigation Company and with the stockholders of the insurance company known, the 21 merchants owned at least $210,000 worth of stock in five corporations.

Even the minimal figure is impressive—the more so since the Bank of the United States was excluded because of ignorance of stock requirements for directors—for it represents exactly 10 percent of the nominal capitalization of the five local corporations. Moreover, because the actual capitalization represented by paid-up shares was lower than the nominal figure, the investment commitment of the 21 merchants was undoubtedly much higher than 10 percent. The Bank of Louisiana did not market the full $600,000 in stock authorized by its charter, which was amended to allow the bank to operate when subscriptions for $300,000 in shares were received. Advertising extensively, the bank's promoters pointed out the advantages of a "home-owned" institution to both merchants and planters. An editorial in the *Louisiana Gazette* conjured up a view of the Bank of the United States, about to open a branch in New Orleans, reminiscent of later Jacksonian criticism of the second bank. According to the editor: "The Bank of the United States is owned chiefly by Europeans . . . all the profits arising from that Bank . . . will be drawn away from us . . . and it must in the end leave us poorer than it found us – whereas the Louisiana Bank, being owned altogether by the inhabitants of the country, all the profits which it may make will be divided among them & remain in the country." [9] After the war, when the second bank sought subscriptions, investment from New Orleans at $315,000 ranked below thirteen other cities includ-

[9] New Orleans *Louisiana Gazette*, December 28, 1804.

ing such smaller places as Wilmington, Delaware; Lexington, Kentucky; and Cincinnati, Ohio. Richmond, Virginia subscribed to about five times more stock and Charleston, South Carolina, almost eight times more than New Orleans. But in 1811 stock for the Bank of Orleans and Louisiana Planter's Bank was taken up rapidly.

The record of political participation reflected in column 4 of Table XI does less than full justice to several of the merchants. Some, like Fortier, Cavalier, Tricou, Callendar, Shepherd, Nott, and Labutat, were apparently politically inactive, at least prior to 1815. Others who did not serve on the city council held other positions. Thomas Urquhart, a member of the territorial House of Representatives, was elected speaker in 1808–10, elected to the territorial constitutional convention in 1812, and to the United States Senate from which he resigned in 1815. His brother David sat on the municipal council from 1806 to 1808. Benjamin Morgan and William Kenner received appointments to the legislative council from Governor Claiborne in 1804. James Pitot and Nicholas Girod were mayors of New Orleans, the former serving in 1804–05, the latter from 1812 to 1814. Pitot was appointed parish judge in 1812. Peter Dubourg was Collector of Customs between 1813 and 1815.[10] Francis Duplessis was a member of the Spanish Cabildo and treasurer of the city in 1800. Beverly Chew held down several positions: justice of the territorial Court of Common Pleas, territorial postmaster, and Collector of Customs from 1816 to 1829.

There were few men in New Orleans possessed of greater economic power or political influence than those appearing in Table XI. Most were established prior to the assumption of control by the United States and were either sufficiently eminent at that time or enjoyed such influential backing in the United States to attract the attention of the new sovereigns. Among the fifteen men recommended as possible directors of the branch bank by Collector Trist were Chew, Kenner, Callendar, Morgan, Fortier, Lanusse, and Dubourg. Several of the remaining eight have been encountered previously: John McDonogh, William Donaldson, Gerome Lechiapella, J. F. Merricult, and Charles Patton of Meeker, Williamson & Patton. William Taylor of Baltimore worked diligently for the appointment

10 Dubourg launched the New Orleans *General Weekly Price Current* in 1816.

of a member of Shepherd, Brown to the board of the branch bank. John McDonogh was disqualified because of his connection with the Bank of Louisiana. Chandler Price, a director of the parent bank, at the suggestion of Benjamin Morgan and Taylor, saw to the selection of Shepherd Brown in 1805. Morgan, Kenner, Callendar, Chew, McNeil, and Cavalier (all in Table XI) were also chosen along with John Palfrey—associated at that time with Rezin D. Shepherd, who was appointed to the board in 1808—George T. Phillips, Nathaniel Evans, and three others.

The political organization imposed on Louisiana by the United States proved unsatisfactory to some and gave rise to a degree of political factionalism between the so-called "French" and "American" parties. The elite furnished leadership to the factions, both of which maintained a certain liveliness during the territorial and war years, feeding on unsettling events such as the Burr conspiracy, the embargo, and finally the war and subsequent British invasion. Claiborne and other federal officials at the center of the strife were opposed by such as Edward Livingston, Daniel Clark, Jr., and Evan Jones. Factionalism was serious and substantive during the earlier years but degenerated into a matter of personal antagonism and pique during the later years of the period. In 1804 Claiborne's offers of appointments to the legislative council were refused on principle by Evan Jones, Daniel Clark, Étienne de Boré, Colonel Bellechaise, and others. Morgan, Kenner, Dr. John Watkins, James Mather, Julien Poydras, William Wikoff, and Gaspar Dubuys (Dubourg and Dubuys) were among those willing to accept appointments.

How far the political division carried over into economic affairs and with what impact is not a matter of record. Only one of the known opponents of territorial policy, Pierre Sauvé, was considered for appointment to the board of the branch bank. However, Sauvé, Edward Livingston, and Evan Jones, along with John McDonogh, Nicholas Girod, Paul Lanusse, Benjamin Morgan, and Michel Fortier were among the original promoters of the Bank of Louisiana in 1804–05. Sauvé was apparently sufficiently acceptable to the regime by 1805 to prompt his appointment to the legislative council, serving as its president in 1806, succeeding J. Noel Destrehan and succeeded by Colonel Bellechaise, both dissidents in 1804. Evan Jones served as the first president of the Bank of Louisiana and in 1810 as president of the branch Bank of the United States. So tenuous were the political allegiances that the defeat of Jones, erstwhile leader of the "French" faction in 1804, and the election of Benjamin Morgan as president of the branch bank in 1811 was considered a victory for the "French" faction.

Men associated with both factions served concurrently as the directors of several corporations. There is no evidence that such divisions penetrated the boards. As directors, the men guiding the companies were capitalists rather than politicians, entrepreneurs not factionalists, intent on maximizing profits and exploiting the services offered by the companies. The local banks were not established to provide a profitable source of investment for surplus capital nor did men invest in anticipation of large dividends. Their purpose was to deepen the well of credit available to the investors, thus augmenting the capital of each investor in proportion to his credit (reputation) and means. Merchants with access to bank credit were no longer limited in their ventures by their actual capital resources. Through the issue of bank notes and acceptance paper, banks multiplied the operating capital of the community and somewhat relieved merchants of the inconvenience of making and receiving payments in bullion. Given the crucial services dispensed by the banks, it was an obvious advantage to a merchant to participate in the policy making of those institutions. The houses in Table XII controlled numerical majorities in three of the four banks before 1812.

Of the two nonbanking corporations, the insurance company promised the greatest immediate returns from dividends. In view of the fact that the navigation company had first to sow before it could reap, motivation for investment in it is elusive. Any improvement in the transportation and port facilities of the city would benefit merchants and advance both public and private interests. Property along the line of the improvement would also rise. Kenner and Henderson owned property fronting Bayou St. John. Kenner served as a director of the improvement company and it is likely that other stockholders and directors had similar property interests between Lake Pontchartrain and the river. Both the insurance and improvement ventures were capital pools, the former for protection and the latter for construction. The insurance company contributed to the capital resources of the community by keeping insurance premiums at home. This was the import of the patriotic cry: "Citizens of America, insure yourselves." [11] It could just as easily have read "Citizens of New Orleans." Such reasoning mixed with a pinch of Anglophobia partially explains the annual tax of $1,000 levied in 1818 by Louisiana on the New Orleans branch of the Phoenix Insurance Company of London. Such sentiments also resulted in the adoption of a resolution in 1819 by the state House of Representatives to investigate the expediency and constitutionality of taxing the New Orleans branch Bank of the United States.

Except for the Bank of the United States, the corporations in New Orleans, were home-owned and home- and investor-controlled. With few exceptions, their affairs were managed by merchants—by relatively few merchants at that. Merchants established in New Orleans prior to 1803 occupied some 65 percent of all directorships in four corporations to 1810. While there is no evidence to support the contention that the directors sought their positions for the purpose of self-aggrandizement, it can be assumed that they managed the institutions in a manner reconcilable with both institutional policy and self-interest. Bank directors, among other functions, decided whether notes would be accepted for discount and negotiated with those seeking credit. Directors of the insurance company made decisions regarding the insurability of an applicant's ship and cargo and established premium rates. Each separate decision was of supreme importance to the applicant and at the same time the balance and accuracy of each corporate decision determined the degree of success experience by the corporation. There were few positions in the city of a more sensitive nature than that of director.

The function of an elite depends upon the fostering society, its customs and traditions—or its historical value structure—and evolving needs, which may or may not clash with historic patterns. Great hunters and warriors filled the council halls of the Chickasaw planning forays against the less aggressive Choctaw. But the convergence

[11] Charleston *Gazette*, n.d., quoted in New Orleans *Louisiana Gazette*, September 29, 1809.   .

of the paths of England, Spain, and France in the land of the Chickasaw, Choctaw, and other tribes disrupted hoary patterns of conflict, giving rise to the politician-Indian who played one European nation against the other in an effort to achieve some security for his tribe or tribal faction. The French elite consisted of administrator-soldiers, appointed by the crown to defend and advance the territorial dominions of the king. Ranking below the governors and intendants were the members of the Superior Council, largely colonists but restricted in their role to an advisory capacity and certain judicial functions. Local power and some wealth accrued to members of the council and caused fierce competition for a place on that body. Below the council, a handful of merchants and planters or planter-merchants achieved some prosperity. Du Breuil, de Pradel, Father Beaubois, Paul Rasteau, Pictet, Caminada, and a few others gained local notoriety for their wealth but served in no leadership capacity except perhaps as members of the local militia. Outlets for leadership ability were few and restricted to those with influence rather than capacity.

Spanish institutions, particularly the Cabildo, the large influx of Anglo-Saxons into the city, and the pragmatic application of Spanish commercial law by local officials vastly extended the potential field of endeavor for ambitious individuals. Members of the Cabildo assumed tasks previously executed with small results by French governors and intendants. The responsibilities of the Cabildo were monumental compared with those of the Superior Council, and the Spanish properly filled this body with the most prominent residents of the city and surrounding countryside. The city existed for the first time as a corporate entity; the Cabildo existed as a potential reward for prominence. Cabildo members were preeminently merchants and the mercantile community, availing itself of legitimate and illicit trading opportunities, advanced rapidly in wealth. Many newcomers, especially British and Americans, took up residence, a movement that was accelerated with the winning of independence by the American colonies, the dependence of New Orleans upon the United States for foodstuffs, and the outbreak of the French Revolutionary wars.

By the 1790s the solid nucleus of an American elite operated in

New Orleans. Evan Jones drifted into New Orleans from Mobile in 1765, selling his vessel, making contact with local merchants, and establishing a business in New Orleans by 1790. Oliver Pollock gained General O'Reilly's favor, establishing the firm of Pollock and Wraught by the early 1770s and bringing his brother George to the city in the 1780s. [James] Mather and [George] Morgan set up shop in 1776. Mather was heavily involved in the Indian trade by the mid-1780s, about the time Daniel Clark, Jr., arrived from Philadelphia. Clark and William E. Hulings, merchant, served as unofficial consular agents for the United States in New Orleans in the late 1790s. By this time, Joseph McNeil and Shepherd Brown were both solidly established in business. These merchants—officially unrecognized and regarded with suspicion by the Spanish government—joined with such French merchants as Francis Duplessis, Michel Fortier, Nicholas Girod, and Paul Lanusse to provide the basis for a ruling commercial class by the turn of the century.

Immigrants arriving between 1800 and 1803 provided additional personnel for the elite which assumed control of the most strategic sectors of economic life in New Orleans subsequent to the Louisiana Purchase. Beverly Chew and Richard Relf, William Kenner and Thomas Callendar were among the arrivals of those years. The elite group evidenced no dramatic growth from 1805 through the conclusion of the War of 1812. Membership in the group was a factor of economic success and stability. Vincent Nolte, in a barbed statement descriptive of the prewar years, maintained that none of the American merchants possessed any capital worth mentioning. Singling out Amory and Callendar as exceptions to the generality of American trader, Nolte described that firm as possessed of integrity and "a certain distrust of all undertaking which involved the least risk . . . two qualities which are rather rare in American business circles . . . ." [12]

Compared with New York, Philadelphia, or Boston, Nolte's judgment regarding the capital resources of the city was incontrovertible. Still, merchants in the city invested about two million dollars in five corporations and certainly more than that sum if subscriptions

[12] Vincent Nolte, *Fifty Years in Both Hemispheres, or Reminiscences of the Life of a Former Merchant* (New York, 1854), 90. Nolte failed in 1825–26.

to the water works and the steamboat company are included. Nicholas Girod purchased $30,000 in insurance company stock while Thomas Callendar subscribed to $10,000 worth of stock in the same firm. Benjamin Morgan owned, at a bare minimum, $22,000 worth of stock in three corporations. Obviously, the wealth of these merchants is unimpressive if contrasted with Stephen Girard or Alexander Brown but, unlike Philadelphia and Baltimore, New Orleans was just beginning to experience sustained economic growth.

Nolte was less than charitable in his judgment of the integrity and stability of merchants in New Orleans. One can assume that there were firms with less than the proper measure of both ingredients, but there is no evidence to support the contention that most or even many of the merchants in the city lacked integrity. Nolte's judgments reflect the application of European standards of behavior to business life in New Orleans. American merchants were more venturesome than French merchants. More Americans than French were involved, at least as directors, in the new forms of corporate enterprise introduced into New Orleans. The corporate form of business was less common in France than in England or the United States where the economy was less fettered by the encumbrances of arbitrary government, class distinctions, and internal barriers. French merchants were less attracted by high potential profits if the risk factor was abnormally high. To engage in traditional patterns of trade, American merchants, as colonists and after independence, were forced to accept risk as the norm. If they had not done so, there would have been no trade with the foreign West Indies or Spanish Main. They would not have come to New Orleans while it was a Spanish city.

The stability of a business can be judged in part by its capacity for survival; the character and reputation of a merchant by his ability to rebound after a serious business reverse. The elite merchants in New Orleans measure up well in both instances. Of the original 149 merchants, 15 failed between 1803 and 1815. Four of the failures were included in group one and represent three firms: H. and A. Amelung, George T. Phillips, and Palfrey and Shepherd. Phillips died; the Amelungs were operating again within two years; Palfrey turned to planting; and Shepherd became a senior partner in Shepherd, Brown, and Company. The individuals in Table XI and the firms they represent survived the fall of Napoleon. They survived a period of time when America's neutrality was ignored, the port of New Orleans closed to foreign trade for two years, and the United States engaged in a war against the premier naval power in the world.

These firms entered the postwar world with confidence as did the nation in general. Times had never looked better. The world was at peace. Demand for cotton was great and prices high. The Mississippi River Valley was the destination for thousands and thousands of settlers whose only route to market passed New Orleans. Steamboat service spread rapidly throughout the valley. New banks and insurance companies were organized in the city. New adventurers, braving the fever, invaded the town. It was the beginning of a new era and the eleventh hour for the old. The demise of the old was sped along by the Panic of 1819 and the subsequent years of depression.

The old guard, the original elite, lost their rather complete control of economic affairs while the nation and the city worked itself out of depression. Paul Lanusse failed in 1823 and died in Mexico in 1825 trying to recoup his fortune. William Kenner and Company collapsed in 1825. T. and D. Urquhart barely survived a series of severe blows. Benjamin Morgan died in 1826. The survivors shared their positions of influence and power with new men. John Palfrey placed two of his five sons, Henry and William, with merchants in New Orleans. Henry learned business from Chew and Relf and in 1819 joined with William Taylor as Palfrey and Taylor.[13] As the hinterlands of New Orleans became more productive and business expanded in the city, the numbers of the elite were augmented and economic power somewhat diffused. More men possessed more capital to invest in a greater variety of enterprises. Mobility and fluidity engendered by extraordinary growth displaced the relative stability enjoyed by the business community during the first American years. Lists of vestrymen and managers of dramatic groups serve less well in identifying this new elite.

[13] Henry Palfrey, Maunsel White, and Rezin D. Shepherd were among the delegates from New Orleans to the railroad convention held in New Orleans in January, 1852. Two others in attendance antedated the War of 1812, E. J. Forstall and James W. Zacherie.

17

A Century of Economic Growth

N 1803 no city in the United States possessed a commercial hinterland so vast as that served by New Orleans. While the Mississippi River and its tributaries provided access to the sea for an expanding population a thousand miles to the north, the major ports along the eastern seaboard of the United States chaffed at the restrictions imposed by the Appalachian barrier. New York, Philadelphia, Boston, and Baltimore vied with one another for the trade of narrowly circumscribed but rather densely populated back countries and for a share in the foreign trade. New York, for instance, was still largely confined to the Hudson River Valley and areas only slightly west and north of Albany and had made few inroads into the commerce of Boston or Newport along the northern shore of Long Island Sound. A glance at a map convinced many New Orleans residents in the early decades of the nineteenth century that their city was invulnerable to competition.

At the conclusion of the first decade of American rule, almost a century had passed since Bienville and his comrades first paddled up the Mississippi River searching for a suitable site upon which to raise a city. From the very beginning of their occupation, the French enjoyed a vision of Louisiana's future greatness to which New Orleans was quickly appended and then made central. The idea of New Orleans as a great metropolis was defined and described in all its component parts, based upon the magnificent position of the town, astride the Mississippi, with potential command of the trade of a continent. To be sure, such expectations hardly described reality. Life was hard in New Orleans and the anticipated growth of commerce and agriculture was obstructed by wars, natural disasters, governmental priorities, and human and monetary scarcities.

Still, New Orleans' destiny as a staple town was charted during the period of French control. Crop possibilities were tested and a plantation economy was developed with strength sufficient to survive numerous calamities. Commercial connections were regularized with France and her colonies as well as with other parts of the world. Spain inherited a small but established society.

Economic growth had been slow—distressingly so—during the French period. Louisiana could not prosper under the French regardless of the system imposed for the simple reason that France lacked the resources necessary to exploit such distant frontiers. France was not powerful enough, nor was the power that she commanded flexible enough to develop and defend Canada, Louisiana, the Antilles, and India while simultaneously pursuing traditional diplomatic objectives in Europe. She lacked three basic elements: capitalists willing to invest surplus funds in an undeveloped region such as Louisiana; a navy adequate to her colonial pretensions; and a population willing to emigrate. Spain had much less of each of these three elements necessary to the successful exploitation of Louisiana.

New Orleans emerged as a major staple port during the period of Spanish ascendancy. Forgotten by most Frenchmen and unimportant to most Spaniards, Louisiana was discovered economically by the British during their efforts to establish control in the West Floridas and the Illinois country and was incorporated within their informal trading empire. British economic interest sustained the colony until the American Revolution. Eventually involving both France and Spain, the American Revolution resulted in such a reshuffling of geographic possessions in North America as to finally provide the elements necessary for economic development in New Orleans and her hinterlands.

A new nation was born to the north, Spain reconquered the Floridas and conquered much of that portion of Louisiana which had gone to Great Britain in 1763. The Anglo-Saxons, for all the nervous tension they aroused in the Spaniards, supplied the mobile population, potential source of capital, and entrepreneurial skills that Spain herself was unable to provide. Although the Spanish viewed the sweep of Americans across the Appalachians as a threat to New

Spain, this movement created the first productive hinterland for New Orleans in the Upper Mississippi Valley and ultimately contributed to the populating of the lands in and around Louisiana.

The American presence did not mean that New Orleans and Louisiana would become an economic asset to Spain. Americans accompanied their goods. Even though New Orleans demonstrated a greater growth rate in the last fifteen years of the eighteenth century than in the entire preceding period, the profits did not flow into Spanish coffers but rather into the pockets of indigenous merchants and newly arrived entrepreneurs. New Orleans and the province, an economic backwater even within the economically backward Spanish colonial empire, was not worth accommodating before prosperity arrived. With prosperity it became unassimilable because the nature of its commerce worked at cross purposes to and functioned in spite of the established system. Louisiana's transfer to France and then to the United States hastened the economic metamorphosis of the region and its urban center.

One economic historian has suggested that the timing and pace of the development of the economy of the United States was determined by the success of its export sector, the characteristics of the export industry, and the disposition of the income received from the export sector.[1] An economy is successful, Douglass North suggests, if an expansion of the external market provides the means for an increase in the size of the domestic market, growth in money income, the spread of specialization, and the division of labor. In the unsuccessful economy, the increment to income from the expansion of the export industry leads to an increase in the supply of the major export commodity but not to the broadening of the economy. It may be useful to conclude this study of colonial New Orleans by considering the region in the light of North's model.

During the late Spanish period there is evidence of a widening of the export base with the introduction of new staples—cotton, sugar, and grain products—of greater potential value than the major staples of the French period—tobacco, indigo, and furs. Tobacco was retained as an export commodity but its center of production shifted

[1] Douglass C. North, *The Economic Growth of the United States, 1790–1860* (Englewood Cliffs, 1961).

out of Louisiana. Technological progress in Europe and North America contributed to the successful conversion to cotton and sugar while a growing population in the Upper Valley, engaged in the cultivation of grains and tobacco, provided in addition a large domestic market for New Orleans. This latter development was exploited by New Orleans to its fullest extent only after the War of 1812 with the initiation of regular steamboat connections with the Upper Valley. In the immediate vicinity of New Orleans, profitable operations in cotton and sugar attracted large numbers of planters and slaves (as had been the case during the tobacco boom of the Spanish period). Thus, there was a change in the nature and size of the agricultural economy served by New Orleans from a restricted plantation economy to an enlarged plantation and mixed-farming economy, spread from the English Turn west to the Teche and north to the Ohio River Valley.

Factors included in North's description of the unsuccessful economy persisted, however, into the early American period. New Orleans and the area it served suffered from an adverse balance of payments during the entire French period and most of the Spanish. Subjective evidence indicates that this condition was ameliorated by about 1800 but not wholly rectified during the next troubled decade. Money and credit were always scarce but the reasons for the deficit appear to have changed from the French to the American period. In the former, inadequate capital was available to maintain more than a static level of commerce. In the latter period, the demands of an expanding economic base outran the supply of development capital. One response was the chartering of the Bank of Louisiana and other banks in later years. As suggested by Fritz Redlich, such banks were created not because capital was seeking investment but because men without capital and credit wanted loans.[2]

Moreover, there was only a small and relatively insignificant development of residentiary industry in New Orleans that was not directly connected with the processing and movement of staple crops. Of the industries that flourished, the most heavily capitalized were service firms such as banks and insurance companies. Job-

[2] Fritz Redlich, *The Molding of American Banking: Men and Ideas* (2 vols.; New York, 1951), I, 43.

generating industries appeared only slowly—cotton presses, found-
ries, and the like—and frequently employed slave labor. White labor
was largely confined to service functions, crafts, and construction.
The plantation economy, then, did not stimulate the evolution of an
urban center in the nineteenth century as fully diversified in nature
as were urban centers in the Northeast or the cities which rose in
the Northwest in the middle of the nineteenth century. However
active New Orleans was economically, it was a commercial rather
than commercial-industrial metropolis. In this sense, the economic
functions of the city remained constant from its foundation through
the coming of the Civil War.

This is not to say that such a developmental course was less advantageous economically than some other pattern—say, a partial diversion of capital into industry—at least not in the short run and
certainly not in the eighteenth and early nineteenth centuries. In an
era when industrialization appears to have been the dominant causa-
tive force in the creation of an affluent society, the temptation is
great to apply this criterion to all points in the past. If such an approach is selected, then there is an inherent obligation to define in
detail the feasible hypothetical alternatives available to New Orleans, the region, or the nation as the case may be. In short, what the
better course would have been must be spelled out, and it must be
demonstrated that the effort would have been worth the costs involved both for the individuals concerned and for society as a whole.

North's model of success applies largely to a preindustrial economy and it is relevant to that extent in the specific case of New
Orleans. But it must be remembered that there is no such thing as
an archtypical balanced economy (which I assume North's successful economy to be). A balanced economy is one which uses its
resources most efficiently at a given time. What appears to later
generations as an overconcentration on a single sector of the economy may have been the most expedient course for the contemporary
generation, given its location and resources. In other words, imbal-
ance may be the only road to economic growth in certain situations.
It may be that success was the equivalent of survival and the eventual
achievement of a static economic level during the French period.

In discussing a colonial economy there is present a built-in factor
which impinges upon growth; that is, outside control or an absence

of choice at the local level. This need not be detrimental to the colonists if colonial officials read the environment correctly or govern weakly. For the Louisiana colony, the problem was that assessments of the potentialities of the environment (if hitherto totally undeveloped) were made from the frame of reference of the metropole, a frame of reference that was politically as well as economically inspired and which had within its view the total colonial system. Political ambitions, territorial objectives, security pressures generated along the frontiers of the mother country restricted the degree of attention given to Louisiana by both France and Spain. Colonial officials—Bienville, Maurepas, Vaudreuil, Gálvez, and Carondelet—recognized the potential value of the colony but were able to act only partially and fitfully in ways conducive to development. During the French and Spanish eras, the fiscal structure of the state—itself a blend of sociological, political, and economic variables—influenced economic decisions relative to the colony in ways harmful to the latter but advantageous to the mother country or another colony. Policies formulated to regulate the tobacco trade illustrate this tendency.

But at the same time, the colony survived and the flexibility of resident Spanish officials promoted its growth, albeit outside of the Spanish colonial system. Despite the fact that the economy may have been imbalanced or relatively undiversified, it had realized a degree of stability and had formulated patterns of commerce which the Americans utilized and supplemented. Even though the concentration on staples intensified, it is unrealistic to describe the economy of New Orleans and its hinterlands as unsuccessful. Although the history of New Orleans and Louisiana is to a degree one of frustration and misplaced hopes during the French and Spanish periods, the settlement of the Upper Valley by hundreds of thousands of Americans and the arrival of Americans in New Orleans introduced a new and vital dynamic into the life of the city. This dynamic—compounded of unabashed idealism, a vision of an unexampled future for the city, uninhibited opportunism, directed materialism, and technical competence—operated in a milieu relatively free from restraint and enjoying the advantages of French and Spanish beginnings. The mixture of this dynamic with residual qualities produced the New Orleans of antebellum days.

Notes on Sources

Workers in the field of Louisiana history must forever be indebted to such intrepid researchers as Alcée Fortier, François-Xavier Martin, and Charles Étienne Arthur Gayarré. Although their works are considered by some to be hopelessly outdated, filled with errors, and impossible to read, I used them whenever necessary throughout this work both as a general guide and as a source of information.

No less important for the French period were the two principal works of N. M. Miller Surrey, *Calendar of Manuscripts in Paris Archives and Libraries Relating to the History of the Mississippi Valley to 1803* (2 vols.; privately printed, 1928) and *The Commerce of Louisiana During the French Regime, 1699–1763, Columbia University Studies in History, Economics, and Public Law,* LXXI (New York, 1916). The *Calendar* enabled me to locate manuscript materials in transcript form in French Colonial Documents, Library of Congress; and Mississippi Provincial Archives, French Dominion, Mississippi Department of Archives and History, Jackson, Mississippi, as well as the Archives Nationale, Paris. The bulk of the material for chapters 1 through 8 derives from these sources, involving hundreds of letters, numerous memoirs and other lengthy accounts, census materials, etc. In the first draft of this work, reference material was footnoted in the conventional manner, running seventy to ninety footnotes per chapter. Because no suitable criteria occurred to me for the deletion of one reference vis-a-vis any other, I decided to delete all locational citations.

Supplementing Surrey's *Calendar* were three particularly useful reference works: Olivia Blanchard (tr.), *Regulations, Edicts, Declarations and Decrees Concerning the Commerce, Administration of Justice and Policing of Louisiana and other French Colonies in America, Together with* The Black Code (New Orleans, 1940); Joseph M. White (comp.), *A New Collection of Laws, Charters and Local Ordinances of the Governments of Great Britain, France, and Spain, Relating to the Concessions of Land in Their Respective Colonies* . . . (2 vols.; Philadelphia, 1839); and Laurence C. Wroth and Gertrude L. Annan (comps.), *Acts of French Royal Administration Concerning Canada, Guiana, the West Indies, and Louisiana, prior to 1791* (New York, 1930).

Two of the most essential printed collections of primary materials were: B. F. French (comp.), *Historical Collections of Louisiana, embracing translations of Many . . . Documents Relating to the Natural, Civil and Political History of that State* (7 vols.; New York, 1846–75); and Dunbar Rowland and Albert Godfrey Sanders (eds.), *Mississippi Provincial Archives, 1704–1743: French Dominion* (3 vols.; Jackson, 1932). Among the items found in the former were the memoirs of Bernard de La Harpe, M. Dumont, and the Chevalier de Champigny. The Rowland and Sanders work contains many translations of materials cited in Surrey's *Calendar*. Archival materials consulted for the French period included the Loudon Papers, Vaudreuil Letters, Henry E. Huntington Library, San Marino, California; and Louisiana Superior Council Records (Mss microfilm) and Rosemonde E. and Emile Kuntz Collection, both in Tulane University Library, Manuscript Division. The Superior Council Records are extremely difficult to read because of faculty reproduction and the poor condition of the original manuscript. Fortunately, some of this material has been published in various volumes of the *Louisiana Historical Quarterly*. Apparently, the original manuscripts are locked away forever in a vault in the Presbytere at New Orleans. The Council records are indispensable to an understanding of the day-to-day routine of economic activity in New Orleans during the eighteenth century.

Other primary data useful through chapter 3 were: Sr. Bougues, *Colonie de la Louisiane: Journal historique* (1722), Tulane University Library, Manuscript Division; [Jean Bernard] Bossu, *Travels through that part of North America formerly called Louisiana*, translated by John F. Forster (2 vols.; London, 1771); *Memoir of Charles Le Gac, Director of the Company of the Indies in Louisiana, 1718–1721*, translated from the French by Olivia Blanchard (n.p., 1937–38); P. D. Charlevoix, *Journal of a Voyage to North America* . . . , edited and translated by Louise Phelps Kellogg (2 vols.; Chicago, 1923); A. S. Le Page du Pratz, *The History of Louisiana . . . with An Account of the Settlements, Inhabitants, Soil, Climate, and Products* (2 vols.; London, 1763);

Thomas Jefferys, *The Natural and Civil History of the French Dominions in North and South America . . .* (Charing Cross, 1760); and Richebourg G. McWilliams (tr. and ed.), *Fleur de Lys and Calumet: Being the Pénicaut Narrative of French Adventure in Louisiana* (Baton Rouge, 1953).

A large number of secondary works figure in these early chapters as well as those that follow. Among those utilized to this point that deal specifically with French Louisiana are: J. Hanno Deiler, *The Settlement of the German Coast of Louisiana and the Creoles of German Descent* (Philadelphia, 1909); Henry Folmer, *Franco-Spanish Rivalry in North America, 1524–1763* (Glendale, Calif., 1953); Guy Frégault, *Le Grand Marquis, Pierre de Rigaud de Vaudreuil et la Louisiane* (Montreal, 1952); Marcel Giraud, *Histoire de la Louisiane Française* (3 vols.; Paris, 1953—) and "La France et la Louisiane au debut du XVIII siècle," *Revue historique*, CCIV (October–December, 1950), 185–208. Giraud's multi-volume study, when completed, will be a comprehensive and probably definitive study of French Louisiana. The value of the first three volumes is enhanced by the author's close attention to continental and world-wide affairs. Other valuable secondary works include: Clarence P. Gould, "Trade between the Windward Islands and the Continental Colonies of the French Empire, 1683–1763," *Mississippi Valley Historical Review*, XXV (1939), 473–91; Henri Gravier, *La colonisation de la Louisiane à l'époque de Law: Octobre, 1717–Janvier, 1721* (Paris, 1904); James D. Hardy, "The Transportation of Convicts to Colonial Louisiana," *Louisiana History*, VII (1966), 207–20 and Hardy, "Law in French Louisiana," in *Proceedings of the Ninth Annual Genealogical Institute* (Baton Rouge, 1966); Pierre Heinrich, *La Louisiane sous la Compagnie des Indes, 1717–1731* (Paris, 1908); Charles Wilson Hockett, "Policy of the Spanish Crown Regarding French Encroachments from Louisiana, 1721–1762," in Charles W. Hockett, G. P. Hammond, *et al* (eds.), *New Spain and the Anglo-American West: Historical Contributions Presented to Herbert Eugene Bolton* (2 vols.; Los Angeles, 1932), I, 107–145; and Charles E. O'Neill, *Church and State in Colonial Louisiana* (New Haven, 1966).

Helpful in conceptualizing the French colonial experience in general were: D. K. Fieldhouse, *The Colonial Empires: A Comparative Survey from the Eighteenth Century* (New York, 1967); Earl J. Hamilton, "The Role of Monopoly in the Overseas Expansion and Colonial Trade of Europe before 1800," *American Economic Review*, XXXVIII (May, 1948), 33–53; H. Hauser, "The Characteristic Features of French Economic History from the Middle of the Sixteenth Century to the Middle of the Eighteenth Century," *Economic History Review*, IV (1933), 257–72; and Frederic C. Lane, "Force and Enterprise in the Creation of Oceanic Commerce," *Journal of Economic History*, X, supplement (1950), 19–31.

Information relevant to specific French colonial and domestic history was obtained from: H. Carré, *Le règne de Louis XV, 1715–1774* in Ernest Lavisse (ed.), *Histoire de la France depuis les origines jusqu' à la revolution*, (9 vols.; Paris, 1909–11), VIII; Charles Woolsey Cole, *Colbert and a Century of French Mercantilism* (2 vols.; New York, 1939); Dom H. Leclerq, *Histoire de la Régence pendant la minorité de Louis XV* (3 vols.; Paris, 1921), II; E. Levasseur, *Histoire du commerce de la France* (2 vols.; Paris, 1911), II; Richard Pares, *War and Trade in the West Indies, 1739–1763* (Oxford, 1936) and Pares, *Yankees and Creoles: The Trade Between North America and the West Indies before the American Revolution* (Cambridge, Mass., 1956); and Herbert Ingram Priestley, *France Overseas Through the Old Regime: A Study of European Expansion* (New York, 1939). For financial and monetary history, see: P. Harsin, *Les doctrines monétaires et financières en France du XVI au XVIII siècle* (Paris, 1928); "La banque et le systeme du Law," in J. G. Van Dillen (coll.), *History of the Principal Public Banks accompanied by Extensive Bibliographies of the History of Banking and Credit in Eleven European Countries* (The Hague, 1934), 273–300, and Harsin (ed.), *John Law: Oeuvres complètes* (3 vols.; Paris, 1934); Herbert Lüthy, *La banque Protestante en France de la révocation de l'édit de Nantes à la Révolution* (2 vols.; Paris, 1959–61); and Marcel Marion, *Histoire financière de la France depuis 1715* (2 vols.; Paris, 1914–17), I. For the Company of the Indies and earlier monopolies, see: Pierre Bonnassieux, *Les grandes compagnies de commerce: Étude pour servir à l'histoire de la colonisation* (Paris, 1892); Joseph Chailley-Bert, *Les compagnies de colonisation sous l'Ancien Régime* (Paris, 1898); Wilbert Harold Dalgliesh, *The Company of the Indies in the Days of Dupleix* (Easton, Pa., 1933); Albert Girard, "La reorganisation de la Compagnie des Indes, 1719–1723," *Revue d'histoire moderne et contemporaine*, XI (1908–1909), 5–34, 177–97; Gaston Martin, "Nantes et la Compagnie des Indes, 1664–1769," *Revue d'histoire économique et sociale*, XV (1927), 25–65, 231–53; and Leon Vignols and Henri Sée, "Les ventes de la Compagnie des Indes à Nantes, 1723–1733," *Revue de l'histoire des colonies françaises*, XIII, 4 trimestre (1925), 489–550.

The basic data for these chapters were found in French Colonial Documents, Library of Congress; Mississippi Provincial Archives, Mississippi Department of Archives and History, and Rowland and Sanders (eds.), *Mississippi Provincial Archives, 1704–1743*. Chapter 4 relied heavily on materials from the Archives Nationale, AC., B55, 56–58, 60, 62, 64–69, 71, 75, 77, and 86, including letters from Maurepas to the Chamber of Commerce at La Rochelle, marine officials in various French ports, merchants—notably Rasteau, père—and to colonial officials in New Orleans, particularly Bienville and Salmon. Chapter 5 utilized the Louisiana Superior Council records, especially microfilm reels #79–81, 83, 85–86, 91–92, 98–104, 108, 112–13, and 116, including correspondence between merchants, contractual agreements, invoices, etc. A. Baillardel and A. Prioult (eds.), *Le Chevalier de Pradel, Vie d'un colon Français en Louisiane au XVIII siècle: D'apres sa correspondance et celle de sa famille* (Paris, 1928) illustrates the marketing problems of a major Louisiana planter.

Among the more useful secondary sources was Arthur M. Wilson, *French Foreign Policy During the Administration of Cardinal Fleury, 1726–1743: A Study in Diplomacy and Commercial Development* (Cambridge, Mass., 1936). Wilson is appreciative of the pacific foreign policy of Fleury and the great strides made in the overseas commerce of France. H. Carré, *Le règne de Louis XV*, and G. Lacour-Gayet, *La marine militaire de la France sous le règne de Louis XV* (Paris, 1902), among others, are critical of Fleury's English-oriented foreign policy. The studies of Richard Pares, Herbert Lüthy, Marcel Marion, and E. Levasseur (see Notes on Sources, chapters 1–3) again proved valuable. Further data were derived from: Ella Lonn, "The French Council of Commerce in Relation to American Trade," *Mississippi Valley Historical Review*, VI (1919), 192–219; Louis-Phillippe May, *Histoire économique de la Martinique, 1635–1763* (Paris, 1930); J. Saintoyant, *La colonisation Française sous l'Ancien Régime, du XV siècle à 1789* (2 vols.; Paris, 1929), II; and Henri Sée, *L'evolution commerciale et industrielle de la France sous l'Ancien Régime* (Paris, 1925) and Sée, *Histoire économique de la France: Le Moyen Âge et l'Ancien Régime* (Paris, 1948).

The paragraphs in chapter 4 dealing with the French ports were based upon: Philippe Barrey, "Le Havre et la navigation aux Antilles sous l'Ancien Régime: La question coloniale, en 1789–1791," in Julien Hayem (ed.), *Mémoires et documents pour servir à l'histoire du commerce et de l'industrie en France* (9 vols.; Paris, 1911–25), V. P. Boissonnade, "La marine marchand, le port et les armateurs de La Rochelle à l'époque de Colbert, 1662–1683," in *Comité des Travaux Historiques et Scientifiques, Bulletin de la Section de Géographie*, XXXVII (Paris, 1922), 1–45; Emile Garnault, *Le commerce Rochelais au XVIII siècle d'apres les documents composant les anciennes archives de la Chambre de Commerce de la Rochelle* (4 vols.; La Rochelle, 1888–98), III–IV; Theophile Malvezin, *Histoire du commerce de Bordeaux depuis les origines jusqu' à nos jours* (4 vols.; n.p., 1892); Francisque Michel, *Histoire du commerce et de la navigation à Bordeaux* (2 vols.; Bordeaux, 1866–70), II; Gaston Rambert, *Histoire du commerce de Marseille, 1660 à 1789*, vol. IV of Gaston Rambert (ed.), *Histoire du commerce de Marseille* (6 vols.; Paris, 1954—), part 2; Henri Sée, *Le commerce de Saint-Malo au XVIII siècle d'apres les papiers des Magon* in Hayem (ed.), *Mémoires et documentes*, IX; and J. T. Viaud and E. J. Fleury, *Histoire de la ville et du port de Rochefort* (2 vols.; Rochefort, 1845).

CHAPTER 6

Most of the data for this chapter were gleaned from numerous letters to and from Maurepas, Salmon, Lénormant, Bienville, and Vaudreuil. These were found in French Colonial Documents, Library of Congress; Mississippi Provincial Archives, Mississippi Department of Archives and History; Loudon Papers, Vaudreuil Letters, Henry E. Huntington Library; and Archives Nationale. AN. AC. B70, 72, 77–78, 82, and 86.

The effort to place the monetary and financial crises of French Louisiana within the context of general colonial monetary problems was aided by my reading of: Stuart W. Bruchey, *The Roots of American Economic Growth. An Essay in Social Causation* (New York, 1965); E. James Ferguson, "Currency Finance: An Interpretation of Colonial Monetary Practices," *William and Mary Quarterly*, X (April, 1953), 153–80; Curtis P. Nettels, *The Money Supply of the American Colonies Before 1720, University of Wisconsin Studies in the Social Sciences and History*, No. 20 (Madison, 1934); Douglass C. North, *Growth and Welfare in the American Past: A New Economic History* (Englewood Cliffs, 1966); and Jacob Viner, "Power Versus Plenty as Objectives of Foreign Policy in the Seventeenth and Eighteenth Centuries," *World Politics*, I (1948), 1–29.

For the French background, works previously mentioned, such as

Lüthy and Marion, were supplemented by Raymond de Roover, *L'evolution de la lettre de change XIV–XVIII siècles* (Paris, 1953) and Henri Lévy-Bruhl, *Histoire de la lettre de change en France aux XVI et XVIII siècles* (Paris, 1933).

CHAPTER 7

Correspondence among and between merchants and French resident and colonial officials supplied most of the information for this chapter. French Colonial Documents, Library of Congress, contains the relevant correspondence between French colonial officials and their superiors at home. Vaudreuil's letters to Maurepas are in the Loudon Papers and other information relative to Vaudreuil's administration is in Frégault, *Le Grand Marquis*. Ministry of the Marine communications, memoirs, orders, and the like are in Archives Nationale, AN. AC. B55–57, 61–62, 64–66, 72–75, 77–79, C9, and F3. Commercial routine at New Orleans may be traced through the Louisiana Superior Council records at Tulane, especially reels #81, 83, 85–86, 88, 91–92, 95, 103–104, 108, and 113, and the translations in the *Louisiana Historical Quarterly*.

Although most of the data on the slave trade came from the above sources, Elizabeth Donnan, *Documents Illustrative of the History of the Slave Trade to America, Carnegie Institution of Washington, Publication No. 409*, (4 vols.; Washington, 1931), II, IV, and Lucien Peytraud, *L'esclavage aux Antilles Françaises avant 1789* (Paris, 1897) were useful.

Numerous secondary works contributed material for this chapter. Among those previously cited, E. Levasseur and Arthur Wilson provided a general framework. Richard Pares, N. M. Miller Surrey, and Emile Garnault provided relevant facts about more specific areas of trade and commercial patterns. To these should be added the article by Clarence P. Gould, "Trade between the Windward Islands and the Continental Colonies of the French Empire," May, *Histoire économique de la Martinique (1635–1763)*, and Jules Ballet, *La Guadeloupe: Renseignements sur l'histoire . . . le commerce, l'industrie . . .* (5 vols.; Basse-Terre, 1899), II (1715–74). An overview of the specie-dynamic in world trade is found in Louis Dermigny, "Circuits de l'argent et milieux d'affaires au XVIII siècle," *Revue historique*, CCXII (October–December, 1954), 239–78.

CHAPTER 9

A few of the primary sources consulted for the French period served equally well for the Spanish era. This was especially true for the Louisiana Superior Council Records, reels #113–17, 120, and 128, which provided some insight into the difficulties faced by New Orleans merchants during the transition from French to solid Spanish control. Wroth and Annan (comps.), *Acts of French Royal Administration*, noted earlier, was useful in following the French solution to the monetary crisis caused by the Seven Years' War. The relevant *arrêts* are cited in this work and are available at the John Carter Brown Library, Brown University, and the New York Public Library, among other places. Joseph White, (comp.), *A New Collection of Laws of the Governments of Great Britain, France, and Spain Relating to the Concessions of Land in Their Respective Colonies*, and Arthur P. Whitaker (ed. and tr.), *Documents Relating to the Commercial Policy of Spain in the Floridas with Incidental Reference to Louisiana, Publications of the Florida State Historical Society*, No. 10, (Deland, 1931) afford the researcher access to the developing land and commercial policy of Spain in Louisiana.

Great Britain's efforts to establish herself in West Florida and the Illinois as well as to preempt the trade of Louisiana and undercut New Orleans may be traced in: Great Britain, Colonial Office Papers, Series C.O.V., vols. 574–622 (dealing with British West Florida) and 597–98 (especially concerned with Louisiana); and Clarence W. Alvord and Clarence E. Carter (eds.), *The Critical Period, 1763–1765, The New Regime, 1765–1767,* and *Trade and Politics, 1767–1769, Collections of the Illinois State Historical Library*, X, XI, XVI [British Series, I–III] (Springfield, 1915–16, 1921); and Alvord (ed.), *Kaskaskia Records, 1778–1790, Collections of the Illinois State Historical Society*, Vol. V [Virginia Series, vol. II] (Springfield, 1909). Equally valuable collections of documents relevant to the Spanish experience in the Mississippi Valley were: Louis Houck (ed.), *The Spanish Regime in Missouri* (2 vols.; Chicago, 1909); Lawrence Kinnaird (ed.), *Spain in the Mississippi Valley, 1765–1794*, Vols. II and III of the *Annual Report of the American Historical Association* (4 vols.; Washington, 1945–49); and Herbert Eugene Bolton (ed. and tr.), *Athanase de Mézières and the Louisiana-Texas Frontier, 1768–1780* (2 vols.; Cleveland, 1914).

Among the manuscript sources consulted, none are more important for the entire Spanish period than the five books of Spanish (and English translation) of *Records and Deliberations of the Cabildo, 1769–1803,* in the New Orleans Public Library. This source was used extensively in chapters 9, 11, and 13; it was the major source for chapter 13. Supplementing the Cabildo Records, and housed just across the street, are Miscellaneous French Records, 1732–69, in the Notarial Archives, Civil Courts Building. Unfortunately, there is only one volume of *acts* prior to 1764. These were used more extensively for the American period. The name of the notary identifies each volume. The Kuntz Collection, Tulane University Library, was again useful, especially the "Report of François Bouligny, July–August, 1769." The Reggio Family Papers, 1771–1860, in Louisiana State University Archives, Baton Rouge, contains an extremely long and important letter descriptive of conditions in 1771. The William Dunbar Papers, in Mississippi State Department of Archives and History, pertain to an early Mississippi planter-merchant and contain much information about marketing crops. The three volumes of John Fitzpatrick Letter Books, 1768–1800, in the New York Public Library were invaluable for their wealth of data regarding mercantile procedures and English influence in New Orleans. The regime of Gálvez was documented in "Confidential Dispatches of Don Bernardo de Gálvez, Fourth Spanish Governor of Louisiana, Sent to His Uncle Don Jose de Gálvez, Secretary of State and a ranking Official of the Council of the Indies" (Typescript translation in Tulane University Library).

As in the French chapters, many secondary books contributed to my knowledge and understanding of the period. Gayarré and Wilson served once again. Among the studies providing a European setting, I consulted: A. S. Aiton, "Spanish Colonial Reorganization Under the Family Compact," *Hispanic American Historical Review*, XII (1932), 269–80, which is descriptive of the role of France in urging and supporting meaningful reforms not only to improve the position of France vis-a-vis England but to strengthen Spain for the next war with England; Vera Lee Brown, *Studies in the History of Spain in the Second Half of the Eighteeth Century, Smith College Studies in History*, XV (Northhampton, Mass., 1929–30), and Brown, "Anglo-Spanish Relations in America in the Closing Years of the Colonial Era, 1763–1774," *Hispanic American Historical Review*, V (1922); and Earl J. Hamilton, *War and Prices in Spain, 1651–1800* (Cambridge, Mass., 1947).

Most of the scholars consulted agree that the reforms of Charles III furthered the centralization of power in the crown. G. Desdevises du Dezert, *L'Espagne de l'Ancien Régime* (3 vols.; Paris, 1897–1904), II, III, and Fieldhouse, *Colonial Empires*, view the reforms as an effort to increase revenues for the crown. François Rousseau, *Règne de Charles III d'Espagne, 1759–1788*, (2 vols.; Paris, 1907), and Robert Jones Shafer, *The Economic Societies in the Spanish World, 1763–1821*, (Syracuse, 1958) emphasize the accommodationist nature of the reforms as does

Herbert Ingram Priestley, *José de Gálvez: Visitor-General of New Spain, 1765–1771, University of California Publications in History*, V (Berkeley, 1916). Richard Herr, *The Eighteenth-Century Revolution in Spain* (Princeton, 1958), and Roland Dennis Hussey, *The Caracas Company, 1728–1784: A Study of Spanish Monopolistic Trade* (Cambridge, Mass., 1934) come around to the centralization thesis by maintaining that Colbertism came to Spain during this century. These scholars also point out that much that was done, especially in the colonies, was forced upon Spain by the vicissitudes of foreign affairs. Hussey and C. H. Haring, *The Spanish Empire in America* (New York, 1963) refer to the foreshadowing of the major reforms in the economic writings of José Campillo y Cossio in 1741. His recommendations were similar to those of the committees in 1764 and 1765. Silvio Zavala, *The Colonial Period in the History of the New World*, abridgement in Engish by Max Savelle (Mexico, D.F., 1962) sees Spain caught up in the intellectual, commercial, and industrial ferment of European society in the eighteenth century.

Works more directly focused on Louisiana and New Orleans were: Pierre H. Boulle, "French Reactions to the Louisiana Revolution of 1768" in John Francis McDermott (ed.), *The French in the Mississippi Valley* (Urbana, 1965), 143–57; David K. Bjork, "Alexander O'Reilly and The Spanish Occupation of Louisiana, 1769–1770" in Hockett, Hammond, et al, *New Spain and the Anglo-American West*; John W. Caughey, *Bernardo De Gálvez in Louisiana, 1776–1783, University of California at Los Angeles Publications in Social Sciences*, No. 4 (Berkeley, 1934); G. Desdevises du Dezert, "La Louisiane à la fin de XVIII siècle," *Societé de l'histoire des colonies françaises* (Paris, 1914); James Alton James, *Oliver Pollock: The Life and Times of an Unknown Patriot* (New York, 1937); E. Wilson Lyon, *Louisiana in French Diplomacy, 1759–1804* (Norman, 1934); and Arthur P. Whitaker, "The Commerce of Louisiana and the Floridas at the End of the Eighteenth Century," *Hispanic American Historical Review*, VIII (1928), 190–203.

CHAPTERS 10–11

The notes and letters, books and memoirs of sojourners in New Orleans and the Lower Valley provided a wealth of data for these two chapters. Some are more reliable than others, just as some are more insightful in their descriptions and analyses of the people among whom they visited and often worked. Unfortunately there is no assurance that those most acute in their analysis of Louisiana life were also accurate when counting flatboats, masts, or bales of cotton. One can only weigh the statistics gathered by these peripatetics against what seems reasonable and then accept or reject them. Among the more interesting were: Berquin-Duvallon, *Travels in Louisiana and the Floridas . . . 1802 . . .* translated from the French by John Davis (New York, 1806) [Prefect Laussat thought this man's account of Louisiana society to be grossly distorted. It was, at the least, highly critical of Creole life and culture]; Georges Henri Victor Collot, *A Journey in North America . . .* (2 vols.; Paris, 1826); Baudry des Lozières, *Second voyage à la Louisiane . . . 1794 à 1798* (2 vols.; Paris, 1803) [Lozières was one among many Frenchmen who advocated the retrocession of Louisiana to France]; Perrin du Lac, *Travels through the Two Louisianas . . . translated from the French* (London, 1807); Thomas Hutchins, *An Historical Narrative and Topographical Description of Louisiana . . .* (Philadelphia, 1784); E. Wilson Lyon, "Moustier's Memoir on Louisiana," *Mississippi Valley Historical Review*, XXII (1935), 251–66; Captain Philip Pittman, *The Present State of the European Settlements on the Mississippi* (London, 1770); John Pope, *Tour through the Southern and Western Territories of the United States of North America . . .* (Richmond, 1792); "The Journal of Dr. John Sibley, July–October, 1802," *Louisiana Historical Quarterly*, X (1927), 474–512; and Henri Delville de Sinclair (tr.), *Memoirs and Correspondence of Pierre Clement de Laussat* (n.p., 1940). In addition, excellent travel accounts were found in James Alexander Robertson (tr. and ed.), *Louisiana Under the Rule of Spain, France, and the United States, 1785–1807: Social, Economic, and Political Conditions of the Territory Represented in the Louisiana Purchase* (2 vols.; Cleveland, 1911); and Reuben Gold Thwaites (ed.), *Early Western Travels, 1748–1846* (32 vols.; Cleveland, 1904–1907).

The documentary materials collected by Alvord, Bolton, Houck, and Kinnaird were used in conjunction with David K. Bjork (ed.), "Documents Relating to Alexander O'Reilly and an Expedition Sent Out By Him from New Orleans to Natchez, 1769–1770," *Louisiana Historical Quarterly*, VII (1924), 20–39; Charles H. Cunningham, "Financial Reports Relating to Louisiana, 1766–1788," *Mississippi Valley Historical Review*, VI (1919), 381–97; Dunbar Rowland (ed.), *Official Letter Books of W. C. C. Claiborne, 1801–1816* (6 vols.; Jackson, Miss., 1917); and Heloise H. Cruzat (tr.), "Letters, in Journal Form, Written to Don Estevan Miro, Ex-Governor of Louisiana, by Don Joseph Xavier de

Pontalba in 1792," *Louisiana Historical Quarterly*, II (1919), 393–417. The translations of this laborer in Louisiana History are indispensable to students.

Previously cited manuscript material that served me in these chapters were: "Confidential Dispatches of Gálvez"; Great Britain, Colonial Office Papers; Kuntz Collection; Dunbar Papers; Fitzpatrick Letter Books; Reggio Family Papers; and the Cabildo Records. In addition, the James Brown Papers, 1764–1811, Louisiana State University, Department of Archives; Dispatches from United States Consuls in New Orleans, 1798–1807, in National Archives, Microcopy T225, Roll 1; and [Julien Poydras], "Private and Commercial Correspondence of an Indigo and Cotton Planter, 1794–1800," in Library of the Louisiana State Museum, New Orleans, all contain pertinent data.

A few secondary works figured in these chapters. They were: Caroline Maude Burson, *The Stewardship of Don Esteban Miro, 1782–1792* (New Orleans, 1940); Max Savelle, *George Morgan, Colony Builder* (New York, 1932); Arthur P. Whitaker, *The Spanish-American Frontier, 1783–1795: The Westward Movement and the Spanish Retreat in the Mississippi Valley* (Boston, 1927); Whitaker, *The Mississippi Question, 1795–1803: A Study in Trade, Politics, and Diplomacy* (New York, 1934); Whitaker, "Reed and Forde: Merchant Adventurers of Philadelphia," *Pennsylvania Magazine of History and Biography*, LXI (July, 1937), 237–62; and Minter Wood, "Life in New Orleans in the Spanish Period," *Louisiana Historical Quarterly*, XXII (1939), 642–709.

CHAPTERS 12–13

The archives of Louisiana State University and of Tulane University house a number of collections which I relied upon heavily in composing these chapters. At the former are located: the Richard Butler Papers; John Bisland Papers, 1763–1895; Ellis-Farrar Papers; Butler Family Papers; Nathaniel Evans and Family Papers, 1791–1932; Gras-Lauzin Family Papers, 1783–1864; George Mather Account Books, 1782–1836; New Orleans Municipal Records; William J. Minor and Family Papers; and A. P. Walsh Papers, 1789–1826. At Tulane are: the Collins Family Papers, 1774–1824; John McDonogh Papers, 1802–50; Minor Family Papers (tentative title of an uncatalogued collection of Xeroxed manuscripts); Robert Smith and Nicholas Low Papers, 1782–1811; and Dispatches of the Spanish Governors of Louisiana, 1776–94, typescript and in translation. At the New Orleans Public Library, the City Council,

Proceedings of Council Meetings, 1803–1814, 5 volumes in French and English, pick up the story of municipal government from the Cabildo Records.

The French Colonial Documents, Library of Congress, cited in conjunction with the French period yielded letters and reports from the French commissioners assigned to New Orleans and their superiors at home, such as de Villars, *Mémoire en faveur de la rejouise de la Louisiane par la France* (1778). Some use was made of *Ships' Registers and Enrollments of New Orleans, Louisiana 1803–1870* (6 vols.; Baton Rouge, 1942–45).

Previously cited manuscript collections that were used again included: Consular Dispatches, National Archives; Fitzpatrick Letter Books, New York Public Library; and Poydras Correspondence, Louisiana State Museum. The edited works by Alvord, Kinnaird, Robertson, Rowland, de Sinclair, and Whitaker along with the "Dispatches of Gálvez" were used extensively, as were the travel accounts cited earlier. "William Johnson's Journal," *Louisiana Historical Quarterly*, V (1922), 34–50, should be added to that group.

Several secondary works aided me: C. Richard Arena, "Philadelphia-Spanish New Orleans Trade in the 1790's," *Louisiana History*, III (1961), 429–45; Harry Bernstein, *Origins of Inter-American Interest, 1700–1812* (Philadelphia, 1945); and [the most fun to read] Henry A. Kmen, *Music in New Orleans: The Formative Years, 1791–1841* (Baton Rouge, 1966).

CHAPTERS 14–16

Manuscript collections relevant to the first decade of American rule are plentiful. Several of the collections span the Spanish and American periods and were noted earlier, such as the Richard Butler Papers, John McDonogh Papers, Minor Family Papers, William J. Minor and Family Papers, and the New Orleans Municipal Records. Also noted previously, and indispensable for chapter 14, were New Orleans City Council Proceedings, in New Orleans Public Library.

Previously uncited collections at Tulane include: Coxe-Lewis Letters, 1806–1807, typescript; Louisiana Historical Association Collection; New Orleans Collection; New Orleans Municipal Papers; Records of Dividends Paid By a New Orleans Insurance Company, 1806–49; and David Rees Papers, 1804–1965. At Louisiana State University: Thomas Butler and Family Papers; Benjamin Kendrick Papers, 1806–94; Manuel Lopez

Papers, 1802–55; William Machette Letter Books, 1807–20; Meeker, Williamson, and Patton Correspondence, 1807–1808; William T. Palfrey and Family Letters, 1806–21; John M. Pintard Papers, 1796–1825; Hudson Tabor and Family Papers; Charles L. Thompson Collection, 1699–1949; and David Weeks and Family Papers, 1782–1894. Also valuable were the Thomas Williams Papers, 1800–35, New York Public Library; and the Bank of the State of Mississippi Papers, Mississippi Department of Archives and History. Information was gained from the correspondence of the Secretary of the Treasury with Collectors of Customs, 1789–1833, Letters to and from the Collector of New Orleans, October 11, 1803–April 11, 1833, in The National Archives, Microcopy No. 178. Roll No. 16 is available on microfilm. Interesting correspondence of James Brown was published in James A. Padgett (ed.), "Letters of James Brown to Henry Clay, 1804–1835," *Louisiana Historical Quarterly*, XXIV (1941), 921–1177.

Travellers contributed their observations: F. Cuming, *Sketches of a Tour to the Western Country . . . 1807 . . . 1809* (Pittsburgh, 1810) and T. M. Harris, *The Journal of a Tour into the Territory Northwest of the Alleghany Mountains* (Boston, 1805) are both conveniently reprinted in Thwaites (ed.), *Early Western Travels*, Vols. IV and III, respectively. See in addition: William Darby, *A Geographical Description of the State of Louisiana . . .* (Philadelphia, 1816); Vincent Nolte, *Fifty Years in Both Hemispheres, or Reminiscences of the Life of a Former Merchant* (New York, 1854); and Christian Schultz, *Travels . . . through . . . Louisiana, Mississippi, and New Orleans . . . 1807 and 1808* (2 vols.; New York, 1810), II.

Legislation can be found in *Acts* of the Legislative Council and *Acts* of the Legislature, published in New Orleans between 1804 and 1818. Newspapers added a variety of information. See *Le Moniteur de la Louisiane* (1802); New Orleans, *Louisiana Gazette and New Orleans Advertiser* [title varies] (1805–20); New Orleans *Le Télegraphe, Commercial Advertiser* [title varies] (1804–1807, 1811); and New Orleans *Union, Orleans Advertiser and Price Current* (1803–1804).

Among the secondary works consulted for information or inspiration were: Carl Bridenbaugh, *Cities in the Wilderness. Urban Life in America, 1625–1742* (New York, 1964) and Bridenbaugh, *Cities in Revolt. Urban Life in America, 1743–1776* (New York, 1964); John G. Clark, *The Grain Trade in The Old Northwest* (Urbana, 1966); W. Freeman Galpin, "The Grain Trade of New Orleans, 1804–1814," *Mississippi Valley Historical Review*, XIV (1928), 496–507; Lewis Cecil Gray,

The History of Agriculture in the Southern United States to 1860 (2 vols.; Gloucester, Mass., 1958); Bray Hammond, *Banks and Politics in America from the Revolution to the Civil War* (Princeton, 1957); Douglass C. North, *The Economic Growth of the United States, 1790–1860* (Englewood Cliffs, 1961); Fritz Redlich, *The Molding of American Banking: Men and Ideas* (2 vols.; New York, 1951; Joseph Clarke Robert, *The Tobacco Kingdom: Plantation, Market, and Factory in Virginia and North Carolina* (Durham, 1938); J. Carlyle Sitterson, *Sugar Country: The Cane Sugar Industry in the South, 1753–1950* (Lexington, 1953); and Richard C. Wade, *The Urban Frontier: Pioneer Life in Early Pittsburgh, Cincinnati, Lexington, Louisville, and St. Louis* (Chicago, 1964).

Contributing specific points of information were: William B. Hatcher, *Edward Livingston: Jeffersonian Republican and Jacksonian Democrat* (Baton Rouge, 1940); John S. Kendall, "Shadow Over the City," *Louisiana Historical Quarterly*, XXII (1939), 142–65; Harry A. Mitchell, "The Development of New Orleans as a Wholesale Center," *Louisiana Historical Quarterly*, XXVII (1944), 933–63; Joe Gray Taylor, "The Foreign Slave Trade in Louisiana After 1808," *Louisiana History*, I (1960), 36–43; and Harris Gaylord Warren, "The Firebrand Affair: A Forgotten Incident of the Mexican Revolution," *Louisiana Historical Quarterly*, XXI (1938), 203–12.

Index